Prophetic Literature

Prophetic Literature

From Oracles to Books

Ronald L. Troxel

WILEY-BLACKWELL

A John Wiley & Sons, Ltd., Publication

This edition first published 2012
© 2012 Ronald L. Troxel

Blackwell Publishing was acquired by John Wiley & Sons in February 2007. Blackwell's publishing
program has been merged with Wiley's global Scientific, Technical, and Medical business to form
Wiley-Blackwell.

Registered Office
John Wiley & Sons Ltd, The Atrium, Southern Gate, Chichester, West Sussex,
PO19 8SQ, UK

Editorial Offices
350 Main Street, Malden, MA 02148-5020, USA
9600 Garsington Road, Oxford, OX4 2DQ, UK
The Atrium, Southern Gate, Chichester, West Sussex, PO19 8SQ, UK

For details of our global editorial offices, for customer services, and for information about how to
apply for permission to reuse the copyright material in this book please see our website at
www.wiley.com/wiley-blackwell.

The right of Ronald L. Troxel to be identified as the author of this work has been asserted in accordance
with the UK Copyright, Designs and Patents Act 1988.

Wiley also publishes its books in a variety of electronic formats. Some content that appears in print may
not be available in electronic books.

Designations used by companies to distinguish their products are often claimed as trademarks.
All brand names and product names used in this book are trade names, service marks, trademarks
or registered trademarks of their respective owners. The publisher is not associated with any product
or vendor mentioned in this book. This publication is designed to provide accurate and authoritative
information in regard to the subject matter covered. It is sold on the understanding that the publisher
is not engaged in rendering professional services. If professional advice or other expert assistance is
required, the services of a competent professional should be sought.

Library of Congress Cataloging-in-Publication Data

Troxel, Ronald L., 1951–
Prophetic literature : from oracles to books / Ronald L. Troxel.
    p.   cm.
  Includes bibliographical references and index.
  ISBN 978-1-4051-8846-3 (hardcover : alk. paper) – ISBN 978-1-4051-8845-6 (pbk. : alk. paper)
1. Bible. O.T. Prophets–Criticism, interpretation, etc.   I. Title.
  BS1505.52.T76 2012
  224'.06–dc23

                                            2011026336

A catalogue record for this book is available from the British Library.

This book is published in the following electronic formats: ePDFs 9781444354126;
ePub 9781444354133; Mobi 9781444354140

Set in 10/12.5pt Galliard by SPi Publisher Services, Pondicherry, India
Printed in Singapore by Ho Printing Singapore Pte Ltd

1   2012

To my parents
The late Rev. James R. Troxel (1921–2011)
and Mrs Rosemary E. Wolfe Troxel

Contents

Preface

There are many ways to read a prophetic book. Early readers often cited individual oracles in the same way as today's tabloids cite statements attributed to Nostradamus. For instance, a treatise written by the group that lived at the ancient site of Qumran, on the shores of the Dead Sea, quoted Isaiah 40:3's call to prepare a way in the wilderness as anticipating their community (1QS 8.14), and the Synoptic Gospels (Matthew, Mark, and Luke) quoted the same passage as presaging the work of John the Baptist (Mark 1:3; Matt. 3:3; Luke 3:4).

Another long-standing way of reading identifies a book's structure and themes as keys to its messages. Characterizing a book's literary units under terms like "judgment," "salvation," or "covenant" is one way of epitomizing its messages. Sometimes this type of reading presupposes that the prophets were vehicles of divine communication, but it has also been used in an attempt to evaluate an individual book's contributions to a collection like the 12 shorter prophetic books or the entire corpus of prophetic books.

The prophets have also frequently been read as moral guides. This is consonant with their repeated emphasis on "justice and righteousness," their calls for attending to the needs of society's most vulnerable, and their criticisms of those who misuse religion, authority, and power for their own ends. The books' varied forecasts of an age when injustices will be set right and flaws in the world's structure cured imply ethical ideals. Dr Martin Luther King, Jr, is probably the best-known exponent of this way of reading the prophets.

Conversely, it is possible to highlight the ideas and values in these books that strongly conflict with modern ethical standards. Feminist critics have rightly called attention to passages that ascribe degrading roles or qualities to women, since historically many men have used these to justify despicable treatment of women. Likewise, the prophets' notion that the LORD sponsors or wages war grates on our sense of morality and deserves to be critiqued, and its use today scrutinized. The same is true of the notion that some nations enjoy divine favor while others do not, an idea already challenged by the prophet Amos. Highlighting these issues rightly cautions us against adopting the prophets' norms without thinking critically about what their words endorse or have been used to justify.

In recent decades, a strong interest in studying the prophets as literature has arisen. Some readers look for literary devices betokening structural coherence that permits reading them as wholes. Whether such readings imagine how a book was understood by audiences in a particular historical period or suggest how the finished product can be read today, the focus is on how the book functions as literature.

While the current literary form of these books is the necessary starting point for any attempt to understand them, reading them on the literary plane alone leaves questions. How, for example, did the book of Nahum become part of the collection of the prophets when it takes such delight in the gory defeat of Nineveh? Why is the prophet Hosea ordered to take "a wife of whoredom and have children of whoredom" (Hos. 1:2) and then told to take her back after losing her to another man (Hos. 3:1)? How do we explain Amos's abrupt shift in tone in 9:11–15 where, after consistently condemning his audience in 1:1–9:14, he suddenly forecasts Jerusalem's restoration and an ideal age (9:11–15)? How do we account for distinctive phrases that are shared among multiple books, such as, "The LORD roars from Zion, and utters his voice from Jerusalem," in Joel 3:16 and Amos 1:2?

This book addresses questions such as these in light of what we can perceive about how the prophetic books were composed. Doing so involves detecting editorial expansions, perceiving how oracles were arranged, and noting embedded "hyperlinks" to other books. Even if many traces of editing were so smoothly executed that they are undetectable, and the way back to the original wording of a particular passage is barred, enough hints survive about how the books evolved to shed light on their origins. Answering questions about what gave rise to these books does not provide the key that unlocks them, for the questions they raise are too many and varied to yield to one key. Nevertheless, addressing questions about what lies behind these books offers one way of reading them to be used alongside others.

The notion that these books arose through editing and expansion might seem sacrilegious to some readers. However, such observations, afforded by biblical scholarship, have led many people of faith to reframe rather than abandon confessions that these books mediate divine communication. This is not the place to pursue those questions, but a variety of helpful discussions of such issues are available (see, for example, Barton, 2007; McKenzie, 2005a; Roberts, 1979).

A couple of notes on terminology used in this volume might be helpful. The prophetic books stand in a collection most widely known as the Old Testament. That label, however, presumes a collection called the New Testament. The opposition of New Testament to Old Testament was constructed by Christian clerics of the third century to demean the older collection in favor of writings by early Christians. Owing to the resultant religious bias that the phrase "Old Testament" carries, contemporary scholars refer to this collection as "the Hebrew Bible," a title recognizing that most of these books were written in Hebrew.

In the same vein, rather than identifying dates under the rubrics of BC and AD – the former meaning "before Christ" and the latter representing the Latin *anno domini*, "in the year of the Lord," intended as a reference to Jesus of Nazareth – this book will utilize the more inclusive abbreviations commonplace in scholarship: BCE, "before the common era" (of Judaism and Christianity), and CE, "the common era."

The English translation of the Bible used, unless otherwise indicated, is the New Revised Standard Version (NRSV), published by the National Council of Churches (1989). I am deeply grateful to the Division of Christian Education of the National Council of Churches for granting permission to quote this translation extensively. Verses will be cited by the chapter and verse divisions found in English translations rather than by those found in medieval Hebrew manuscripts, which sometimes differ significantly.

Reading this book with the NRSV in hand will prove beneficial. The benefit of the NRSV, beyond its translation of Hebrew into contemporary English, is that its translators paid special attention to **textual criticism** (bold will be used for the first occurrence in a chapter of a word treated in the Glossary). Textual criticism is the art of evaluating differences in wording between manuscripts that have survived from as early as 200 BCE, with the goal of recovering the most likely wording for a passage. The NRSV does much of that legwork for us, although I will occasionally note that I prefer a different manuscript reading than the NRSV has chosen.

The NRSV, like most translations, uses small caps with LORD or Lord GOD. The personal name of Israel's God, equivalent to the four English consonants YHWH (thus, called the **Tetragrammaton**, "four letters"), came to be considered too sacred to pronounce. In its place the religious community uttered a form of the Hebrew word for "lord." Correlatively, it is conventional for translations to represent the Tetragrammaton with LORD. When the simple Hebrew word for "lord" stands before the Tetragrammaton, the convention is to translate the phrase with "Lord GOD."

Occasionally it will prove useful to represent Hebrew words in English characters. In place of the technical system of transliteration used by scholars, I will use phonetic equivalents that are (hopefully) user-friendly for non-specialists.

Many people helped see this book to completion. The undergraduates in Prophets of the Bible, which I taught at the University of Wisconsin-Madison for 20 years, forced me to think regularly about the books of the prophets and how best to convey issues in studying them to non-specialists.

Andrew Humphreys of Routledge, formerly an editor at Wiley-Blackwell, first approached me with questions about what I would like to see in a textbook on the prophets and later offered me the opportunity to write the book. Upon his departure from Wiley-Blackwell, I gained the benefit of Rebecca Harkin as editor. She has been a wonderful support and sounding board. The entire process of conceiving and writing this book was greatly assisted by the numerous readers Andrew and Rebecca secured to read and comment on chapter drafts. I cannot express deeply enough the debt I owe these readers and editors.

During the final year of writing I was fortunate enough to have a graduate student as a project assistant. Mr Aaron West read every chapter, wrote detailed comments, pointed out weak arguments, corrected verse references, suggested clearer wording, and saved me from a multitude of embarrassments. In the final stages of preparing the manuscript for publication, Ms Laurien Berkeley scrutinized the text again, providing valuable refinements and removing additional problems. Having benefited from all this assistance, I am forced to acknowledge surviving flaws as mine alone.

My wife, Jacki, has been a steady support during the three years I have worked on this book, and she remains my closest confidant on all matters that are truly important. My sons, Ben and Bryan, provided me with visible reassurance that I have brought other projects to successful completion, so I could expect to finish this one, as well. Without a doubt, the project of seeing them to adulthood has been the most significant and rewarding of my life.

Among those to whom I owe the largest debt of gratitude are my parents, Mrs Rosemary E. Wolfe Troxel and the late Rev. James R. Troxel. From early on they taught me to cherish the Bible, acquainting me with its words more than any other book. When I was a child, Jeremiah, Isaiah, and Ezekiel were as familiar to me as family, even though their words filled me with mystery and fear. For the impetus to study the Bible and its prophets I am forever and profoundly grateful to my parents, who in so many ways set me on the path I have taken. In particular, with the death of my father fresh as I write, I am reminded that he was the first to teach me that the Bible must be studied in its original languages and historical contexts. To his memory and to my mother I lovingly dedicate this book.

R.L.T.
Madison, Wisconsin
July 2011

Resource Acknowledgments

New Revised Standard Version Bible, copyright 1989, Division of Christian Education of the National Council of the Churches of Christ in the United States of America. Used by permission. All rights reserved.

The maps were created with Accordance Bible Atlas, © 2008 Oak Tree Software. Reproduced with permission.

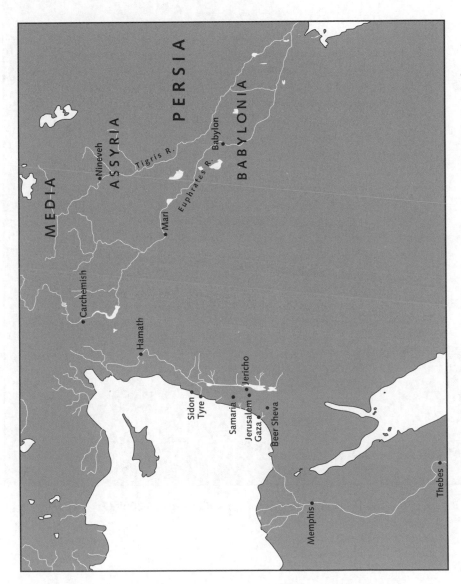

Map 1 The ancient Near East (created using Accordance Bible Atlas, ©2008 Oak Tree Software)

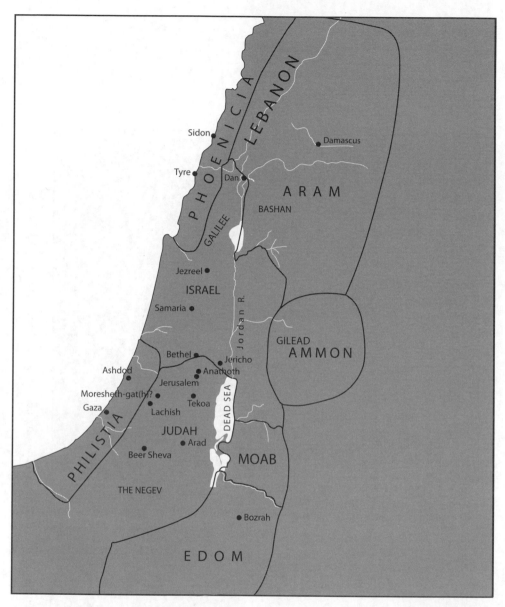

Map 2 Israel and Judah (created using Accordance Bible Atlas, ©2008 Oak Tree Software)

1

What Is a Prophetic Book?

In the pages to come …

The prophets have long fascinated people for their stinging criticisms of society, their defense of the vulnerable, and their visions of the future. But where did their books come from? Our understanding of the role of writing in semi-literate cultures, our knowledge of the creation and editing of literature in the **ancient Near East**, and evidence of records of prophets' words among Israel's neighbors have all grown significantly in recent years. This chapter will make clear how applying these gains in knowledge to the prophetic books is changing the way scholarship views them.

At first blush, the strategy for reading a biblical prophetic book seems intuitive: you follow the logic of the prophet's words, much as you would follow any speech, looking for the key points of the rhetoric. And in fact, some passages read like highly developed oratory. For instance, Isaiah 40:12–31 mounts a sustained challenge to a group whose estimation of their God is implied to be deficient. Verse 12 speaks of Israel's God as a colossus who dwarfs his creation, vv. 13–14 describe him as beyond human instruction, and vv. 15–17 measure him against the nations, who are paltry by comparison. The prophet then voices the question "To whom then will you liken God?" (v. 18). He adduces idols for comparison, deconstructing them as nothing more than human confections of wood and metal (vv. 19–20). He summons his audience to recall what they already know: the LORD dominates his domain, bringing human rulers to naught (vv. 21–24). And then the question recurs: "To whom then will you compare me, or who is my equal?" (v. 25), with the speaker immediately denying comparison to the stars (v. 26). In this light, how dare Jacob's children

Prophetic Literature: From Oracles to Books, First Edition. Ronald L. Troxel.
© 2012 Ronald L. Troxel. Published 2012 by Blackwell Publishing Ltd.

(Israel) question whether their ever-attendant, inexhaustible god has lost sight of them (vv. 27–31)? Such oratory means to revive confidence in the LORD by replacing defeatism and weariness with strength to "mount up with wings like eagles."

But most of the material found in the prophetic books doesn't read as smoothly as Isaiah 40. Isaiah 1 is more representative, in that it seems disjointed and hard to follow. After vv. 2–3 complain that the people's rebellion against the LORD shows them lacking the sense of brute beasts, v. 4 upbraids them for turning from the LORD, while vv. 5–6 address them as masochists inviting further beatings, despite having a (collective) body already battered and bloodied. After vv. 7–8 make this imagery concrete by describing Judah as savagely destroyed and Jerusalem bereft of its satellite cities, the speaker laments, "If the LORD of hosts had not left us a few survivors, we would have been like Sodom, and become like Gomorrah" (v. 9). But then he pivots quickly, using Sodom and Gomorrah with a different tone: "Hear the word of the LORD, you rulers of Sodom! Listen to the teaching of our God, you people of Gomorrah!" (v. 10). The implied comparison is no longer "we were nearly annihilated like Sodom and Gomorrah" but "you and your rulers are as *wicked* as Sodom and Gomorrah." This wickedness is defined in terms of worship, with the LORD rejecting the people's sacrifices, owing to their entanglement with evil, from which they can free themselves if they "seek justice, rescue the oppressed, defend the orphan, plead for the widow" (v. 17). The LORD then calls them to a dialogue with himself that would result in their eating "the good of the land"; but if they remain rebellious, they will be eaten by the sword (vv. 18–20). Surprisingly, vv. 21–26 state that such judgment will not annihilate them, but will restore the city to its former righteousness. Verses 27–28 forecast that "Zion shall be redeemed by justice, and those in her who repent, by righteousness," but its rebels and sinners will be destroyed. Such sinners delight in "oaks and gardens" (v. 29) – apparently a form of illicit worship – and their fate will be (ironically) to become like a dead oak or a withered garden (vv. 30–31).

Although it is possible to track a series of relationships in these verses, they lack the rhetorical coherence of Isaiah 40. It is not just the abrupt switch in the use of Sodom and Gomorrah that presents difficulties. For example, it is curious that while v. 9 laments the decimation of Judean society nearly to extinction, vv. 21–28 do not assume a hobbled state, but one that thrives under the reign of a corrupt aristocracy. And although vv. 5–9 state that the people's unchanged behavior invites further calamities that would bring complete destruction, vv. 21–26 stipulate that hardship will not destroy Zion/Jerusalem but save it by purging its wicked rulers and replacing them with righteous ones (compare vv. 27–28). Nevertheless, vv. 4–6 define the *entire* population as wicked, and vv. 7–8 describe a land devastated rather than recuperating from a surgical removal of the wicked.

There are also questions about who is at fault. In the latter half of the chapter it is clearly the aristocracy. Even though v. 10 takes aim at both the rulers and the people, vv. 11–17 have in view upper-class religious practices, since the remedy (attending to the rights of the widow and the orphan, v. 17) is in their power. This is the same ruling class that has sullied Jerusalem's pedigree as a "righteous and faithful city" (vv. 21–26). And yet, the chapter begins by characterizing *all* the LORD's children as a "sinful nation, people laden with iniquity, offspring who do evil, children who deal corruptly, who have forsaken the LORD, who have despised the Holy One of Israel, who are utterly estranged" (v. 4) and who, despite having suffered the consequences, are making themselves vulnerable to further disaster (vv. 5–6). There is variation in identifying who is responsible for Israel's peril.

Similarly, religious crimes are described differently throughout this chapter. On the one hand, vv. 11–17 denigrate religion as reduced to sacrifices and festivals while spurning justice for the vulnerable. On the other hand, the chief religious crime of vv. 29–31 is inappropriate delight in oaks and gardens.

In short, when reading the prophetic books, we far more often face these sorts of incongruity between adjacent statements than the type of coherent oration we find in Isaiah 40. Although many readers consider such incongruities inevitable features of prophetic books, scholars have sought to understand why these books contain them. Before starting to address that question, we must be clear about how these books fit with other biblical literature about prophets and within the Bible as a whole.

Prophetic Books and Prophetic Literature

The Hebrew Bible contains three divisions: the **Torah** (Genesis–Deuteronomy), the Prophets, and the Writings (Psalms, Proverbs, Ruth, Daniel,[1] 1 and 2 Chronicles, etc.). The Prophets embraces two collections:

The former prophets	The latter prophets
Joshua	Isaiah, Jeremiah, Ezekiel
Judges	Hosea, Joel, Amos, Obadiah, Jonah
1 and 2 Samuel	Micah, Nahum, Habakkuk, Zephaniah
1 and 2 Kings	Haggai, Zechariah, Malachi

The ancient rabbis attributed authorship of the book of Joshua to Moses' successor, Joshua (considered a prophet), Judges and the books of Samuel to the prophet Samuel, and the books of Kings to Jeremiah (*b. Baba Batra* 14a).[2] Although those attributions have not stood the test of time, the tradition of considering these books prophetic literature endures.

Among the "latter prophets," Isaiah, Jeremiah, and Ezekiel each consumed one **scroll** and so came to be called the "major [i.e., larger] prophets." The remaining 12 books could fit on a single scroll – called, for that reason, "the **Book of the Twelve**" – and earned the moniker "the minor [i.e., smaller] prophets."[3]

At the same time, while the latter prophets contain mostly **oracles** (messages from the deity), 1 Samuel through 2 Kings and 1 and 2 Chronicles (henceforth, "Chronicles") also contain *narratives* about prophets. While such narratives often report oracles, their images of prophets differ from those in the latter prophets. For example, 2 Kings 20 reports that, as King Hezekiah lay ill and was told by Isaiah to set his affairs in order, he reminded the LORD of what a good king he had been (vv. 1–3). Isaiah, already on his way out of the palace, was stopped in his tracks by a divine order to tell the king he would recover and live another 15 years (vv. 4–6). When Hezekiah asked for a sign confirming this, Isaiah caused the sun to backtrack 10 intervals on the royal sundial (vv. 8–11). This narrative depicts Isaiah as a wonder-worker, similar to Elijah and Elisha in 1 and 2 Kings, but different from his image in the book of Isaiah, where he is the speaker of oracles.[4]

Sometimes such narratives have been viewed as less "prophetic" than the books containing oracles. By that standard, however, we could question whether the book of Jonah (entirely narrative) is truly prophetic, even though no one raises a similar question about Haggai, which is also structured as a narrative. It seems wiser, then, to consider oracles and narratives simply as different types of prophetic literature (Floyd, 2003a).

Narratives about prophets are diverse in themselves: stories of a prophet's miraculous deeds that secure his reputation as a holy man, stories of his involvement in political events, stories offering ethical lessons, and stories of prophets suffering for fidelity to their task (Rofé, 1988). In 1 Samuel through 2 Kings different types of narrative are combined to portray prophets as wonder-workers and to stress the effectiveness of the LORD's word through the prophet by detailing its fulfillment (e.g., 1 Kings 13:1–3 and 2 Kings 23:16) (Long, 1973; Römer, 2005).[5]

Narratives included in the latter prophets have their own distinctive features. A prophet is portrayed as a wonder-worker only in the stories that Isaiah 36–39 share with 2 Kings 19–20. More typical are accounts of the conditions under which the prophet received his call (Isa 6; Jer 1:4–19), stories of confrontations between a prophet and an opponent (Jer 28:1–17; Am 7:10–17), the response of the audience to a prophet (Jer 36; Hag 1:12, 14), and reports of symbolic actions (Isa 20:1–6; Ezek 5:1–4), called **sign acts**.

Such narratives embody different ways of portraying prophets, all of which can be classified as types of prophetic *literature*.[6] The prophetic *book*, however, is a distinctive type of prophetic literature that can contain narratives, but focuses especially on prophetic oracles. More significantly, a *book* has a clear beginning and end, and offers a viewpoint that differentiates it from other documents (Ben Zvi, 2003). A *prophetic book* features the words of a single prophet as the LORD's word (Ben Zvi, 2000a), over against the former prophets' concern to integrate prophets into the larger story of Israel's life.

This is not to say that prophetic books are of one type. In exploring these works, it will become evident that while some books feature oracles, others report a sequence of events in which a prophet is an actor, although always speaking at least one oracle (in the case of Jonah). But who composed these books: the prophets themselves or others?

Prophets and Writing

For much of the twentieth century, scholars viewed a prophetic book as a repository of utterances by the prophet named at the outset, even if those are encrusted with additions that obscure their meanings. The goal of identifying the original words of the prophet was inspired partly by Romanticism's fascination with "great men" who propounded ground-breaking ideas (Tull Willey, 1997). And based on an assumption that "primitive" cultures were oral rather than literate, coupled with a belief that poetry was the primal form of oral expression, scholars believed that prophets must have spoken poetry. Scholars posited that the words of the prophets stood at the core of an onion-like structure whose outer layers (later editors' expansions) could be peeled away to reveal the pristine oracles.

An analytical method called "form criticism" promised to isolate these oracles. This method recognized that certain passages show a similar structure. For instance, often prophets lament the peril facing a group of people, as in Isaiah 5:8: "Ah, you who join house to house, who add field to field, until there is room for no one but you, and you are left to live alone in the midst of the land!" The word translated "ah" frequently introduces speech of the sort used to bemoan the passing of a friend, suggesting that prophets borrowed this type of speech to announce the peril hanging over members of their society. Because such laments are at home in funeral orations, the prophets' imitation of laments was seen as a mark of prophetic speech.

A fundamental flaw in this sort of reasoning is the assumption that such imitations of speech must reflect *spoken* words. There is no reason that a writer could not have attributed such language to a person he portrayed as speaking. Nor is there reason to assume that reports of speeches must have been written by the prophet. In fact, research into literacy in ancient societies – not just how many people were literate (which turns out to have been few) but also *which* people (namely, those whose professions required it) – has undermined assumptions that prophets or those around them would have written texts.[7]

The assumption that such people must have been literate is problematic. Literacy is common only when copies of texts can be produced inexpensively and sufficient resources are dedicated to teaching the populace to read (Young, 1998a). Those the Bible portrays writing or reading are typically **scribes**, kings, priests, and other bureaucrats (Carr, 2005). Most Israelites would not have been literate (Young, 1998b), even if some might have been able to write their name.

Although it is not unthinkable that some prophets were literate, we find few hints of this, and likely "in most cases oracles originally spoken by prophets who did not write were subsequently written down by scribes who did" (Floyd, 2008, 223). It is instructive to note how Jeremiah executes the LORD's command to "take a scroll and write on it all the words that I have spoken to you" (Jer 36:2): "Then Jeremiah called Baruch son of Neriah, and Baruch wrote on a scroll at Jeremiah's dictation all the words of the LORD that he had spoken to him" (Jer 36:4). Jeremiah's employment of a **scribe** (a professional writer) accords with how most documents were written in the ancient world (compare Esther 8:8–9).

Furthermore, rather than posting the dictated scroll on a kiosk for public review, Baruch took it to the temple and read it aloud to those arriving to observe a fast (36:9–10). And when the scroll was brought to the king, it was read aloud (36:21). Two features of this scene accord with what we know of writing and literacy. First, reading a document aloud reflects the prime way written words were "published" when literacy was an uncommon skill (Carr, 2005). Second, the prophet's report "I am prevented from entering the house of the LORD" (36:5) explains why Baruch must read these oracles rather than Jeremiah speak them.

At the same time, the depiction of a scroll that contains "all the words that I have spoken to you against Israel and Judah and all the nations … from the days of Josiah until today" (36:2) seems a bit artificial. Given that Jeremiah 1:1 dates the start of his work to Josiah's thirteenth year (627 BCE) and 36:1 specifies this record was written in the fourth year of Jehoiakim (605 BCE), the scroll would have contained oracles spanning more than two decades. Even allowing for some incompleteness in the record (see 36:32), this scenario raises the question under what conditions those visiting the temple could be expected to listen to such a lengthy scroll and whether reading a compendium of old oracles would be the most effective way of persuading them to "turn from their evil ways" (v. 3) (Davies, 1996). Therefore, this report seems interested in imagining how a written collection of Jeremiah's oracles arose in the first place, a concern that surfaces elsewhere in the book.

In Jeremiah 29 the prophet writes a letter (or has one written) to those already in **exile**, admonishing them not to suppose that Jerusalem will escape Babylon's clutches.[8] In a similar manner, he sends a scroll to Babylon via an emissary, who is instructed to read the oracles aloud and then throw the scroll, weighted with a stone, into the river (Jer 51:59–64). In both instances writing is – at least partly – a substitute for Jeremiah's voice.

The other mention of writing is in 30:2–3, where the prophet is commanded to "write in a book all the words that I have spoken to you," for one day "I will restore the fortunes of my people, Israel and Judah, says the LORD, and I will bring them back to the land that I gave to their ancestors and they shall take possession of it." The reason for this record is stated in the chapter's final verse, addressed to the people: "In the latter days [i.e., the future] you will understand this" (30:24). This record is meant for those presently incapable of understanding, but who will one day grasp the prophet's words. Once again this document substitutes for the prophet's voice.

References to writing in the book of Isaiah point to a somewhat different use, but one that fits the function of texts in Jeremiah. Chapter 8 carries the first mention of writing:

> 1: Then the LORD said to me, "Take a large tablet and write on it in common characters, 'Belonging to Maher-shalal-hash-baz,' 2: and have it attested for me by reliable witnesses, the priest Uriah and Zechariah son of Jeberechiah." 3: And I went to the prophetess, and she conceived and bore a son. Then the LORD said to me, "Name him Maher-shalal-hash-baz; 4: for before the child knows how to call 'My father' or 'My mother,' the wealth of Damascus and the spoil of Samaria will be carried away by the king of Assyria."

Whatever the original relationship between vv. 1–2 and vv. 3–4,[9] v. 4 defines the meaning of the legal document as much as it does the child's name (Maher-shalal-hash-baz = "quick is booty, swift is plunder").[10] The crucial observation is that this tablet is *not* a transcript of the prophet's words; it is a legal document.

The specter of a legal document appears again in 8:16–18:

> 16: Bind up the testimony, seal the teaching among my disciples. 17: I will wait for the LORD, who is hiding his face from the house of Jacob, and I will hope in him. 18: See, I and the children whom the LORD has given me are signs and portents in Israel from the LORD of hosts, who dwells on Mount Zion.

"Binding up" and "sealing" are terms proper to the handling of documents (Carr, 2005), although here they are likely used metaphorically of preserving memory of Isaiah's teaching.[11] Given the prophet's implied intention to withdraw from engagement with society and await the LORD's action (v. 17), the idea is that his teaching, vouchsafed with his disciples,[12] bears witness to those who have refused to listen. It strains the text's language to extrapolate this as evidence that Isaiah's disciples transmitted *written* reports of his words (Davies, 1996).[13]

The final reference to writing in Isaiah runs in a similar vein. A scolding of "rebellious children" who suppose that they can rely on Egypt's aid (Isa 30:1–5) and a characterization of such hope as futile (vv. 6–7) are followed by the command

> 8: Go now, write it before them on a tablet, and inscribe it in a book, so that it may be for the time to come as a witness[14] forever. 9: For they are a rebellious people, faithless children, children who will not hear the instruction of the LORD; 10: who say to the seers, "Do not see"; and to the prophets, "Do not prophesy to us what is right; speak to us smooth things, prophesy illusions, 11: leave the way, turn aside from the path, let us hear no more about the Holy One of Israel."

Precisely what is to be recorded is unclear, but it constitutes a witness in the future. Much like Isaiah's teaching sealed among his pupils, this writing preserves the prophet's voice until a time when those unwilling to listen to him now might do so.

To cite one more example, the prophet Habakkuk is instructed, "Promulgate the vision on tablets, so that the one reading it may run" (my translation). The main action of the reader is running: he runs, reading the vision (Andersen, 2001). The image is that of a town crier (van der Toorn, 2007), a role well attested in ancient Mesopotamia (Schaper, 2009). As with Jeremiah's scroll, this document serves proclamation (see further below, p. 119).

In each instance, writing (or its use as a metaphor) conveys a prophet's words to an audience remote, whether geographically or in attitude. Although no prophet is said to assemble oracles for use after the lifetime of his audience (van der Toorn, 2007), the eventual collection of prophets' words into the books we possess attests someone's belief that prophets' voices needed to address hearers beyond the prophet's day (Jeremias, 1996l).

The concluding verse of Hosea epitomizes this role of preserved prophetic words, inasmuch as it commends the book as cherished by those who acknowledge that "the ways of the LORD are right" and "walk in them" (Hos 14:9). Implicit in this endorsement is a defense of these words as a means for learning the LORD's ways with Israel, and it presupposes a group of scholars who study the composition to derive its meaning for them (Davies, 1996).

Zechariah 1:2–6 similarly exhorts its audience to heed the prophets of the past:

> 2: The LORD was very angry with your ancestors. 3: Therefore say to them, "Thus says the LORD of hosts: Return to me, says the LORD of hosts, and I will return to you, says the LORD of hosts. 4: Do not be like your ancestors, to whom the former prophets proclaimed, 'Thus says the LORD of hosts, Return from your evil ways and from your evil deeds.' But they did not hear or heed me, says the LORD. 5: Your ancestors, where are they? And the prophets, do they live forever? 6: But my words and my statutes, which I commanded my servants the prophets, did they not overtake your ancestors? So they repented and said, 'The LORD of hosts has dealt with us according to our ways and deeds, just as he planned to do.'"

Although this does not appeal to a specific collection of prophecy, it assumes a tradition of oracles whose effects outlived the prophets who uttered them. Not only is this an implicit claim that the oracles of this book align with the earlier ones, but it also implies the need to attend to those oracles because they proved true. It is this sort of esteem for the words of past prophets that stands behind the composition of the prophetic books.

But who undertook this task? If the prophets did not record their oracles for posterity, then who did? We can gain a foothold in answering this question by comparing what we know of written reports of prophets' words elsewhere in the ancient Near East.

Oracle Reports in the Ancient Near East

A collection of over 1500 tablets from the eighteenth-century BCE city of **Mari**, located on the Euphrates river (see Map 1), includes 50 administrative reports to King Zimri Lim of oracles spoken by prophets.[15] The official reports how he or she learned of the prophecy, gives the name or title of the prophet, identifies the deity the prophet invoked, and states the occasion. Occasionally several oracles are grouped together, while still preserving them as separate oracles, suggesting that such groupings were merely a matter of convenience (van der Toorn, 2004).

The reports use the letter format common in the Mari documents (Parker, 1993) but also betray individual scribes' habits, so that some stylistic traits belong to an individual scribe rather than the speech of a prophet (Nakata, 1982). The committal of oracles to writing makes them different than a simple transcript of speech (Nissinen, 2000). In fact, only exceptionally does an official claim to offer a verbatim report (van der Toorn, 2000a).

Speech vs. Reported Speech

Linguists point out that oral and written forms of communication are structurally different (Kelber, 2007), as can be deduced from reflecting on newspaper reporting. Although reporters do their best to report accurately, "they must conform to the conventions of their craft, and there is always slippage between their choice of words and the nature of an event as experienced or perceived by others" (Darnton, 2008). Even if reporters frequently quote their sources, they often paraphrase; and even direct quotations are not always precise, as anyone who has seen their words reported can attest. The casting of speech into written form (unless it is a transcription) subjects it to a different medium and a distinct set of rules (Davis, 1989, 20–25).[16]

On the other hand, among the documents surviving from the archives of the palace in the Assyrian capital of Nineveh (in the seventh century BCE, just after Micah and Isaiah) are four anthologies of oracles having to do with King Esarhaddon. These anthologies reflect individual oracle reports, with each report attributing its oracle to a specific prophet, but omitting the circumstances in which it was spoken, most likely because the collection was aimed at providing validation for the recently ascended king (van der Toorn, 2000b).[17] Similar to the Mari letters, these reports use a common form, suggesting that they were composed according to literary models rather than as transcripts (Nissinen, 2000; Van Seters, 2000).

Even more instructive is evidence that such reports were distinctively shaped by those who composed them. The Mari letters preserve two reports of oracles uttered by the same prophetess, on the same day, warning King Zimri Lim against an alliance with the king of Eshnunna. In the first report, her warning is summarized by an official named Sammetar:

> A *qammatum* [a type of prophet] of Dagan of Terqa came to me and spoke to me in the following terms: "Beneath the straw the water is running. They keep sending messages proposing peace, and they even send their gods, but it is a very different wind they are planning in their hearts. The king must not commit himself without (first) asking the god." ... She also gave her oracle in the chapel of Belet-ekallim to the priestess Inibshina.[18]

We are fortunate to have that priestess's own report of the oracle delivered to her:

> Now a *qammatum* of Dagan of Terqa came to me and spoke to me in the following terms: "The friendship of the Man of Eshnunna is a fraud: beneath the straw the water is running. In the very net which he knots I will collect him, and his possession from of old I will put to utter waste." This is what she said to me. Now take care of yourself. Do not enter the treaty without an oracle.

Common to these reports is a proverbial warning against trusting appearances: "beneath the straw the water is running." The second oracle contains a reassurance of Eshnunna's defeat that is absent from the first, although this might have been a feature of the oracle as spoken before the priestess. More significant, however, is the first report's warning (within the oracle) against the king committing himself to the alliance without divine approval. The identical warning appeared in an oracle Sammetar, this official, reported earlier, suggesting that he inserted it again here to underscore what he saw as the oracle's thrust (Parker, 1993). The official's interpretation of the meaning thus became part of the oracle, whereas in the priestess's report it stands as her advice to the king, based on the oracle.

The book of Jeremiah gives evidence that this type of prophecy and report was practiced in ancient Israel. And helpfully, it also contains two reports of an oracle. That these report the same event is evident from similarities in their introductions:

7:1–2: The word that came to Jeremiah from the Lord: 2: Stand in the gate of the Lord's house, and proclaim there this word, and say, Hear the word of the Lord, all you people of Judah, you that enter these gates to worship the Lord.	26:1–2: At the beginning of the reign of King Jehoiakim son of Josiah of Judah, this word came from the Lord: 2: Thus says the Lord: Stand in the court of the Lord's house, and speak to all the cities of Judah that come to worship in the house of the Lord; speak to them all the words that I command you; do not hold back a word.

While 26:1 assigns a date for the oracle, 7:1 mentions only the prophet's name. And while 7:1 commands the prophet to speak in the gates of the temple, 26:1 specifies the temple court as the venue. Nevertheless, the command to take up position in the temple and address all Judeans entering to worship the Lord is the same.

More significant differences appear in the succeeding sections. 7:3–11 lambaste the people for treating the temple as if it would protect them from punishment, despite their behavior. In the parallel section of chapter 26, the LORD sets before Jeremiah the prospect that the people might change their ways, enabling him to relent from punishment. Thereafter the parallels between the reports resume:

7:14: therefore I will do to the house that is called by my name, in which you trust, and to the place that I gave to you and to your ancestors, just what I did to Shiloh.	26:6: then I will make this house like Shiloh, and I will make this city a curse for all the nations of the earth.

The threat to treat the temple after the manner of Shiloh appears only in these passages in the Bible, confirming that they report the same incident. And yet, as with the reports of oracles from Mari, there is variation in phraseology and content, leaving us with two different forms of the oracle (van der Toorn, 2007). This suggests that the author(s) of Jeremiah did not feel bound to present verbatim transcripts.

The fundamental difference between the oracle reports from Mari and Assyria and the biblical prophetic books is that the latter compile large sets of oracles and attribute them to a single prophet. How is it that while the rest of the ancient Near East has left us isolated prophetic oracles, ancient Israel has left us prophetic books?

Prophetic Literature

Earlier I noted the frequent narratives about prophets within the Bible. Numbers 22–24 tell the story of Balaam, son of Beor, who is portrayed as an **intermediary** between humans and the divine, hired by the king of Moab to curse Israel. The LORD thwarts this plan, compelling Balaam to utter a blessing instead.

This story is not the only one about Balaam, however. Another survives in fragments of a text written in plaster on the wall of a building on the eastern side of the Jordan (Deir 'Allā), whose ruins can be dated to the early eighth century BCE (around the time of Amos and Hosea).[19] It portrays Balaam as a prophet to whom the gods revealed a set of cataclysms that would befall his land. Most remarkable, for our purposes, is its introduction, which resembles the headings in the latter prophets: "The book of Balaam, son of Beor, a Seer of the Gods" (Weippert, 1991). Unlike most prophetic books, however, the text is (as far as can be determined from the fragments) entirely a narrative. Among the biblical prophetic books, only Jonah and Haggai are narratives.

Even the description of this as "the *book* of Balaam, son of Beor" distinguishes it from most of the latter prophets, only one of which labels itself similarly: "The *book* of the vision of Nahum of Elkosh" (Nahum 1:1b); the remainder introduce themselves as "the words" or "vision" of a prophet. Nevertheless, whereas the texts from Mari and Neo-Assyria are written *reports* of prophecy, the Balaam text and the biblical prophetic books are *literary* prophecy (Lange, 2006). Literary prophecy sets oracles within a narrative (as in the story of Balaam) or juxtaposes them in such a way that they gain new meaning(s) by their association with one another, without giving any indication of their original context (Jeremias, 1996k).[20]

For example, Amos 3:11 issues this ominous forecast: "Thus says the Lord GOD: An adversary shall surround the land and strip you of your defense; and your strongholds shall be plundered." The statement of v. 12 is but loosely connected: "Thus says the LORD: As the shepherd rescues from the mouth of the lion two legs, or a piece of an ear, so shall the people of Israel who live in Samaria be rescued, with the corner of a couch and part of a bed." In contrast to the straightforward warning of calamity in v. 11, this is shot through with irony that undermines the claim of deliverance by likening any rescue to a shepherd who manages to "save" only fragments of a lamb from a lion.

These two warnings assume different backgrounds. The threat of v. 11 specifies the consequences resulting from v. 10's accusation that the people of Samaria have "stored up violence and robbery in their strongholds." The ironic imagery of v. 12, on the other hand, seems to counter an expectation that the LORD would deliver Israel whole from its enemies. There is no obvious or necessary connection between v. 12 and vv. 10–11, as is signaled also by the introductory "Thus says the LORD" at the head of each oracle. However, because the circumstances of these oracles are not reported, the literary context replaces whatever distinct contexts they may have had originally, forcing them to be read *as if* they were connected.

As a modern analogy, imagine reading the following report of an argument between a teenager and his parents: "Thus say the parents: 'Repeated lies will result in severe penalties.' Thus say the parents: 'The only party you're going to is the one we're arranging for you alone in your room!'"

These statements appear extracted from a larger conversation, or even different conversations, but give no indication of what those settings would have been. The reader extrapolates a relationship between them based on literary context: the threatened prohibition against attending parties must be related to lying (Jeremias, 2002). The sequence of oracles in Amos 3:10–12 involves a similar association of words, extracted from their situation.

Such associations, lacking context, enable a reader to apply statements to her situation, as if they were addressed directly to her (Floyd, 2006). For this reason, prophetic *books* are broader than a collection of oracles, involving extended passages sharing an overarching point of view and a distinctive voice. Producing these was not the expertise of speakers like prophets, but of scribes like Baruch, whom Jeremiah employed.

The Role of Scribes

Scribes were not mere copyists. Their role in society was to transmit and inculcate the traditions of their culture, as much by oral recitation as through writing (Carr, 2005). Their work involved not just preserving traditions but also revising and expanding them, making them as involved in the production of works as in preserving them (Carr, 2005). The famed Epic of Gilgamesh from ancient Mesopotamia offers a prime example of a work assembled from diverse stories and developed in multiple retellings over nearly 500 years, leaving concrete evidence of the modifications and expansions to the work over time (Tigay, 1985a).

A fundamental problem for us in comprehending this is that we are accustomed to mass-produced books. Gutenberg's invention of the printing press in the fifteenth century made the printed text the standard for preserving ideas and introduced notions of authorship and composition not imaginable in the ancient Near East, where no two copies of the same work were exactly the same. In fact, the gulf between our view of texts and that in the ancient world is so profound that speaking of scribes "writing and editing" entails modern assumptions (Kelber, 2007). What we call "editing" in the ancient world might better be understood by comparing "sampling" and "remixing" music today. Sampling involves reformulating a song so as to give it new meaning – as in Sean Diddy Combs's transformation of The Police's sinister "I'll Be Watching You" into the rap ballad "I'll Be Missing You" (or the incorporation of strains from Luther's "A Mighty Fortress" within the fourth movement of Mendelssohn's Symphony No. 5, the Reformation Symphony) – while remixing involves insinuating one's own contributions into an existing work, as with Sean Kingston's remix of Fergie's "Big Girls Don't Cry" (or Shakespeare's bawdy version of Ovid's story of Pyramus and Thisbe in *A Midsummer Night's Dream*). When we talk of the "editing" of the prophetic books, it is such creative sampling and remixing of traditions that we should imagine rather than the narrower revisions undertaken by a modern copy-editor. The fact that such sampling and remixing of traditions left a much deeper mark on these books than the mere correction of punctuation or the replacement of a word makes perceiving how editors shaped these works key to understanding them.

An important qualification to this comparison, however, is that while we can observe differences between the original and a sampling or remix, doing so in texts whose "originals" we do not possess is difficult. And even when we detect earlier and later layers within a book, we cannot fully trace the path back from the book's current form to an earlier stage. In part this is because, when editors do their best work, they create seamless joints between what they add and what they began with (Fox, 1991).

It is equally important to understand that while reading and writing are commonplace for us, in the largely pre-literate culture that produced the Bible, writing often bore a mysterious quality. Some cultures considered writing a gift of the gods (such as the Egyptian god Thoth or the Greek god Hermes). Chronicles' ascription of the writing of historical narratives to prophets (as in 1 Chr 29:29; 2 Chr 12:15, 13:22) is in this vein, but less likely suggests that prophets wrote books than that scribes viewed writing as analogous to prophecy (Floyd, 2000). The elevated role of scribes in ancient society helps account for such views.

Scribes were the learned class who wrote in service of the official institutions, chiefly the palace and the temple, although some likely operated from household workshops (Carr, 2005). Most would have been located in urban or administrative settings, which helps explain the preservation of oracles that promised support for Jerusalem and its ruler, oracles against foreign nations, and even oracles announcing judgment on the northern kingdom of Israel, since all the prophetic books were shaped in the southern state of Judah (Floyd, 2008). The need for educated scribes would have been great during the era of Judah's monarchy, from the eighth century on. However, the evidence for scribal activity virtually ceases after the fall of Jerusalem until well into the Persian period, when Jerusalem may have served as an administrative center for the Persians (Ben Zvi, 1997).

Such scribes played a significant role in shaping the prophetic books. The varied themes and perspectives in prophetic literature reflect diversity of thought among the scribes as much as among the prophets. We must understand that the writing of prophetic books would not have been a cottage industry; it was undertaken by a class of professionals who had their own concerns about the shape of society, viewed from fundamentally urban and aristocratic perspectives.

The most significant evidence of scribal involvement in the composition of the prophetic books comes from the **superscription** (Latin for "written above") to each book. At a minimum, these attest that someone other than the prophet shaped the way a book was introduced.

Biblical Superscriptions

When we open a modern book, we encounter a page bearing its title, the name of the author, and the publisher. The copyright date and other publication data stand on the reverse side. Not far behind is a preface via which the author discloses her/his reasons for writing and acknowledges help that he/she has received. Consequently, by the time we begin chapter 1, we know a good deal about the book's origins.

Many prophetic books provide what seems similar information: a title that includes, minimally, the prophet's name and some definition of what follows (such as, "the words of …"). Some superscriptions provide fuller information, as in the case of Zephaniah 1:1: "The word of the Lord that came to Zephaniah son of Cushi son of Gedaliah son of Amariah son of Hezekiah, in the days of King Josiah son of Amon of Judah." As unpromising as such skeletal information seems for thinking about the composition of these books, it enables some useful preliminary inferences.

First, four of the 15 books lack a superscription. Jonah 1:1 launches directly into its story: "Now the word of the Lord came to Jonah son of Amittai, saying …." Three other introductions that move directly into their body include a date:

> In the thirtieth year … the heavens were opened, and I saw visions of God. (Ezek 1:1)

> In the second year of King Darius … the word of the Lord came by the prophet Haggai to Zerubbabel son of Shealtiel, governor of Judah, and to Joshua son of Jehozadak, the high priest. (Hag 1:1)

> In the eighth month … the word of the Lord came to the prophet Zechariah son of Berechiah son of Iddo, saying … . (Zech 1:1)

In these three books similar introductions are prefixed to subsequent sets of oracles. Thus, the formula in 1:1 of each book introduces just its initial oracle, not the entire book.

Second, the remaining headings appear to have been composed in the latter stages of editing the books (Wahl, 1994). They are grammatically incomplete phrases that (with one minor exception) stand aloof from the body of the book and bear a clinical tone that vanishes once the prophet's words commence (Floyd, 1995).[21] Moreover, each superscription casts its prophet as a figure of the past, as is especially clear in those superscriptions that name the kings who reigned in the prophet's time (Isaiah, Jeremiah, Hosea, Amos, Micah, and Zephaniah). The prophet's words have been given a setting by someone who viewed the prophet as living in a bygone era (Floyd, 2000).[22]

Third, many superscriptions contain information deducible from the book's contents, as is the case with the superscription to Amos (1:1):

> The words of Amos, who was among the shepherds of Tekoa, which he saw concerning Israel in the days of King Uzziah of Judah and in the days of King Jeroboam son of Joash of Israel, two years before the earthquake.

Although some awkwardness in the sentence is palpable in English, the Hebrew is more clearly contorted, owing to the two relative clauses: "who was … which he saw." The statement about Amos being "among the shepherds" may have been deduced from Amos's description of himself as a herdsman in 7:14–15 (Blenkinsopp, 1996).

Equally peculiar is that the precisely phrased "two years before the earthquake" follows the broader time frame of "the days of" Uzziah and Jeroboam. An analogous statement might be "During the Presidency of Lyndon Johnson and the Secretariat of Leonid Brezhnev, two years before I entered college, I took a chemistry class." While it seems relevant to say that I took the class two years before I started college, it is unclear what Johnson and Brezhnev have to do with anything. The mention of rulers in Amos is similar: Uzziah is nowhere else mentioned in Amos, while Jeroboam appears only incidentally in 7:9–11. The image of an earthquake, on the other hand, figures prominently in Amos 9:1. Setting his words within the reigns of Jeroboam and Uzziah likely expanded a superscription that read, "The words of Amos, which he saw concerning Israel, two years before the earthquake" (Schmidt, 1965, 170). The designation of Amos working during the reign of Jeroboam is deducible from the mention of Jeroboam in Amos 7, while placing him during the reign of the southern king Uzziah involves a simple correlation of Jeroboam's reign with Uzziah's (see 2 Kings 15:1, where Azariah = Uzziah).

In fact, even the sequence "Uzziah … Jeroboam" is noteworthy, inasmuch as the king of Judah is mentioned before the king of Israel, despite the fact that Amos addressed the kingdom of Israel. The same phenomenon occurs in the superscription to Hosea (1:1):

> The word of the LORD that came to Hosea son of Beeri, in the days of Kings Uzziah, Jotham, Ahaz, and Hezekiah of Judah, and in the days of King Jeroboam son of Joash of Israel.

Given that Hosea was a northerner, listing the southern king first betrays that this superscription was written by a Judean scribe, like the superscription to Amos (Andersen and Freedman, 1989).

Thus, the six superscriptions that specify a prophet's era show signs of having been composed during the editing of the books.

The five remaining superscriptions contain only the prophet's name:

> The word of the LORD that came to Joel, son of Pethuel. (Joel 1:1)

> The vision of Obadiah. (Obad 1)

> An oracle concerning Nineveh. The book of the vision of Nahum of Elkosh. (Nah 1:1)

> The oracle that the prophet Habakkuk saw. (Hab 1:1)

> An oracle. The word of the LORD to Israel by Malachi. (Mal 1:1)

In contrast to the other prophetic books, none of these names appears again in its book (or the rest of the Bible), with the exception of Habakkuk, whose name stands in the superscription to the psalm that concludes the book (3:1). Without these superscriptions, we would lack names for the voices in the books.

The case of Malachi is especially noteworthy, since Hebrew names typically combine a divine name (such as "Lord") with another word, typically a verb. Whereas "Isaiah" means "the Lord saves" and "Ezekiel" means "God seizes," "Malachi" means "my messenger," making it more of a title than a name. And notably, *malachi* appears again at the start of chapter 3: "See, I am sending *my messenger* (*malachi*) to prepare the way before me ..." (3:1; my italics).

The rest of Malachi 1:1 is equally distinctive among the superscriptions: "An oracle. The word of the Lord to Israel by Malachi." The only similar superscriptions are Zechariah 9:1 – "An oracle. The word of the Lord against the land of Hadrach, and Damascus is where it will rest" – and 12:1 – "An oracle. The word of the Lord concerning Israel" (my translations).[23] Because Zechariah 9–13 lack features characteristic of Zechariah 1–8, take up entirely new topics, and reflect a different time period, they appear to be late addendums to that book. Malachi, with its similar superscription, constitutes something of a third addendum. Its distinction is that a scribe found it desirable to associate its four chapters with someone who bears, if not a name, at least a title, and so supplied "Malachi" to designate the speaker, based on the *malachi* of 3:1.

Deserving equal attention is Nahum 1:1, which begins with "An oracle concerning Nineveh." That title is followed by a second: "The book of the vision of Nahum of Elkosh." Curiously, the first title is similar to many headings for oracles that appear in Isaiah: "An oracle concerning Moab" (Isa 15:1), "An oracle concerning Damascus" (17:1), "An oracle concerning Egypt" (19:1; compare 21:1, 11, 13; 22:1; 23:1; 30:6). Isaiah 13:1 is the only case in which the name of the prophet is included: "The oracle concerning Babylon that Isaiah son of Amoz saw." However, chapters 13–14, which forecast the downfall of Babylon to the Medes (see especially 13:17), are likely from someone much later than Isaiah (Blenkinsopp, 1996). Correspondingly, while the oracles of the book Nahum give no reason to doubt (or confirm) the existence of a prophet by that name, 1:2's singular designation of this as a "book" suggests that a scribe was as concerned to attach a name to this collection as the one who attributed Isaiah 13 to Isaiah or the one who provided "Malachi" as the name for the voice in that book.

In summary, the superscriptions of the 15 prophets are varied, but show similar impulses. First, they share an interest in identifying collections of oracles with a single prophet, even to the point of creating a pseudonym. Second, the majority make the identity of the prophet concrete in some way, by identifying either his father, his city, the time when he worked, or some combination of these. Third, several show signs of being formed from information gleaned from the book. Fourth, each treats the prophet as a figure of the past. Finally, the majority of superscriptions are distinct from the body of the books they introduce, serving as headings.

How did these superscriptions arise? The Mari letters mention the name of the prophet and the circumstances under which the oracle was delivered. Neo-Assyrian records also identify the prophet's name. In both cases, the name provides a means of authenticating the oracle.[24] However, they do not preserve record of a set of oracles ascribed to a single prophet. And even though the superscription to the narrative about Balaam from Deir 'Allā is similar to those of the prophetic books, it does not introduce a collection of oracles from one prophet.

The most apt comparison for these superscriptions is the attribution of authorship in some Egyptian texts (Tucker, 1977). For instance, this superscription is prefixed to the Precepts of Ptah-hotep: "The Instruction of the Mayor and Vizier, Ptah-hotep, under the Majesty of the King of Upper and Lower Egypt; Izezi, living forever and ever" (Pritchard, 1969, 412). The attribution of the aphorisms in this document to an official of the 5th dynasty (circa 2200 BCE) is a literary device that casts "Ptah-hotep" as an "honorary author" for a collection of wise sayings, even as Proverbs 1:1 attributes the aphorisms of chapters 1–9 to Solomon, despite chapters 1–9 having been composed between 500 and 300 BCE, long after Solomon (Fox, 2000). This superscription enhanced the authority of the sayings by ascribing them to the figure reputed to have been the wisest ruler of Israel.

The same sort of strategy appears in a text from the royal library in Nineveh, dubbed "a catalogue of texts and authors" (Lambert, 1962). Because most Mesopotamian texts lack an attribution of authorship, the catalog sought to compensate by providing a list of titles, some consisting of the first line of the work, together with names of the authors, who are further identified by their vocation and/or the names of their parents (Tucker, 1977). The catalog lists the oldest texts first, assigning their authorship directly to the god Ea (god of crafts and wisdom), followed by the next oldest texts, attributed to legendary figures, and concluding with the youngest texts, credited to famous scholars. The interest seems to be in accounting for the authority of the texts based on their age and the pedigree of their authors (van der Toorn, 2007).

Given what we have seen of the superscriptions to the prophetic books, a similar motive likely lies behind them. A superscription's specification of a prophet does not designate an author for the book but identifies a mediator of the divine word. And if we recall the creation of a "name" for the last of the minor prophets, the likely late attribution of a collection of oracles to Nahum of Elkosh, and the assignment of Isaiah 13–14 to Isaiah of Jerusalem, it becomes clear that naming the authors or editors was less important than associating oracles with identifiable prophets.

This is not to say that all the attributions of the superscriptions are fabrications. There is no reason to doubt that the books of Amos and Hosea contain oracles traceable to those prophets. But the composition of these books, like other scribal compositions from the ancient Near East, involved the preservation *and* elaboration of the tradition to inculcate a certain understanding of Israel's life, drawing on traditions of prophetic oracles to illuminate the LORD's dealings with Israel in the past, the present, and the future (Ben Zvi, 2000b).

Looking Ahead

Although we could study these books in the sequence they appear in the Bible, the strong similarities in the superscriptions of the books of Hosea and Amos – whose prophets are dated the earliest and both of whom spoke to the people of the northern kingdom – make a good case for exploring them first. And because Micah (who addressed the south) is placed not long after Amos and Hosea, and his book's superscription is structured like theirs, we will next consider how that book gained its shape. There is also reason to include Zephaniah in this early survey, since some scholars claim that it underwent editing and development in circles allied with those that produced Hosea, Amos, and Micah.

Having begun with the minor prophets, it will be beneficial to stay with them, since they illustrate the types of material found in prophetic books. By the time we conclude looking at these 12 books, we will have a good sense of the types of literature that fall within the classification of "a prophetic book," preparing us to deal with the major prophets.

Notes

1. Although Daniel was frequently regarded as a prophet in early Judaism and Christianity, it constitutes a different sort of literature than the prophetic books and, thus, will not be treated in this book. For a discussion of its genre, see Collins (1998).
2. The rabbis recognized that this does not account for everything in these books, assigning the report of Joshua's death to Aaron's son Eliezer, and that of Eliezer to the priest Phineas, while reports of events after Samuel's death (1 Sam 25:1) were attributed to Gad the Seer and Nathan the prophet (*b. Baba Batra* 15a).
3. The rabbis dated Hosea before Isaiah and explained why his book follows Isaiah by saying that it was included with the smaller books to prevent it from being lost accidentally (*b. Baba Batra* 14b).
4. This story appears in Isaiah 38, which takes it (along with chapters 36–39) from a source similar to the one lying behind 2 Kings 20.
5. Chronicles lays less stress on the role of prophets as foretellers, even casting them as historians who record and expound the events of their day (Amit, 2006).
6. In early Judaism "prophetic" served as a term equivalent to "inspired," designating any literature regarded as originating after Moses and before Ezra, when prophets were seen as the unique mediums of divine communication (Barton, 1984).
7. For a summary of issues surrounding Israelite literacy see Young (1998a, 1998b).
8. Chapter 29 v. 1 does not explicitly say that Jeremiah wrote the letter himself; it only says that he "sent it" to the exiles in Babylon. Moreover, v. 3 reports that he sent it "by the hand of Elasah son of Shaphan and Gemariah son of Hilkiah, whom King Zedekiah of Judah sent to Babylon to King Nebuchadnezzar of Babylon." We hear of a "Gemariah son of Shaphan the scribe" in 36:10 (where the NRSV translates *sopher* with "secretary"), and quite likely the emissaries Zedekiah sent to Babylon in 29:3 were scribes. They may not only have conveyed Jeremiah's message but also taken it at Jeremiah's dictation, in accord with normal practice in antiquity, even among those who could write (Young, 1998a).
9. The order of this pair of events is odd, inasmuch as the inscription on a large tablet is given no explanation until the birth of the son. Most likely the inscription has been placed first to highlight Isaiah's public pronouncement of reassurance as a backdrop that makes the people's stubbornness stand out starkly (Barthel, 1997).
10. Just as the name "Emmanuel" of 7:14 is defined by a statement about the fate of a conspiracy against Judah (7:16), so the name assigned in 8:3 is explained by the failure of the capital cities of Aram and Israel. For a similar use of children's names, note the name of Isaiah's other son, Shear-Jashub ('a remnant shall return/repent'), in 7:3 and the assignment of names to Hosea's children in Hosea 1:2–9.
11. Compare the characterization of his oracles as "teaching" or "instruction" in 1:10, 5:24, and 30:9.

12.   The word translated "disciples" comes closer to the sense of "pupils." Throughout the ancient Near East, teachers were frequently referred to as "fathers" (less often "mothers") and their pupils as "children," most likely because the home was the primary educational institution (Carr, 2005). While these pupils could be a group of followers Isaiah had taken under his wing, his reference to "the children whom the LORD has given me" in v. 18 leaves open the possibility that these "pupils" were his own children, to whom he refers elsewhere (Isa 7:3, 8:3).

13.   Williamson's argument (1994, 99) that the language of 8:16–18 can only refer to a document is unconvincing, for it demands that metaphors must be marked, when they seldom are.

14.   The NRSV assumes the commonly accepted **emendation** of *la'ad* ("forever") to *le'ed* ("for a witness"), in accord with the majority of ancient translations.

15.   The speaker "could be a private person, but usually was a cultic functionary whose duties were specifically associated with such oracular activity" (Ellis, 1989, 135).

16.   For the application of this observation to the prophetic books see Becker (2004, 37).

17.   The turbulence surrounding Esarhaddon's ascension likely made the collection of these oracular validations of his rule politically useful (Nissinen, 2000).

18.   This translation and the next are from van der Toorn (2000a).

19.   However, the layout of the text indicates that the story was copied from a scroll (van der Toorn, 2007).

20.   As noted by Beck (2006), the closest analogy to this in the ancient world was the development of anthologies in Hellenistic culture. The blending of received epigrams with ones composed in imitation by the editors so as to address their own eras through their collections began in the second and first centuries BCE (Gutzwiller, 1998).

21.   "And he said" in Amos 1:2 relies on v. 1 for the identification of "he." However, v. 2 is not part of the body of the book, but a sort of "motto" given to it (found also in Joel 3:16 (Heb 4:16)) that was likely supplied only after the superscription was already prefixed to the book (Tucker, 1977).

22.   Ben Zvi (1999) rejects concluding from this view of the prophet as a historical figure that the book has been edited, objecting that this conclusion unjustifiably assumes that the books were initially written by the historical prophets. It is not necessary to assume that an editor has prefixed the superscription to a prophet's own words, only that (1) the words assume, on some level, a tradition of a prophet's words; (2) the book has been constructed by recipients of that tradition.

23.   The prepositions in "to Israel," "against the land," and "concerning Israel" are not as distinct in meaning in Hebrew as they appear in translation.

24.   Sometimes oracles are further authenticated by sending with the report a lock of hair, a fingernail, or the hem of the prophet's garment (Huffmon, 2000; Moran, 1969).

2

The Book of Hosea

In the pages to come ...

The prophets Hosea and Amos share two characteristics. First, both were active around the middle of the eighth century BCE, when the northern kingdom of Israel (the tribes that split from the southern state of Judah) were prospering from trade but also beginning to feel the hot breath of the Mesopotamian powerhouse, Assyria, as it began extending its rule westward. Also true of both prophets is that they addressed the northern kingdom, the only two among the prophets in these books to have done so.

The book of Hosea is probably best known for a salacious story about a promiscuous prophet's wife, called "a wife of whoredom" (1:2). This image, prominent in chapters 1–3, shapes the reader's comprehension of the entire book. An important question, however, is whether this theme is as crucial to the book as a whole as it seems. And tied to this question is that of how the book came to have such a characterization at the hand of its authors. To answer these questions, we will begin in a different place than the book leads us to: chapters 4–14. After exploring selected sections from those chapters we will return to 1–3 to understand their role in the book and what they can teach us about how the book was composed.

The book's **superscription** tells us nothing about Hosea beyond his name and that of his father. We can infer that Hosea was a citizen of the northern kingdom, since he mentions only its cities and addresses its affairs (see, for example, 5:8, 9:8). Nevertheless, the superscription introduces his words from a southern perspective, naming Judah's kings before those of Israel.

Prophetic Literature: From Oracles to Books, First Edition. Ronald L. Troxel.
© 2012 Ronald L. Troxel. Published 2012 by Blackwell Publishing Ltd.

The first three chapters are markedly different from the remainder of the book, in so far as they are steeped in the images of marriage, children, sexual promiscuity, and renewed relationships. Although promiscuity appears again occasionally in chapters 4–14, at times as a metaphor for the people's behavior (4:10–12, 15; 5:3; 6:10; 9:1) and sometimes designating the concrete behavior of individuals (4:13–14, 18), it never carries the resonances of marriage and family that unify chapters 1–3. Because the tightly focused discourse in chapters 1–3 sets the reader's perception of the book, it will be useful to read chapters 4–14 on their own terms first.[1]

Although chapters 4–14 do not have the thematic unity of 1–3 – in fact, their **oracles** are closer in form to the reports from Mari and Nineveh – they have their own structure. Chapters 12–14 are distinguished from 4–11 by unique phrases, such as the exclamation "I am the LORD your God since the land of Egypt" (my translation), which appears only in 12:9 and 13:4. At the same time, chapters 4–11 and 12–14 follow a similar progression – from accusation, to threat, to promise of restoration – suggesting that they were given shape by **scribes** with like inclinations (Wolff, 1974).

Chapters 4–11

While we cannot consider every section in chapters 4–11, we will explore two of its larger units. We will first probe the structure and themes of 4:1–6:6 for hints of how these chapters were composed, noting signs of modification and expansion that suggest how they have been shaped into a book, without speculating about what forms oracles might have had before their inclusion in their present contexts. These verses compose two literary units: 4:1–19 and 5:1–6:6.

4:1–19: The Culpability of Priests and People

Chapter 4 vv. 1–3 contain indications that they were formulated as a preface to chapters 4–11. The summons to "hear the word of the LORD" (4:1) marks the beginning of this unit. Although a similar call, "hear this," stands in 5:1, the phrase "the word of the LORD" occurs only in 4:1 and in the book's superscription (1:1). The only similar phrase in this section is "says the LORD," which stands at the end of this unit (11:11), creating a bookend to 4:1 (Jeremias, 1996c). The address of the listeners as "people [sons] of Israel" appears only here in chapters 4–14, but stands earlier, in 1:10, 11; 3:1, 4, 5.

The list of misdeeds in v. 2 focuses on social crimes: abuse of one's neighbor "breaks out" owing to lack of "loyalty" and "knowledge of God," terms that will be developed further in 4:6 and 6:4–6 (Wolff, 1974), and social misdeeds will be the focus in 6:9–10 and 7:1 (Jeremias, 1983). Such misdeeds corrupt the land and its inhabitants, including "the wild animals … the birds of the air … the fish of the sea" (v. 3), the three essential realms of land, sky, and sea (Ben Zvi, 2005b), anticipating the more targeted threats in 4:10, 8:7, and 9:4, 12, 14, 16. The distinct, formal introduction of v. 1 and the foreshadowing of themes and motifs in vv. 2–3 indicate that these verses were fashioned to serve as an introduction to chapters 4–11 (Jeremias, 1996c).

The Role of Inference in Reasoning about Composition

The Enlightenment introduced an innovative way to read texts: as products of particular times and cultures, with meanings that can be counter-intuitive for a modern reader. Following that agenda, biblical scholars developed methods for uncovering how biblical books were composed and why. One such method, **redaction criticism**, looks for signs of how scribes composed and shaped biblical books. Some scholars consider such study too speculative to be useful (Ben Zvi, 1996b; Floyd, 2000). However, any attempt to reconstruct a past activity (even in our own lives) involves speculation. So do attempts to understand the meaning(s) books would have held for their **implied audiences** (Ben Zvi, 2000b).[2] Reconstructing scribes' activity from features in the book is no more speculative than other types of reading, as long as we do not claim to be able to uncover all the building blocks they used in composing the book.

Redaction criticism relies on inferential reasoning, a common reading strategy (Yule and Brown, 1983). All communication involves occasional gaps between the communicator's assumptions and that of the audience, leaving the latter to infer how those gaps are to be bridged, if the speaker/author cannot be interviewed. Even when gaps are exacerbated by our lack of knowledge of the communicator's culture (see, for example, "raisin cakes" in Hosea 3:1 – a type of cultic offering rather than a snack bar!), it is possible to infer logical relationships, as long as there are no abrupt shifts in sentence structure or topics.

When faced with such abrupt shifts, however, inferring that these evince editorial activity is not a recourse of desperation, but a conclusion guided by our knowledge of how oracles were preserved at **Mari** and Nineveh, as well as how scribes composed and expanded literature in the ancient world (see especially the essays in Tigay, 1985b). The fact that scholars have proposed different accounts of editorial processes for a book no more discredits such study than the plethora of literary interpretations offered for a book discredits that approach. And in fact, discoveries of ancient texts have frequently given evidence that confirms previously drawn inferences about the editing of a book (Fox, 1991; Tov, 1985).

The remainder of chapter 4 addresses and describes various groups. Verses 4–6 accuse the priests of failing their duty to teach the people "knowledge"; vv. 7–11a describe a group that proliferates sin, which will result (ironically) in their inability to proliferate; vv. 11b–13b detail the people's "whorish" religious practices; vv. 13c–15 announce the exoneration of the addressees' daughters and daughters-in-law for illicit sexual liaisons, since the men are just as promiscuous; vv. 16–19 describe Israel's stubborn devotion to licentious religious practices. Despite sharing motifs, these verses bear marks of being composite.

For instance, vv. 4–6 *address* priests under the guise of an individual priest who has failed his duties, while vv. 7–8 *describe* a group whose growth is matched by its increasing exploitation of the people. Verse 9 provides a bridge to the theme of the people's profligate behavior via the phrase "like people, like priest": priest and commoner are equally guilty and face the same punishment. Verses 11–16 describe the behavior of "my people" as "whorish": using divining rods, sacrificing at inappropriate sites, and engaging in improper sexual liaisons. Not only does this list have no apparent connection with the charges against religious and civil leaders (vv. 4–8), but it also competes with them, since it lays blame directly at the people's feet, rather than the leaders' misbehavior. These competing attributions of guilt suggest that v. 9's equation of the people's crimes with those of the priests is a mortar mixed to join the accusations of vv. 11–16 with the chastisement of the priests in vv. 4–8 (Jeremias, 1996c).

A similar conclusion is apt for v. 10. The word translated "multiply" is the same one translated "break out" in v. 2 (part of the three verses constructed as an introduction), its only other appearance in Hosea. And nowhere else in the book does the phrase "forsake the LORD" appear,[3] and not even the verb translated "forsaken" appears again in Hosea, despite being common throughout the Bible. On the other hand, the motif of "forsaking the LORD," especially in tandem with "playing the whore," is at home in the book of Jeremiah (for example, Jer 1:16; 5:7, 19), whose language may have influenced Hosea's scribal authors (Jeremias, 1996c).

In short, vv. 4–6 and 7–8 likely juxtapose two oracles stressing the culpability of the priests, while vv. 9–11a are editorial links to bind those charges closely with the descriptions of the people's behavior, placed under the rubric of "whoredom" in vv. 11b–19 (Jeremias, 1983). This is similar to a musical medley, which places songs in a series (such as excerpts from a Broadway musical), joining them through changes from one key to another. Using that analogy, vv. 4–6 and 7–8 are two songs compatible enough to blend without changing key, while vv. 9–10 modulate to broader charges against the people in vv. 11–19.

Traces Left by Editors

An important criterion in detecting traces of editors is unique wording in the book under study. The issue is not just that the language is unique within the book, since any author can use a phrase only once. More significant is language characteristic of *another* composition and bearing its distinctive ideology. In this case, the combination of the phrase "forsake the LORD" and the concept of "whoring" or "going after other gods" bears the stamp of Jeremiah.

Within those verses, vv. 11b–14 appear composite, since 11b–13b (ending with "because their shade is good") *describe* the people's behavior, while vv. 13c–14 *address* Israelite men. Prior to this the only addressees have been the priests, who will be addressed again in 5:1. Verses 11b–13b and 13c–14, then, appear to be an amalgam of oracles, conjoined (via "therefore") because of their shared theme of illicit religious practices, characterized as "whoredom."

The concluding statement of v. 14 – "thus a people without understanding comes to ruin" – is a peculiar summation for the rejection of the fathers' outrage at the scurrilous behavior of their young women, especially since the people's lack of insight has not previously been a topic in the address. The statement has the character of a literary cap, casting an eye back to v. 11b's assertion that "wine and new wine take away understanding" and, ultimately, to v. 6's description of the people as "destroyed for lack of knowledge."

There is a notable shift between vv. 11–14 and vv. 16–19 (Jeremias, 1996c). Verse 15 interrupts the description of Israel's plight to voice a desire that Judah not be plagued by the same perversity. Given that Hosea was a native of the northern kingdom, which is the focus of every other statement of this chapter, v. 15 is like a thunderbolt from a blue sky. It is one of several statements in Hosea and Amos that make sense only as scribal asides to a Judean audience. The commands against pilgrimages to Gilgal or Beth-aven are meant to dissuade Judah from falling prey to Israel's sins (Jeremias, 1996i).

Verses 16–19 emphasize Israel's intransigence in a way that brings together themes from vv. 11b–14. The assertion that "a wind has wrapped them in its wings" (v. 19) drives home the point that Israel's perversity is so engrained that she is held captive by it.

The composition of this literary unit from distinct oracles, its literary mortar joints, and clear editorial additions show that it is the work of scribes who did more than just hand on reports of oracles.

5:1–6:6:   The Reality of Judgment

Chapter 5 opens with a call to hear, similar to 4:1, but its addressees include the priests, the "house of Israel," and the king's court, marking this as the start of a new unit. Whether the concluding statement of v. 2 – "but I will punish all of *them*" – involves a copyist's error for "all of *you*" (as suggested by Wolff, 1974) or has been deliberately modified to aid the transition to vv. 3–4, those next two verses turn from addressing the leaders to describing the people. They reprise motifs from chapter 4, particularly in their accusation that the people have "played the whore" (4:10, 12) and have been overcome by "a spirit of whoredom" (4:12), but distinctly emphasize that such behavior has made return to the LORD impossible. Moreover, vv. 5–7 describe the engrained perversity that alienates the LORD from the people in a way reminiscent of 4:16–19,[4] which emphasized the stubborn confirmation of Israel in its waywardness, inviting calamity (Jeremias, 1996c). This provides a prelude to the extended description of assaults on Israel's territory that opens in v. 8.

Chapter 5 v. 8 calls on an unnamed group to sound the alarm of war. From here through 7:16 we find reflections of the latter stages of the Syro-Ephraimite Crisis of 733–732 BCE (Alt, 1959). Most remarkably, the call to sound the alarm (vv. 8–9) is not directed to cities in the northern regions of Israel – where Assyria's armies attacked – but to cities on Israel's southern border with Judah. They foresee an attack by Judah that will bring about the north's destruction. The accent on the validity of this forecast ("I declare what is sure!") suggests that the thought of an attack that would imperil "all the tribes of Israel" was unthinkable to the prophet's contemporaries (Alt, 1959).

The "Syro-Ephraimite Crisis"

Just after the mid-eighth century, Israel was pressed by its northern neighbor, Aram, to join a coalition against Assyria. After the assassination of King Menahem of Israel, Aram installed Pekah as its puppet king in Samaria and pressed Judah to join them by threatening to replace its ruler, Ahaz, with a king supportive of their plot. Aram and Israel marched on Judah, placing it in a peril from which it extricated itself by appealing to Assyria for help. Assyria subjugated Aram, while Judah assisted in pacifying Israel. Pekah was assassinated and replaced by King Hoshea, who reinstated Israel's submission to Assyria (Miller and Hayes, 2006).

Verse 10 voices a different perspective. Whereas vv. 8–9 still anticipate the attack as "the day of punishment" – and thus an appropriate measure – v. 10 assumes that the action has already reached beyond the southern territories of v. 8, capturing land long held by Israelites (Alt, 1959), making Judah's rulers guilty of violating the boundaries (see Deut 27:17). The distinction between an attack considered justified and one judged excessive suggests that two oracles with different perspectives have been juxtaposed (Jeremias, 1996c).[5]

Verse 11's declaration of Ephraim as "oppressed, crushed" likewise assumes that calamity has already fallen, most likely the *Assyrian* attacks (Jeremias, 1983; Wolff, 1974). These are portrayed as apt punishment for Israel's determination "to go after vanity,"[6] perhaps an allusion to Israel's alliance with Aram (Alt, 1959). Accordingly, vv. 8–9, 10, and 11 address different circumstances but have been joined to characterize Hosea's message during this crisis (Jeremias, 1996c).

While the NRSV introduces v. 12 with "Therefore" to create a logical sequence between vv. 11 and 12, the Hebrew says simply, "*And* I am like pus [NRSV: maggots] to Ephraim and like rottenness to the house of Judah." The Lord's identification of himself with destructive forces is paralleled in v. 14 by his declaration that he is like a lion to Ephraim and the house of Judah. Between these, v. 13 asserts that Ephraim and Judah have recognized their plight and sought treatment, but in the wrong place: Ephraim appealed to "the great king," a title frequently used by Assyrian kings (Alt, 1959; compare Isa 36:4).[7] This tactic is faulted for failing to recognize the Lord's hand, leading him to plot a more devastating and direct attack: "I myself will tear and go away, I will carry off, and no one shall rescue" (v. 14).

"I will return," at the start of v. 15, translates a phrase using the same verb translated "[I will] go away" in v. 14. Even though the image has changed from a lion who takes away his captured and torn prey to that of the Lord withdrawing until they recognize their guilt, it is difficult to dissect this verse neatly from vv. 12–14, on the one hand, and 6:1–6, on the other; it introduces a new phase of the action begun in vv. 12–14 and anticipates an appeal to the Lord, as voiced in 6:1–3. Also uniting 6:1–3 with 5:12–15 is the people's confession that "it is [the Lord] who has torn," which plays on the Lord's resolve to "tear" them (5:14), while their belief that he will heal them echoes their request for healing from "the great king" (5:13) (Wolff, 1974). Their expectation is that the Lord will act quickly ("after two days") to rescue their life. The way vv. 1–3 reprise earlier language – "Let us return" (6:1) / "I will return" (5:15); "he has torn" (6:1) / "I will tear" (5:14); "he will heal" (6:1) / "to heal" (5:13) – suggests that the words attributed to the people have been created for this context by the scribe who joined these statements into a literary unit from the beginning.[8]

Despite the people's confession that the LORD has torn them and that healing comes from him, v. 4 finds their appeal inadequate, denigrating their piety by use of the same natural phenomena they used to voice their confidence in the LORD: they consider the LORD's appearance as certain as the dawn and the spring rain (v. 3), but he considers their love as ephemeral as a cloud that appears at dawn (Wolff, 1974). This criticism is poignant, but seems ill-defined, at least until we reach v. 6, which keys in on their claim to pursue "knowledge of the LORD" (v. 3), declaring it of the wrong sort, since it focuses on burnt offerings rather than "the knowledge of God" (v. 6; compare 4:6). Accordingly, sacrifices are set in antithesis to "steadfast love." Their confident expectation that the LORD can be counted on to appear as assuredly as the dawn and as fully as rain embodies a sort of mechanical conception of religious practice: "we offer sacrifice, and the LORD comes through." While the LORD implies healing for them if they return to him (v. 3), their notion of return as a mechanism is not the sort of "seeking" he requires.

In effect, vv. 1–6 portray the people's response to the summons to seek the LORD (5:15) as proving as inadequate as was Israel's diplomatic attempt to remedy its peril (5:13). The full explanation of this inadequacy is delayed until v. 6 in order to allow the connection between Israel's abysmal piety to be connected directly to its fate: "*Therefore* I have hewn them by the prophets, I have killed them by the words of my mouth" (v. 5; my italics). Thus, the answer to Israel's dilemma is not simply to identify the source of their trouble correctly, but to respond in accord with his demands delivered through the prophets, whose words have brought destruction upon them, owing to their disobedience.

What makes 5:12–6:6 remarkable is that its network of vocabulary ("heal," "tear," "I will go," "return," "know/knowledge of the LORD," "love") and its two-stage identification of Israel's inadequate responses to its predicament – the first a diplomatic solution (5:13), the second religious (6:4) – occupies a lengthy passage, in contrast to the juxtaposition of oracles in 5:8–11. This *literary* complexity points to this as a written composition from the outset, rather than a transcript of rhetoric delivered on a particular occasion (Jeremias, 1996c).

In sum, 4:1–6:6 consists of carefully arranged oracles, sometimes introduced with summary statements and connected by editorial links; but more often, oracles are simply juxtaposed, leaving readers to infer connections between them. Periodically, statements apply these oracles to a Judean audience. Accordingly, these chapters offer a literary representation of Hosea's message to be contemplated by those who read (and heard) it, as 14:10 admonishes (see below, p. 30).

11:12–12:14: Traditions about Jacob

Chapter 11 v. 12–chapter 12 v. 14 forms a self-contained unit, distinguished by its use of traditions about Israel's forefather Jacob. Chapter 12 vv. 3–4 view Israel's crimes through stories about Jacob supplanting his brother while still in the womb

(Gen 25:26, 27:36) and his struggle with a divine messenger (Gen 32:24–32). Both of these acts are cast as sinful, prefiguring the misdeeds of the nation that came to bear his name.

11:12–12:6:   Israel as Jacob Redivivus

The unit opens with the LORD's complaint about Ephraim's treatment of him: they surround him with lies and pursue fruitless alliances (11:12–12:1). By contrast, the assertion that the LORD levels "an indictment against *Judah*" (12:2; my italics) ill fits the context. Not only does it contrast with the approval of Judah's fidelity to "the Holy One" in 11:12, but vv. 3–4 contend that Jacob (the northern kingdom) merits punishment, while the remainder of the chapter recounts the north's misdeeds, without mentioning sins committed by Judah (Jeremias, 1983). Accordingly, there is a strong argument that "Israel" was the original term in v. 2 but was replaced with "Judah" by a scribe who wanted to state that Judah's fate mirrored the north's (Jeremias, 1983; Wolff, 1974).

The relationship of 12:5–6 to vv. 2–4 is initially obscure. Verse 5 is a **doxology**, formulated like Exodus 15:3 ("The LORD is a warrior; the LORD is his name") and similar to Amos 5:8 and 9:6, whose hymns end with "the LORD is his name." However, whereas those doxologies cap literary units, Hosea 12:5 stands prior to this unit's conclusion (v. 6).

Verse 6 presents its own problems, inasmuch as it addresses an unnamed individual, whereas earlier verses spoke of Ephraim (11:12–12:1) or Jacob (12:2–4).[9] Nevertheless, after v. 4's report that Jacob "wept and sought his favor," it is reasonable to assume that the remainder of that verse reports the response to Jacob, with "he" meaning God (or his angel): "he met him at Bethel, and there he spoke with him." In that case, v. 6 contains the words addressed to Jacob, while v. 5 is a scribe's clarification that the speaker is "the LORD God of hosts," similar to the way that "blessed be He" accompanies mention of the LORD in some contemporary religious speech. The title "the LORD God of hosts" appears nowhere else in Hosea and contrasts with the solitary "LORD" and "God" used otherwise in this context, thereby marking v. 5 as supplied by a later scribe (Jeremias, 1983).

12:7–9:   Ephraim, the Trader

Chapter 12 verse 7 opens a new section. At first glance, the description of "a trader, in whose hands are false balances" and who "loves to oppress," seems parallel to the recitation of Jacob's deeds in vv. 3–4. Verse 8 reveals the traitor to be Ephraim, at the same time that we learn the nature of his crime: he maintains his innocence by denying that his business practices have caused him to incur guilt. In response, the LORD asserts that he will make them live in tents again. This is not equivalent to sending them back to Egypt, although Hosea makes such a threat elsewhere (8:13, 9:3, 11:5). Although the temporal phrase "as in the days of the appointed festival" (v. 9) brings to mind a religious celebration, this is unlikely, since the phrase "as in the day(s) of" throughout Hosea introduces analogies to Israel's past (2:3, 15, 17; 9:9; compare 10:9). Accordingly, the Hebrew word (*moʿed*) is better translated "(as in the days of) meeting," a reference to Israel's meeting with the LORD in the wilderness (Wolff, 1974), elsewhere cited as the ideal era that will be relived after Israel is sent into the wilderness to renew her relationship to the LORD (2:14–15; compare 9:10). Accordingly, the vow to make Ephraim live in tents is not a consignment to punishment but implies the possibility of a fresh beginning, even as the counsel to Jacob was to "return to your God" (v. 6) (Jeremias, 1983).

The relationship between vv. 7–9 and vv. 2–6 is unclear. The naming of the trader as Ephraim breaks with the figure of Jacob, for it presumes Israel's life in its land rather than the period of the **patriarchs**. And whereas v. 6 reports a divine admonition to Jacob, v. 9 addresses the Ephraim of Hosea's day. Moreover, v. 6 assumes that the people hold their fate in their hands, while v. 9 assumes that the only course is for the LORD to eject them from their land. Given these different assumptions about the addressees, these two units can hardly belong to a single address.

Nevertheless, there are vocabulary links between vv. 7–9 and the preceding verses. The LORD's *finding* (NRSV: "met") of Jacob at Bethel (v. 4) is echoed in Ephraim's *finding* (NRSV: "gained") wealth, without any offense being *found* in him (v. 8), each time using the Hebrew verb *matsa'* (Jeremias, 1983). Similarly, the description of the trader as holding "*false* balances" (v. 7; my italics) reprises the same Hebrew word translated "deceit" in 11:12 (*mirmah*) (Wolff, 1974). There are, therefore, **catchwords** that might have made the juxtaposition of these oracles attractive.

12:10–13:   A Contrast of "Guarding"

Verse 10 continues divine speech, but abruptly shifts topic to the LORD's use of the prophets as agents, through whom he will now bring destruction. This motif of prophetic agents is reprised in v. 13, which refers to Israel's first prophet, Moses, sent to be Israel's guardian. But one is hard-pressed to detect how v. 11's disparaging the sacrifice of bulls in Gilgal flows from this or is connected to it (Mays, 1969b).

The job of clarifying the link between vv. 10–11 is accomplished by vv. 12–13, which effect a contrast by playing on a word. The recollection of Jacob's sojourn in Aram, where he acquired a wife by serving her father in lieu of a bride-price (Gen 29:15–30), includes the report "and for a wife he guarded sheep." The NRSV supplies "sheep" to fill out the sense, while the Hebrew reads simply, "for a wife he guarded." It is not that the Hebrew text denies that Jacob tended sheep, but that it focuses attention on the verb "guarded" as a play on words to emphasize the role of the LORD's prophet (Moses) as Israel's guard (v. 13):

12: Israel served for a wife,	and for a wife he guarded
13: By a prophet the LORD brought Israel up from Egypt,	and by a prophet he was guarded

The only differences between the final clauses are the active voice ("he guarded") versus passive ("he was guarded") and "wife" versus "prophet" (Jeremias, 1983).

Just as vv. 3–4 imply that Jacob's misdeeds foreshadowed those of Ephraim, so here the recollection of Jacob's "guarding" refers to Israel's crimes. In examining 4:13–14, we noted the implication that worship entailed sexual activity by men that made adulterous behavior by their daughters and daughters-in-law excusable. The elusive relationship between 12:11–13 finds its clarification in this light. The irony is that while the LORD provided a guard for Israel, the nation (in the mold of its ancestor Jacob) has devoted itself to activities in exchange for women. The people's refusal to heed the LORD's prophets (12:10) finds its precedent in Jacob's rebuff of the LORD by choosing to exercise his "guarding" in exchange for a woman. This crime is set over against the kind of "guard" the LORD has provided Israel in sending his prophets.

12:14:   The Final Word

The last verse of the chapter brings the implications of the indictment against Israel to bear, using a number of terms found only here in the book. For example, the expression "has given (bitter) offense" translates a Hebrew verb (*hik'is*) used often in the **Deuteronomistic History** (see the text box) to speak of offending the LORD, typically by worshipping other gods (see, for instance, Deut 4:25; 9:18; 1 Kings 14:9, 15; 2 Kings 17:11, 17).[10] The word translated "bitter" (*tamruriym*) appears in the Bible only here and in Jeremiah 6:26 and 31:15.

The Deuteronomistic History

In the middle of the twentieth century, a scholar named Martin Noth noticed that the books of Joshua through Judges showed varying degrees of affinity to the book of Deuteronomy. He posited that Deuteronomy, rather than being the final book of the **Torah**, was written as the start of a story of Israel's life from just before it crossed the Jordan until the fall of Judah to Babylon. Although Noth's idea of a history spanning Deuteronomy through Kings and written from a single perspective has been questioned, the web of phrases (such as "offending/provoking the LORD") and ideas in Deuteronomy and Kings is too strong to deny that they, and at least parts of Joshua, Judges, and Samuel, have been shaped by scribes using similar ideas and vocabulary. What is more, the book of Jeremiah seems to have been molded by scribes who utilized many of the same phrases and ideas, and traces of similar language and ideas are found sporadically throughout the prophetic books.

To this list of words found only here in Hosea we can add the designation of the LORD as Ephraim's "lord" (not the **Tetragrammaton**) and the word translated "insults" (*cherpah*). The fact that the verse is composed of expressions not used elsewhere in Hosea and that the phrase "pay him back" reprises the phrase translated "repay him" in v. 2 suggests that this verse was constructed to round off the chapter. The statement redefines Israel's misdeeds by calling them "insults" that deserve repayment, even as it speaks of Ephraim "giving bitter offense." While vv. 6 and 9 suggest the possibility of Israel returning or, in the worst case, being expelled to the wilderness, the rejection of the LORD's counsel through the prophets in the practice of illicit religion bars any possibility of Israel's rehabilitation (Jeremias, 1983).

In summary, chapter 12 contains sayings juxtaposed to create a message that builds to its conclusion. It forms a carefully constructed literary representation of Hosea's message that subsequent scribes made speak to their Judean readers by making clear that Judah faced a similar peril.

Chapter 14:   A Scribe's Hopeful Ending

The report of Ephraim's death at the outset of chapter 13 and the anticipation of Samaria's demise in its final verse provide a frame around it (Jeremias, 1983),[11] while the oracles packed within those boundaries are rife with images of death (Wolff, 1974). By the end of the chapter, any possibility of sparing Israel vanishes, leaving only the expectation that Samaria will "bear her guilt" (13:16), an assertion that is elaborated by three phrases describing the violent death of its inhabitants, voicing an expectation that the final siege of Samaria, already under way, will succeed (Jeremias, 1983).

In the wake of that expectation, chapter 14's summons for Israel to repent, accompanied by the dissipation of the LORD's anger and his promise to heal Israel's disloyalty, is breathtaking. Verses 1–3 call for repentance and provide the words the people should speak, while vv. 4–8 lay the groundwork for them to offer it.[12] Verses 1 and 8 address the people as a unit, under the names "Israel" and "Ephraim," providing a frame around the words of repentance and the LORD's preparation for their return (Jeremias, 1983).

These verses show familiarity with earlier parts of the book: talk of "stumbling" (v. 1) recalls 4:5 and 5:5; the rejection of idolatry (v. 3) echoes 8:3–6 and 13:2; the verb "heal" (v. 4) echoes 5:13, 6:1, and 7:1; and the plant metaphors for Israel in vv. 5–7 recall those of 9:10, 13, 16, and 10:1, 12–13 (Nogalski, 1993a). Most strikingly, talk of the LORD curing "their disloyalty" implies a reversal of the verdict of 11:7 that the people are "bent on *turning away* from me" (the same Hebrew word translated "disloyalty" in 14:4) (Jeremias, 1996d).

Strikingly, this chapter overturns conditions depicted in chapter 13: the withering of Israel as vegetation (13:15) is reversed by its flourishing in 14:5–7, cancelling the LORD's resolve to leave Israel in death's hands (13:14); whereas the LORD denied that he would have compassion on Israel's predicament (13:14), 14:3 confesses, "in you the orphan finds mercy"; while Israel is "like the dew that goes away early" (13:3), the LORD promises, "I will be like the dew to Israel" (14:5); the condemnation of the people worshipping cast images (13:2) finds its resolution in the proffered oath to "say no more 'Our God' to the work of our hands" (14:3) (Nogalski, 1993a). Moreover, 14:1 calls for repentance, whereas earlier chapters repeatedly stressed impediments to it (5:4, 6; 6:4; 7:2, 7, 13–14) (Jeremias, 1983),[13] and the LORD's promise to *cure* Israel's "disloyalty" so as to avert wrath (14:4) differs from his earlier vow not to bring wrath upon Israel *in spite of* their persistent disloyalty (11:7–9), with no expectation of change (Jeremias, 1996d).

One can also find here statements betraying a distinctly Judean viewpoint. The vow the people are told to utter, "we will not ride upon horses" (14:3), is a cardinal case. While Israel's trust in its military and its king for deliverance is belittled in 10:3, 13; 13:9–10, this denunciation of horses finds its only parallel in 1:7, widely recognized as a supplement by a Judean scribe (Jeremias, 1983; Mays, 1969b; Wolff, 1974). "Horses," as shorthand for military power, is characteristic of Isaiah (Isa 2:7; 30:16; 31:1, 3) and occurs in the (Judean) prophet Amos (2:15, 4:10). These marks, taken together, suggest that chapter 14 was composed in Judah after Israel's fall (Jeremias, 1996d).

The concluding verse is a distinctly formatted statement, the first two lines speaking of the "wise" and "discerning" understanding "these things," while the next lines define such wisdom as understanding the ways of the LORD. The implication is that the one who understands this book aright will agree with the LORD's judgments and deeds reported in it (Jeremias, 1983). Given the distinctive form and function of this pronouncement, it was likely appended by an early scribe as an endorsement of Hosea's words and a call to fellow scribes (the wise) to contemplate their meaning (Davies, 1996).

Summary: The Composition of Chapters 4–14

Our samples from chapters 4–14 allow us to see different types of editing that created the literary units. On the one hand, it is often apparent that oracles were juxtaposed and, at times, bound together with a sort of literary mortar mixed by the scribes (4:4–19). At other times, it is clear that a set of verses was a literary unit from the start (5:12–6:6). The introduction to the first unit (4:1–3) appears to have been specially fashioned for its role, and the whole of chapter 14 seems to have been supplied as a counterpoint to chapter 13. The concluding verse directs readers to invest effort so as to profit from the book. And occasionally we stumble across comments meant to help Judean readers apply statements to their own situation. These diverse features show that, whatever basis the book had in oracles delivered by a prophet named Hosea, the book itself is a composite literary work.

Chapters 1–3

The first three chapters provide a backdrop that colors the reader's perception of the book. This, however, proves to be a curious sleight of hand, for their themes and construction differ from chapters 4–14, especially in their use of narrative (chapters 1 and 3) and extended metaphor (chapter 2). These chapters were likely composed after 4–11 (Vielhauer, 2007).

Atypically for prophetic books, the initial unit (1:2–9) does not carry Hosea's words. Rather, it narrates commands to him about whom to marry and what to name his children. Following on that, 1:10–2:1 play off the names assigned to the children, reversing the threats those names embodied in 1:2–9.

Chapter 2's charges of infidelity and its appeals for reconciliation resonate with the command "Go, take for yourself a wife of whoredom and have children of whoredom" (1:2), spurring readers to assume that the unfaithful wife of chapter 2 is the same woman. And Hosea's talk of his relationship with an "adulteress" (3:1) reinforces the assumption that chapters 1–3 reflect Hosea's troubled family life (Andersen and Freedman, 1980). There are, however, several stumbling blocks to this reading.

First, the command to take "a wife of whoredom" (1:2) is given a rationale: "for the land commits great whoredom by forsaking the LORD." The command does not forecast marital shipwreck, but makes the marriage point beyond itself. Just as it would be inappropriate to read the children's names (or their designation as "children of whoredom") as revealing something of their character, so we misapply "wife of whoredom" if we assume that it describes the pedigree of Hosea's wife.

Second, and more important, chapters 1–3 do not tell a single story, but contain three different genres of literature. Chapter 1 vv. 2–9 are a prose narrative *about* Hosea, his wife (Gomer), and childbearing, central to which are divine orders for the children's names, with statements of their significance. Chapter 2 vv. 2–15 are poetry and concentrate on the infidelity of the "mother." While the speaker is the offended husband, it soon becomes apparent these are not Hosea's words. Certainly the proposal to "hedge up her way with thorns so that she cannot find her paths" (v. 6) anticipates action that no human could effect. Similarly, while one might imagine a husband asserting that his wife enjoyed his grain, wine, oil, silver, and gold, the qualification of those by "that *they* used for *Baal*" (v. 8; my italics) suggests a different sort of infidelity. Equally, the speaker's ability to project that he will take back "my grain *in its time* and my wine *in its season*" (v. 9) presupposes his power to frustrate a harvest. These features hint that the speaker is the LORD and lead to the conclusion that the chapter is a complex metaphor (Keefe, 2001) rather than a report of Hosea's troubled family life.

Chapter 3 is autobiographical prose. More specifically, it constitutes a **sign act**, a narrative in which a prophet is commanded to do something extraordinary to convey a message. For example, in Isaiah 20 the prophet is instructed to remove his sackcloth garment and his sandals, walking around naked and barefoot to signify that Egypt will be led away to Assyria disrobed. Such narratives do not address questions we might consider pertinent ("How did Isaiah's reputation fare?"). They focus on the message conveyed by an extraordinary act required of the prophet (Petersen, 1998).

Similarly, Hosea 3 answers none of the questions commonly asked, such as "Was this adulteress Gomer, either before or after her marriage to Hosea?" Themes in this chapter are actually closer to those in chapter 2 than chapter 1. The mention of "love" in 3:1 finds no parallel in chapter 1, but does in 2:5, 7, 10, 12, 13. Meanwhile, chapter 3 makes no mention of the children from chapter 1, which (conversely) lacks the actions the prophet is to take (3:2–3) that mirror the relationship between the LORD and Israel spoken of in 2:6–7, 14–15.

Given these differences and distinctions between chapters 1–3, they do not present a unified saga of the prophet's troubled marital life but propound the LORD's intent to restore Israel to himself (Ben Zvi, 2005b).

A common but increasingly rejected alternative is to read these chapters against a presumed rite in which the powers of fertility (Baal, the Canaanite thunderstorm deity, and Ashera/Astarte/Anat, goddesses of fertility) could be engaged through acts of **cultic** prostitution. Based on Herodotus' report of such practices in Mesopotamia, this reading posits that every woman was required to engage, as a rite of passage, in intercourse with men at the cultic site to invoke the gods and goddesses to be fertile themselves. Accordingly, the command to "take a wife of whoredom" would involve not seeking out a prostitute, but marrying *any* Israelite woman, since all would have submitted to this rite. The children born to her could be characterized as "children of whoredom" because they were conceived by people who participated in this "whorish" religion (Wolff, 1974).

Cultic Prostitution

The theory that prostitution was a sacral rite at shrines rests, in part, on the now discredited assumption that the Hebrew word *qedesha* refers to a "temple prostitute" (as the NRSV translates it in Hosea 4:14). Research has shown that words **cognate** to it in other Semitic languages designated temple officials whose varied duties did not entail sexual relations (Fisher, 1976). Even when this term stands alongside the Hebrew word that does mean "prostitute" (Gen 38:21–22; Deut 23:17–18; Hos 4:13–14), one need not understand these associations as references to cultic prostitutes (Keefe, 2001). What is more, neither biblical nor Mesopotamian literature combines the terms "sacred" and "prostitute" to designate such a class of women (Bird, 1989).

While Herodotus, Strabo, and Lucian speak (long after the fact) of ancient Mesopotamian sexual rites involving all women, such practices are without a trace in the voluminous literature from Mesopotamia (Yamauchi, 1973). Although we have reports of ritual intercourse of a priest and priestess to represent the bond between the deity and his consort, there is no evidence of a generalized system of sacral prostitution at temples (Fisher, 1976). Similarly, although references to sexual activity in connection with the cult in ancient Israel suggest that prostitution might have been used as a source of revenue (directly or indirectly) at cultic sites (van der Toorn, 1989), there is no evidence of the use of cultic prostitution to engage the powers of fertility (Keefe, 2001).

The use of this hypothesis to explain Hosea's language about taking "a wife of whoredom" and his metaphor of adulterous Israel is partly due to preoccupation with the question "What does it mean for Gomer to be called 'a wife of whoredom'?" That question elevates Gomer and her behavior to central issues, despite the fact Gomer and the children are merely mediums for a message, with no role as characters in their own right (Chaney, 2004).

If chapters 1–3 are not interested in the characters themselves, what is the meaning of the language about marriage, children, and whoredom? The verb translated "to play the whore" (2:5, 3:3) means to engage in sexual activity outside of marriage, whether before or during marriage (Bird, 1989). While terms for promiscuity occur 21 times in Hosea, terms that denote adultery specifically appear only six times. When terms for promiscuity (such as "play the whore") and adultery appear together, the term for promiscuity typically stands first (2:2, 4:13) (Chaney, 2004). Within chapters 1–3, words for promiscuity appear five times, and those for adultery occur twice. Even when 3:1 calls its woman an "adulteress," its first description of her is that she "has a lover."[14]

This emphasis on promiscuity is significant for understanding the perspective of the wronged husband in chapter 2, because in a patriarchal culture the question of promiscuity stirs concerns of paternity (Chaney, 2004). This explains why 1:2 closely links children and their mother with promiscuity (Bird, 1989) and why the children are implored to mediate with the mother: "Plead with your mother, plead – for she is not my wife, and I am not her husband" (2:2). It also accounts for why they can be condemned along with their mother as "children of whoredom" (2:4). The children are linked with the wife and not the husband.

There is, however, another reason for the close binding of the woman and her children in chapter 2. As noted earlier, the husband's proposed reprisals reveal that he is not a human, since he can threaten to "hedge up her way with thorns" (2:6) and take back the grain and wine "in its season" (2:9). Equally assumed in these phrases is a portrait of the woman: even though she is said to tread paths to visit her lovers (2:6–7) and to celebrate religious festivals (2:11, 13), she is more often portrayed as passive. She receives bread, water, wool, flax, oil, and drink (2:5, 8), and is blocked from finding her former lovers by her husband's devices (2:6–7). She is threatened with deprivation of the produce given her "to cover her nakedness," revealing her shame before her lovers (2:9–10), just as earlier she was threatened with exposure that would make her "like a wilderness" and turn her "into parched land" (2:3).

Equally noteworthy is how much these images have to do with agricultural processes and products. This hints at an identity for her in agreement with 1:2's command to take "a wife of whoredom" because "the land commits great whoredom by forsaking the LORD." While on one level "the land" represents the people (as also in Amos 7:10), on another level the image of the woman is precisely about the land (the ground) as the recipient of the produce she uses "to cover herself" (the foliage), so that being deprived of them leaves her exposed, suffering drought (2:3), and bereft like an untended forest (2:12).

Equally important is that the people's activity is highlighted. They are the ones who use the land's produce in service of the Baals (2:8) and celebrate the festivals, new moons, and Sabbaths (2:11). Likewise, it is the people who are reprimanded when the woman's adultery is decoded in her belief that her produce is pay from the "lovers" she pursues on "the festival days of the Baals" (2:12–13). The chapter is a deft interweaving of the land's mistaken identification of who provides its produce and an accusation of the people for holding such perceptions.[15]

These observations about chapters 1–3 provide a basis for inferences about their composition. First, 1:2–9 claims to provide a framework for understanding Hosea's message by reporting what "the LORD said *to* Hosea" when he "first spoke *through* Hosea" (my italics). Nevertheless, because the birth of three children assumes the passage of several years, and the report that the conception of Lo-ammi occurred only after his sister had been weaned (v. 8) adds at least two years to the timeline (Wolff, 1974), the characterization of this story as the *beginning* of the LORD's speech through Hosea is less a statement of chronology than an assertion that this narrative constitutes the archetype or model of Hosea's message.

Second, the narrative of naming the children is curious for what it omits. Prior to each report of Gomer conceiving, there is no statement that Hosea "knew/went in to his wife," the typical euphemisms for sexual relations (compare Gen 4:1, 17; 16:4; 38:18) (Ben Zvi, 2005b). The chapter is far more interested in the significance of the children's names than in the characters and their relationship to each other.

Third, the punishments announced via the names make no allusion to "whoredom." The name Jezreel, assigned the first son, gains its significance from "the blood of Jezreel," a reference to the bloody assassination of Queen Jezebel in the town of Jezreel during Jehu's *coup d'état* (2 Kings 9:30–37).[16] Consistently with this, the name Jezreel betokens the downfall of Jehu's dynasty and, with it, the political end of

Israel. Meanwhile, the name of the daughter, Lo-ruhamah, proclaims the end of pity for the house of Israel (v. 6), while the second son's name, Lo-ammi, signals the LORD's disowning of Israel (v. 9). The motif of whoredom appears nowhere in this narrative.

Equally striking is the abrupt shift of tenor in the final two verses of chapter 1 and the first verse of chapter 2. They foresee a voiding of the dire import of these names, which no longer refer to the children, but to Israel. Not only will their identity as "my people" be restored, but their new name, "children of the living God," will cancel the epithet "children of whoredom" (Wolff, 1974). The forecast that Israel will be composed of incalculable throngs reinstates the promise of innumerable progeny issued in Gen 22:17 and 32:12. The recapture of the land ("the place where" the LORD disavowed his relationship with them) will be achieved by Israel and Judah under a single leader. And the great reversals of the people's status (Ammi, "my people"; Ruhamah, "pitied") will be within a community that acknowledges each other as "brother" and "sister" (the Hebrew nouns are in the plural: "your brothers ... your sisters"). While this might reflect Hosea's reformulation of these names later in his work (Wolff, 1974), more likely they were added after the fall of both the northern and southern kingdoms (Jeremias, 1983).

In summary, 1:2–2:1 focuses on the assigned names, while the characterization of the wife and children as promiscuous (1:2) lies dormant until we reach chapter 2, where it is used as a metaphor for Israel that binds chapter 2 tightly with chapter 3, where Hosea's taking a promiscuous woman is fully developed. From that perspective, the "whoredom" motif of 1:2 is extraneous to its narrative. Although this creates a type of foreshadowing, the differences of genre in chapters 1–3 make it probable that these three chapters began life as separate literary units that were brought together by an editor. It was likely during that work that the description of Hosea's wife and children as promiscuous was inserted into 1:2 to integrate the first narrative with the oracles of chapter 2 and the narrative of chapter 3 (Jeremias, 1983).

The narrative of the children's names is exploited again at the end of chapter 2 (vv. 21–23), using a play on the name Jezreel ("God sows") to posit a hopeful future and reversing the force of Lo-ammi and Lo-ruhamah. These follow five verses that envision the successful restoration of Israel's relationship with the LORD (vv. 16–20). Verses 16–23 as a whole are a riff on the prospect of a restored relationship voiced in vv. 14–15.

Two features in vv. 16–23 betray them as scribal extrapolations from the LORD's plan to woo Israel in the wilderness in vv. 14–15. First, while vv. 2–15 consistently speak *about* the wife and the LORD's treatment of her, vv. 16–23 offer a confusion of pronouns, with the LORD addressing her directly in v. 16, speaking *of* her in v. 17, and returning to direct address in vv. 18–20. What is more, vv. 21–23 leave behind the image of the woman per se, with the LORD speaking of the fruitful conditions he will establish and forecasting his treatment of Jezreel, Lo-ammi, and Lo-ruhamah. A second mark that vv. 16–23 are supplements is their repeated use of "on that day" to refer to the distant future (vv. 16, 18, 21) (De Vries, 1995).[17] Verses 14–15 project the LORD's treatment of the unfaithful woman and her response, without removing those acts from the present. The phrase "on that day" occurs elsewhere in the book only in 1:5, which is widely recognized as a scribal expansion (Jeremias, 1983; Wolff, 1974).[18]

Admittedly, readers of the book were not expected to consider how these chapters came to be, but to use the integration of Hosea's family life with the threats and hopes as a lens through which to read the book as a whole (Ben Zvi, 2005b). Nevertheless, we can perceive that these chapters are an amalgam of the complex metaphor of infidelity, the use of a marital metaphor to envision Israel's rehabilitation, a narrative in which Hosea's children are assigned names as vehicles for announcing Israel's doom, and scribal extrapolations from each of these motifs that cycle through condemnation to restoration by the close of each chapter. The positioning of this theme at the outset of the book provides a guide for readers about how to comprehend the more diverse collections of oracles in 4–11 and 12–14. Not only are themes from chapters 1–3 picked up in those chapters, but the pattern of movement from judgment to restoration found in them is established in chapters 1–3. Given that pattern, the denunciations of Israel's life in chapters 4–14 can be comprehended as charges of infidelity, while the visions of a new era can be grasped as the LORD's persistent countervailing desire to renew his relationship with his wayward people.

Summary

Even though the book identifies its words with a prophet of mid-eighth century BCE Israel and carries marks of that era, it is not a compendium of Hosea's words to his compatriots, but an exposition of the meaning of Hosea's message. To take up a musical metaphor again, it is less a period piece than a series of orchestrations of and improvisations on oracles, biographical and autobiographical narratives, metaphorical descriptions of Israel's apostasy, and hymnic refrains. Through the arrangement of these materials scribes gave shape to a book showing that the north merits destruction at the hand of the Assyrians, but also announcing that punishment will not spell Israel's death. In the end, the LORD is more beholden to his love for Israel than to his anger over its unfaithfulness and will transform it into the faithful people he requires.

Notes

1. I concur that the only way to detect contributions of editors in forming the prophetic book is by understanding its **literary structure** (Becker, 2004; Sweeney, 1995, 1999). However, given my goals in an introductory book, I will postpone dealing with chapters 1–3 to show how the book is structured by disorienting the reader from what they have come to expect.
2. The "implied author" is equally a construct of the reader; many "implied authors" are possible (Ben Zvi, 1996b, 149).
3. The NRSV's "forsaking their God," in v. 12, is more literally translated, "they played the whore from beneath their God."
4. The final clause of v. 5 ("Judah also stumbles with them") is gratuitous and was likely added after Jerusalem fell (Jeremias, 1983; Wolff, 1974).
5. Positing a conversation between Hosea and his audience to explain the transition from vv. 8–9 to v. 10, Wolff (1974) introduces a sleight of hand.
6. The NRSV here justifiably follows the **Septuagint** (an ancient Greek translation), reading *shav'* in place of the MT's *tsav*, "command"(?).

7. Lying behind this is likely the capitulation to Assyria by Pekah's assassin and successor, Hoshea (2 Kings 15:30), as reported in the annals of the Assyrian king Tiglath-pileser III (Pritchard, 1969, 284).

8. Although it has been suggested that vv. 1–3 is a hymn of repentance used by priests in times of crisis (Wolff, 1974), these verses do not follow the pattern of such laments (such as Lam 3:40) and more closely approximate a resolve to conduct pilgrimage to a holy site, with an expectation of reward (compare Isa 2:3, 5) (Jeremias, 1983).

9. The only other addressee later in the chapter is Ephraim (vv. 8–10), and there the speaker is clearly marked: "I am the LORD your God" (v. 9).

10. It also occurs in statements about the people's offenses 11 times in Jeremiah (7:18, 19; 8:19; 11:17; 25:6; 25:7; 32:29, 30, 32; 44:3, 8), but only four times in such statements in other prophetic books (Ezek 8:17, 16:26; Isa 65:3; Hos 12:15).

11. Ben Zvi (2005b) argues that the reference to Israel's death as past in 13:1 suggests that it concludes the unit begun in 11:12. However, the opening words of 13:2, "and now they keep on sinning," would be a peculiar start to a new unit, especially since its subject is unspecified. Since the remainder of chapter 13 shows no connections with chapter 12, 13:1–16 constitutes a separate unit (Jeremias, 1983; Wolff, 1974).

12. While vv. 4–8 might seem to assume that the people have uttered the prayer, three observations preclude that (Jeremias, 1983). First, the LORD's words are not directed to Israel but are spoken about it. Second, the LORD's vow to "heal their disloyalty" (v. 4) suggests that he will effect the *preconditions* for their return. Third, the LORD's question to Ephraim about confusing him with idols (v. 8) presupposes that their "disloyalty" has not yet been cured.

13. The one seeming exception is 12:6. However, that address is directed to the patriarch Jacob, and the failure of Israel to heed the exhortation given him is underscored in the next two verses.

14. I thank Aaron West for pointing this out.

15. This does not demand dissociation of the LORD from the processes of fertility, in favor of a more transcendent deity (Keefe, 2001), but recognition of *which* deity invests the land with fertility.

16. Vielhauer's argument (2007, 139–40) that the condemnation of Jehu is a direct refutation of the positive evaluation of Jehu in 2 Kings 9–10 is unconvincing. There is, in fact, no good explanation for the oracle against Jehu if the core of chapter 1 was composed in Judah, weakening Vielhauer's argument that it was written in Judah to explain the northern kingdom's fall. In fact, Wolff's attribution of vv. 5 and 7 to a later editor (Wolff, 1974) and the identification of these as directed to a Judean audience (Jeremias, 1983) make it more likely that the passage had already received its fundamental shape before reaching Judah.

17. The distinctive role of this phrase in chapter 2 is further accented by "says the LORD," which follows it in vv. 16 and 21.

18. More difficult to detect is the relationship of vv. 14–15 to vv. 2–14. Admittedly, these bear a similarity to vv. 6–7, which Vielhauer (2007) considers secondary. However, Vielhauer rejects suggestions that vv. 6–7 might have been utilized in binding vv. 2–5 and 8–13 (Jeremias, 1983) by reasoning quite rigidly about what could be conceived as self-standing oracles. In the end, Vielhauer identifies only vv. 2a, 5b, and 10 as the core of vv. 2–13, attributing everything else to later expansions. He is much more confident about our ability to detect editorial layers than am I.

3

The Book of Amos

In the pages to come ...

While Amos, like Hosea, spoke to the northern kingdom, he was not a northerner. He was a resident of Tekoa, south of Jerusalem. The only location the book portrays him visiting is Bethel, just across Judah's border with Israel (see Map 2). And the report of his encounter with the priest at Bethel's **shrine** portrays him as quickly making himself unwelcome (7:10–17).

The book of Amos falls into three literary units: chapters 1–2, 3–6, and 7–9. Features in chapters 1–2 show that the unit was composed in tandem with chapters 7–9. The intervening chapters possess distinct characteristics, not closely connected with either 1–2 or 7–9. Nevertheless, the book is united by a set of **doxologies** and ends with a series of addenda forecasting a reversal of the harsh judgment Amos proclaims (9:7–15). This chapter will explore these units and how their constituent parts were shaped, and consider the literary relationship between the books of Amos and Hosea.

As noted in Chapter One, the earliest form of the **superscription** to Amos probably read, "The words of Amos, which he saw concerning Israel, two years before the earthquake." But even that seems composite. The phrase "the words of Amos, which he saw" contrasts with the characterization of the book of Hosea as "the word of the LORD that came to Hosea son of Beeri,"[1] since what Amos "sees" are his own words.[2] The closest parallels to "the words of Amos" are superscriptions like "the words of Agur son of Jakeh" (Prov 30:1), "the words of King Lemuel" (Prov 31:1), "the words of Qoheleth" (Eccl 1:1),[3] and "the words of Jeremiah son of Hilkiah" (Jer 1:1) (Paul, 1991).[4] Most likely, the earliest form of the book's superscription blended two originally distinct superscriptions (Wolff, 1977).[5] "The words of Amos" correlates

Prophetic Literature: From Oracles to Books, First Edition. Ronald L. Troxel.
© 2012 Ronald L. Troxel. Published 2012 by Blackwell Publishing Ltd.

well with the content of chapters 3–6, while "[that] which he saw two years before the earthquake" corresponds to the vision reports of chapters 7–9. We will explore the latter of these first, since tracing its structure and development is relatively straightforward.

7:1–9:10:   The Vision Reports

At the heart of chapters 7–9 are reports of visions Amos received,[6] the first four of which he introduces as "what the Lord GOD showed me" (7:1, 4, 7; 8:1), while the last he presents simply as what "I saw" (9:1), marking the culmination of the series of visions (Jeremias, 1996h). A narrative about Amos's confrontation with a priest at Bethel intervenes between the third and the fourth reports (7:10–17), and a series of **oracles** stands between the fourth and the fifth (8:3–14). By contrast, the first three reports appear in quick succession (7:1–9). The common structure among these raises suspicion that the fourth (8:1–2) once followed closely on the first three (Wolff, 1977).

Indeed, the first four vision reports form matched pairs. In the first pair Amos sees images of calamity: locusts eating "the latter growth" (7:1; the harvest stored as food for the year) and "a shower of fire" that devours "the great deep and … the land" (7:4; i.e., a drought). In both cases, he pleads that the LORD have pity on Jacob (7:2, 5), and the LORD relents (7:3, 6).

The third and fourth visions differ from the first pair in two ways. Rather than the prophet averting judgment with a plea, he is told in advance that the LORD "will never again pass them by" (7:8, 8:2). Second, rather than the meaning of each vision being transparent to the prophet, its meaning becomes clear only when the LORD explains it.

In the third vision (7:7–9) Amos sees the LORD standing beside a wall erected with the aid of a plumb line (a string with a weight attached, used to gauge whether a wall is perpendicular).[7] The LORD says that he will place that tool in the midst of the people, implying that he will measure their rectitude. However, given that the LORD rules out any possibility of a reprieve ("I will never again pass them by," v. 8), his "setting a plumb line in the midst of my people Israel" *presumes* that they merit judgment (Jeremias, 1998a).

Like the third vision, the fourth's image of a basket of summer fruit requires interpretation, and this one hinges on a play on words. The Hebrew word for "summer fruit" is *qayits*, based on which the LORD announces that an "end," Hebrew *qets*, "has come upon my people Israel" (8:2).[8] And as in the third vision, the LORD declares that he will no longer pass Israel by.

The arrangement of the first four visions in pairs leaves the fifth isolated. After reporting what he sees (9:1), Amos neither protests nor engages in dialogue. The details of the scene present a number of problems, but the envisioned menace is clear: the LORD topples the columns of the sanctuary onto people, after which he undertakes a vigorous campaign to annihilate those who survive. This scene envisions judgment in concrete form.

Considering these five visions as a unit yields several important observations. First, there is an implied progression. While in the first pair of reports Amos's intercessions successfully avert the foreseen danger, such intervention is ended in the second pair (the phrase "never again" presupposes a time when the LORD did "pass them by"). And while the second pair of visions anticipates judgment, that judgment takes form only in the fifth vision, making it the culmination of the series (Jeremias, 1996j).

Second, consistently with the passage of time implied in this series, the visions themselves assume different stages in the calendar year. The Gezer Calendar, a tablet from the tenth century BCE that lists the months of the year, titles the third month "latter growth" and the eighth month "summer fruit," using the same terms found in 7:1 and 8:1, respectively (Jeremias, 1998a). Like the story of the naming of the children in Hosea 1, these visions imply a passage of time that has been compressed in the literary presentation of the visions.

Third, there is an implied change in the role of the prophet in the course of these visions. In the first two, Amos stands with the people, pleading on their behalf. In the later visions, Amos simply witnesses what the LORD will do, with no power to alter it but implicitly assigned the task of forecasting a calamity that will touch the sanctuary itself (Jeremias, 1996m).

Fourth, these reports seem composed to be read in sequence, even if the fourth vision is now separated from the third by a narrative (7:10–17) and the fifth is postponed by a series of oracles (8:3–14). The paired structure of the first four visions, followed by their climax in the fifth, points to these having been fashioned as a unit, prior to the insertion of the narrative and the series of oracles.

Finally, it is important to observe the relationship between the notice in 1:1 that Amos spoke "two years before the earthquake" and the fifth vision. While the shaking of the thresholds and the consequent death of those present befits an earthquake, this vision does not merely predict a geological event; it forecasts the destruction of a temple, considered an emblem of divine protection (Mays, 1969a), as temples commonly were in the ancient world (compare Jer 7:1–4). The LORD's malicious pursuit of those not directly affected by the temple's collapse marks an end to the LORD's role as protector of the people (Jeremias, 1996h).

Accordingly, while 1:1 dates Amos's work to "two years before *the earthquake*," the look back to Amos's words in light of an earthquake the **scribe** knew implies that (in his view) Amos's visions began to be realized in that event (Jeremias, 1996j). However, this image of an earthquake appears even before chapter 9, within the book's initial two chapters, which bear additional marks that they are closely connected to chapters 7–9, more so than they are to chapters 3–6.

1:3–2:16: Oracles against the Nations

Just as the individual vision reports in 7:1–8, 8:1–2, and 9:1–4 have a shared literary structure, so do these oracles. Common to each are: the **messenger formula** ("thus says the LORD"), the **graduated numerical saying** ("for three … and for four"), a list of crimes committed, and a detailing of the consequent punishment. But there are also features shared by only five of these oracles, while distinctive features common to the other three indicate that they were added to the collection secondarily (Wolff, 1977).

The most notable distinction of the oracles against Tyre (1:9–10), Edom (1:11–12), and Judah (2:4–5) is the absence of the concluding formula "says the LORD." And those three share other peculiarities. A glance at the chart on pp. 40–41 reveals that whereas the oracles against Damascus, Gaza, the Ammonites, and Moab

---

The "Messenger Formula" and the "Graduated Numerical Saying"

Remarkably, the prophets seem to have developed little terminology of their own, having appropriated most of their forms of speech from other institutions (Jeremias, 1996k). For example, they based the phrase "Thus says the LORD" on the phrases messengers used to identify their words as those of the king who sent them: "Thus says the king of ——" (see, for example, 2 Kings 18:19). Accordingly, this phrase is called the messenger formula.

The graduated numerical saying ("for three crimes of … and for four") finds its home in the observations of "the wise" about how life works. Notice how Proverbs 30:15b–16 (for instance) uses the form "Three things are never satisfied; four never say, 'Enough': Sheol, the barren womb, the earth ever thirsty for water, and the fire that never says, 'Enough.'" The graduated numerical saying typically catalogs phenomena in this way.

---

offer succinct statements of the crimes committed and then detail the punishments, the oracles against Tyre, Edom, and Judah have more detailed lists of crimes but succinct and identically formulated statements of punishment. In fact, while the other oracles use simple sentences to denominate the crimes, these three list varying numbers of crimes in clauses conjoined by "and" (Schmidt, 1965).

On the other hand, the oracle against Israel enumerates "four transgressions," while the oracles against Damascus, Gaza, the Ammonites, and Moab specify only one crime. Significantly, the fourfold indictment in the oracle against Israel is structured as follows (Wolff, 1977), using my own translation to reflect more precisely the Hebrew word order:

1. because they sell the righteous for silver and the needy for a pair of sandals – they who trample the head of the poor … and the case of the poor they pervert;
2. and a man and his father go in to the same girl, so that my holy name is profaned;
3. and on garments taken in pledge they lay themselves down beside every altar;
4. and wine bought with fines they imposed they drink in the house of their God.

The initial clause states the crime, accompanied by a relative clause ("they who") to describe those who "sell the righteous for silver." Then follow three additional clauses, each headed by "and" plus a noun (once preceded by a preposition) – a word order that Hebrew uses to isolate clauses from each other, as opposed to clauses begun with "and" plus a verb, which are used to narrate a series of actions (as in the indictments of Tyre, Edom, and Judah).[9]

In effect, the single-count indictments of Damascus, Gaza, Ammon, and Moab, by citing only *one* crime, even though four are expected, set in relief the list of four crimes attributed to Israel (Jeremias, 1998a). Parallel to the progression in the vision reports of chapters 7–9, those four oracles lead to the indictment of Israel and the announcement of judgment through earthquake and irresistible attack (Jeremias, 1996h).

Place	Crimes	Punishments	"says LORD"
Damascus 1:3–5	they have threshed Gilead with threshing sledges of iron [1 crime]	I will send a fire on the house of Hazael, and it shall devour the strongholds of Ben-hadad. I will break the gate bars of Damascus, and cut off the inhabitants from the Valley of Aven, and the one who holds the scepter from Beth-eden; and the people of Aram shall go into **exile** to Kir	Present
Gaza 1:6–8	they carried into exile entire communities to hand them over to Edom [1 crime]	I will send a fire on the wall of Gaza, fire that shall devour its strongholds. I will cut off the inhabitants from Ashdod, and the one who holds the scepter from Ashkelon; I will turn my hand against Ekron, and the remnant of the Philistines shall perish	Present
Tyre 1:9–10	they delivered entire communities over to Edom and did not remember the covenant of kinship [2 crimes]	I will send a fire on the wall of Tyre, fire that shall devour its strongholds	–
Edom 1:11–12	he pursued his brother with the sword and cast off all pity; he maintained his anger perpetually, and kept his wrath forever [4 crimes]	I will send a fire on Teman, and it shall devour the strongholds of Bozrah	–
Ammon 1:13–15	they have ripped open pregnant women in Gilead in order to enlarge their territory [1 crime]	I will kindle a fire against the wall of Rabbah, fire that shall devour its strongholds, with shouting on the day of battle, with a storm on the day of the whirlwind; then their king shall go into exile, he and his officials together	Present

Moab 2:1–3	he burned to lime the bones of the king of Edom [1 crime]	I will send a fire on Moab, and it shall devour the strongholds of Kerioth, and Moab shall die amid uproar, amid shouting and the sound of the trumpet; I will cut off the ruler from its midst, and will kill all its officials with him	Present
Judah 2:4–5	they have rejected the law of the LORD, and have not kept his statutes, but they have been led astray by the same lies after which their ancestors walked [3 crimes]	I will send a fire on Judah, and it shall devour the strongholds of Jerusalem	–
Israel 2:6–16	because they sell the righteous for silver, and the needy for a pair of sandals – they who trample the head of the poor [*into the dust of the earth*[10]], and push the afflicted out of the way; father and son go in to the same girl, so that my holy name is profaned; they lay themselves down beside every altar on garments taken in pledge; and in the house of their God they drink wine bought with fines they imposed [1 crime]	So, I will press you down in your place, just as a cart presses down when it is full of sheaves. Flight shall perish from the swift, and the strong shall not retain their strength, nor shall the mighty save their lives; those who handle the bow shall not stand, and those who are swift of foot shall not save themselves, nor shall those who ride horses save their lives; and those who are stout of heart among the mighty shall flee away naked in that day	Present

Each oracle contains a phrase reminiscent of the visions: "I will not revoke the punishment" (more literally, "I will not turn it back"). The refusal to rescind punishment appears in no other prophet's oracles against foreign nations and is absent from Amos 3–6 (which also lack any intimation of an earthquake). It finds a parallel only in the LORD's vow never again to "pass them by" in Amos's third and fourth visions (7:8, 8:2) (Jeremias, 1996h).

Finally, within this set of oracles we find an allusion to an earthquake even clearer than in 9:1. Chapter 2 vv. 13–16 announce this punishment to Israel: "So, I will press you down in your place, just as a cart presses down when it is full of sheaves" (2:13). Although the verb translated "press down" appears only here in the Bible, languages akin to Hebrew (**Ugaritic** and Arabic) have the same word in their vocabulary, and the word shows up in later eras of Hebrew. Based on comparisons to these words, the verb translated "press you down" by the NRSV more likely means "I will break open." Consequently, the following phrase, "in your place" (Hebrew, "beneath you"), is best understood to mean "the ground beneath you" (Wolff, 1977). The comparison to the cart clarifies the imagery: the earth beneath their feet will break open as it does when the wheels of a heavily loaded cart incise ruts in the ground. The fact that vv. 14–16 then assert that judgment will be inescapable makes the parallel to 9:1–4 striking.

The structuring of both chapters 1–2 and 7–9 with five original components, their climactic portrayal of an earthquake as judgment, their denial of escape from calamity, and their claim that the LORD will not relent support the surmise that the oracles against the nations and the vision reports were fashioned in tandem (Jeremias, 1996h).

Expansions to the Oracles and the Visions

The Oracles against Tyre, Edom, and Judah

The similar characteristics of the oracles against Tyre, Edom, and Judah – especially the multiple but varied number of crimes, the brief and stylized punishment ("I shall send fire on … and it shall devour the strongholds"), and the lack of the concluding formula "says the LORD" – suggest that these were added secondarily (Schmidt, 1965).

The first clause of the Tyre oracle ("they delivered entire communities into exile"; my translation) closely resembles the charge leveled against Gaza in v. 6, but with a difference: while the Hebrew of v. 6 accuses the Philistines of uprooting an entire community to hand over to Edom, v. 9 accuses Tyre of handing over *previously* uprooted people (Paul, 1991). In other words, whereas Gaza is charged with shipping prisoners of war to Edom, Tyre is accused of slave trafficking. Parallel to this, Ezekiel 27:13 indicts Tyre for dealing in human cargo, while Joel 3:6 accuses Tyre, Sidon, and the region of the Philistines of having "sold the people of Judah and Jerusalem to the Greeks, removing them far from their own border." While it is plausible that Edom should have had an interest in acquiring slaves, given its large copper mining and smelting industries (Paul, 1991), and while there is no reason that they should not have looked to Tyre for such slaves, the storied career of Tyre as a trading hub of the Mediterranean makes connecting the criminality of its slave trade uniquely to its dealings with Edom peculiar.

Important in this connection is the qualification of Tyre's misdeed as failure to "remember the covenant of kinship" (literally, "covenant of brothers"). The similarity between forgetting "the covenant of brothers" and the impropriety of Edom viciously pursuing his "brother" (v. 11) prompts suspicions that the "covenant" Tyre violated involved the fraternal relationship between Israel and Edom (based on the tradition that their forefathers Jacob and Esau were twins born to Isaac and Rebecca, according to Genesis 25–33).[11] The fact that the word "brother" appears only in the oracles against Tyre and Edom within the book of Amos deepens this suspicion. We must, therefore, compare the oracle against Tyre with that against Edom.

The victim of Edom's violence is identified as its "brother." Although no other known voices in Amos's day level charges against Edom for violating its kinship with Israel, the prophet Obadiah, speaking in the wake of Jerusalem's destruction, does so: "for the slaughter and violence done to your brother Jacob, shame shall cover you, and you shall be cut off forever" (Obad 10). Despite occasional conflicts between Israel/Judah and Edom throughout their histories, only Obadiah's invective parallels the resentment voiced in Amos 1:11. Similarly, the only parallels we have to the caustic charges against Tyre in vv. 9–10 date from around 600 BCE onward (Ezek 26:1–28:19; Isa 23; Joel 3:4–8) (Wolff, 1977). Most likely, then, the oracles against both Tyre and Edom were products of that era.

The oracle against Judah (2:4–5) likely derives from the same age. While the other oracles cite either war crimes or (in the case of Israel) social injustices, the oracle against Judah condemns impiety: "they have rejected the law of the LORD, and have not kept his statutes, but they have been led astray by the same lies after which their ancestors walked" (v. 4). The association of rejection of the LORD's law with failure to keep "his statutes" appears in Deuteronomy 4:8 and 17:19 in reference to the prescriptions of Deuteronomy. Similarly, the talk of the people being "led astray by the same lies after which their ancestors walked" is allied with Deuteronomy's warnings against "following other gods" (Deut 6:14, 8:19) (Schmidt, 1965). In fact, this forecast of doom for Judah concurs with the verdict of 2 Kings that Judah suffered destruction owing to its rejection of the LORD's commandments, statutes, and law (2 Kings 17:13–20, 22:16–17). The greatest probability (especially given the likely dating of the Tyre and Edom oracles) is that the fire that would "devour the strongholds of Jerusalem" had already fallen (in the form of the Babylonian assault of 587) by the time this oracle was penned (Schmidt, 1965).

In short, the author of these three oracles applied Amos's words to his day, playing off the mention of Edom in the oracle against Gaza to create the oracles against Tyre and Edom and fashioning the oracle against Judah as a counterpart to the oracle against Israel (Jeremias, 1996i).

The Vision Reports

As noted earlier, an original set of five visions appears to have been expanded by insertions after visions three and four. Chapter 7 vv. 10–17 interrupts the first-person reports with a narrative of Amos's encounter with Amaziah, the priest of the sanctuary at Bethel, just north of Israel's border with Judah (see Map 2). While biographical accounts are common in the prophetic books, this is the only narrative in the book of Amos. There is no reason why the story could not have been cast in autobiographical form to accord with the first-person vision reports if it had been integral to them (Williamson, 1990).

Not surprisingly, readers have mined this narrative for information about Amos. Only here do we get an explicit indication of when he worked: the reign of Jeroboam (the superscription's dating of Amos to his era probably derives from this narrative). Only here is Amos identified as an agricultural entrepreneur from Tekoa, and only here are we told that Amos spoke at the sanctuary of Bethel.[12]

Nevertheless, this narrative does not exist to provide biographical information. Its focus is Amos's rebuff of the priest's attempt to control him by appealing to royal authority ("it is the king's sanctuary, and it is a temple of the kingdom") and dismissing him as just another prophet. Amos rejects Amaziah's directive to return to Judah, asserting that the LORD's commission of him trumps the priest's order. He reinforces his assertion that Israel will go into exile with a forecast of exile specifically for Amaziah, who has rejected not just Amos, but the LORD's word.

An important question is the relationship of v. 9 to this narrative. The third vision seems to conclude with 7:8, inasmuch as the LORD's pronouncement "I will never again pass them by" is paralleled at the end of the interpretation of the basket of summer fruit in 8:2. But this leaves v. 9 dangling between the third vision report and the narrative. Although v. 8's poetic structure makes v. 9 appear part of the third vision report, three elements within v. 9 attest its closer bond with the narrative. First, its term "sanctuary" appears again in the book only in v. 13 ("the king's sanctuary"). Second, Amaziah's prohibition of preaching against "the house of Isaac" (v. 16) employs a name that appears elsewhere only in v. 9. Third, vv. 9 and 11 are the book's only references to Jeroboam, and they both speak of a threat "by/with the sword." There is, however, a significant difference in how that threat is phrased.

According to v. 11, "Jeroboam will die by the sword." Verse 9, on the other hand, threatens his dynasty: "I will rise against the *house* of Jeroboam with the sword." According to 2 Kings 14:29, "Jeroboam slept with his ancestors, the kings of Israel; his son Zechariah succeeded him." The formula "slept with his ancestors" is used only when the deceased king's son follows him on the throne in an orderly succession (Bin-Nun, 1968). Assassinations, on the other hand, are duly noted, as in the case of Jeroboam's son Zechariah: "Shallum son of Jabesh conspired against him, and struck him down in public and killed him, and reigned in place of him" (2 Kings 15:10). Accordingly, the sword proved to be a threat not to Jeroboam himself (as v. 11 asserts), but to his heir (his "house"), as v. 9 forecasts.

In this light, v. 9 accomplishes two aims. First, it allows the threat Amaziah attributes to Amos to be heard as a threat against Jeroboam's heir, thereby enabling Amos's oracle to prove true. Second, its poetic structure connects the narrative to the third vision (Jeremias, 1998a). That connection is strengthened by additional verbal links between the narrative and the third vision, two of which are noteworthy.

First, the final phrase of the third vision, "I will *never again* pass them by" (v. 8), is echoed in Amaziah's prohibition "but *never again* prophesy at Bethel" (v. 13). Amaziah's dictum explains why the LORD refuses to hear further petitions (Utzschneider, 1988). The state's refusal ever again to hear the word of the LORD through Amos illuminates the LORD's resolve "never again" to pass them by (Jeremias, 1996m).

The second connection involves the LORD's declaration that he will place a plumb line "*in the midst of* my people Israel" (7:8) and Amaziah's report to the king that "Amos has conspired against you *in the midst of* the house of Israel" (v. 10). The first instance states the LORD's plan to manifest Israel's waywardness; the second places Amos within Israel (Jeremias, 1998a). Amos becomes the plumb line, while the rejection of the LORD's word through him reveals that the "wall" is crooked (Williamson, 1990). In these ways, the inserted narrative explicates the LORD's resolve at the end of the third vision report.

Turning to 8:3–14, two features indicate that this series of oracles was developed from oracles found elsewhere in the book to serve as a commentary on the fourth vision's proclamation that the Lord has planned an inescapable end for Israel. In 8:4–6 the addressees are characterized as those who "trample on the needy" (v. 4) and who buy "the poor for silver and the needy for a pair of sandals" (v. 6), phrases that echo 2:7 ("they who trample the head of the poor") and 2:6 ("they sell the righteous for silver and the needy for a pair of sandals"). But strikingly, in the midst of these charges of abusing the poor, v. 5 speaks of merchants impatiently awaiting the end of religious observances so that they can conduct fraudulent sales. Such complaints about unscrupulous business practices are common in the Bible (compare Prov. 11:1, 16:11; Deut. 25:13–15), but here are oddly sandwiched between references to abuse of the poor. Even if the poor suffered at the hands of unscrupulous vendors, this complaint is broader than "buying the poor" (v. 6). Most likely, the author of v. 5 appropriated the phrases from chapter 2 to form a frame around his complaint about unscrupulous businessmen (Jeremias, 1998a).[13]

The next unit, 8:7–8, shows similar relationships to other parts of the book. The introduction of an oath with the phrase "The Lord has sworn by the pride of Jacob" is both reminiscent of and at odds with 6:8: "The Lord God has sworn by himself (says the Lord, the God of hosts): I abhor the pride of Jacob and hate his strongholds; and I will deliver up the city and all that is in it." While elsewhere the Lord swears by his name (Jer 44:26), his holiness (Ps 89:35), or some other connection to his person, the prophet's portrayal of him taking an oath based on an evil he earlier inveighed against ("the pride of Jacob") is less likely than that the scribe who employed that phrase here interpreted it in light of its use elsewhere to refer to Israel's land (compare, for example, Ps. 47:4; Nah 2:2). What is more, the oath itself invokes an earthquake: "Shall not the land *tremble* on this account, and everyone mourn who lives in it, and all of it rise like the Nile, and be tossed about and sink again, like the Nile of Egypt?" (v. 8). The likening of the land trembling to the annual rise and fall of the Nile betokens geological undulations.

However, this is not the primary announcement of punishment in these verses. Verse 3, which forms a bridge to vv. 4–14 (Jeremias, 1996n), unpacks the forecast of an end to Israel by detailing a dearth of joy and a flowering of calamity: "'The songs of the temple shall become wailings in that day,' says the Lord God; 'the dead bodies shall be many, cast out in every place. Be silent!'" Strikingly, just as swearing by "the pride of Jacob" in v. 7 echoes 6:8, v. 3's images appear derived from 6:9–10:

> If ten people remain in one house, they shall die. And if a relative, one who burns the dead, shall take up the body to bring it out of the house, and shall say to someone in the innermost parts of the house, "Is anyone else with you?" the answer will come, "No." Then the relative shall say, "Hush! We must not mention the name of the Lord."

Chapter 8 v. 3 speaks of such a proliferation of bodies that, as in 6:10, it spurs a warning not to speak, out of fear that lamentation will invoke more death and devastation.

Evidence from these first several verses of the postscript to the fourth vision indicates, then, that they are a remix of language from Amos 2:6–7 and 6:8–10. The remaining verses of this addendum betray similar origins and show signs of having been attached to vv. 3–8 in stages, using an introductory formula referring to events that will take place in "that day" (vv. 9, 13) or in "coming days" (v. 11) (Jeremias, 1998a). This set of appendices teases out "the end" forecast in v. 2 (Jeremias, 1996n).

3:1–6:14:　The Words of Amos

Whereas the oracles against the nations and the vision reports were shaped as literary units, chapters 3–6 contain individual oracles closer in form to those from **Mari** and Nineveh. Like the oracles in Hosea 4–14, however, they have been woven into a literary structure rather than simply cataloged.

Immediately obvious is the refrain "Hear this word" in 3:1, 4:1, and 5:1. However, 4:1 differs slightly from the latter two, where "hear this word" is followed by a relative clause identifying the speaker and his audience: "that the Lord has spoken against you, O people of Israel" (3:1), "that I take up over you in lamentation, O house of Israel" (5:1) (Koch, 1976).[14] What is more, the name of the addressee in 3:1 ("people of Israel") sets the pattern for chapters 3–4 (3:1, 12; 4:5), while 5:1 establishes the addressee ("house of Israel") for chapters 5–6 (5:1, 4, 25; 6:1, 14) (Jeremias, 1998a). In short, then, the parallel phrases in 3:1 and 5:1 introduce sets of oracles, as indicated also by the doxology of 4:13 that concludes the first set (see further below).

These two sections are structured around distinctive themes or terms, as exemplified by the oracles against Samaria in 3:9–4:3. Chapter 3 vv. 9–11 constitute a judgment speech (a statement of crimes, followed by "therefore" and the imposition of punishment), with "strongholds" being its common motif (twice in v. 9, once in v. 10, and once in v. 11) (Melugin, 1978). In vv. 13–15, a call to unnamed hearers to "hear and testify against the house of Jacob," reinforced by a notice that this is divine speech, is followed by a vow to punish Israel's sins on the "altars of Bethel" and to destroy luxurious houses. Chapter 4 v. 1 calls on the "cows of Bashan" (the wealthy, complacent women of Samaria) to hear the Lord's oath that they will be deported by their enemies (vv. 2–3). The abrupt changes in subject matter or tone and the repeated assertions of divine speech (3:10, 11, 12, 13, 15; 4:2, 3) point to these statements having once existed independently, but having been conjoined owing to their focus on Samaria (3:9, 12; 4:1), mentioned elsewhere only at 6:1 and 8:14 (Jeremias, 1998a). Together, they attack the wealthy of Samaria (Jeremias, 1988).

There is also a hint that at least one of these oracles is, itself, composite. Chapter 3 v. 12, introduced by the messenger formula, seems to stand on its own, since v. 13's call to listen is followed by a new assertion that this is divine speech ("says the Lord God, the God of hosts"). Moreover, while v. 14, which is connected with v. 13, speaks of destroying altars, in v. 15 the Lord vows to destroy winter house and summer house, houses of ivory, and numerous houses, the dwellings of the wealthy. Verse 12 placed a similar focus on the wealthy, sarcastically promising the sort of "rescue" a shepherd can make of a sheep attacked by a beast: a corner of a couch or part of a bed (6:4 makes it clear that "bed" and "couch" are items of furniture common among the wealthy). Quite likely, vv. 12 and 15 once formed a single oracle, denying any escape to Samaria's wealthy, who could expect only the destruction of their property. A scribe spliced vv. 13–14 into that unit, so as to include the cultic site of Bethel in the forecast of destruction (Jeremias, 1998a), much as a musical medley can begin and end with the same song, creating bookends around another song.

Other verses modify Amos's words still more distinctly, as in 3:3–8. Verses 3–6 pose a series of rhetorical questions based on cause-and-effect relationships, most frequently with the effect stated first (for example, v. 3, "Do two walk together unless they have made an appointment?"). At the conclusion of these questions, Amos points to the inference he wants his audience to draw: "The lion has roared; who will not fear? The Lord GOD has spoken; who can but prophesy?" (v. 8). In other words, those who dispute Amos's credentials should infer the cause from its effect: Amos prophesies because he has heard the LORD speak.

In the midst of these rhetorical questions stands a peculiar statement. Following the implied claim (via a question) that standing behind disaster that befalls a city is the LORD's action (v. 6), v. 7 claims, "Surely the Lord GOD does nothing, without revealing his secret to his servants the prophets." This is the only declarative sentence in 3:3–8, and the relationship between its clauses is not cause and effect ("without revealing his secret" designates a precondition for such action, not its cause). Additionally, in the book of Amos the phrase "his servants the prophets" appears only here. It is most at home in 2 Kings (9:7; 17:13, 23; 21:10; 24:2) and Jeremiah (7:25, 26:5, 29:19, 35:15, 44:4), where it regularly makes the point that the LORD has sent fair warning through the prophets, exactly what Amos 3:7 claims. Verse 6 asserts that disaster befalls a city because the LORD initiates it, but says nothing about the people being forewarned. Verse 7 insinuates that notion by stating that the LORD reveals his plans to "his servants, the prophets" (Jeremias, 1998a).

In short, chapters 3–6 are no haphazard collection. By the selection, arrangement, and expansion of oracles attributed to Amos, scribes synthesized and re-presented his preaching. Rather than situating oracles within their historical and social context, they arranged and elaborated them literarily to convey a message for their audience (Jeremias, 1988).

The Interspersed Hymns (1:2, 4:13, 5:8, 9:5–6)

The use of a lion roaring as an image for the LORD's speech in 3:8 is anticipated by 1:2: "The LORD roars from Zion, and utters his voice from Jerusalem ...." In contrast to the articulate divine speech Amos references in 3:8, however, 1:2 describes the LORD's roar as withering Carmel, a place proverbial for its vegetation (see, for example, Isa 35:2; Nah 1:4). The idea that this roaring emanates from Zion betrays a Judean perspective, since it assumes that Jerusalem is the LORD's dwelling, something that would not have been conceded in the northern kingdom (Mays, 1969a). Moreover, this verse's construction is similar to language found in the Psalms that anticipates the LORD's action originating from Zion (Ps 20:2; 53:6, 128:5, 134:3). It is not the lone example of **liturgical** material incorporated into the book.

Doxologies (statements praising the deity's virtues or deeds) appear at several points in Amos. After 4:12 summons Israel to "prepare to meet your God," v. 13 extols him: "For lo, the one who forms the mountains, creates the wind, reveals his thoughts to mortals, makes the morning darkness, and treads on the heights of the earth – the LORD, the God of hosts, is his name!" This creates a fitting capstone for chapters 3–4.

Amos 5:6–7 exhort the people to seek the LORD, warning that he will attack them with fire, assaulting those who derail righteousness. Verse 8 then extols his deeds: "The one who made the Pleiades and Orion, and turns deep darkness into the morning, and darkens the day into night, who calls for the waters of the sea, and pours them out on the surface of the earth, the LORD is his name." Such acts underscore the LORD's power to effect the judgment threatened in vv. 6–7 (Wolff, 1977).

The book's final doxology (9:5–6) elaborates on the shaking of the thresholds by evoking the image of the Nile's undulations.[15] Not only are these verses formed according to the pattern typical for doxologies (introducing descriptions with the phrase "[he] who …"), but this hymn concludes exactly like 5:8: "who calls for the waters of the sea, and pours them out upon the surface of the earth, the LORD is his name." These similarities signal that 4:13, 5:8, and 9:5–6 derive from a single hymn (Jeremias, 1998a). The fact that they have been distributed across the second and third sections of the book, and that another hymnic unit has been prefixed to the book, suggests that these were supplied to help unify chapters 1–9. Indeed, 9:5–6 likely ended the book at one time, and vv. 7–15 were appended later (Jeremias, 1998a).

The liturgically styled announcement of the LORD's roar issuing from Zion in 1:2 may have been supplied by the same hand that introduced these doxologies. In effect, it serves to identify the ultimate voice of the oracles against the nations that follow (Wolff, 1977).

9:7–15: Judgment Reconceived and Reversed

The utter and inescapable destruction foreseen in 9:1–4 and underscored by the doxology of vv. 5–6 elicited two supplementary comments in vv. 7–10. The first (vv. 7–8) relativizes Israel's status by likening the LORD's deliverance of them from Egypt to his extraction of the Philistines and the Arameans from their prior locations. Correlatively, a nation's rectitude is the LORD's sole criterion for judgment; no nation holds a privileged position.

The succeeding caveat turns the logic of that pronouncement on its head: "except that I will not utterly destroy the house of Jacob, says the LORD" (v. 8). Its intent becomes apparent in the metaphor of Israel being funneled through a sieve that permits no pebble to fall to the ground, an image v. 10 explains as separating out Israel's sinners for punishment. Consequently, Israel's vulnerability to judgment, said to be equal to that of other nations, is softened by a scribe who directs punishment solely at its sinners (Nogalski, 1993a).

Still more surprising is the forecast of glorious days ahead, formulated in two stages, the first introduced with "on that day" (v. 11), the second with "the time is surely coming" (v. 13). While talk of rebuilding "the booth of David that is fallen" might anticipate the restoration of the Davidic dynasty, the phrase "booth of David" would be the only occurrence of this metaphor (for which "house of David" is characteristic),[16] while repairing its "breaches" (broken sections of the walls) and rebuilding its "ruins" fit better the image of a city. What seems in view, therefore, is the rebuilding of the city of David to once again rule over Edom and the nations (Wolff, 1977). Most notably, the anticipation of Jerusalem's reconstruction presupposes its fall, so that these verses could have been added only after the Babylonian assault of 587.[17]

The second stage of this expansion, which foresees agricultural prosperity and the rebuilding of ruined cities, likewise reflects the devastation of 587, while the divine promise that "they shall never again be plucked up out of the land that I have given them" (v. 15) presupposes that Judeans have been expatriated.

In any event, these forecasts of glorious days ahead have moved beyond even the limitation of judgment to the wicked in vv. 9–10. Judgment of no kind is anticipated; only the flourishing of Jerusalem, its cities, and its crops lies ahead. These expectations are distinct from the stress on the inescapability of judgment in the rest of the book.

Amos and Hosea

One final factor must be taken into consideration in thinking about the composition of Amos: its relationship to the book of Hosea.[18]

Hosea 8:11–13 bewail Ephraim's multiplication of altars that turned into occasions for sinning, at the same time that they considered the LORD's own instruction foreign, prompting him to reject their sacrifices and vow punishment for their sins. Even though the initial charge of v. 14 ("Israel has forgotten his Maker") is consistent with the preceding verses, the evidence of this "forgetting" – the building of palaces – is not, since it departs from the topic of sacrifices. The foreignness of the bulk of v. 14 becomes even more obvious when the charge is extended to Judah: "and Judah has multiplied fortified cities." Evidence that this concern for the building of fortified cities has been imported from Amos is in the LORD's final declaration, "I will send a fire upon his cities, and it shall devour his strongholds." Those words derive from the punishments slated for the nations in Amos 1:4, 7, 10, 12, 14, and 2:2, 5 (Jeremias, 1996a).

Hosea 11:10 is equally distinct from its context, which otherwise is a coherent series of statements by the LORD. Even when v. 11 speaks of the people "trembling like birds" from Egypt and Assyria, the concluding statement, "I will return them to their home," makes clear that the LORD is the speaker. Although v. 10 speaks similarly of the LORD's children "trembling from the west," the first statements of the verse speak of him in the third person: "They shall go after the LORD, who roars like a lion." The LORD describes himself as a lion in Hosea 5:14 and 13:7, but the Hebrew word in 11:10 (*'aryeh*) differs from the one used in those passages (*shachal*) and yet is the same one used in Amos 3:4 and 8, where it is accompanied by the verb translated "roar" here – a verb that is otherwise absent from Hosea. Accordingly, v. 10 bears the marks of an addition minted under the influence of the book of Amos (Jeremias, 1983).

The most important feature of each of these verses is that they are distinguishable from their context, which means they were inserted after their host passages had been composed (Jeremias, 1996a). By contrast, language borrowed from Hosea in the book of Amos is often woven into the book's fabric.

For example, we have seen that Amos 7:9 was formed as a bridge between the third vision and the narrative of 7:10–17, using terms from that narrative. There are, nevertheless, distinctive features in its terms. While Amaziah prohibits Amos from preaching against "the *house* of Isaac" (v. 16), v. 9 forecasts the desolation of "the *high places* of Isaac," a term designating (illegitimate) sacred shrines that appears nowhere else in Amos. Allied with this is that while Amaziah refers to Bethel as "the king's sanctuary" (singular), v. 9 foresees the destruction of "the sanctuaries [plural] of

Israel." Anticipation of the destruction of Israel's sanctuaries and high places is found in Hosea 10:8, and the association of the crown's guilt with the cult is characteristic of Hosea (Jeremias, 1996a). Thus, the editorial bridge of Amos 7:9 shows influence from the book of Hosea.

We have noted that Amos 3:1, with its summons to "the people of Israel" to "hear this word," serves as the heading for chapters 3–4. We can now add that terms in 3:2 betray the influence of Hosea. For instance, while Amos disparages the people because "they do not *know* how to do right" (3:10) and the LORD claims to "know how many are your transgressions, and how many are your sins" (5:12), the verb "know" bears a very different meaning in 3:2: "You only have I *known* of all the families of the earth." The use of "know" in the sense of "choose" occurs nowhere else in Amos, while Israel's unique standing among the nations (assumed here) is disputed in 9:7 (Jeremias, 1996b). It is Hosea who assumes divine election of Israel (11:1) and uses the verb "know" to express it in 13:4.[19]

Similarly, although Amos has much to say about "transgressions" (1:3, 6, 13; 2:1, 6; 4:4; 5:12), only in 3:2 do we find the term "iniquity," a term that is commonplace in Hosea (4:8; 5:5; 7:1; 8:13; 9:7, 9; 10:10; 12:8; 13:12) (Jeremias, 1996b).[20] There is, therefore, reason to think that 3:1–2 are a heading an editor created for chapters 3–4 (Jeremias, 1988), with v. 2 betraying influence from Hosea's language (Jeremias, 1996a).

These examples suggest that the shapers of the book of Amos were influenced by Hosea, while themes from Amos appear in Hosea only as later additions. The book of Hosea was probably well formed by the time it came under the influence of traditions from Amos, whereas the process of creating the book of Amos was influenced by knowledge of Hosea (Jeremias, 1996a).

Summary

The resultant message(s) of the book of Amos can hardly be equated with the preaching of Amos himself. Whatever features hint that Amos's conviction of the inevitability of judgment dawned on him over time (as suggested by the contrast between the effectiveness of his petitions in the first pair of visions and the LORD's vow of "never again" in the second set), the overall tenor of the book's message is doom. Only the concluding verses raise hopes for a bright future in the restoration of Jerusalem's and Judah's fortunes and the securing of its people within their borders. But even that is possible only because those who supplied those verses already knew of a day when the people were subjected to the sort of ruin that Amos forecast.

The book has been created from previously existing literary units, two of which show signs of having been formulated in tandem (chapters 1–2 and 7–9) and the other (chapters 3–6) shows a carefully organized structure that weaves oracles into literary units, without regard for their original setting. The expansions in chapters 1–2 and 7–9 give evidence of interpretations to which these already elaborated units were subjected, while the inserted doxologies evince an attempt to weld these three units into a whole.

While the reliance on traditions of Amos's words – much like the reliance on traditions of Hosea's words in that book – suggests that literate contemporaries considered (at least) some oracles worth recording (whether as a report to authorities or out of esteem for the prophet), the way the oracles address the fall of Samaria and play out its implications for Judah shows that the confirmation given them by Samaria's collapse became the prime impetus for the creation of this book, like that of Hosea (Jeremias, 2002). What is more, the evident mutual influence between the books of Amos and Hosea indicates that their elaboration as literary works was carried out, in some measure, in overlapping circles of scribes.

Notes

1. Compare the superscription to Habakkuk as "the oracle that the prophet Habakkuk saw" (Hab 1:1), or the epitome of Isaiah's oracles as "the word that Isaiah son of Amoz saw concerning Judah and Jerusalem" (Isa 2:1).
2. Even the superscription to the book of Isaiah as "the vision of Isaiah son of Amoz, which he saw concerning Judah and Jerusalem" (1:1) differs from Amos seeing his own words.
3. "Qoheleth" is a transliteration of the Hebrew word often translated "the teacher," as it is in the NRSV.
4. In the case of Jeremiah 1, the prophet himself is later described as one "to whom the word of the LORD came" (1:2), but this is kept separate from the phrase "the words of Jeremiah."
5. Such a blend of titles is hardly unimaginable. A financial institution in my area, the People's State Bank, recently merged with another, the Community Bank, resulting in the composite name, the People's Community Bank. Even if the compound superscription to the book of Amos was formed less elegantly, the process is analogous.
6. See below, pp. 143–144, on the evaluation of such vision reports.
7. Since medieval times, the third vision has been understood as involving a "plumb line," based on the supposition that the Hebrew word 'anak means "iron," designating the weight at the end of the string. However, Landsberger (1965) demonstrated that Hebrew 'anak is **cognate** with a term in the ancient language of **Akkadian** that means "tin." Since tin is hardly a suitable weight for a plumb line, alternative interpretations were proposed. Recently, however, compelling arguments have rehabilitated the image of the plumb line on several grounds. On the one hand, we cannot be entirely certain that "tin" and "lead" were always distinguished in the **ancient Near East** (Williamson, 1990). Second, Zechariah 4:10 describes Zerubbabel, leading the rebuilding of Jerusalem's temple, as having in his hand "a tin stone." Even though some scholars have suggested that Zechariah's "tin stone" played a role different from a "plumb line," the earliest translations of the Hebrew Bible (into Greek, Syriac, Aramaic, and Latin) understood it as a plumb line, just as they did the metal referred to in Amos's third vision. While these observations do not vanquish doubt, identifying this as a plumb line seems less speculative than other suggestions (see Williamson, 1990, 105–110).
8. The image is not significant in and of itself, but forms the basis for a wordplay, just as in Jeremiah 1:11–12 the prophet reports seeing "a branch of an almond tree (*shaqed*)," based on which the LORD announces, "I am watching (*shoqed*) over my word to perform it."
9. The four accusations fall under the rubrics of: (1) sponsoring indentured servitude and harsh treatment of the poor, (2) breaches of sexual taboos, (3) violation of safeguards for those working off debt (compare Deut 24:12), and (4) the misuse of funds for one's own benefit.
10. This phrase, syntactically problematic in Hebrew, is widely considered an addition meant to clarify in what sense "the head of the poor" was trampled (Wolff, 1977, 133).

11. While the use of "brothers" for partners in compacts throughout the ancient Near East has spurred suggestions that the "covenant of brothers" refers to commercial or political treaties (Paul, 1991), a complaint about failing to abide by such an agreement would reduce Tyre's crime to a contractual lapse. That raises the question why only Edom is mentioned, given what we know of Tyre's large network of trading partners. Therefore, it seems that the covenant with brothers was more specific than a generic agreement.

12. Even more has been deduced from Amos's refutation of Amaziah's assumption that he is a card-carrying prophet ("I am not prophet or *the son of a prophet*" – i.e., a member of a prophetic band, 1 Kings 20:35; 2 Kings 2:3). The classic question posed has been, is Amos denying that he is a prophet or that he is a prophet for hire of the sort Amaziah supposes?

13. The reuse of previously existing material in reverse order from its earlier appearance is a well recognized practice of ancient scribes, known as "Zeidel's law" (see Beentjes, 1982).

14. Chapter 4 v. 1, on the other hand, addresses its audience directly: "hear this word, you cows of Bashan." As becomes clear, this metaphor refers to the wealthy women of Samaria, the city addressed in the two preceding oracles (3:9–11, 12–15) as a subset of the "people of Israel."

15. The reference to the rising and falling of the Nile in 9:5 reprises the reference to the rise and fall of the Nile in 8:8, but with noteworthy differences. While in 9:5 the Nile's undulations are linked with the just-stated responses of the earth to the LORD's touch, the Nile imagery in 8:8 is only loosely connected with the oath of v. 7. What is more, its format as a rhetorical question is equivalent to an assertion that the quaking of the earth is inescapable, given the people's misdeeds. In this sense, 8:8 simply takes for granted the earthquake 1:1 cites, making its use of image of the undulating Nile gratuitous and suggesting that it was borrowed from 9:5 to foreshadow 9:1–4 (Jeremias, 1996j).

16. Isaiah 1:8 describes *Jerusalem* standing "like a booth in a vineyard."

17. There is no forecast of its fall in the book that would prepare the way for this expectation.

18. Needless to say, the fact that Amos and Hosea addressed the northern kingdom in roughly the same era has spurred comparisons of the two prophets. The oldest layer of oracles in Hosea (2:4–15, 4:4–5:7) presumes the same prosperity and lack of Assyrian influence assumed by Amos (Jeremias, 1983, 1998a). Nevertheless, whereas Amos inveighs repeatedly against the social injustices of his day, Hosea mentions such issues infrequently and typically as matters associated with cultic places (see, for example, Hos 5:1) (Jeremias, 1996i). This disparity is so striking that some have sought to find in Hosea's talk of promiscuity a code for a royal socio-economic program (Chaney, 2004) or, more generally, the political conditions that the royal cult authorized (Keefe, 2001). However, these proposals require imposing an understanding of Hosea 1–3 from the outside. We must interpret Hosea's imagery from within the book's concern for the proper conception of religion, including the attacks on the bull image at Bethel (8:5–6, 10:5–6, 13:2). Strikingly, the bull image never arises in Amos, even though he spoke at Bethel (Jeremias, 1996i). Such differences likely have their roots in the different foci of the prophets themselves (Jeremias, 1998a).

19. This assumes reading "knew," based on the **MT**, rather than "fed," as found in the Greek and Syriac translations, which the NRSV follows (see Jeremias, 1996b, 44).

20. The Hebrew term *'avon* is variously translated by the NRSV: "guilt" (Hos 5:5), "corruption" (Hos 7:1), " offence" (Hos 12:8).

4

The Book of Micah

In the pages to come …

The book's superscription places Micah in the late eighth century BCE, a half-century after Hosea and Amos and in the same era as Isaiah. In contrast to Isaiah, he is not from Judah's capital, Jerusalem, but from a village in Judah's western hinterlands, near the border with the Philistines.

The book comprises four sections, distinct in themes and tenor. Chapters 1–3 condemn the Judean aristocracy, telling them that they will receive their just deserts when Jerusalem falls. Chapters 4–5 envision the restoration of glory to Israel and Jerusalem once **exiled** Judeans return home. Meanwhile, the nations will submit to the LORD either willingly or by force. In 6:1–7:7 the vision of a bright future for Jerusalem disappears, replaced with renewed condemnation of Judean society. In 7:8–20, the fourth section, the prophet's voice vanishes, along with the complaints of the preceding section. The voice is now that of the community, speaking in a style at home in the book of Psalms, asking for the LORD's vindication and expressing confidence that he will act. The challenge in this chapter will be to consider how these diverse sections form a single prophetic book.

The distinct characteristics of the book's sections obscure bonds by which **scribes** have united them. For example, while chapters 4–5 focus on the restoration of Jerusalem and its people, 2:12–13 already anticipate the gathering of all "the survivors of Israel," with the LORD ruling over them as a single flock. Moreover, while 7:8–20 are composed of hymns like those found in the Psalms, fragments of hymns appear already in 1:3–4 and 5:9. Equally, the summons of the world's peoples to hear the

Prophetic Literature: From Oracles to Books, First Edition. Ronald L. Troxel.
© 2012 Ronald L. Troxel. Published 2012 by Blackwell Publishing Ltd.

LORD's witness against them from his temple (1:2), followed by a description of the LORD wreaking havoc on the earth (1:3–4), is reprised in the LORD's threat of "vengeance on the nations that did not obey" (5:15) and the forecast of the earth's desolation for the crimes of its inhabitants (7:13) (Jeremias, 1971). Accordingly, there is reason to characterize the book as a network of motifs that reflect a complex compositional process (Jeremias, 1971; Wolff, 1990).

Given that the call of all peoples to hear the LORD's witness in 1:2 is matched by the LORD's vow in 5:15 to "execute vengeance on the nations that did not obey [Hebrew: hear]," 1:2–5:15 form a unit (Wolff, 1990). We will begin with chapters 4–5, whose **oracles** are the easiest to demarcate and describe. From there we will return to 1:2–3:12 to see how those verses form a whole with chapters 4–5, despite their differences. Afterwards we will consider the role of chapter 7 in the book (with a side glance at chapter 6).

Chapters 4–5:   Mixed Oracles concerning Israel and the Nations

Drawing conclusions about how these chapters were composed requires noting their sharp twists and turns. The scene of the nations flocking to Jerusalem for the LORD's instruction and arbitration (4:1–4) and Israel being restored under his rule (4:5–8) is followed by anticipation of Jerusalem's destruction and exile (4:9–10), its victory over nations arrayed against it (4:11–13), its gain of a new leader from David's home town (5:1–6), its victory over its foes (5:7–9), and its purification from earlier flaws (5:10–14). In counterpoint to the nations' willing submission in 4:1–4, the unit concludes with the LORD vowing vengeance against "nations that did not obey" (5:15).

The abrupt contrasts in these chapters (Israel's exile and defeat versus victory over the nations; the nations' voluntary submission to the LORD versus their forced submission) makes for a convoluted scenario, comprising three subunits: (1) the vision of an era when the nations and Israel will be united under the LORD's rule in Jerusalem (4:1–8); (2) Israel's current crises that will result in triumph over its foes (4:9–5:9); (3) a purge of Israel's wickedness, along with the LORD's wreaking vengeance on the nations "that did not obey" (5:10–15). Surveying the course of these units will provide a foundation for considering their composition.

4:1–8:   Israel and the Nations Will Unite under the LORD's Rule

The image of Jerusalem as the world's center, to which all nations come for instruction and from which the LORD rules them (4:1–4), stands in sharp contrast to the forecast of 3:9–12 that Zion/Jerusalem would become a plowed field and a heap of stones. A buffer between these is provided by the introductory phrase "in days to come" (4:1), a phrase that projects this scenario into the future, without presupposing some sort of an "end of the world" (van der Ploeg, 1972). Nevertheless, the remarkable changes forecast for Jerusalem and the world merit labeling this scene **eschatological** (see the text box).[1]

What Is Eschatology?

Although "eschatology" is often popularly defined as forecasts of "the end of the world," passages typically labeled eschatological are not really concerned with an end, but with the transformation of life on the other side of a decisive turning point (Collins, 1974). Accordingly, "eschatology" is better defined as a vision of a new era, introduced by God, that definitively realizes the loftiest divine and/or human ideals (Troxel, 2008).

That description of an ideal future is interrupted, however, by a group confessing their resolve to "walk in the name of the LORD our God forever and ever" (v. 5). The speakers posit a contrast between themselves and others: even if the peoples will one day aspire to walk in the *ways* of the LORD (v. 2), the speakers vow to "walk in his *name*."[2] Their present confession of the LORD as "*our* God" distinguishes them from the nations, who walk "each in the name of *its* god," making it clear that the speakers represent Israel. The prospect of submission to the LORD one day being commonplace among the nations is a spur for Israel to set itself apart by vowing its submission now.

On the other hand, the renewed focus on the future in vv. 6–8 describes what will happen to Israel in the era when the nations submit. The LORD's equation of "those who have been driven away" with "those whom I have afflicted" (v. 6) implies that it is he who "drove them away." Now the LORD promises to consolidate them into a strong nation he will rule (v. 7), the reverse image of his pacifying strong nations so that they do not threaten each other (vv. 3–4). The upshot is not Israel's domination of the nations, but its parallel submission to the LORD's rule. Jerusalem's recovery of sovereignty (v. 8) is not tantamount to mastery over the nations, but provides the foundation for the LORD's rule over both Israel and the nations.

4:9–5:9:   Israel's Current Crisis Will End in Triumph

In contrast to the image of peoples pacified under the LORD's rule, 4:9–5:9 spotlights Jerusalem's current distress in scenes introduced by "now" (4:9, 10, 11; 5:1), with each scenario moving to a resolution of the crisis.

At first glance, 4:9 seems to chide the people for too dire a view of their circumstances, as if they should take courage from the fact that they still have a king and counselor. And yet, v. 10's exhortation to "writhe" confirms that their anguish is justified, suggesting that v. 9 merely mocks their predicament. The comparison of the city to "a woman in labor" is a cliché for suffering (e.g., Isa 13:8, 42:14; Jer 6:24, 22:23, 30:6), here caused by imminent deportation. Nevertheless, the concluding lines soften the severity by designating Babylon as the very place where "the LORD will redeem you from the hands of your enemies."

These two verses betray much about their origins. The assumption that Jerusalem would be deported to Babylon does not fit the era of Micah in the late eighth century and would have been unintelligible for his audience. Judah faced threats from Assyria, not Babylon, whose glory days (the era of Hammurabi, in the nineteenth century) had long since passed. Prospects of exile in Babylon would have been as inscrutable in Micah's day as a forecast today that Britain will conquer the United States. The threat of Babylonian exile became intelligible only after 604 BCE, when a new group in Babylon wielded power in the region. Verses 9–10 date to that era.

The next scene introduced by "now" (vv. 11–13) is sharply dissonant with the last, inasmuch as it presumes that Jerusalem is surrounded by enemies that it can whip handily. These nations' devotion of their treasure "to the LORD of the whole earth" (v. 13) is due not to their mass conversion but to the LORD equipping Zion to "beat in pieces many peoples," having assembled the nations "as sheaves" for Jerusalem to thresh (v. 12). In contrast to the earlier portrayal of Jerusalem's attraction of the peoples to receive the LORD's instruction and rule, the city now serves as an ambush for the nations, who are forced into subjugation. This sharp difference suggests that vv. 11–13 are of a different origin than vv. 9–10, although the role they assign to Jerusalem is equally at odds with the destroyed city envisioned in 3:12.

Chapter 5 opens with a new scene of distress, introduced again with "now."[3] Jerusalem is again under a siege, spoken of as an assault on "the ruler of Israel." Verse 2's expectation of a new ruler suggests that this "ruler of Israel" is either the LORD (Ben Zvi, 2000a) or Jerusalem itself. The promise of a new ruler is addressed to Bethlehem of Ephrathah, recalling David's pedigree as "the son of an Ephrathite of Bethlehem" (1 Sam 17:12). The description of "his origin" as "from of old, from ancient days" likewise describes Bethlehem, as the venerable home town for Judah's ruling dynasty. The assumption is that a new David is needed, and the only source left to supply that is Bethlehem, much as Isaiah 11:1 speaks of a new ruler arising from the stump of Jesse.

Verse 3's statement, introduced by "therefore," reflects on the peril to Jerusalem in v. 1, but through the eyes of v. 2: the LORD will "give them up" in expectation of the birth of this ruler.[4] And yet, its expectation that an anonymous woman's completion of labor will mark the end of the LORD's abandonment of them is puzzling. The most immediate link is with the birthing described in 4:9–10, even though that focuses on suffering.[5] If v. 3 is read against that background, then it is not a matter of waiting for the ruler to be born, but for the time of distress to reach its end.[6] It is *then* that "the rest of his kindred shall return to the people of Israel."[7] And it is through him that the LORD will provide sustenance and security for Israel (v. 4).

The problems of vv. 5–6 are many, but suffice it to say that the reference to "peace" is broader than the absence of warfare; it entails general welfare, implicitly for Israel. Thus, v. 6 speaks of ruling over the Assyrians and of deliverance from them. While the reference to the Assyrians might seem better rooted in Judah's situation than the anachronous reference to Babylon in 4:10, Assyria is used by some prophets as a code name for later Mesopotamian kingdoms (see, for example, Zech 10:10–11), inasmuch as Assyria had become the "poster child" for ruthless aggression (Wolff, 1990). Thus, 5:1–6 anticipates a return of exiles (v. 3), just like 4:7; deliverance from enemies, just like 4:10; and the establishment of a secure state by the defeat of foes, just like 4:13. However, these verses posit that these effects will be achieved through a new Davidic ruler rather than by the LORD on his own.

Israel's own role is accented in 5:7–8, speaking in two stages of "the remnant of Jacob" among the peoples. Verse 7 attributes to them the same divine origins as the dew and rain, which appear without human assistance (Wolff, 1990). Verse 8 permits them the same prowess among the nations that lions enjoy among other animals, attacking at will and without deterrence.

Verse 9 employs metaphors not previously met in the book: the image of a hand or arm lifted frequently expresses dominance in battle (e.g., Deut 32:27; Isa 26:11; Ps 89:13, 118:16), as the talk of enemies being "cut off" confirms for this occurrence. More striking, however, is that its addressee goes unnamed. Although the words could be addressed to those just described as routing the nations,[8] what are to be "cut off" in vv. 10–14 are the addressees' weaponry, cities, and religious objects, rather than their adversaries. Moreover, v. 10 is set off from v. 9 by its introductory "In that day, says the LORD." The better option is to construe the Hebrew verb forms of v. 9 as expressing (as they can) a wish: "May your hand be lifted up over your adversaries, and all your enemies cut off" (Ben Zvi, 2000a). This petition serves as a fitting conclusion to the scenes of distress that began with 4:9. Nevertheless, looking back over 4:1–5:9, it is possible to detect an overarching structure.

4:1–5:9:   In Retrospect

Chapter 4 vv. 1–8 anchor the passage with its parallel forecasts of the nations' voluntary submission to the LORD and the revival of scattered and afflicted Israel under the LORD's rule. At the fulcrum of that forecast is the confession of allegiance to the LORD offered for the audience's adoption. That distinction between the idealized future and present reality is further underscored in the vignettes of vv. 9–10, 11–13, and 5:1–6, each of which is introduced by "now" and projects Israel as delivered or victorious. That theme is reinforced by two images in 5:7–8, one portraying "the remnant of Jacob" as created by the LORD's actions, the other touting Israel's power to conquer surrounding nations. The prayer for victory (5:9) provides a conclusion to the unit in a way similar to the hymns of Amos 4:13 and 9:5–6.

The literary flow of these verses partially mutes differences concerning whether the nations submit willingly or are forced, whether Israel is at peace or at war, whether its deliverance is the work of the LORD, the people as a group, or a new Davidic ruler. Yet hopefully our close inspection has shown that these shifts in perspective are real, making it difficult to explain these verses as an original literary unit. Indeed, there is no reason to assume that its components were from a single source.[9]

Many of these verses reflect a time later than Micah. They assume that Israel has suffered at the hands of the nations – even Babylon – and that its people must be gathered back to their homeland. Likewise, the forecast of a new ruler from Bethlehem assumes that the line of descendants from David must be renewed, a circumstance that would have been unimaginable in Micah's day.

5:10–15:   Purgation of Israel and Vengeance against the Nations

Verses 10–14 diverge from the motif of restoration that dominates 4:1–5:9. More significantly, they carry themes like ones we saw in Hosea and Amos. The *removal* of "horses and chariots" (v. 10) recalls the disparaging of horses in the scribal additions of Hosea 1:7 and 14:3, a theme native to Amos 2:15 and 4:10 and frequent in the book of Isaiah.[10] The mention of "strongholds" in v. 11 is solitary within Micah but at home in Amos, which speaks of the destruction of "palaces/fortresses" (Amos 1:4, 7,

14; 2:2; 3:11; 5:9; 6:8; compare the scribal insertion in Hosea 8:14). The removal of "sorceries" and "soothsayers" (v. 12) is different than Micah's castigation of "diviners" in 3:7, where he places them alongside "prophets" and "seers," without singling them out as distinctively evil. The removal of such mediators is, however, of special concern to Deuteronomy 18:10, just as worshipping "the work of your hands" (v. 13) is **Deuteronomistic** language that we already saw injected into Hosea 14:3 (see above, p. 29). Likewise, the removal of "**pillars**" and "sacred poles," mentioned nowhere else in Micah, is a Deuteronomistic concern (Deut 7:5, 12:3; 1 Kings 14:15, 23; 2 Kings 17:10, 18:4, 23:14). There is good reason, then, to regard vv. 10–14 as a later scribal expansion (Jeremias, 1971).[11]

Besides 5:10–14 presenting the reader with a jarring transition, they also show signs that they serve as supplements to 4:1–5:9. They are introduced with the phrase "on that day," a common scribal device for joining additions to an existing text (compare Am 8:9, 13; 9:11; and see De Vries, 1995). Their persistent talk of "cutting off" suggests that they have been appended via this **catchword** to "all your enemies shall be cut off" in v. 9 (Wolff, 1990). These verses introduce into chapters 4–5 a precondition to Israel's enjoying its new era: its purification from former flaws (see Albertz, 2002).

Chapter 5 v. 15 ("And in anger and wrath I will execute vengeance on the nations that did not obey") is a peculiar sequel to vv. 10–14, which specify crimes peculiar to Israel/Judah (Wolff, 1990). And it makes for an equally odd fit with the images of restoration and victory over the nations that otherwise characterize chapters 4–5. Here the LORD vows to take vengeance against a well-defined subset of the nations: "the nations that did not obey." This hearkens back to earlier passages: most recently, the vision of nations streaming to Jerusalem for instruction and, more distantly, 1:2's summons of all peoples to "hear," which translates the same Hebrew word translated "obey" in 5:15 (Wolff, 1990). In fact, 5:15 functions with 1:2 as a frame around chapters 1–5, so that we must view chapters 4–5 in connection with chapters 1–3, to which we now turn.

Chapters 1–3: Castigation of the Ruling Class

The opening pronouncement of 1:2 summons the earth and all its peoples to witness the LORD's judgment on Israel and Judah. This suggests that their fate is to be an example and lesson for the nations. Neither the word for "peoples" nor its synonym "nations" appears again in chapters 1–3, but the two appear 15 times in chapters 4–5,[12] leading to the surmise that 1:2 introduces chapters 1–5 as a whole, but especially with an eye to 5:15.

The first chapter announces calamities to befall Israel and Judah, but says little about their causes. Chapter 2 vv. 1–5 laments (mockingly) the fate of those who have wrongly appropriated others' property, while vv. 6–11 rebuts objections raised against the prophet's words. In vv. 12–13 the LORD promises to gather all "the survivors of Israel" as a single flock. Chapter 3 reports a series of oracles spoken to and about the leaders of Israel, castigating them for their mistreatment of the people and serving notice that Jerusalem itself will be reduced to rubble. A closer look at these chapters will shed light on how they were composed and how they relate to each other.

Chapter 1:   Judah's Downfall as a Corollary to Israel's Collapse

The LORD's "holy temple" is the site from which he strides to bear witness, with the earth convulsing under his foot (vv. 3–4). This depiction is cast as a hymn, as is typical for **theophanies** (descriptions of a deity's arrival and appearance).[13]

The phrase "all this," at the start of v. 5 ("All this is for the transgression of Jacob and for the sins of the house of Israel"), identifies the theophany as punishment for Israel. However, whereas "Jacob" and "Israel" both refer to Judah in 3:1, 8, and 9, 1:5 identifies "the transgression of Jacob" with *Samaria* (the capital of the northern kingdom), making "Jacob" designate a more restricted group than elsewhere in the book. Meanwhile, rather than Jerusalem being equated with "sins of Judah," it is "the *high place* of Judah." This is the only reference in the book to a high place (recall Amos 7:9 and Hosea 10:8),[14] and nowhere else does Micah charge Judah with **cultic** sins. The specification of "the high place of Judah" as Jerusalem's crime betrays a scribe's interest in assigning to Judah the same sort of cultic sins that we found prominent in Hosea.

Vocabulary choices in v. 7 betray a similar interest. The word for "images" occurs again only in 5:13, where it stands alongside "pillar" and "the works of your hands," both of which are Deuteronomistic terms found also in Hosea 3:4, 10:1–2, and 11:2. Similarly, the words "wages" and "prostitute" are found only in 1:7,[15] but are familiar from the book of Hosea (see especially Hos 2:12, 9:1).

Verse 6, on the other hand, lacks these images and introduces an abrupt change of speaker. Whereas vv. 2–4 described the LORD and his actions, and an unspecified voice identified the transgressions of Jacob and Israel in v. 5, the LORD unexpectedly speaks in v. 6.[16] This abrupt shift in speakers suggests that v. 6 did not originally follow what precedes it.[17] Verses 5 and 7 appear to have been constructed by scribes who wanted to link v. 6's forecast of Samaria's fall with cultic crimes and portray those as infecting Judah also.

The phrase "for this," at the start of v. 8, introduces a lament based on v. 6 (the destruction of cult items in v. 7 would hardly induce the prophet to lament!). Verses 8–16 announce impending calamity to Judean villages. The fact that these verses still anticipate Samaria's destruction and are able to address Gath as a Judean city (which it was only until 711 BCE) makes a reasonable prima facie argument that this is an early Micah tradition (Wolff, 1990). The litany of disasters to befall these villages is conspicuously linked to v. 6 by the reference to Samaria via "*her* wound is incurable" (v. 9). Not only Samaria's helplessness is in view, but also the fact that her distress "has come to Judah [and] to Jerusalem." This is what induces the prophet to mourn. Notably, however, neither the perpetrator of this disaster nor its occasion is identified.

Nevertheless, the perpetrator is implied in vv. 3–4, while the cause is provided to the reader by the editorial additions of vv. 5 and 7 and v. 13, the latter of which is an editorial riff on the evils of chariots and horses of the same sort that we noted in 5:10 (Wolff, 1990).

In short, the scribes who shaped Micah 1 have expanded the early Micah tradition with statements making clear that Jerusalem's destruction was due to the same sort of crimes and infidelities that ensnared Israel.

Chapter 2: Lament, Opposition, and Promise for Survivors

Chapter 2 comprises three sections: vv. 1–5 lament (mockingly) the fate of those who have confiscated others' property; vv. 6–11 present interaction between the prophet and his opponents; and vv. 12–13 foresee a return of exiles.

The chapter's first two verses are straightforward: the powerful who while away their time planning and executing illicit seizures of others' properties are in peril. The judgment introduced with "therefore" (v. 3) corresponds to the crime, inasmuch as its evil, "devised" by the LORD, matches the wickedness they have "devised." Awkward, however, is the phrase "this family." First, it is difficult to detect a reason for the shift from talking *about* "this family" to speaking of judgment as an evil "from which *you* cannot remove your necks" (as well as "*you* shall not walk haughtily"). Second, to describe those who have plotted such actions as "this *family*" is peculiar. The Hebrew word *mishpachah* (appearing only here in Micah) regularly designates blood relations, making its use for people associated only through their behavior strained.[18]

Greater problems plague v. 4, although the NRSV has hidden some of them from the reader's view. While the verse leads us to expect words spoken "against" or "about" the addressees (presumably, the same people on whom v. 3 pronounces judgment), the speakers describe the loss of their *own* property. Moreover, 4b complains that "the LORD alters the inheritance of *my* people." Elsewhere in Micah "my people" refers to those who have been wronged by the powerful, with the pronoun "my" typically referring to the prophet (see, for instance, 1:9, 2:8). So who speaks here?

Some argue that while the first half of v. 4 projects that the foes will one day be lamented, the second half is not the content of that lament, but a flashback to the complaint uttered by the victims of the oppressors mentioned in vv. 1–2 (Andersen and Freedman, 2000; Nasuti, 2004). However, this is strained; the second half of v. 4 is more naturally construed as the lament introduced earlier in the verse. Yet, even then we are left with the problem of *who* voices this lament and *what* they lament. To answer this, we must examine v. 5.

The primary problem in v. 5 is its implied logical connection with the lament "*Therefore* you will have no one to cast the line by lot in the assembly of the LORD." It would be strained to see this punishment as a *consequence* of the lament. What is more, the notion of having someone "to cast the line by lot in the assembly of the LORD" recalls the stories of the distribution of the land when Israel took it, casting lots (equivalent to drawing straws) to determine which tribes and families were allotted which properties (Num 26:55–56, 33:54; Josh 14:2). When ownership of land is addressed following this division of property, it is a matter of *inheriting* and retaining land that was apportioned earlier (Num 36:1–9). In that light, being deprived of one to "cast the line" (i.e., someone to determine property boundaries) in the apportionment of land seems anachronistic for Micah's day, inasmuch as it assumes that the land awaits parceling.

Finally, we should note that while all of the "you" pronouns in vv. 3–4 are in the plural (i.e., they address a group), "you" in v. 5 addresses an individual.

These problems find no easy solution, whether one tries to make sense of them as they stand (e.g., Ben Zvi, 2000a; Nasuti, 2004) or posits that they reflect successive additions (e.g., Jeremias, 1971; Wolff, 1990). Nevertheless, a few observations can shed some light on them.

First, the term "family" in v. 3 shifts the castigation from a group of aristocrats who have used their power to amass property to the fate of people related by kinship. Most likely, "against this family" was inserted to expand the scope of addressees beyond the wicked of the ruling class to include Israel as a whole (Jeremias, 1971; Wolff, 1990).

As for the tangle of statements in v. 4, the phrases "we are utterly ruined" and "among our captors he parcels out our field" are probably placed in the wrongdoers' mouths, mocking them with the very laments once used by those whose properties they had confiscated (Lescow, 1999). Their howls at their own land being appropriated creates an ironic twist, parallel to the LORD's vow to "devise" evils in response to the wickedness they "devised" against others (Wolff, 1990).

In this connection, it is noteworthy that "the LORD" has been supplied by the NRSV (it is not in the Hebrew) as a subject for the verbs (the clauses could also be translated "the inheritance of my people is altered … how it is removed"). This statement ironically echoes Micah's lament that *his* people's property was being snatched from them. For these oppressors, "my people" has a much narrower scope, designating their immediate families.[19]

Finally, v. 5 addresses a different circumstance than the crimes of officials. The assumption that the land awaits apportioning assumes the circumstance v. 4 laments: because the "inheritance" has been torn away, a new apportionment is needed. The introduction of vv. 4–5 with "in that day" marks this as a bridge supplied by a scribe (De Vries, 1995).

The features highlighted here likely reflect a situation later than Micah's era. They update his traditions in light of the aftermath of Jerusalem's destruction by the Babylonians, when the entire *family* had been deprived of its inheritance through divine judgment, leaving them to anticipate its redistribution *by lot*

Textual Criticism

Because what would become the biblical books had to be copied by hand, it became inevitable that changes would creep in over time. Besides problems like damage to a **scroll** or fading ink making a copyist's task difficult, forms of some letters could be difficult to distinguish (for instance, the Hebrew letters for "d" and "r" are similar), words placed too close together could lead to connecting a consonant with the wrong word, words similar in appearance to neighboring words could be skipped over accidentally, or a copyist could be influenced by what he expected the text to read. Consequently, the surviving Hebrew manuscripts and translations (such as the **Septuagint**, a translation into Greek produced in the final two centuries BCE) offer evidence of Hebrew texts whose words differed at times. Textual criticism is the art of evaluating such differences to recover the wording that most likely approximates the earliest text of a book. Micah seems to have suffered a high number of copyists' errors and, thus, requires careful text-critical evaluation (Hillers, 1984). Fortunately, the NRSV has taken advantage of such work and therefore provides a good basis for our study.

among those who returned, just as it had been when Israel first claimed its land (Jeremias, 1971; Wolff, 1990).

Verses 6–11 are plagued with several copyists' errors that confound a straightforward reading of the Hebrew (Hillers, 1984; Williamson, 1997a). The NRSV has adopted (for the most part) well-founded proposals for resolving these problems (see the box on **textual criticism**). What is more, its provision of quotation marks for v. 6 (Hebrew does not have such marks) appropriately recognizes that the phrase "thus they preach" marks Micah's citation of his opponents' words (Ben Zvi, 2000a). Nevertheless, the quotation should probably be seen as extending through the third question of v. 7, "Are these his doings?"

Verses 6–7 reject attempts to censor prophetic oracles. The Hebrew verb translated "do not preach" addresses a group, suggesting that this attack was aimed against a number of prophets whose message was found objectionable (Hillers, 1984). The kind of prophet the opponents would prefer, in Micah's estimation, would preach falsehoods and expound the virtues of wine and beer (v. 11; compare Isa 30:9–11).[20] In the intervening verses Micah reveals the objections of these speakers that betray the chasm between his message and their beliefs. They contend that those who forecast Israel's disgrace malign the LORD's patience with Israel. Micah, for his part, accuses the speakers of dismissing such words as merely vindictive and defends his words as doing "good to one who walks uprightly."

Micah sharpens his attack on those appropriating others' property by depicting the effect their actions have on "the women of my people" and "their young children" (2:9).[21] This reprise of a theme from vv. 1–2 does not make vv. 1–11 a single oracle or even two oracles uttered in a single day's work (Wolff, 1990). Most likely, vv. 1–5 and 6–11 have been juxtaposed owing to their similar charges, just as 3:1–3 (which likely abutted v. 11 before 2:12–13 was insinuated[22]) charge the rulers with "tearing the skin off my people" and eating "their flesh," parallel to the charge of vicious opportunism in 2:8.

Verse 10 offers special challenges. In particular, who is addressed? Most likely, v. 10a is addressed to the oppressors, prohibiting them from inhabiting their amassed properties (Andersen and Freedman, 2000).[23] The second half of the verse, "because of uncleanness that destroys with a grievous destruction," should likely be read slightly differently to mean "because of uncleanness *you will be destroyed* with a grievous destruction" (see Andersen and Freedman, 2000, 325). Employing a slight **emendation** that supports this reading,[24] the verse pronounces judgment on the oppressors whose words are rejected in the foregoing rebuttal.

The final two verses of the chapter (vv. 12–13) stand out as scribal additions, not only because of their sudden shift from doom-and-gloom for Israel, but also owing to their anticipation of a gathering of Israel's "survivors," reminiscent of promises of Israel's reconstitution in chapters 4–5 (Wolff, 1990).

Chapter 3: Consequences of the Leaders' Crimes

Chapter 3 falls into three sections: vv. 1–4 take to task the rulers for their abuse of the people, vv. 5–8 address abuses by prophets, and vv. 9–12 charge the ruling class with misuse of their offices. Each section details the leaders' crimes, after which it enumerates their punishments, introducing them with "then" (v. 4) or "therefore" (vv. 6, 12).

All three sections contain the Hebrew word for "justice" (vv. 1, 8, 9), found elsewhere in the book only in 6:8 and 7:9 (where the NRSV translates it "judgment") (Jeremias, 2000b).

In addition to these features common to all units, vv. 1 and 9 begin with similar addresses:

> Listen, you heads of Jacob and rulers of the house of Israel! (v. 1)
> Hear this, you rulers of the house of Jacob and chiefs of the house of Israel. (v. 9)

Equally notable, vv. 4 and 7 impose similar punishments: "he will not answer" the rulers (v. 4), while the prophets will find "no answer from God" (v. 7). While a lack of an answer to a prophet implies failure to receive a response to a query submitted to the LORD on behalf of a client, the situation that would spur rulers to seek a response is when they cry out to the LORD at a time of threat to their city, the very circumstances Jerusalem's rulers claim will never befall them (v. 11) but that Micah forecasts (v. 12). Accordingly, the full ramifications of the punishment for the rulers voiced in v. 4 become clear only in v. 12 (Jeremias, 2000b).

Also striking is the accusation that the leaders should "know justice" (v. 1). Their failure to do so is described in images of butchering and cooking meat, implicitly equating the rulers with cannibals, as a metaphor for their abuse of the people. As with the phrase "he will not answer them," the precise meaning of their failure to "know justice" awaits vv. 9–11, where their misdeeds are stated concretely (Jeremias, 2000b). In both of these respects, the chapter propels the reader to its end, where v. 11 ties together the addresses to rulers and prophets, and v. 12 pronounces the supreme punishment of Jerusalem's reduction to uninhabited ruins.

Alongside this evidence of the unity of this chapter, phrases unique to it betray its connection with the larger prophetic tradition. The accusation that the rulers "hate the good and love the evil" (3:2) echoes Amos 5:15's exhortation to "hate evil and love good" (the only other place where this phraseology occurs in the Bible), followed by Amos's command to "establish justice in the gate," just as Micah's description follows the accusatory question "should you not know justice?" (v. 1) (Jeremias, 2000b). Likewise, Micah 3:11's ridicule of the corrupt rulers' boast "Surely the LORD is with us! No harm shall come upon us" parallels Amos's warning that "the LORD, the God of hosts, will be with you" only if "[you] seek good and not evil" (Am 5:14) (Jeremias, 2000b).

Still more striking is the degree to which v. 10 mirrors Habakkuk 2:12 (I offer my own translation to bring out the similarities in Hebrew):

> who build Zion with bloodshed and Jerusalem with iniquity (Mic 3:10)
> who build a town with bloodshed and found a city with iniquity (Hab 2:12)

The chief difference is Micah's identification of the "town" and "city" as Jerusalem.[25]

Similarly, the phrase "because they have acted wickedly" (literally, "because they made their deeds evil," 3:4) uses phraseology that is especially common in the book of Jeremiah (4:4; 21:12; 23:2, 22; 25:5; 26:3; 44:22) (Jeremias, 2000b).[26]

Although these specimens show that whoever gave chapter 3 its coherence used phrases similar to ones found elsewhere in the prophets, that does not mean that this chapter is a pastiche of borrowed phrases. The fact that the chapter is keyed to v. 12's announcement of the same destruction that was forecast for Samaria in 1:6 and whose fulfillment is assumed by the oracles in chapters 4–5 (since there can be no restoration of a Jerusalem that has not been destroyed) suggests that this forecast, at least, is among the oldest layers of traditions attributed to Micah (Jeremias, 2000b).[27]

A set of assumptions underlying vv. 5–8 suggest that they, also, likely derive from the oldest layers of the Micah traditions. His accusation that the prophets adjust their messages to please paying clients shares assumptions about prophets found in a story of Saul's encounter with a "man of God" in 1 Samuel 9. Having failed to locate his father's lost donkeys, Saul prepares to head home when his servant suggests that they consult the local "man of God" whose words always prove true (1 Sam 9:6). Although this image of a reliable medium accords with an earlier description of Samuel (1 Sam 3:19–20) and is reinforced by a subsequent report that the LORD had informed Samuel of Saul's impending visit (9:15–16), features of the story offer a different image of this "man of God."

After all, when the servant proposes this consultation to learn the whereabouts of the donkeys (9:6), Saul's objection is that they have nothing to pay the man, a problem the servant remedies by producing a quarter shekel of silver (9:7–8). Implicit is that this "man of God" makes a living fielding queries, much like a modern clairvoyant. This sort of figure deviates from the capital image of prophets in the Bible, as epitomized in Deuteronomy 18, where, after outlawing those trafficking in hidden knowledge gained by practicing **divination** (Deut 18:10), the LORD promises to raise up "a prophet like [Moses] from among their own people; I will put my words in the mouth of the prophet, who shall speak to them everything that I command" (18:18). Curiously, Micah numbers "diviners" among those he attacks (3:7), but without disparaging their craft. And apparently he does not regard such mediators as shams:

Divination and Prophecy

The desire to know the future is human. We consult economists, political pundits, or even palm readers in the hopes of seeing what lies ahead. The ancients regularly looked to experts in reading signs in the internal organs of animals or in the path of the stars, or who performed rites that could force the future to tip its hand. Even though Deuteronomy 18:9–14 proclaims such methods illicit for Israel, hints survive that divination was alive and well. The underlying current in the story in 1 Samuel 9 and the words of Micah 3:7 attest that such diviners could be hired in Israel, even if Deuteronomy, prophetic narratives, and the prophetic books endorse the prophet who hears the LORD's word as the appropriate vehicle for knowing the future (see Jeffers, 2007). Some readers may be confused by these contradictory traditions, but it is important to recognize that while Deuteronomy now forms part of the **Torah**, during the years before the exile it was not necessarily subscribed to or even known by most Israelites.

their deprivation of vision, revelation, and divine answer assumes that they have enjoyed such communication in the past. Obsession with their bottom line is what has perverted their office, allying them with the rulers' failure to uphold justice for similar reasons (Jeremias, 2000b). By contrast, Micah offers himself as a valid mediator, "filled with power ... justice and might to declare to Jacob his transgression and to Israel his sin" (3:8).[28] Nowhere does he call into question the legitimacy of the practices of those he condemns, including the diviners; he condemns only their abuses of their offices. Such offices are condemned per se only in 5:12, part of the late addendum to chapter 5. Chapter 3 reflects the same older notions of prophecy as in the story of Saul's visit to the "man of God," suggesting that it preserves features of an early tradition.

The attack on prophets and the forecast of Jerusalem's dereliction are, then, likely the earliest layers of tradition in Micah 3. Whatever roots the remaining materials might have had in early tradition, they have been carefully reshaped by editors with the help of phrases and ideas found elsewhere in prophetic literature, making "the word of the LORD that came to Micah" dovetail with the word received by other prophets (Jeremias, 2000b).

The Composition of Chapters 1–5: A Complex Warning

Chapters 2–3 and 4–5 are discrete units. Chapter 2 vv. 1–11 take to task aristocrats for disabusing the populace of their rightful landholdings. On the heels of this, in 3:1, the prophet recites his rebuke of the civil and religious leaders for their crimes against their society that nullified justice and would culminate in Jerusalem's destruction.

Chapter 4 v. 1–chapter 5 v. 9 is a pastiche of oracles detailing the relationship between Israel and the nations. The diversity of perspectives on both Israel and the nations suggests that they derive from diverse sources, while their assumption that Israel has been deprived of its land and been exiled in Babylon discloses that the bulk of them were composed after Jerusalem's fall in 587 BCE.

Chapters 1–3 and 4–5 have been joined by three links. First, the theme of rescue from exile has been insinuated into the midst of chapters 2–3 in 2:12–13. Second, chapter 1's insistent diagnosis of Jerusalem's fall as attributable to the same cultic misdeeds and reliance on military prowess that brought Israel to its knees – a theme foreign to the heart of chapters 2–5 and 6–7 – is matched by the addendum to chapter 5 that posits a purge of such practices (5:10–14). Third, the whole of this assemblage has been placed between the summons to all the peoples of the earth to hear the LORD's witness (1:2) and the warning that he will one day "execute vengeance on the nations that did not obey" (5:15).

Chapters 1–5, despite the various components that compose them, are presented as a lesson that the nations are to heed or suffer punishment. The crimes that doomed Israel and Judah included misdeeds by the wealthy and, above all, cultic misdeeds. Notwithstanding these, Israel will be revived and dominate the nations that trammeled it. Both Israel and the nations must seek the LORD's reign and instruction. Those nations that refuse are doomed.

Chapter 7:   Voices of Confidence

The oracles of 6:1–16 present issues similar to what we saw in chapters 1–3. Consequently, we will be better served devoting time to the very different material in chapter 7, whose first seven verses lament the dire prospects announced in 6:9–16 (Reicke, 1967).[29] Their speaker stands apart from the people, and to that extent can be heard as a prophetic voice (Andersen and Freedman, 2000). By contrast, the voice of vv. 8–10 speaks on behalf of a community. Verses 1–7 are, then, more closely bound with chapter 6 than are vv. 8–20. At the same time, v. 7's expression of confidence in the LORD's deliverance provides a natural segue to the explicit announcements of deliverance in the rest of the chapter.

The speaker of vv. 8–13 voices confidence that her subjugation to her enemy is a divine reproach that will one day be overturned, enabling her to celebrate her enemy's defeat. The casting of these as words of a vanquished woman about her enemy likely embodies the community's lament of its defeat by a foe (cities and countries were frequently depicted as women in the **ancient Near East**) (Wolff, 1990).

The tone shifts in vv. 14–17, as the speaker implores the LORD to shepherd his people and enact marvels like those he displayed in their flight from Egypt (vv. 14–15), making the nations tremble and submit to him (vv. 16–17).

The concluding three-verse unit (vv. 18–20) takes yet another form: praise that anticipates the LORD's forgiveness of the people, fulfilling the loyalty he vowed to Jacob and Abraham. As in the rest of chapter 7 (at least since v. 8), the complaints and accusations against the people that dominated chapters 1–3 and 6 have vanished.

The distinct styles of these units make it likely that they were not composed as a set, but were brought together to serve as a capstone for the book (Wolff, 1990). We noted hymns inserted by scribes into Amos, and this chapter simply displays the tendency to incorporate hymns even more extensively (compare Isa 12; Hab 3; Nah 1:2–8; Jon 2). If the three units of vv. 8–20 take us beyond the despair of vv. 1–6, the deliverance they foresee correlates with the trust v. 7 voices.

Scribal additions can be detected within this chapter, including in vv. 1–7. Although the NRSV offers the reader a smooth rendition of 7:4, its footnotes attest that the **Masoretic text** has pronouns in the second half of the verse that conflict with those of the first half: "The day of *your* sentinels, of *your* punishment, has come." Prophets are often compared to "sentinels" (compare Hos 9:8; Jer 6:17; Ezek 33:1–9; Hab 2:1), while calling them "*your* sentinels" suggests that the LORD is the addressee (Wolff, 1990). Similarly, the reference to "*your* punishment" means "the punishment you will execute" (Reicke, 1967).[30] The word "now" signals that the "day of your sentinels," equivalent to "[the day of] your punishment," has arrived (Reicke, 1967). This address of the deity interrupts the bemoaning of conditions in the speaker's day that resumes in vv. 5–6. Verse 4b is, then, probably an editor's interpretation of vv. 1–4a as events fulfilling the judgment threatened by the prophets (Jeremias, 1971; Wolff, 1990), even as in Hosea 12:5 an editorial insertion identifies the speaker of v. 4 as "the LORD God of hosts."

A second scribal addition appears in 7:11–13, which deviates from the individual's lament of vv. 8–10 and does not accord with the addresses to the LORD in vv. 14–20. Verses 11–12 address an unspecified city or country, while v. 13 describes earth's desolation. Most striking is the triple reference to a "day" when the addressee's wall will be rebuilt and its territory enlarged (vv. 11–12a). Most likely, v. 11 has been inserted to respond to the community's complaint, reassuring it that the defeat of the enemy that v. 10 anticipates will bring with it the victim's restoration to grandeur (Wolff, 1990). Parallel to this, v. 12 supplies reassurance for the city of the return of its people from exile (Wolff, 1990).[31] By contrast, v. 13 envisions punishment that encompasses more than just the people's enemy, with the whole earth lying desolate. Such an expectation of worldwide punishment accords with themes we saw in 4:11–13, but surpasses even 7:16–17, which expect simply that the nations will "be ashamed of all their might," "turn in dread to the LORD our God," and "stand in fear of you." Accordingly, vv. 11–13 seem to be an editorial expansion of vv. 8–10.

Even though the **liturgical** materials of chapter 7 provide a coda to the book, they are more than a flourish. Verses 1–7 provide comment on the charges of 6:9–16 that brings with it a note of hope and trust in the LORD, while the remainder of the chapter reprises the expectations of triumph and restoration found in chapters 4–5. The chapter brings the book to a climax by placing before the reader again the proclamation that the LORD will restore his relationship with Israel, while showing the nations their appropriate place in the world, whether through compliance or through forced submission.

Summary

The scribes who shaped Micah have encapsulated cries against the abrogation of justice by those who should exercise it and a denouncement of illicit religious practices within a call to the nations to submit to the LORD's justice. Nations that refuse to heed the LORD's call will suffer the same calamity as Judah, who is now promised restoration and vindication over its enemies.

The scribal arrangement of Micah provides periodic respite from the prophet's harangue against the ruling class. The first is 2:12–13, which promises Jacob the return of its survivors. But that reassurance is short-lived, as Micah launches into his most pointed condemnation of Judah's rulers, culminating in the consignment of Jerusalem to ruins. The extended treatment of Jerusalem's future role (chapters 4–5) reprises the forecast of 2:12–13 that its dispersed citizens will return.

If chapters 1–5 have the nations as their prime addressees, chapters 6–7 are directed to Israel. The summons to hear the LORD's case against his people (6:1) quickly shifts to a plea to his people to realize how mundane and yet profound his demands of them are: "to do justice, and to love kindness, and to walk humbly with your God" (6:8). The absence of such justice among them prompts the prophet to recoil from his society, but not to despair, for he awaits the LORD's salvation (7:1–7). That salvation is, however, assured: the LORD will secure victory over the enemy, subordinate the nations, and pardon his people (7:8–20).

This description of Micah – both in its overall scope and in its details – leads to a conclusion similar to one we drew from study of the books of Hosea and Amos. Namely, a prophetic book is much more than a repository of words from a prophet. Even if one can detect, at points, oracles that might be read as the preaching of a particular prophet, those are so embedded in frameworks and expansions constructed by the scribes who shaped and reshaped the books that the words of the historical prophet – in this case, Micah – are not only beyond recovery, but are rather beside the point. Prophetic books are interested in expounding their messages in conversation with language and ideas from other prophetic books and their audiences. Even if the individual books retain features that distinguish them from each other, they equally contain threads that link them thematically in various ways.

Notes

1. While vv. 1–3 are virtually identical with Isaiah 2:2–4, Micah 4:4 outstrips that passage by depicting the nations' transformation to peace-loving peoples, sitting contentedly under their own vines and fig trees. Equally, vv. 6–8 surpass Isaiah 2 by forecasting the assembly of those "driven away" to be the LORD's subjects in Jerusalem.
2. Despite the similarities with Isaiah 2:5, both verses were likely formulated as editorial links to what follows them, based on language drawn from talk of the "walking" of the peoples (Williamson, 2006). While the "light(*'or*)" of the LORD in Isaiah 2:5 plays off the description of the nations walking in his "paths" (*'orchot*) (v. 3), its address of the "house of Jacob" binds it closely to the accusation of v. 6 that the "house of Jacob" has "forsaken [the ways of] your people," a connection reinforced by "for" at the head of v. 6.
3. The debate over the relationship of 5:1 to 4:9–13, on the one hand, and to 5:2–6, on the other, is complex (see Andersen and Freedman, 2000, 458–459). It is difficult to see v. 1 as the continuation of 4:13, which has already found a successful conclusion to the crisis introduced in v. 11. Moreover, the "therefore" of v. 3 is difficult to explain if it is reliant solely on v. 2.
4. The referents of the pronouns are problematic throughout these verses. "Them" could refer to the inhabitants of the city in v. 1. The subject for the verb "give," under this understanding, would be the LORD.
5. Seeing in this an allusion to the sign of a young woman giving birth to a son in Isaiah 7:14 (Wolff, 1990) is attractive but unacceptably speculative.
6. This interpretation of "when she who is in labor has brought forth" is rooted in the context given us by the editor. It may well be that the phrase had a more precise referent when it was uttered. However, we are left no basis to identify the original referent; we have only the framework the scribes provide for interpreting this statement.
7. The possessive pronoun in "*his* kindred" does not likely refer to the subject of "he shall give," but rather returns to the topic of the anticipated ruler, even as "he shall stand" in v. 4 clearly does: it is the ruler's kindred who "shall return to the people of Israel."
8. This would seem supported by the fact that vv. 10–14 carry on the address and repeatedly use the verb "cut off" (9, 10, 11, 12).
9. A key piece of evidence in this conclusion is the parallel between Micah 4:1–3 and Isaiah 2:2–4. The relationship between these largely identical passages is not as clear-cut as concluding that Micah borrowed from Isaiah, or vice versa. More likely, both books accessed a common source (Andersen and Freedman, 2000; Willis, 1997).
10. Even the command to Lachish has accrued a scribal comment branding such military preparations as "the beginning of sin to daughter Zion" and the equivalent of "the transgressions of Israel" (see Wolff, 1990, 50).
11. The idea of a purge of Israel (vv. 10–14) recalls the deprivations Hosea 3 imposes on Israel to restore her devotion to the LORD, as well as the singling out of sinners for elimination when Israel is "sifted" among the nations in Amos 9:9–10.
12. Only the word translated "nations" (*goyyim*) appears again outside of chapters 4–5 (7:16).

13. Whether vv. 2 and 3–4 represent different stages of editing (Wolff, 1990) is too knotty a question to consider here and perhaps parses the clues of editing too finely.

14. The Hebrew word translated "high places [of the earth]" in 1:3 is rendered "[a wooded] *height*" in 3:12, but in neither place refers to a cultic site.

15. The word translated "idols" also appears only here in the book.

16. The NRSV smoothes over this abrupt change by opening the verse with "therefore," whereas a more literal translation would read, "*and* I will make."

17. It may, however, have come from the Micah tradition. Just as 3:12 – which is attributable to the earliest layers of the tradition – forecasts Jerusalem becoming "plowed as *a field*" and "a *heap of ruins*," so 1:6 anticipates Samaria becoming "a *heap* [the same word translated 'heap of ruins' in 3:12] in the *open country* [the same Hebrew word translated 'field']."

18. While this term is used in the plural ("families") for groups not related by blood in Late Biblical Hebrew (e.g., 1 Chr 2:55, 4:21), no such usage appears in literature from Micah's era.

19. The fact that the first and the final lines of the verse are spoken in the first person *plural*, while the middle two lines are in the first person *singular*, has prompted the suggestion that the middle lines interject a statement by the prophet (Andersen and Freedman, 2000). This seems forced. More likely, the use of "my people" is a parody of the prophet's complaints against the oppressors, now ironically placed in their mouths as laments of their own fate.

20. This involves a wordplay on "falsehoods" (*sheqer*) and "beer" (*shecar*) (Wolff, 1990). Recall the complaint of Hosea 4:11 that "wine and new wine take away the understanding."

21. I concur with Wolff that we should read the Hebrew word for "the bedchamber" rather than "my glory" in v. 9 (Wolff, 1990).

22. The abutment of 3:1–3 to 2:11 would explain the start of 3:1 with "and I said." In fact, the NRSV of 3:2 hides a problem that a more literal translation reveals: "who tear their skin from *them* and *their* flesh from their bones" (i.e., "their" and "them" lack antecedents). The NRSV's "my people" justifiably assumes that "this people" in 2:11 was the original antecedent (Jeremias, 2000b).

23. If the addressees are Micah and others chastised for speaking "heresy," then v. 10 would demand that they cease and desist (Wolff, 1990). However, the assertion that "this is no place to rest" is cryptic if intended as a command to be silent. It is equally difficult to understand "arise and go" as the oppressors' address to the women and children they victimize, with "a place to rest" meaning their houses.

24. It involves merely the transfer of one letter (*waw*) from the beginning of the word for "destruction" to the end of the preceding verb.

25. Three observations suggest that Micah 3:10 was borrowed from Habakkuk 2:12: (1) the terms "bloodshed" and "iniquity" are paired only in these two passages; (2) each verb in Micah 3:9 has a plural subject ("who *are ones* abhorring justice and perverting all equity"), while v. 10 has a single subject ("who *is one* building Zion"), which fits the syntax of Habakkuk 2; (3) what "bloodshed" denotes is unclear in Micah, but is obvious in Habakkuk 2, where vv. 8 and 17 connect "human bloodshed" to the conquest of cities and land (Jeremias, 2000b).

26. This phraseology appears elsewhere only sporadically: Deut 28:20; 1 Sam 25:3; Isa 1:16; Hos 9:15; Zech 1:4; Ps 28:4; Neh 9:35. In Zechariah 1:4 it stands in the midst of a prologue to the book (1:2–6) that offers a review of the words of earlier prophets and the people's refusal to listen to them, urging obedience to this prophet's words (Petersen, 1984). The inclusion of the phrase in Isaiah 1:16 creates literary incongruities that raise the question of whether it was inserted by an editor (Williamson, 2006). No one disputes that Hosea 9:15 is an old element of Hosea tradition.

27. Although the citation of Micah 3:12 in Jeremiah 26:17–19 is considered by some to be verification that this oracle was remembered in Jeremiah's day (Holladay, 1989; Lundbom, 2004), there are reasonable questions about whether these verses were inserted into the chapter secondarily (McKane, 1996).

28. The phrase "with the spirit of the LORD" (which I have omitted) is syntactically problematic in its sentence and invokes a concept of prophecy (as inspired by the spirit) not otherwise found among prophets before the exile. This phrase was likely inserted to buttress the image of Micah by adding a phrase later accepted as a mark of authentic prophetic claims (Wolff, 1990).

29. For the rationale behind viewing v. 7 as the conclusion of the lament, see Wolff (1990, 203) and contrast Andersen and Freedman (2000, 577).

30. Compare "on the day of my punishment" in Exodus 32:34, which means "on the day I bring punishment."

31. This assumes that the Hebrew pronoun of v. 12's "in that day they will come to *you*" should be read as feminine rather than masculine, consistent with "*your* walls" in v. 11.

5

The Book of Zephaniah and the Twelve

Zephaniah

In the pages to come …

Zephaniah is the first of two prophetic books that focus on "the day of the LORD" (the other is Joel). While that event will be a cosmic phenomenon that shakes the world, its primary effect will be the removal of Jerusalem's haughty citizens. The book of Zephaniah has been constructed from various materials, including phrases borrowed from other prophetic books. This chapter will consider how those materials were utilized to offer an exposition of the implications of the day of the LORD for Israel.

The book's superscription is formatted like those in Hosea, Amos, and Micah: "The word of the LORD that came to Zephaniah … in the days of King Josiah son of Amon of Judah" (1:1). The placement of Zephaniah during Josiah's reign has led some to see him protesting conditions prior to the reforms 2 Kings 22–23 attributes to Josiah (Roberts, 1991) or prodding people to support those reforms (Seybold, 1985). Others, however, have questioned whether Zephaniah actually worked during Josiah's reign (Nogalski, 1993a). In principle, there is no reason to assume that the era specified in the superscription is accurate, if evidence within the book undermines that date (Ben Zvi, 1993).

Since Josiah is mentioned nowhere in the book, the only way to confirm the dating given by the superscription is to isolate allusions to circumstances or events unique to Josiah's reign. For instance, the religious practices protested in 1:4–5 have been

Prophetic Literature: From Oracles to Books, First Edition. Ronald L. Troxel.
© 2012 Ronald L. Troxel. Published 2012 by Blackwell Publishing Ltd.

King Josiah of Judah

According to 2 Kings 21:23–24, Josiah was acclaimed king after the assassination of his father, Amon. The chief act attributed to him is a series of reforms based on a book discovered during refurbishment of the temple. According to 2 Kings 23, those reforms included gaining the people's consent to follow the requirements of the newly found "book of the covenant"; the destruction of objects devoted to the Canaanite deities Baal and Asherah, as well as those dedicated to "the host of heaven"; destruction of the **high places** and other cultic establishments prohibited by the discovered book, including those in Israel's old territory; dismissal of the illegitimate priests who served at the high places; and elimination of other practices at variance with the book. Because both Zephaniah and Jeremiah are placed during Josiah's reign (Zeph 1:1; Jer 1:2), scholars have sought to fit these prophets' words into the era of Josiah's reforms (see, for example, Floyd, 2000, 177; Sweeney, 1991a, 391, 406).

compared with ones 2 Kings reports Josiah terminating (Roberts, 1991) and 2:4–15 have been read as an endorsement of Josiah's expansion of Judah at the expense of Assyria (Christensen, 1984). Such attempts to fit Zephaniah within Josiah's reign presume that 2 Kings's account of Josiah's reforms is accurate and then correlate statements in Zephaniah with it (Ben Zvi, 2005a). However, doubts have been raised about 2 Kings's account, such as whether the destruction of high places was as thoroughgoing as depicted (Hardmeier, 2005; Uehlinger, 2005) or was even undertaken by Josiah (Na'aman, 2002).[1]

Even apart from these questions, dating Zephaniah to Josiah's reign faces difficulties. While Zephaniah assumes that Jerusalem will soon suffer attack, there is no known foe capable of doing that during Josiah's reign, nor is there a good explanation of why Zephaniah would have spoken so harshly of Moab and Ammon (Zeph 2:8–11) during that era (Williams, 1963). These difficulties are surmounted if we accept the more likely scenario that Zephaniah worked during the reign of Josiah's successor, Jehoiakim (Nogalski, 1993a; Williams, 1963). But that raises the question why, then, Zephaniah 1:1 would place this prophet in Josiah's reign. To answer this, we need to note the superscription.

Zephaniah is given an unusually long pedigree: "son of Cushi son of Gedaliah son of Amariah son of Hezekiah." The enumeration of four generations of ancestors is without parallel in the other superscriptions and is unusual for genealogies in the **ancient Near East** (Nogalski, 1993a). The fact that Zephaniah's genealogy is traced back to Hezekiah, immediately after which stands "in the days of King Josiah son of Amon," hints that this Hezekiah does not simply happen to bear the same name as Josiah's great-grandfather; this genealogy wants to connect the reigns of Hezekiah and Josiah (Nogalski, 1993a). The unusual measures taken to create this link mean that we cannot take the dating at face value and make it impossible simply to identify conditions protested by Zephaniah with 2 Kings's reports of Josiah's deeds.

Nevertheless, whoever created this superscription wanted its forecast of a terrifying "day of the LORD" to be understood as delivered on the brink of the downward spiral of Judah's life following Josiah's death in 609 BCE.

The Book's Structure

Because the superscription's placement of Zephaniah in Josiah's reign is likely artificial, more significant for understanding the book is its structure, which is typically seen as comprising three sections: judgment against Judah and Jerusalem (1:2–2:3), **oracles** against foreign nations (2:4–15), and deliverance for Jerusalem (3:1–20) (Childs, 1979; Soggin, 1976). However, this division presents problems. For instance, 2:7 and 9b interrupt the posited proclamation of judgment to speak of Judah as its beneficiary (Sweeney, 1991a). Conversely, 3:1–8 lament Jerusalem's persistent wickedness rather than promise its deliverance, for which reason some have joined these verses with those against the nations in chapter 2 (Leclerc, 2007; Nogalski, 1993a), although others have connected them with the remainder of chapter 3, despite the chapter's focus on good days for Jerusalem (Blenkinsopp, 1996; Roberts, 1991). The customarily identified boundaries between units make it difficult to explain statements that fit better in another unit.

A more persuasive description of the book's structure identifies its center as the exhortation to seek the LORD before the day of wrath (2:1–3) (Sweeney, 2007a; Weimar, 1998). The preceding unit, 1:2–18, presents the day of the LORD and its consequences as reasons to flee (Sweeney, 1991a), while 2:4–3:13 reinforce that exhortation by explaining that the goal of divine wrath is not simply the subjugation of the nations and the elevation of Judah's remnant, but a purge of what is alien to worship of the LORD, both in Jerusalem and among the nations. While some see that unit extending to 3:20, 3:14–20 surpass urging submission to the LORD to exhorting readers to rejoice in the achievement of the LORD's goals (Floyd, 2000). The effect this perception of structure has on reading the book becomes evident by tracing its flow.

1:2–18:   The Coming Day of the LORD

The first five verses following the superscription startle the reader by announcing the LORD's intent to annihilate all living creatures, beginning with the wide swath of humanity and animals (vv. 2–3) and then turning more specifically to Judah, where those slated for elimination are worshippers of Baal, the host of heaven (the stars), and Milcom (an Ammonite deity), as well as those who have ceased seeking the LORD (vv. 4–6).[2]

Verses 7–18 label this calamity "the day of the LORD" (vv. 7, 14) or "the day of the LORD's wrath" (v. 18), also referred to as what will happen "on that day" (vv. 9, 10, 15).[3] Nevertheless, these verses have a focus different from vv. 2–6, highlighting the LORD's plan to punish wrongdoers (vv. 8–9, 12, 17) and describing the day's devastating effects (vv. 10–11, 13, 14–16, 18). These verses emphasize the *nearness* of the day (vv. 7, 14), preparing the way for the soon-to-follow exhortation of the humble to seek the LORD (2:1–3).[4] The refrain "the day of the LORD is near" at the head of vv. 7–13 and at the start of vv. 14–18 distinguishes two units.

Verses 7–9 describe the day of the LORD as a sacrifice, characterizing the LORD's slaughter of humans and beasts as a sacred act (much like calling warfare an act of worship), even as in Ezekiel 39:17–20 the LORD summons the birds and the animals as guests at a sacrificial feast of foes slain in battle. This characterization continues through v. 13 by repetition of the phrases "on that/the day" (vv. 8, 9, 10) and "at that time" (v. 12).

Verse 14 begins a new section by announcing, "The great day of the LORD is near, near and hastening fast." Verse 7's accent on the day's nearness ("For the day of the LORD is at hand"[5]) is now highlighted through a riff on "near," with the adjective placed first in both phrases: "*Near* is the great day of the LORD, *near* and hastening fast" (my translation, reflecting the Hebrew word order). Verses 15–16 further characterize that day through repetition of "a day of," while vv. 17–18 sketch the dimensions of the distress it will bring,[6] with v. 18 reprising the theme of vv. 2–4 by declaring "a full, a terrible end" for "all the inhabitants of the earth." This echo of the chapter's beginning, together with the intertwined assertions of destruction on the day of the LORD, indicates that this chapter has been artfully composed (Weimar, 1998).[7]

The diversity of the chapter's components is evident in the different settings presupposed. Verse 7 precedes the announcement of the day of the LORD as a sacrificial meal with the command "Be silent before the Lord GOD!" This resembles a summons heard at a cultic site, as is evident from comparing Habakkuk 2:20: "the LORD is in his holy temple; let all the earth keep silence before him!" (Beck, 2005; Bergler, 1988). Verses 8–9 abruptly switch to divine speech, with the transition provided by the temporal phrase "and on the day of the LORD's sacrifice" (v. 8a). The fact that this is followed by three additional forecasts using "on that day" (vv. 9, 10–11) or "at that time" (v. 12) – phrases that often serve as editorial links – suggests that v. 8's distinctive phrase "on the day of the LORD's sacrifice" has been created to link vv. 8–9 with v. 7 (Roberts, 1991).

The content of these verses is equally diverse. Whereas in vv. 8–9 the LORD identifies those to be punished, v. 10 forecasts lamentation in various sectors of Jerusalem, culminating in v. 11's call to bewail the loss of merchants in their sector. Verse 12 returns to the LORD's stated intent to bring punishment, taking aim at those confident that he will not act. The figure of "searching Jerusalem with lamps" accents that this crime is not overt but more subtle: a crime of indifference. Verse 13's culmination of these forecasts in terms of the plundering of wealth and houses reinforces the perception that the punishments are directed at the upper class.

The similarity of v. 13b–c to Amos 5:11 is noteworthy:

Though they build houses, they shall not inhabit them; though they plant vineyards, they shall not drink wine from them. (Zeph 1:13b–c)

… you have built houses of hewn stone, but you shall not live in them; you have planted pleasant vineyards, but you shall not drink their wine. (Am 5:11b–c)

Most likely, the editor pressed the statement from Amos into service as a suitable climax to the vows of punishment in vv. 10–12 (Beck, 2005; Holladay, 2001).[8]

The upshot of these observations is that vv. 8–13 comprise four units that enumerate the calamities of the day of the LORD but assume a different background than v. 7's call to silence. In fact, this set of verses follows a pattern frequent in descriptions of the day of the L ORD in the prophets: its initial description is as a universal phenomenon, expanded by addenda that detail the concrete effects of divine judgment (Bergler, 1988).

By contrast, vv. 14–16 describe the day of the L ORD in abstract terms.[9] Even the references to "fortified cities" and "lofty battlements" assume an affliction affecting multiple, unspecified cities, whereas vv. 8–13 focus on a single city: Jerusalem (Beck, 2005).[10] Nevertheless, v. 14 reinforces v. 7's note of impending doom ("near and hastening fast"), creating a bracket around vv. 8–13 that places their calamities under the rubric of "the day of the L ORD" (Beck, 2005).[11]

Verse 17 reinstates the L ORD as the speaker and returns to concrete description with his vow to make humans who have sinned against him blind and shed their blood as if it were dust.[12] The denial that even money will be able to save them (v. 18) befits the pledge of retribution "on the day of the L ORD's wrath," a phrase unique to the book of Zephaniah that reprises the description of the day of the L ORD as a day of wrath in vv. 14–16 (Beck, 2005).

Meanwhile, the recapitulation of vv. 2–4 in v. 18's vision of a world-encompassing event effectively frames Jerusalem's fall, via a **hyperbole**, as the collapse of creation itself.[13] Indeed, vv. 7–16 constitute reflection on "the day of the L ORD" that states the punishments threatened for individual wrongdoers in starker terms than we have seen in other prophetic books. And given that this unit stands under the title of "the word of the L ORD to Zephaniah," set artificially in "the days of King Josiah," it seems likely that these oracles portend the calamitous judgment to be realized in Babylon's sack of Jerusalem. Moreover, since the hyperbolic description of this as the overturning of creation is limited to chapter 1 and stands at odds with the offer of escape for the humble in 2:1–3, most likely 1:2–3 and 18b specially interpret the oracles of doom in light of the fall of Jerusalem in 587 BCE (compare Beck, 2005).

2:1–3:13:   The Goals of Divine Wrath

While there are strong connections between 2:1–3 and chapter 1 (Neef, 1999), they show stronger ties to 2:4–15. First, the conjunction "for" at the start of v. 4 links 2:1–3 tightly with the rest of chapter 2 (Floyd, 2000; Sweeney, 1991a). Second, because 2:1–3 offer "the humble of the land, who do his commands" a path to escape the disaster forecast in 1:2–18, they prepare for the forecast of Judah's restoration in chapter 3 (Sweeney, 1991a). To that degree they undercut chapter 1's claim of inevitable, universal disaster (Bergler, 1988).

At the same time, features of 2:1–3 anticipate 3:1–13: the address to "the humble of the land, who do his commands" (2:3) accords with the character of those who will be left in Jerusalem, according to 3:12; the exhortation of a group in 2:3 is resumed in 3:8's call to "wait for me … for the day when I arise as a witness"; the address of Israel as "shameless nation" in 2:1 is echoed in the description of Jerusalem as unwilling to bend to correction in 3:1–7; the urgency of taking action *before* the onset of divine wrath, announced in 2:2, anticipates an assault whose effect is the removal of "your proudly exultant ones," reported in 3:11. In these ways, then, 2:1–3 is more closely bound with 2:4–3:13 than with chapter 1.

Chapter 2 v. 4 introduces a set of oracles that depict the day of the L ORD unleashed against the Philistines (vv. 4–7), Moab and Ammon (vv. 8–11), Ethiopia (v. 12), and Assyria (vv. 13–15), nations that mark the four points of the compass (west, east, south, and north) around Judah (Floyd, 2000). The oracles do not simply announce calamity for these nations, but expect that their defeat will result in Judah's remnant gaining territory, anticipating the forecast of Judah's restoration in 3:14–20 (Sweeney, 1991a).

Hyperbole in Zephaniah

Even though 1:2–3, 18, and 3:8 speak of a complete destruction of creation, that description seems an exaggeration for effect (hyperbole). When chapter 2 announces judgment against the Philistines (2:4–7), Moab and Ammon (2:8–11), Ethiopia (2:12), and Assyria (2:13–15), each is treated as an individual target. And while in 3:6 the LORD speaks of having cut off nations, he refers to this as a series of acts against individual nations that should have made Jerusalem change course. Even though nations are singled out for judgment, the calamities of "the day of the LORD" do not befall them as a group, so that talk of wholesale destruction of the world likely means to stress – through hyperbole – the severity of the judgment that will afflict the wicked.

Chapter 3 vv. 1–5 set a different trajectory than the oracles against the nations, inasmuch as they lament Jerusalem's failure to heed and trust the LORD (vv. 1–2), contrasting the wickedness of its leaders (vv. 3–4) with the LORD's righteousness (v. 5) (Floyd, 2000). In vv. 6–7 the LORD reprises v. 2's lament that Jerusalem refused to accept "correction." Rather than learning from the fate of the nations, "they were the more eager to make all their deeds corrupt" (v. 7). The consequence is a summons of the nations to punish the city's wicked (v. 8), in the wake of which he will purify the nations' language so as to spur united worship of him (vv. 9–10). Jerusalem will be purified of its "proudly exultant ones," its haughtiness, and its wicked speech, for the LORD will leave within it only "a people humble and lowly" (vv. 11–13).

Accordingly, 2:1–3:13 unfolds in five stages: (1) the call for the humble to seek the LORD for possible refuge when his wrath falls (2:1–3); (2) an explication of what that day of wrath will be like via a summary of judgment on those to the east, west, south, and north, with consequent benefits for "the remnant of the house of Judah" (2:4–15); (3) a lament of Jerusalem's refusal to accept correction, even when faced with the LORD's acts against the nations (3:1–7); (4) a renewed exhortation to the upright to await the LORD's punishment of the wicked (3:8);[14] (5) anticipation of the nations' transformation into devotees of the LORD, as well as the cleansing of Jerusalem, so as to leave "a people humble and lowly ... the remnant of Israel," no longer under the threat of enemies (3:9–13).

The complexity and yet coherence of this unit reveals the same investment in literary design we noted for chapter 1. However, it also carries marks of construction from disparate pieces. The connection that "for" (2:4) makes between 2:1–3 and the announcement of judgment on the Philistines is ambiguous, since v. 4 certainly does not provide the reason that "the humble of the land" should seek the LORD (Roberts, 1991). On the other hand, 2:4 is syntactically and formally separate from

vv. 5–6, which begin with the particle "ah" (*hoy*), which is characteristic of a lament (compare 3:1) and reports words of the LORD himself. Moreover, while v. 4 *describes* what will happen to Philistine cities, vv. 5–6 *address* Philistine citizens. Not surprisingly, therefore, some scholars have perceived v. 4 as having been dislocated and they relocate it after either v. 5 (Roberts, 1991) or v. 6 (Holladay, 2001). It seems more likely, however, that v. 4 (whatever its origins) was placed here as a segue into the judgment oracles against the nations in vv. 5–15 (Sweeney, 1991a). In fact, the whole of those oracles appear to be a collage.

Chapter 2's oracles against the four nations shift from third-person description (v. 4) to an address of a nation (vv. 5–6), revert to third-person description (v. 7), then adopt first-person speech (vv. 8–9), return to third-person description (vv. 10–11), resume a mode of address (v. 12), and wind up with third-person description (vv. 13–15), without any evident rationale behind the switches. At the same time, the extremely brief oracle against the Ethiopians (v. 12) is connected with the preceding oracle only loosely by "also" (Sweeney, 1991a). Such twists and incongruities, especially in contrast to the coherence in 3:1–13,[15] suggest that 2:4–15 is a set of disparate oracles, arranged around the points of the compass (west, east, south, then north).

Especially striking within chapter 2 are vv. 10–11, which shift from first-person speech about Moab and Ammon (in vv. 8–9) to a third-person explanation of their fate, described as an assault on "the gods of the earth" that will result in worship of the LORD by "all the coasts and islands of the nations." While v. 10 cites as the basis for Moab's and Ammon's punishment the same scoffing against "the people of the LORD" with which they were charged in v. 8 ("taunted and made boasts" translate the same Hebrew words as do "scoffed and boasted" in 2:10), such behavior is epitomized as "their pride," the same fault attributed to those who will be purged from Jerusalem and replaced by the humble and lowly (3:11–12; compare 2:3). Additionally, these verses appear to be cast as prose, as opposed to the poetry of the surrounding verses (Holladay, 2001). These distinctive features of vv. 10–11 are grounds for suspecting that they have been fashioned and integrated into this collage to underscore the idea that pride and arrogance are the chief of humanity's crimes.

It is also noteworthy that the description of Nineveh as "the *exultant* city" (2:15) employs the same adjective used in 3:11's forecast of the removal of "your proudly *exultant* ones," a phrase found elsewhere only in Isaiah 13:3, even as the adjective "exultant" appears outside this phrase only in Isaiah 22:2, 23:7, 24:8, and 32:13. Additionally, the modifying phrase "that lived secure, that said to itself, 'I am, and there is no one else'" appears in precisely the same form in Isaiah 47:8. Accordingly, just as vv. 10–11 were formulated as a cap to the oracles against Moab and Ammon, so v. 15 was fashioned, drawing on this phraseology from Isaiah, to cap the lament over Nineveh (Holladay, 2001).

3:14–20:   Goals Realized

Verses 14–18a exhort Zion to rejoice in what the LORD has done and its effects, while vv. 18b–20 forecast details of the LORD's deliverance (Floyd, 2000).[16] Overlapping this shift is a change from the words of the prophet (vv. 14–18a) to the voice of the LORD, reassuring the people by enumerating his coming acts of salvation (vv. 18b–20). Nevertheless, vv. 14–20 are remarkably symmetrical: the initial summons of Jerusalem to rejoice (v. 14) is matched by the forecast of the LORD rejoicing over her (vv. 17c–18a); the announcement of deliverance from enemies (v. 15a–b) is complemented by the reference to the LORD giving victory (v. 17b); the declaration of the LORD in Jerusalem's midst in v. 15c is echoed in v. 17a; and the assurance of no more fear of disaster (v. 15d) is mirrored in an exhortation to be spoken to Jerusalem in the future (v. 16b) (Floyd, 2000).[17] At the center of these verses is the prose introduction of v. 16a, introducing a prophetic oracle that will be uttered only in the future (Floyd, 2000): "on that day it shall be said to Jerusalem." Given that v. 20 concludes with "says the LORD," it is reasonable to read vv. 18b–20 as a continuation of the future prophetic speech introduced in v. 16, with the prophet shifting his voice from a description of the LORD's deeds (vv. 17–18a) to present the LORD's words directly (Sweeney, 1991a). The fulcrum of the unit is v. 16's proclamation of what will be said to Jerusalem "on that day." The whole unit is so tightly constructed as to disallow explaining it as a collage of diverse components.[18]

Summary

The book pivots on the exhortation to prepare for the "day of the LORD['s wrath]" (2:1–3) that was announced in chapter 1. The effects of that event will yield a Jerusalem purged of its haughty citizens, with consequent flourishing of the LORD's people and reprogramming of the nations to worship him. As we have seen, the tight construction of the book permits occasional glimpses into the process of scribal authoring and editing that produced it, but just as often blocks perception of how each piece was fashioned into the whole, let alone detecting how each functioned originally.

   Chapter 1 is a carefully constructed reflection on the theme of the day of the LORD, held together by bookend statements that describe it as the annihilation of all living things (1:2–3, 18) that, in turn, enfold a series of statements on the character of the day of the LORD, each beginning with "on the day of the LORD's sacrifice" (v. 8) – a phrase molded to match the call to attend a sacrifice in v. 7 – "on that day" (vv. 9, 10) and "at that time" (v. 12). The series also incorporates a quotation of Amos 5:11 (vv. 13b–c).

   Chapter 2 holds a series of oracles against foreign nations that, judging from their awkward connections with each other, have been joined together to characterize the effects of the LORD's judgments on the nations surrounding Israel. The function of this survey is literary, since it forms the basis for the LORD's reflection on Jerusalem's failure to take note of how he executed his vengeance against the nations (3:6–7). Indeed, there is a strong bond between chapters 2 and 3, inasmuch as the call for "the humble of the land" to seek the LORD so as to find – at least potentially – shelter on the day of the LORD reaches its fulfillment in the removal of "your proudly exultant ones," leaving "a people humble and lowly" (3:11–12). The phrase "your proudly exultant ones" betrays dependence on Isaiah 13, on which we shall find the book of Joel to draw also.

   Accordingly, Zephaniah is a literary work composed of disparate components. The uniting of these in treating the topic of the day of the LORD anticipates the fuller development of this motif in the book of Joel. Before we can explore that work, however, we must consider in what sense the books we have studied thus far might represent the initial stages in forming a collection of 12 short prophetic books.

A Book of the Twelve?

In the pages to come ...

The books of Hosea and Amos evince having been shaped with an eye to each other, while the similarities in the superscriptions of Hosea, Amos, Micah, and Zephaniah suggest that they were edited in the same scribal circles. Some suggest that these four books once formed a unified collection of their own. Could this be the tip of the iceberg? Have the 12 smaller prophetic books been compiled to be read as a whole, so that they must be read sequentially, unfolding themes in a progression that requires us to view them not as 12 distinct books but as a **"Book of the Twelve"**?

An obvious commonality among the four books we have studied thus far is that their superscriptions locate their prophets within the reigns of specific kings.[19] Hosea and Amos are set within the reigns of both northern and southern kings, and their superscriptions have two rulers in common: King Uzziah of Judah and King Jeroboam of Israel. Additionally, Hosea shares with Micah the names of Uzziah's three immediate successors: Jotham, Ahaz, and Hezekiah. Zephaniah 1:1 places its prophet during the reign of Josiah, son of Ammon, but also identifies him as the great-grandson of Hezekiah, one of the kings mentioned in Hosea and Micah. Some scholars have deduced from these similarities that these four books composed a literary core around which the (minor) prophets took shape (Albertz, 2002; Nogalski, 1993a; Schart, 1998; Wöhrle, 2006a). In their view, this compilation transcends a mere collection, inasmuch as the constituent books were edited jointly so as to reflect on the meaning of "the word of the LORD" that proclaimed the end of Israel and Judah. They were fitted with **catchwords** at the end and beginning of adjacent books so as to fashion a "Book of the Four" (Albertz, 2002; Nogalski, 1993a).

Parallel to this "Book of the Four," runs the hypothesis, was a distinct Haggai–Zechariah collection. The creation of the "Book of the Twelve" involved merging these two collections and interspersing other prophetic books so as to form a unified literary work. The various scenarios that have been offered to account for the details of this merger are less important for our purposes than the overall contention that the "Book of the Twelve" is not a haphazard collection but a carefully shaped set, meant to form a single book whose individual components function like chapters.

Before commenting on the details of this hypothesis, it will be helpful to consider how these books were viewed in antiquity. Is there a long-standing perception of these 12 as a single book?

The Testimony of the Past

The earliest references to the 12 prophets speak of them as a group of the same stature as Isaiah, Jeremiah, and Ezekiel. Chapters 44–49 of the Wisdom of Ben Sira (a compendium of guidance written for the pious around 190 BCE) are devoted to extolling Israel's ancestors.[20] Following references to Enoch and Noah, and then brief paeans to Abraham and Isaac, Ben Sira gives extended praise to Moses and Aaron and then lauds other ancestors. Sirach 48:23–25 describe Isaiah's actions and characterize his message, followed by a similar summary for Jeremiah (49:7) and Ezekiel (49:8). While in each case his information derives from the book of the prophet, it is the individual prophet he describes rather than the book.[21]

The minor prophets, however, he speaks of as a group: "May the bones of the Twelve Prophets send forth new life from where they lie, for they comforted the people of Jacob and delivered them with confident hope" (49:10). However, to conclude from this that Ben Sira "pictured the Twelve as a unity ... as a *book* which 'comforted the people of Jacob'" (Coggins, 1994, 66; my italics) stretches the evidence. Although Ben Sira's characterization reflects his familiarity with the Twelve as a unit, he portrays them as a group of *prophets* (Petersen, 2000), as indicated by the plural pronoun serving as subject: "*they* comforted ... and delivered." Even though he ascribes to them a unified message, his summary of it amounts to a caricature, since it hardly does justice to the individual books or the collection as a whole. In the end, Ben Sira attests only that the 12 minor prophets were handed down as a collection by 190 BCE. He tells us nothing about how the collection was read.[22]

The Babylonian Talmud tractate *Baba Batra* stipulates that, in copying the scriptural **scrolls**, four blank lines must separate each book of the **Torah** and each of the prophets, save for the Twelve, where three blank lines suffice (*b. B. Bat.* 13b). While this reduction in blank lines has been offered as evidence that the Twelve were considered a literary unit (Nogalski, 1993a), it actually indicates the opposite. The instruction preserves a distinction between *books*, as opposed to units that are marked out in a composition like Proverbs, where "the proverbs of Solomon" (10:1) and "the words of Agur son of Jakeh" (30:1) introduce sections of a single book, with no more than a single blank line intervening (Ben Zvi, 1996b).

Moreover, while *Baba Batra* 14b speaks of the Twelve alongside Isaiah, Jeremiah, and Ezekiel, it does not assume that the Twelve constitute a fixed literary unit (Beck, 2005). In fact, inferring from the report "the LORD first spoke through Hosea" (Hos 1:2) that Hosea was the first of the prophets in his period (Hosea, Isaiah, Amos, Micah), it asks why, then, Hosea does not stand before Isaiah. Its answer – that the work is so small that it might be lost if not placed with the others – treats Hosea as a distinct composition whose placement is simply to guarantee its preservation (Ben Zvi, 1996b).

The perception of Hosea's independence is reinforced by its superscription, which distinguishes it from other books (Ben Zvi, 1996b). The fact that each book is distinguished by a superscription and contains distinctive themes supports the perception that the Twelve present *different* articulations of the divine word.[23] Above all, there is no superscription for the collection of the Twelve as a whole (Ben Zvi, 1996b). Accordingly, the earliest preserved traditions about the Twelve fail to substantiate the hypothesis that they were meant to be read as a single book, while prominent features that mark off each from the other equally undermine that hypothesis. What, then, of recent perceptions of links between the books said to signal that this collection constitutes a "Book of the Twelve"?

Recent Perceptions

Recent arguments for regarding the Twelve as a unified book highlight words and phrases at the end of one book and the beginning of the next signaling that they are to be read sequentially. For example, the occurrence of the phrase "The LORD roars from Zion and utters his voice from Jerusalem" in both Joel 3:16a and Amos 1:2 has long been identified as coupling them (Cassuto, 1973). More recently, scholars have observed that addressees in Joel 3 (Tyre, Philistia, Edom, and Jerusalem) are also targets in Amos's oracles of 1:3–2:16 (Nogalski, 1993a). This combination of links has been cited as evidence that Amos is the sequel to Joel rather than a distinct book.

Catchword links have also been noted between Joel and the book that precedes it, Hosea. The call for Israel to "return" occurs four times in the concluding chapter of Hosea (14:1, 2, 4, 7) and becomes Joel's chief exhortation to his people (2:12, 13, 14; 3:1, 4, 7) (Cassuto, 1973). To this can be added that the Hebrew words for "inhabitants," "wine," "vine," and "grain" appear in the first 12 verses of Joel and in the concluding verses of Hosea (14:4–9) (Nogalski, 1993a). What is more, argues Nogalski, the call to "hear this" that begins Joel's address of the elders and inhabitants of the land (1:2) is best read as a reference back to the concluding statement of Hosea that "those who are wise understand *these things*" (Hos 14:9), which Nogalski suggests refers to Hosea's call to return to the LORD, joined with the LORD's promise to heal Israel's disloyalty and restore it to prosperity (Hos 14:2–8). Understood against that backdrop, Joel's question "Has such a thing happened in your days, or in the days of your ancestors?" is a blunt acknowledgment that the promise remains unfulfilled, leading the prophet to diagnose the problem as a failure to repent, an action he urges the people to undertake (Nogalski, 1993b). Nogalski identifies similar verbal links between books among the Twelve, identifying them as clues that the books are to be read sequentially, as a unit.

Despite the appeal this approach has generated, it has weaknesses. On the one hand, even if every link between one book and the next could be confirmed, that would merely show that the *arrangement* of the books is deliberate; it cannot show that they are to be read sequentially. One may read them that way, and many proposals to do so have been offered (Coggins, 1994; Rendtorff, 2000; Sweeney, 2000). Even some who are skeptical about these perceived links acknowledge a progression from announcements of judgment to triumph in the course of the Twelve (Petersen, 2000). However, to detect something approaching an unfolding plot in the Twelve requires finding a pattern of themes and phrases that transcends each book, at the expense of each book's distinctive themes (Ben Zvi, 1996b).[24]

Even at that, however, the perceived links are not uniformly compelling. For instance, while the phrase "The LORD roars from Zion and utters his voice from Jerusalem" occurs in Joel 3:16a and Amos 1:2, its occurrence appears to be a superficial addition to each book. Its role in Amos 1:2 is to identify the "real" voice behind the oracles against the nations (Wolff, 1977). However, it is foreign to that context, since its description of the LORD roaring from the temple betrays a Judean point of view (whereas Amos spoke in the north), while its style is more at home in the Psalms (see above, p. 49). Accordingly, it seems to be a secondary editorial introduction to the oracles against the nations in Amos 1–2.

A similar conclusion applies to Joel 3:16a. Whereas 3:12 agrees with 3:2 in depicting the nations assembling in "the Valley of Jehoshaphat" (v. 14's "valley of decision"), where the LORD will meet them in judgment, v. 16a has him launching judgment with a roar *from Jerusalem* (Beck, 2005).[25] This switch in the place of the LORD's attack is abrupt.

More tellingly, v. 15 takes up verbatim Joel 2:10b: "The sun and the moon are darkened, and the stars withdraw their shining." And immediately following v. 16a we find language from 2:10a: "and the heavens and the earth shake." The reference to the LORD roaring from Zion is a syntactically awkward (in Hebrew) interruption of the phrases taken from 2:10 (Beck, 2005).[26] Nevertheless, the use of 2:10b in v. 15 and 2:10a in 3:16b – thus encapsulating v. 16a – parallels Amos 8:4–6, where we saw v. 4 utilize Amos 2:7a and v. 6 use Amos 2:6b as brackets around the new saying in 8:5 (see above, p. 46).[27] Although one might still reasonably argue that Joel 3:16a has been inserted to form a link to Amos 1:2, the way it has been inserted – as if within brackets – suggests that this took place at a late stage in editing (Beck, 2005; Jeremias, 2007); it is not integral to the structure of the book of Joel and, thus, does not signal a thematic link joining the books as part of a unified composition.

In fact, it is not clear that there was widespread early recognition that Amos followed Joel, for other ancient traditions attest alternative orders (Fuller, 1996). For example, 2 Esdras 1:39–40, composed in Hebrew toward the end of the first century CE, and manuscripts of the **Septuagint** cite the first six books in the order: Hosea, Amos, Micah, Joel, Obadiah, Jonah. Another first-century work composed in Hebrew, *The Martyrdom and Ascension of Isaiah*, lists the first six minor prophets as follows: Amos, Hosea, Micah, Joel, Nahum, Jonah (*Mart. Ascen. Isa.* 4:22). Finally, the first-century Greek composition *Lives of the Prophets*, which offers biographical information for each prophet, treats the first six in the order: Hosea, Micah, Amos, Joel, Obadiah, and Jonah. Accordingly, while Joel precedes Amos in the most commonly known arrangement, other orders were known in antiquity, with no indication that there was an original, set order (Jones, 2000). We cannot, therefore, presume that Joel and Amos were widely (much less originally) considered closely bound. Variant orders for others of the Twelve raise similar problems for the perception of a plot unfolding from one book to the next (Ben Zvi, 1996b).

Still less compelling are perceived catchwords like "inhabitants," "wine," "vine," and "grain" in Hosea 14:4–9 and the first 12 verses of Joel. Given that these are common words in the Bible, their occurrences in thematically different contexts within the two books cannot be used as indications of deliberately placed bonds between them. Even the use of "return" in Hosea 14 and its employment in Joel 2–3 cannot be considered a marked bond between books, given how frequently the call to "return" is in the prophets. And if the question "Has this happened in your days" (Joel 1:2; my translation) referred to the grand restoration forecast in Hosea 14, it is striking that the hearers are exhorted merely to inform their children and grandchildren of its failure to materialize. An exhortation to "return" so as to induce the restoration would provide more effective guidance and a clearer link with Hosea 14. On the whole, the identified catchwords between books are too scattered and imprecise to support the contention that they usher readers from one book into the next (Ben Zvi, 1996b).

Themes Common to the Twelve

To affirm the distinction of each book does not mean that the Twelve have no commonalities. We have already noted that Amos and Hosea have been shaped in light of each other, revealing an attempt to make those prophets speak in accord (Jeremias, 1996b). Although common themes appear in all the prophetic books, certain themes enjoy notable prominence in the Twelve. Problems arise, however, when these are considered unifying motifs.

For example, several of the Twelve utilize the confession of Exodus 34:6–7:

> The LORD, the LORD, a God merciful and gracious, slow to anger, and abounding in steadfast love and faithfulness, keeping steadfast love for the thousandth generation, forgiving iniquity and transgression and sin, yet by no means clearing the guilty, but visiting the iniquity of the parents upon the children and the children's children, to the third and the fourth generation.

This formulation appears explicitly in Joel's exhortation "Return to the LORD, your God, for he is gracious and merciful, slow to anger, and abounding in steadfast love, and relents from punishing" (2:13). This characterization of the LORD is the foundation for Joel's question "Who knows whether he will not turn and relent?" (2:14).

This confession figures also in Jonah's explanation of his refusal to go to Nineveh: "That is why I fled to Tarshish at the beginning; for I knew that you are a gracious God and merciful, slow to anger, and abounding in steadfast love, and ready to relent from punishing" (Jon 4:2). This characterization underlies the king's urging all citizens to repent: "Who knows? God may relent and change his mind; he may turn from his fierce anger, so that we do not perish" (3:9). Correlatively, Jonah's action of taking up a position nearby "to see what would become of the city" (4:5) assumes the alternative potential in "Who knows?", tacitly invoking Exodus 34:7's vow that the LORD "will by no means clear the guilty." In both Joel and Jonah the characterization of the LORD as "gracious and merciful" and "relenting from punishment" forms the basis for a *chance* at divine favor.[28]

One other passage strikes some as reliant on Exodus 34:6–7. At the close of Micah stands this **doxology**: "Who is a God like you, pardoning iniquity and passing over the transgression of the remnant of your possession? He does not retain his anger forever, because he delights in steadfast love"[29] (Mic 7:18). If this echoes Exodus 34:6–7 as van Leeuwen (1993) suggests, it does not simply offer the *potential* of divine forgiveness but the basis for reassurance: "He will again have compassion upon us; he will tread our iniquities under foot. You will cast all our sins into the depths of the sea. You will show faithfulness to Jacob and unswerving loyalty to Abraham, as you have sworn to our ancestors from the days of old" (Mic 7:19–20).

Those who judge all these passages to rely on the confession from Exodus 34 suggest that it is the means by which the Twelve jointly justify the LORD's destruction of Samaria and Jerusalem and lay the groundwork for hope (van Leeuwen, 1993). Hosea 14:9 is the prime point through which to correlate these passages: "Those who are wise understand these things; those who are discerning know them. For the ways of the LORD are right, and the upright walk in them, but transgressors stumble in them."

The assertion that "the wise" acknowledge "the ways of the LORD" provides the backdrop for Joel 2:14, "Who knows whether he will not turn and relent?", and Jonah 3:9, "Who knows? God may relent and change his mind," for the wise already know "YHWH's bipolar ways of mercy and justice" (van Leeuwen, 1993, 38). Equally, the question "Who knows?" and the declaration that "those who are wise ... know" create "a brilliant wordplay" with "Who is a God like you?" in Micah 7:18, the answer to which the wise know (van Leeuwen, 1993). Accordingly, Hosea 14:9 provides the integration point for the allusions to Exodus 34:6–7.

The prime question is whether all these passages reflect Exodus 34:6–7 and each other. While Joel 2:13 and Jonah 4:2 clearly reflect Exodus 34, any echo of it in Micah 7:18 is muddled, despite the use of similar words. And why should we detect a link between the questions "Who knows?" in Joel 2:14 and Jonah 3:9, and Micah's "Who is a God like you?" (7:18).[30] Micah's question emphasizes that there is no god whose willingness to forgive equals the LORD's, a notion far different from those of Joel 2:14 and Jonah 3:9, which cast the LORD's willingness to forgive as a mere possibility.

Why, similarly, should we posit that Hosea 14:9 was oriented to the use of Exodus 34:6–7 in Joel and Jonah? There are no verbal ties between them, while a call to recognize the rightness of the LORD's dealings need not assume the LORD's willingness to forgive. Therefore, the argument that Exodus 34:6–7 provided the controlling motif in the editing of the Twelve is unconvincing.

Another motif frequently said to unify the Twelve is "the day of the LORD," which appears three times each in Amos 5:18–20 and Zephaniah 1:7, 14, five times in Joel, and once each in Obadiah 15 and Malachi 4:5. The argument that it constitutes a unifying motif in the Twelve is weakened by the fact that 10 of its 13 occurrences are in just three books.[31] It can be expanded into a unifying motif only by considering the phrases "on that day" and "in those days" as its equivalents, on the grounds that they "can refer to a day when YHWH acts or days which manifest the effects of YHWH's activity, and thus relate to the day of YHWH" (Nogalski, 1999, 619). Comprehending this broadly, one can consider "the day of the LORD" a motif reflecting "at least a shared orientation on the part of [those who edited] these twelve writings" (Nogalski, 1999, 622). However, does any occurrence of "day" in a passage that describes the LORD's intervention convey the same idea as "the day of the LORD"?

Let us take as an example Hosea 11:1, which places the reunification of Israel and Judah under one ruler on "the day of Jezreel." According to Nogalski (1999), this reunification makes this "day of Jezreel" equivalent to "the day of the LORD." To adduce a parallel, imagine the media reporting, "The president declared Monday a day of remembrance for those who lost their lives in the hotel fire." Now suppose that a subsequent report states, "Friday the president visited California for a day of celebration with his daughter, who was graduating from UCLA," or "He visited Utah Wednesday, because on that day he wished to recognize the service of the retiring governor." Even though all three of these "days" involve presidential action, they do not necessarily refer to the same day. A "day of remembrance" is different than a "day of celebration," while "on that day" in the third report simply marks the occasion of an event. For the same reason, expanding the theme of the "day of the LORD" to comprehend all phrases that include "day" and speak of the LORD's intervention forces them into a mold that ignores the particular context of a "day."[32] "The day of

Jezreel," as the occasion when north and south are reunited, is hardly allied with calamities labeled "the day of the LORD" in Zephaniah and Joel.

Even allowing that some occurrences of "that day" refer to "the day of the LORD," as judged from their context, this motif cannot be said to unite the Twelve, for it appears only sporadically outside Joel and Zephaniah.

Summary

It is indisputable that similar phraseology permeates the Twelve, and the influence of themes from one book on another has been clearly demonstrated. The question is what these phenomena signal. The various proposals to attribute similar phrases or ideas to an impulse to unite the Twelve fail to do justice to the individual books.[33] However, the tradition of handing down these books in a single scroll requires some sort of explanation.

Ancient scrolls could hold multiple books without assuming a literary connection between them (Ben Zvi, 1996b). The lack of a superscription for the whole of the Twelve, at the same time that a separate superscription is prefixed to each work, argues against assuming that this scroll presents a unified composition. On the other hand, while the Babylonian Talmud's explanation of the placement of Hosea with the 11 other short books to guarantee its preservation lends support to the suggestion that the Twelve constitute a "collection," that term seems too bland for a set of writings that share themes and motifs, not to mention the image of prophets as the LORD's spokesmen.

An attractive alternative is Petersen's (2000) description of them as "a thematized anthology,"[34] whose enumeration as *12* books is attributable to a desire to match the ideal number of Israel's tribes. The phrase "*thematized* anthology" implies that the works are joined because they share themes.

Even if we cannot detect a scheme according to which the Twelve were organized, their present order begs explanation. The fact that only the superscriptions to Hosea, Amos, Micah, and Zephaniah specify the kings during whose reigns the prophet spoke, and the fact that they share the concept of a divine "word" delivered through the prophets, provide prima facie evidence that those books constituted a "Book of the Four" as the earliest stage in compiling the Twelve (Albertz, 2002, 2003b; Nogalski, 1993a, 1993b; Schart, 1998; Wöhrle, 2006a).[35] However, this does not account for why (for example) the book of Joel intervenes between Hosea and Amos. Even if Joel is variously placed in attested orders for the books, its position between Hosea and Amos in today's Bibles (based on the **Masoretic text**) begs the question of its relationship to them.

In this case, it is noteworthy that Joel's superscription uses the notion of the "word of the LORD" reaching the prophet. The fact that no other book in the Twelve (outside the Four) uses this idiom suggests that Joel is associated closely with the Four (Wöhrle, 2006a). This does not amount to reinstating the argument that it was formulated to stand between Hosea and Amos, however, since this is a feature it shares with Hosea, Micah, and Zephaniah equally (Amos's superscription varies slightly).[36] On the other hand, even if Joel 3:16 and Amos 1:2 were inserted into their books at late stages, this may reveal part of the process by which Joel became linked to Amos in one ordering of the anthology.

In a similar way, we can question how Micah came to be separated from Hosea and Amos by the insertion of Obadiah and Jonah, as well as how Nahum and Habakkuk came to be inserted between Micah and Zephaniah. In my view, however, most of these processes are too inscrutable to permit a comprehensive account of how the Twelve came to be ordered as we know them.[37] And yet, given the varied orders found in lists of the minor prophets noted earlier, we should likely consider that varied orders (plural) was the rule from early on, rather than suppose that an original order was modified by later editors (Guillaume, 2007; Jones, 2000).

Notes

1. In particular, the notion of a revolt against Assyria that led to a wide expansion of Judah's territory has been questioned by research into the political climate after 627, when Assyrian power waned and Egypt became the strongman (Ben Zvi, 1993). This is not even to broach the question of whether 2 Kings 22 and 23 are one piece or whether the discovery of "the book of the covenant" was the trigger for whatever reform Josiah may have undertaken (Hardmeier, 2005).
2. Although there is a distinction in the focus of vv. 2–3 and 4–5, it is inappropriate to refer to them as embodying distinct theologies. Least of all should such a judgment arise from inferred allusions to Genesis 1 and 6 (Nogalski, 1993a), since the phrases "humans and animals," "birds and fish," and "from the face of the earth" are not distinctive enough to conclude that they were drawn from Genesis (Sweeney, 2007a).
3. For the legitimacy of regarding "the day of the LORD's wrath" as a synonym of "the day of the LORD," see Beck (2005, 43–44).
4. The only other place in the prophets where "before" follows an imperative is Jeremiah 13:16, which Holladay (2001) judges dependent upon Zephaniah 2:2.
5. "At hand" translates the same word rendered "near" (*qarob*) in v. 14, where it stands at the head of its clause: "for *near* is the day of the LORD."
6. Although the NRSV's translation of v. 17 appears to introduce a new section by shifting to a statement of the LORD's intentions, that statement is bound to v. 16 by a Hebrew verb formation (the *waw*-consecutive perfect) that links v. 17 closely with v. 16.
7. Beck (2005) distinguishes the latter half of v. 18 (after "on the day of the LORD's wrath") from vv. 17–18, arguing that the reference to a complete destruction of the earth is a later addition that effects a connection with vv. 2–3. This is too speculative to substantiate.
8. Phrases b and c of v. 13 stand in logical tension with 13a, since they assume the possibility of an action already barred according to 13a. Given that 13b–c show a catchword association ("houses") (Beck, 2005), they could either form part of the initial compilation that produced vv. 7–16 or be a subsequent addition.
9. Some have suggested that vv. 14–16 once followed v. 7 directly, since both describe the day of the LORD as near (e.g., Neef, 1999). However, vv. 14–16 do not play out v. 7's anticipated sacrificial meal through the plundering of the victim, which has already been accomplished in vv. 8–13 (Beck, 2005). Rather, they characterize the day of the LORD as a day of terror and wrath (Bergler, 1988).
10. Similar is Isaiah 2:12–17, in which the LORD is said to have "a day against all that is proud and lofty," followed by a series of phenomena that exemplify this, such as "all the cedars of Lebanon," "all the high mountains," and all the large, ocean-going vessels ("ships of Tarshish").
11. While it is possible that v. 15's description of the day of the LORD as "darkness and gloom" is dependent on Amos 5:20 ("Is not the day of the LORD darkness, not light, and gloom

with no brightness in it?") (De Vries, 1995; Schart, 1998), the Hebrew terms "darkness" and "gloom" are not so rare as to compel the conclusion that Amos was the source of this language (Beck, 2005).

12. The phrase "because they have sinned against the LORD" is probably a later insertion to justify the LORD bringing upon them such hardships (Beck, 2005). The subsequent reference to the LORD in the third person ("on the day of the LORD's wrath") is likely due to its use in a fixed formula (Beck, 2005).

13. Compare Psalm 74, which juxtaposes the destruction of Jerusalem with the scene of cosmic chaos prior to the LORD creating an orderly world (Levenson, 1988).

14. While some see in v. 8b a later addition that transforms the assembly of the nations into an assault on them (Nogalski, 1993a; Schart, 1998), it seems more reasonable to identify those on whom the LORD pours his anger as the city's evildoers mentioned in vv. 3–4 and 7 (the NRSV's "all the earth" in v. 8 is better translated "all the land"). Even though vv. 1–7 focus on the character of the city, the training of judgment on the city's wicked fits the book's motif of the "humble and lowly" surviving judgment. Note that the final lines of v. 8 pick up the words used in 1:18.

15. While 3:1–5 describe Jerusalem in words that speak *about* the LORD (vv. 2, 5), their close ties with vv. 6–13 – cast entirely as divine speech – make it reasonable to conclude that the divine address is embedded in a larger speech (Sweeney, 1991a).

16. As stated in the Preface, the NRSV is the translation used throughout this book, including in Zephaniah 3:17–18, which presents many textual difficulties, for which many solutions have been offered. The **emendations** assumed by the NRSV are reasonable, even if they lead to a break of subunits between v. 18a and 18b not typically found in discussions of this passage.

17. In distinction from Floyd (2000), I find the theme of the LORD's removal of judgments and defeat of enemies (v. 15a–b) echoed in the identification of the LORD as "a warrior who gives victory" (v. 17b) rather than postponed until v. 19.

18. Some have suggested that vv. 18–20 are an expansion of vv. 14–17 (Nogalski, 1993a) or that vv. 19–20 are a prose addition to the hymn of vv. 14–18 (Curtis, 2000). Both proposals assert that the verses were added to integrate Zephaniah with other works in the "Book of the Twelve." However, it is difficult to disentangle these verses from vv. 14–17 and, more so, to establish that they were part of an editorial process that spanned several books. Curtis's (2000) demonstration of the different prose particle density of vv. 19–20 as against vv. 14–18 is striking, but there is no reason to assume that the more prosaic description of the LORD's actions could not have been constructed by the author of vv. 14–18.

19. The only other prophetic books to provide such a dating are Isaiah and Jeremiah.

20. The book of Ben Sira is also called Sirach or Ecclesiasticus.

21. For example, Jeremiah is described as one who "even in the womb had been consecrated a prophet, to pluck up and ruin and destroy, and likewise to build and to plant" (Sir 49:7), language taken from Jeremiah 1 to characterize the prophet as a figure.

22. Other ancient witnesses to the existence of a collection of the Twelve are even less informative. Based on the numbers of biblical books mentioned by first-century writers (Josephus, *Contra Apionem* 1.40; 4 Ezra 14.42–46), a collection of the Twelve was recognized, but we find no indication as to how it was read.

23. This is true even if the phrase "the word of the LORD came to *x*" in the superscriptions of several books implies that the words of the prophets represent a univocal communication by the LORD (Albertz, 2003b).

24. Sweeney's contention (2000, 56) that "the placement of the individual books within the Book of the Twelve necessarily compromises their communicative autonomy and subsumes them to the overall communicative outlook of the book as a whole" holds weight only if one establishes on other grounds that they are meant to be so read.

25. By contrast, the assertion that "I, the LORD your God, dwell in Zion, my holy mountain" (v. 17) reflects a traditional formulation of the divine presence "dwelling" in Jerusalem (compare Isa 8:18, 33:5; Ps 74:2, 135:21) and is, thus, of a different order than the (novel) formulation of the LORD roaring "from Zion" (Beck, 2005).

26. The phrases "The LORD roars from Zion and utters his voice from Jerusalem" interrupt the syntactic sequence by interjecting a waw + noun sequence regularly used to provide background information in Hebrew.

27. Such inversion of phrases borrowed from elsewhere is a common phenomenon in the Bible, often called "Zeidel's law" (Beentjes, 1982; Fishbane, 1985, 504 n. 11). The use of inverted phrases to insert this phrase makes it more likely that it is a late insertion than that it is an original formulation for this place in Joel.

28. The parallels between these passages are best explained in terms of Jonah borrowing from Joel (Dozeman, 1989) (see below, pp. 127–128).

29. NRSV: "delights in showing clemency." The Hebrew noun translated "clemency" (*chesed*) is the same one translated "steadfast love" in Joel 2:13 and Jonah 4:2.

30. The questions in Joel and Jonah express uncertainty about the outcome, even as they tacitly argue that the attempt to assuage divine wrath is worthwhile. Why should we suppose that the reader's contemplation of the challenge of Hosea 14:9 should short-circuit that uncertainty?

31. The phrase appears in the major prophets, in Isaiah 13:6, 9; Jeremiah 46:10; Ezekiel 13:5; 30:3.

32. For a careful consideration of which phrases qualify as references to this theme and on what basis, see Beck (2005, 43–44). In a context where "the day of the LORD" is the topic, "on that day" may refer to it, as it does in Zephaniah 1:9, 10, 15. However, for "on that day" and "at that time" as simple temporal phrases in the prophets, see Beck, 2005, 93 n. 119.

33. This raises the question of whether the individual books were meant to be read as literary works, having a plot in whose service the author orchestrated his book (Davies, 1996).

34. The assembly of other works into anthologies before the turn of the era provides analogies to this way of conceiving of the Twelve (Beck, 2006).

35. I remain skeptical about how much of the editorial process of combining these we can recover. As Albertz observes, "there is still no scholarly consensus ... as to the criteria that must be met before we can speak of a deliberate compositional linkage ... in contrast to random verbal echoes," nor is it clear how we discern what sort of intention lies behind the editorial additions that have been posited as joining the books into a whole (Albertz, 2003b, 208; compare Wöhrle, 2006a, 20–21). Despite Albertz's attempt to provide criteria for his own reconstructions, his detections of editorial links rely on the *assumption* that the editor(s) sought to create a flow from one book to the other. For example, his contention that the redactor of the Four expanded the introduction of the book of Micah to convey that the judgment Hosea and Amos forecast for Israel now extended to Judah assumes that the redactor intended Micah to be read as a sequel to Hosea and Amos (Albertz, 2003b). Nogalski (1993a) argues that the kings reigning in the era of each of these prophets were specified to induce the readers' perception of these four books as unfolding the same story of the people's fate caused by their rejection of the prophets' message. However, this argument is compelling only if one accepts Nogalski's larger theory about the Twelve.

36. The notion of a "Joel-related layer" (Nogalski, 1993b) that binds together a "Book of the Four" (so also Wöhrle, 2006a) or that constitutes the overarching bond for a "Book of the Twelve" (Schart, 1998) rest on (what I consider) untenable theories for the composition for Joel (see Chapter Six).

37. Jonah's position in the Qumran scroll of the Minor Prophets (4QXII[a-g]) raises the possibility that it once followed Malachi (Fuller, 1996; Jones, 1997; however, contrast Guillaume, 2007). Jonah likely came to be associated with the prophets from the eighth century only secondarily, on the grounds that "Jonah, son of Amittai" in 2 Kings 14:25 worked during the reign of Jeroboam II (Schart, 2000). Even so, chronology was only one factor in ordering the books (Sweeney, 2000), even as other ancient anthologies seem to have used chronology as but one strategy for arranging their contents (Beck, 2006).

6

The Books of Joel and Obadiah

Joel

In the pages to come …

The interest in the day of the LORD that we saw in Zephaniah sharpens in Joel, where it becomes the central motif. The book's **superscription** shares with the books we have studied thus far – and with them alone – the phrase "The word of the LORD that came to …." It does not, however, locate Joel in a specific time, spurring various proposals that place him between the mid-eighth through the mid-fourth centuries BCE, although most scholars consider the latter part of that range more likely (Beck, 2005). However, we must ask whether trying to assign a date to Joel as a historical figure is pertinent, given questions about whether the book is a collection of a prophet's **oracles** or a collage of materials drawn from various prophetic books. An equally pressing question is whether the book was composed in a single effort, or if 2:28–3:21 is a late expansion of 1:1–2:27. We will tackle the latter of these questions first.

The Book's Structure: Two Halves or a Narrative Whole?

Following a summons to the elders and the people to pay attention, a voice touts the uniqueness of the book's contents: "Has such a thing happened in your days, or in the days of your ancestors?" (1:2). The audience is instructed to relay what they hear to their children and grandchildren (1:3). In keeping with this hint of a story to be handed down, the reader finds something approaching a narrative, detectable in three pivotal statements.

Prophetic Literature: From Oracles to Books, First Edition. Ronald L. Troxel.
© 2012 Ronald L. Troxel. Published 2012 by Blackwell Publishing Ltd.

The first statement occurs in the wake of 2:1's alert to a calamity worse than those chapter 1 described as having already befallen the people. After vv. 2b–11 portray a frightful army invading the land, v. 12 calls for penitence: "Yet even now, says the LORD, return to me with all your heart" (2:12). "Even now" marks this exhortation as pivotal, for it suggests that this peril – although imminent – is not inevitable, since the LORD might still "turn and relent, and leave a blessing behind him" (v. 14). Whereas chapter 1 enumerated calamities past, chapter 2 describes an impending threat that repentance might turn aside.

Not long afterwards we find the second pivotal statement: "Then the LORD became jealous for his land, and had pity on his people" (2:18). This verse abruptly shifts to reporting deliverance, without saying whether the people gathered for repentance. In vv. 19–27 the LORD announces the expulsion of the invading army (v. 20) a restoration of crops (vv. 23–26b) and removal of the people's shame (vv. 26c–27).

Immediately after this reassurance stands the third pivotal statement: "Then afterward, I will pour out my spirit on all flesh; your sons and your daughters shall prophesy, your old men shall dream dreams, and your young men shall see visions" (2:28). While the restoration of crops in 2:19–27 resolved the calamities that had either occurred or were impending, 2:28–3:21 expands on the removal of the people's shame (announced in vv. 26c–27) through a decisive defeat of their enemies, accompanied by deliverance from the day of the LORD for all who call on him and idyllic fruitfulness for the land of Judah.

This pivot carries another notable shift: the day of the LORD that was directed against Judah in the book's first half (1:1–2:27) is now aimed at other nations (2:28–3:21).[1] The LORD's summons of the nations to "the valley of Jehoshaphat" (3:2) brings crisis upon them and ushers in paradisiacal fruitfulness for Judah (3:18). This shift in tone and substance between 1:1–2:27 and 2:28–3:21 has prompted assertions that the book's second half was composed by a **scribe** who extrapolated ideas from the book's first half into a still more dramatic scene (Barton, 2001; Beck, 2005; Plöger, 1968).[2]

Possibly supportive of this perception are phrases from the book's first half that recur in the second. For example, in chapter 2 the warriors who leap on the city's walls and enter its houses produce terrifying effects: "The earth quakes before them, the heavens tremble. The sun and the moon are darkened, and the stars withdraw their shining" (2:10). These ominous effects reappear in the LORD's attack on the nations, when the sun is "turned to darkness and the moon to blood" (2:31), while (as in 2:10) "The sun and the moon are darkened, and the stars withdraw their shining … and the heavens and the earth shake" (3:15–16).

More noteworthy than the recurrence of this image, however, is that in both halves of the book it is associated with "the day of the LORD." This phrase so pervades Joel (1:15, 2:2–11, 2:30–32, 3:14) as to constitute its signature theme (Jeremias, 2002; Wolff, 1977). In chapter 1 the day of the LORD is presaged by agricultural catastrophes that have occurred, while in chapter 2 it designates a supra-historical event, a time of "darkness and gloom" that brings with it a grotesque, horrific army. In chapter 3 it is directed against the nations.

Those who characterize the day of the LORD as more radical in 2:28–32 and 3:14 than in 1:1–2:27 downplay the fact that the LORD's assault on the nations in chapter 3 is no more extraordinary than the army of chapter 2, whose "like has never been from of old, nor will be again after them in ages to come" (2:2) and is led by the LORD himself (2:11). Neither is the bestowal of the divine spirit in 2:28 more sublime than the restoration of divine oversight and protection in 2:18–27.[3]

Correlatively, the claim that "then afterward" only "loosely connects" 2:28–32 to the preceding verses (Beck, 2005, 180) overlooks how this phrase functions elsewhere. The phrase translated "afterward" (*'acharey ken*) appears elsewhere in the latter prophets only in Jeremiah 16:16, 21:7, 34:11, 46:26, and 49:6, and only in Jeremiah 49:6 is it part of a scribal expansion. More importantly, wherever the full phrase found here (*waw* + *hayah* + *'acharey ken*) appears elsewhere, it signals a new stage in a narrative (Judg 16:4; 1 Sam 24:5; 2 Sam 2:1, 8:1 [= 1 Chr 18:1], 10:1 [= 1 Chr 19:1], 13:1, 21:18; 2 Kings 6:24). Accordingly, there is no reason to conclude that "then afterward" marks an expansion of the passage.

In accord with this, reviewing the features identified as reasons to consider 2:28–3:21 a late expansion mutes their force. As has often been noted, 2:28–3:21 contains reversals of language and themes found in 1:1–2:27. For instance, in 2:3 the land is "like the garden of Eden" ahead of attackers who leave it "a desolate wilderness," while in 3:18 it becomes extraordinarily fruitful, while Egypt and Edom become "a desolate wilderness" (3:19) (Bergler, 1988). And whereas 2:3 describes the devouring horde as leaving "nothing [that] escapes" (*peletah*), 2:32 announces that there will be "those who escape" (*peletah*) in Mount Zion and Jerusalem (Wolff, 1977). But similar reversals appear already within the first half of the book. For instance, the promise of 2:25 ("I will repay you for the years that the swarming locust has eaten, the hopper, the destroyer, and the cutter") uses the same four names for locusts found in 1:4. Chapter 2 v. 24 promises an abundance of grain and wine, reversing chapter 1's laments of their destruction. It seems more accurate, then, to say that the book presents a crisscrossing network of images depicting the destruction of produce and its restoration (Deist, 1988).

Equally supportive of reading 2:28–3:21 as integral to the book is the observation that, if the day of the LORD is spent by the end of Joel 2:27 (under the thesis that this marks the original end of the book), then it differs surprisingly from its contours in Zephaniah, where the day of the LORD is still future, ominous, and incomprehensible. And yet, Joel's call to escape the brunt of the day of the LORD by repentance (2:12–17) is similar to Zephaniah's call to the humble to "seek ... [to] be hidden on the day of the LORD's wrath" (Zeph 2:3), while this measure is given no more guarantee of success in Joel ("who knows whether he will not turn and relent?", 2:14) than in Zephaniah ("perhaps you may be hidden on the day of the LORD's wrath," 2:3). These parallels give reason to expect that the character of the day of the LORD in Joel will parallel that in Zephaniah. But this proves true only if all three chapters of Joel are original to it.

Correlatively, we should also note that, unless the book of Joel does more than recount a day of the LORD in the past, it is unclear why the audience is asked to view the calamities it brings as unprecedented (1:2), since those described in chapter 1 were commonplace in ancient Israel. If, however, the second half is integral to the book's treatment of the day of the LORD, the demand placed on the hearers makes sense. Indeed, the most horrific aspect of the day of the LORD – the assault by a divinely led army – is suspended in chapter 2, while it is portrayed as inevitable in chapter 3. And in both cases the day of the LORD arises without specific provocation: the call for the people to appeal to the LORD in 2:12–17 names no crimes that brought on such peril,[4] nor does 2:30–32 identify what occasions the day of the LORD that people in Jerusalem must escape, so that only the nations are vulnerable. The report of 2:18, that the Lord "had pity on his people," does not mean that the threat of the day of the Lord was exhausted after removal of the people's guilt. The second half of the book makes clear the lesson to be drawn from the first half by subsequent genera-tions (1:2–3), promising that, when faced with a new manifestation of the day of the Lord, "everyone who calls on the name of the Lord shall be saved" (2:32), even as 2:18 implies happened in the past.[5]

In sum, the arguments for judging the book composed of two distinct units, the second of which was added late, are placed in doubt by the detection of a narrative thread running through the book, consideration of interrelationships within it, and observations about the trajectory established in the initial call to heed and transmit the story. Although it remains possible that the second half of the book is a later elaboration, it has been so integrated into the structure of the book as to make that assertion highly speculative.

Reuse of Earlier Oracles

Another common feature of the book deserves consideration: its reuse of language and motifs from other books. Chapter 2 v. 32 is most explicit: "Then everyone who calls on the name of the Lord shall be saved; for in Mount Zion and in Jerusalem there shall be those who escape, *as the Lord has said*" (my italics). The promise on which this offer rests is found in Obadiah 17: "But on Mount Zion there shall be those that escape."[6]

Quotations, Allusions, and Echoes

A growing interest within biblical studies is the way scribes reused earlier materials. This phenomenon is often called "intertextuality," although that term focuses on relationships between texts recognized by the reader. An author's intention to remind the reader of another passage is more properly called "allusion" (Sommer, 1998; Tull Willey, 1997). An explicit case is apparent in Joel 2:32, where the author cites a text with "as the Lord has said." A more subtle allusion occurs when an author uses a phrase or phrases found uniquely elsewhere. A problem arises when phrases are short or only approximate other passages. For instance, some have suggested that Joel 2:5's warning of a threat from "a powerful army arrayed for battle" alludes to "a people coming from the land of the north … arrayed like a man for battle" in Jeremiah 6:22–23 (Beck, 2005). However, the language of arraying an army for battle is commonplace (see Judg 20:22; 1 Sam 17:2, 8), even if the passive form "*arrayed* (for battle)" is unique to Joel 2:5 and Jeremiah 6:22–23. What confirms the identification of Jeremiah 6:22–23 as the source for Joel 2:5 is that Joel later refers to its army as "the northern one" (2:20), language distinctive to Jeremiah. Such issues must be considered when pondering whether an author is alluding to another passage (Leonard, 2008), since similarities may be merely incidental, making them mere "echoes."

Another case of reuse is the description of the day of the LORD as "a day of darkness and gloom, a day of clouds and thick darkness" (2:2), taken from Zephaniah 1:15 (Barton, 2001; Beck, 2005; against Nogalski, 1993a). The phrase "the mountains shall drip sweet wine" in 3:18 seems derived from Amos 9:13, where it is also followed by talk of the hills flowing with liquids. Joel 3:10's summons to the nations, "Beat your plowshares into swords, and your pruning hooks into spears," is an ironic reversal of Micah 4:3's "they shall beat their swords into plowshares, and their spears into pruning hooks" (= Isa 2:4) (Coggins, 1996). Just as striking is the reliance of Joel 1:15 ("Alas for the day! For the day of the LORD is near, and as destruction from the Almighty it comes") on Ezekiel 30:2c–3a ("Wail, 'Alas for the day!' For a day is near, the day of the LORD is near") and Isaiah 13:6 ("Wail, for the day of the LORD is near; it will come like destruction from the Almighty!") (Beck, 2005). Similarly, the promise of 2:27 ("You shall know that I am in the midst of Israel, and that I, the LORD, am your God and there is no other") owes its diction to Ezekiel and Isaiah. Specifically, the phrase "you (or they) shall know that I am the LORD" appears four times in Exodus, twice in 1 Kings, and twice in Isaiah, but 56 times in Ezekiel. Meanwhile, the assertion "and no other" is dependent on Isaiah 45:5, 6, 18, 22; 46:9, the only other passages that contain the phrase "I am the LORD/God, and no other" (Wolff, 1977). Most strikingly, the transition from the forecast that Israel will recognize the LORD in their midst (v. 27) to the outpouring of the spirit (v. 28) likely alludes to Ezekiel 39:28–29: "Then they shall know that I am the LORD their God because I sent them into **exile** among the nations, and then gathered them into their own land. I will leave none of them behind; and I will never again hide my face from them, when I pour out my spirit upon the house of Israel, says the Lord GOD" (Wolff, 1977).

Joel's frequent ties to other prophetic books correlate with its infrequent claim to convey a fresh divine word. Despite the superscription's assertion that "the word of the LORD … came to Joel," the only explicit claim to speak the divine word is the use of the **messenger formula** to underscore the appeal for repentance in 2:12. Other references to divine speech appear only in the narrative report "In response to his people the LORD said …" (2:19), and in the recollection of a divine word delivered earlier: "for in Mount Zion and in Jerusalem there shall be those who escape, *as the LORD has said*" (2:32). The book's authority rests primarily on the reuse of oracles (Jeremias, 2002). The degree to which such reuse shapes the warp and woof of the book becomes evident from a survey of its two sections.

Joel 1:1–2:27:   Repentance that Staves Off Catastrophe

Acknowledging Joel's narrative framework is not equivalent to identifying a plot, for nothing as schematic as that underlies the book. Chapter 1 vv. 5–13 call on four groups to bewail the nation's calamities: drunkards (vv. 5–7); an unnamed woman, most likely personified Jerusalem (vv. 8–10; Wolff, 1977; Crenshaw, 1995); farmers and vine dressers (vv. 11–12); and the priests (vv. 13). While v. 14 continues to address the priests, it no longer exhorts them to lament but urges them to assemble the people for a communal lament. Verses 15–18 offer the lament the people are to utter, calling the peril they face "the day of the LORD," while vv. 19–20 provide a model prayer to address to the LORD.

Curiously, both the lament and the prayer characterize the predicament as a drought, with no mention of locusts: "all the trees of the field are dried up" (v. 12), "the seed shrivels under the clods, the storehouses are desolate; the granaries are ruined because the grain has failed" (v. 17); "the watercourses are dried up" (v. 20). Minus the waves of locusts mentioned in v. 4 (and again in 2:25), there is no basis for associating the failure of crops with locusts (Bergler, 1988).[7] And yet, v. 4 has a decisive impact on the reader, causing him or her to envision the destruction of crops as due to a locust invasion.

The Locusts: Focus or Distraction?

A possible hint at the work of locusts in chapter 1 is in vv. 6–7, which describe a nation with teeth like a lion that has "laid waste my vines, and splintered my fig trees ... stripped off their bark and thrown it down," leaving the branches white. The NRSV's use of plural nouns ("vines ... fig trees") leaves the impression of an attack on multiple plants, but the Hebrew nouns are grammatically singular: "my vine ... my fig tree ... its bark ... its branches." And given the possessive pronoun "my" after the identification of the object of attack as "*my* land," this is most likely meant as the LORD's lament over the devastation of his land and people, under the image of a vine (Bergler, 1988, 55), a frequent metaphor for Israel (Isa 5:1–7, 27:2–6; Jer 2:21, 8:13, 12:10; Ezek 19:10; Hos 10:1; Ps 80:8–18).[8] This portrayal more likely assumes an attack by a foe, anticipating chapter 2, where the LORD will call for sounding the alarm of an attack "on my holy mountain" (Jeremias, 2002). By combining laments over land despoiled by an enemy, laments of drought and crop failure, and images of a locust plague, the editor has created a terrifying scenario of mass destruction.

Following the carefully crafted call to lament, summons for an assembly, and the provision of a prayer for that service, one might expect a report of a resolution of the crisis. However, chapter 2 launches into an extended description of the day of the LORD (2:1–11) before the call for repentance is reprised (2:12–17) and a resolution reported (2:18–27). Moreover, while chapter 1 focused on agrarian disaster, 2:2b–11 depicts an immense invading army under the mien of horses and chariots. And whereas chapter 1 described devastation already past, chapter 2's call to "blow the trumpet in Zion; sound the alarm on my holy mountain" alerts people to a still-impending day of the LORD (vv. 1–2).

The description of a fearful fighting force arriving on the day of the LORD seems to be based on Isaiah 13 (Bergler, 1988; Müller, 2008).[9] Even though the superscription to Isaiah 13 identifies it as "an oracle concerning Babylon" (13:1; my translation), Babylon comes into view only in vv. 19–22. Most likely this description of Babylon's defeat by the Medes (introduced in vv. 17–18) and the superscription "An oracle concerning Babylon" were added as a specific case of the day of the LORD, which vv. 2–16 describe in the abstract (Jeremias, 2000a). Isaiah 13:2–5 reports the LORD mustering an army "from the end of the heavens" who will "execute my anger" and "destroy the whole world." Chapter 13 v. 6 (quoted verbatim in Joel 1:15) calls for wailing because "the day of the LORD is near," following which vv. 7–8 describe the dismay and distress of humanity faced with the onslaught of divine wrath (compare Joel 2:6). Isaiah 13:9 refocuses attention on this as the day of the LORD, using phraseology appropriated again in Joel 2:1 ("See, the day of the LORD comes"). Following that, v. 10 describes the darkness of stars, sun, and moon, while v. 13 speaks of the heavens trembling and the earth being "shaken out of its place," similar to Joel's description of the effects of the approaching divine army: "The earth quakes before them, the heavens tremble. The sun and the moon are darkened, and the stars withdraw their shining" (Joel 2:10). The number of parallels between Joel 2 and Isaiah 13 and the fact that Joel 1:15 quotes Isaiah 13:6 make it likely that the author of Joel 2 used Isaiah 13:2–16 as his template (Beck, 2005; Bergler, 1988; Jeremias, 2000a; Müller, 2008).

Also important to note is the background to the image of locusts introduced in 1:4, reprised explicitly in 2:25 and tacitly invoked in 2:2b–11. Although the image of a threatening army distinguishes chapter 2 from chapter 1, the military onslaught that turns a land "like the garden of Eden" into "a desolate wilderness" (2:3) is reminiscent of the anguished cry that invaders have "laid waste my vine" and "my fig tree" (1:7). More significantly, in 2:9 these warriors run on the city wall and enter houses by coming "through the windows like a thief," an image that seems befitting insects like those of 1:4 more than a human army.[10] Equally significant is the emphasis on the army's uniqueness in 2:2c ("their like has never been from of old, nor will be again after them in ages to come") echoing the query of Joel 1:2: "Has such a thing happened in your days, or in the days of your ancestors?"

Joel's talk of a locust assault bears striking resemblances to Exodus 10. The assertion that this event is distinctive parallels Exodus 10:14's description of the locust plague in Egypt as "such a dense swarm of locusts as had never been before, *nor ever shall be again*" (my italics) (Beck, 2005; Bergler, 1988; Jeremias, 2002).[11] And just as Joel 1:2 commands that hearers relay these events to their children and grandchildren, so Exodus 10:2 admonishes the Hebrews, "tell your children and grandchildren how I have made fools of the Egyptians and what signs I have done among them" (Exod 10:2). The instruction to pass along to posterity an account of singular events and to invoke the specter of locusts suggests that the author followed the pattern of Exodus 10 (Jeremias, 2002).

This combination of calls to lament, varied descriptions of crop failure, and allusions to other passages reinforces the perception that the book of Joel is not so much a collection of an individual prophet's oracles as it is a literary composite fashioned from diverse traditions to expound the day of the LORD (Deist, 1988; Jeremias, 2002), much like a musical work constructed by sampling familiar songs. The first chapter combines the images of a locust infestation (under influence of Exodus 10) and drought as a prelude to the more dramatic image of an invading army, drawn from Isaiah 13 and described as an army from the north, as in Jeremiah (Jeremias, 2000a).

Although the book gives no report of an assembly of the sort urged on the people in the first two chapters, 2:18–19 seems to presume some event like that: "In response to his people the LORD said: 'I am sending you grain, wine, and oil, and you will be satisfied; and I will no more make you a mockery among the nations.'" The assumption that such a gathering preceded the LORD's response is a literary device that relies on the audience's powers of inference.[12] The focus is on calling the people – as much in the future as in the crisis portrayed – to rely on divine mercy in the face of the day of the LORD so as to find the LORD "gracious and merciful ... abounding in steadfast love" (2:13).[13]

Joel 2:28–3:21:   The Day of the LORD Renewed

The extension of the promise of deliverance into an era when the LORD will pour out his spirit upon all Israel reapplies the motif of deliverance from the day of the LORD from the first half of the book. The promise of the bestowal of the spirit in vv. 28–29 deepens the bond the LORD confirms with the people in v. 27, while the specification that it will fall on male and female, slave and free, young and old matches the demand of 2:16 that the aged, children, infants, brides, and bridegrooms participate in an assembly of repentance. In contrast to Micah's assertion that he was the only authentic divinely appointed mediator (Micah 3:5–8), vv. 28–29 expand the prophetic role to all Israel, who are now equipped to understand the portents of the day of the LORD that will appear (2:30–31) (Jeremias, 2002). The deciphered signs will forewarn the community to escape divine wrath by calling "on the name of the LORD" (2:32).

The LORD's answer to the anticipated taunt from the nations in 2:17 ("Where is their God?") appears in two stages (Wolff, 1977), each using the formula "you shall know that ...":

> *You shall know* that I am in the midst of Israel, and that I, the LORD, am your God and there is no other. And my people shall never again be put to shame. (2:27)

> So *you shall know* that I, the LORD your God, dwell in Zion, my holy mountain. And Jerusalem shall be holy, and strangers shall never again pass through it. (3:17)

The first response is directed against the disparagement of Israel as a people whose God has forsaken them, while the second response caps the LORD's forecasts of the nations' defeat with an assertion of his presence in Jerusalem that will entail a reprisal for the disdain the nations have shown: they will be prohibited from entering the LORD's city. Through this two-stage response to the taunt, the LORD makes clear that those who call on him will see any suggestion that he has abandoned them rebuffed.

Woven among these verses are subsequent expansions of the passage. Chapter 3 vv. 4–8, for example, interrupt the LORD's announcement of his intent to assemble the nations for judgment in 3:1–3 and his direct summons of them to prepare for this confrontation in vv. 9–12 (Beck, 2005; Wöhrle, 2006a; Wolff, 1977; contrast Bergler, 1988). The address of Tyre, Sidon, and Philistia (v. 4) as distinct groups differs from talk of "the nations" in general in the surrounding verses, while the epithet "the people of Judah and Jerusalem" contrasts with the broader phrases "my people" and "my heritage" (v. 2) and the description of the nations "casting lots for my people" (v. 3), who are only then divided into "boys" and "girls" traded as merchandise. While "my/your/his people" appears frequently in Joel as a designation for Israel (2:17, 18, 19, 26, 27) and "your heritage" is used synonymously with "your people" in 2:17, the phrase "the people Judah and Jerusalem" occurs for the first time in 3:6. "The people of Judah" appears again in 3:18–21, which also addresses specific countries (Edom and Egypt), at variance with the more general "all the neighboring nations" in v. 12. This observation, coupled with the phrase "And it shall be in that day," a frequent mark of editorial additions, points to vv. 18–21 as a later supplement, parallel to v. 6 (Wöhrle, 2006a, 433; Wolff, 1977).

Summary

The book of Joel is woven of traditions mixed and matched to address the theme of the day of the LORD. Its purpose, indicated at the outset, is to engage hearers in anticipating the inevitable arrival of that day, showing them how they can survive it, as well as what survival will mean in contrast to the fate awaiting the nations. Its invitation to derive instruction from the book is similar to the way Hosea 14:9 implores its readers to be among "the wise" by recognizing the truth of "these things." Joel's implicit narrative gives it a different format than we have encountered, just as its reuse of material from other prophetic books gives it a distinctive weave. It is not constructed from oracles preserved from a historical figure but is composed as a literary work.

The Book of Obadiah

In the pages to come …

Obadiah may be the shortest of the all the biblical books, but that does not make it the least complex. The book takes aim at Edom, accusing it of inappropriate abuse of its kith and kin, Judah. However, as poignant and direct as are the accusations of vv. 11–14, the verses leading up to them bear strong evidence of having been formed from an earlier oracle tradition used also in the book of Jeremiah. And vv. 15–21 evince an even more complex dovetailing of traditions to form the book's conclusion.

The book's superscription is, appropriately, the briefest in all the prophetic books: "the vision of Obadiah," reinforced with "thus says the Lord GOD concerning Edom" (Ben Zvi, 1996a). Given the absence of any vision in the book, "vision" is used as a synonym of "prophecy," much as it is in Isaiah 1:1 and Nahum 1:1 (compare the equation of "the word of the LORD" with "visions" in 1 Samuel 3:1). As for the identification of the prophet simply as "Obadiah," only the book of Malachi is as bereft of information about its prophet. Thus, the attribution of this book to Obadiah seems less an assertion that its oracles stem from a particular individual than an insistence on its independent standing as a book.

A Prophet by Any Other Name

As we have seen, even though scribes associated the oracles of a book with a name, they were willing to include oracles that originated with others. Moreover, although the narratives about Amos and Hosea portray them as individuals, they are more characters in a story than subjects of biography. Even if Amos's vision reports are cast in the first person, their arrangement in two pairs of symmetrical visions, capped by a final vision, raises problems for taking them as candid self-reports.

The difficulties are even more pronounced in Joel and Obadiah, which provide no significant biographical information, lack stories about the prophet, and contain no speeches in the first person. In books that rely so heavily on earlier materials (such as Joel's use of Isaiah 13 and Obadiah's reliance on Jeremiah 49) it seems fruitless to construct a profile of the prophet.[14] The combination of locust plague, drought, and northern army in Joel 1–2 reveals not so much a prophet addressing a specific set of circumstances as a collage of calamities that prefigure the day of the LORD and counsel how to avoid it. Likewise, the book of Obadiah's interweaving of verbal attacks on Edom with an expectation of the day of the LORD reflects scribal composition.

Because scribes were the guardians of written traditions who reshaped them to address their own days, they took on the role of "brokers of the divine" (Ben Zvi, 1996a, 5) in a way parallel to the prophets.[15] Whether oracles in the books of Joel or Obadiah are traceable, in some way, to men who bore those names is immaterial. Apart from the superscriptions, their speakers would be anonymous (compare Carroll, 1986, 48).

The centerpiece of the book is the litany of offenses alleged in vv. 12–14, introduced by the accusation that Edom was complicit in wrongs committed against its brother Jacob (vv. 10–11) (Lescow, 1999). Edom's acts "on the day that" a third party acted against Jacob are enumerated as things Edom "should not have" done (vv. 12–14), that made them "like one of them" (v. 11), exulting in and benefiting from Jerusalem's downfall (v. 13).[16] Even though we lack explicit evidence that Edom formally allied with Babylon as it sacked Jerusalem and ravaged the countryside (Bartlett, 1982), these accusations fit that time better than any other and match the accusations against Edom voiced in Ezekiel 35:1–15 for its part in Jerusalem's fall (Barton, 2001). In fact, those accused may well have been Edomite mercenaries serving Babylon (Wolff, 1986).

Verses 1–9 focus on the impending threat to Edom, without specifying its crimes. The identification of this work as prophetic via the technical term "vision" is reinforced with the formula "thus says the Lord GOD concerning Edom" (Ben Zvi, 1996a). Whereas we might expect the messenger formula of v. 1b ("Thus says the Lord GOD concerning Edom") to be followed by an oracle, instead we find a report of an oracle already received: "We have heard a report from the LORD, and a messenger has been

Prophetic Parody and Sarcasm

Obadiah's reproaches of Edom in vv. 12–14 mirror passages in which a speaker affirms his uprightness by decrying what he has not done (Lescow, 1999), such as Jacob's words to Laban before departing with his wives and children:

> These twenty years I have been with you; your ewes and your female goats have not miscarried, and I have not eaten the rams of your flocks. That which was torn by wild beasts I did not bring to you; I bore the loss of it myself; of my hand you required it, whether stolen by day or stolen by night. (Gen 31:38–39; compare Deut 26:13–14 and Ps 40:9–10)

Obadiah's parody of this form of speech serves to accentuate Edom's guilt, much as Amos's mock call to worship "Come to Bethel – and transgress; to Gilgal – and multiply transgression" (Am 4:4) uses a familiar form to mock Israel's worship as wicked.

sent among the nations: 'Rise up! Let us rise against it for battle!'" These words and those that follow (vv. 2–5) are strikingly similar to Jeremiah 49:14–16 and 49:9:[17]

Obadiah 1–5	Jeremiah 49:14–16, 9
1c: We have heard a report from the LORD, and a messenger has been sent among the nations: "Rise up! Let us rise against her for battle!"	14: I have heard a report from the LORD, and a messenger has been sent among the nations: "Gather yourselves together and come against her, and rise up for battle!"
2: Behold, I will make you least among the nations; *you shall be* despised *utterly.*	15: For behold, I will make you least among the nations, despised *among humanity.*
3: The pride of your heart has deceived you, you who live in the clefts of the rock, whose *dwelling* is in the heights. *You say in your heart, "Who will bring me down to the ground?"*	16: *The terror you inspire and* the pride of your heart have deceived you, you who live in the clefts of the rock, who *hold* the heights of *the hill.*
4: Although you make high like the eagle, *though* your nest *is set among the stars,* from there I will bring you down, says the LORD.	Although you make your nest as high as the eagle's, from there I will bring you down, says the LORD.
5: If thieves came to you, *if plunderers* by night – *how you have been destroyed!* – would they not steal only what they wanted? If grape- gatherers came to you, would they not leave gleanings?	9: If grape-gatherers came to you, would they not leave gleanings? If thieves came by night, they would steal only what they wanted.

The question raised by the divergences between these passages (in italics) is whether either passage derived from the other. Given the lack of any clear motivation for the author of Obadiah to omit a phrase like "The terror you inspire" or Jeremiah to omit

"You say in your heart, 'Who will bring me down to the ground?'", the likeliest scenario is that each took up an oracle that circulated in various forms, much as Isaiah 2:2–4 and Micah 4:1–4 are variant versions of the same oracle (Barton, 2001; Wolff, 1986).

There are two other parallels to Jeremiah 49 in Obadiah, although they are not as transparent. Verse 6 has striking similarities to Jeremiah 49:10 (my translations):

Obadiah 6	Jeremiah 49:10a
How Esau has been *searched*, his *hidden things* searched out!	But as for me, I have *stripped* Esau, I have uncovered his *hidden things*.

The verbs translated "searched" in Obadiah and "stripped" in Jeremiah involve an exchange of place for two consonants: *chaphas* versus *chasaph*. The correspondence between these sentences is clear, whether the variation reflects a copyist's error or a play on words. Second, even though the phrase "his hidden things" translates different Hebrew words in each passage, they have the same meaning.

The other parallel to Jeremiah 49 appears in v. 8:

Obadiah 8	Jeremiah 49:7
"Will it not be on that day," says the LORD, "that I will *destroy* the *wise* from Edom, and *understanding* from Mount Esau?"	Is there no longer *wisdom* in Teman? Has counsel *perished* from the *understanding*? Has their *wisdom* vanished?

Jeremiah's question about the failure of wisdom in Teman (= Edom) is followed by a command to flee the calamity the LORD is about to incite, implying that such flight would be wise. The use of the same vocabulary in speaking of Edom – wise/wisdom, understanding, and destroy/perish (using two forms of the same Hebrew verb) – in the vicinity of other similarities to Jeremiah 49 strongly hints that Obadiah's scribe relied on a tradition similar to what lies behind Jeremiah 49 (Wolff, 1986), modifying it to serve his purposes.[18]

Two emphases in vv. 1–5 without parallel in Jeremiah 49 are striking: (1) the revelation of Edom's presumption at the end of v. 3: "You say in your heart, 'Who will bring me down to the ground?'"; (2) the expansion in v. 4: "Though you soar aloft like the eagle, though your nest is set among the stars" (see Weimar, 1985, 39–40). The latter is especially telling, since its expansion creates awkward syntax in Hebrew. Moreover, while the image of setting "your nest as high as the eagle's" befits the talk of living "in the clefts of the rock" and holding "the height of the hill," the notion of soaring "aloft like the eagle" and the exaggerated idea of a nest "set among the stars" (compare Isa 14:13) makes the added motif of "your proud heart" (v. 3) the central topic. The stress on Edom's haughtiness is uniquely developed in Obadiah.

One further observation substantiates that this development is attributable to whomever fashioned this book. Verses 10–11 make the transition from the forecast of calamity to detailing the crimes that occasion it. The theme of Edom's haughtiness in vv. 2–9 is insinuated into the list of crimes by characterizing them as high-handed treatment inappropriate for kith and kin. Rather than treating Judah as its brother, Edom aligned itself with the abusive aggressors (v. 10). Edom's "pride" is not generic hubris but haughtiness toward Jacob.

The Devil Is in the Detail

Subtler than the reformulations and embellishments of tradition are the verbal links between statements to integrate the oracles against Edom into the larger unit of vv. 1b–9. The lament inserted into v. 5 ("How you have been destroyed!") anticipates the fuller lament of v. 6: "How Esau has been searched, his hidden things searched out!" Similar is v. 7's final pronouncement, "there is no understanding in it," whose only function is to foreshadow v. 8's forecast of the annihilation of wisdom from Mount Esau (Weimar, 1985).[19] In these smaller modifications, as much as the more striking additions, tradition is made to serve new purposes. The insertion of these to fashion a new literary work illustrates what it means to speak of this as literary prophecy rather than a transcript of a prophet's words.

The section that offers the greatest difficulties in accounting for the composition of the book is vv. 15–21. On the one hand, "For the day of the LORD is near against all the nations" (v. 15a) leaves off charges directed specifically at Edom and extends the threat of the LORD's action to "all the nations." Nevertheless, the remainder of the verse addresses an individual, with each pronoun singular in number – "as you have done, it shall be done to you; your deeds shall return on your own head" – thereby resuming the second person singular address of the reproach of Edom in vv. 10–14. By contrast v. 16 uses "you" in the plural: "For as you have drunk on my holy mountain, all the nations around you shall drink." Since the metaphor of "drinking" connotes divine judgment (compare Isa 51:17, 22; Jer 25:15, 49:12; Ezek 23:31–34; Hab 2:16), those who have already drunk this cup "on my holy mountain" are Israel, to whom is given the assurance that "all the nations around you shall drink ... and shall be as though they had never been" (v. 16). Not only does this switch in addressee highlight the odd position of v. 15b, but it also reveals the peculiarity of v. 16 in its context, in so far as nowhere else in the book is Israel addressed directly. Even v. 17, which contrasts with the fate of the nations the deliverance of those "on mount Zion," speaks *about* "the house of Jacob." As a consequence, v. 15b fits better the unit that concludes with v. 14 than the one begun in v. 15a. Not surprisingly, then, a common solution has been to posit that a copyist erroneously transposed the two halves of v. 15: v. 15b was originally the conclusion of vv. 10–14, and v. 15a introduced vv. 16–21 (Wellhausen, 1892; Wolff, 1986).

However, upon closer inspection, the arrangement of v. 15 seems deliberate. First, on other occasions the scribe created links between verses and units by allusions and repeated phrases (see the text box "The Devil Is in the Detail"), fashioning a work that "progresses in overlapping and interlocking steps" (Peckham, 1993, 680). Second, even though v. 15b could reasonably continue v. 14, there is a logic in its present position, inasmuch as its declaration "as you have done, it shall be done to you" is echoed by v. 16's "just as you have drunk ... all the nations around you shall drink" (Ben Zvi, 1996a). The assertion of v. 16 seems to have been selected because it comports with v. 15b, even if it requires that we take in stride a sudden shift to Israel as the addressee. Meanwhile, its talk of "all the nations" drinking from the cup correlates with the announcement of the day of the LORD as directed against all the nations (Weimar, 1985).

At the same time, the announcement of the nearness of the day of the LORD forms a web of relationships with what precedes it. First, owing to the interweaving of this announcement with a prescription of retaliation (v. 16), the day of the LORD brings comeuppance for crimes like those alleged against Edom in vv. 11–14. In that light, the day of the LORD becomes a more specific definition of the period v. 8 introduces with "on that day" (Weimar, 1985). And correlatively, the recurring references to Israel's "day of misfortune/distress/calamity" in vv. 10–14 foreshadow the day of the LORD that will afflict the nations who have abused Israel (Lescow, 1999).

Following the broad horizon of "the nations" in vv. 15–16, vv. 17–18 and v. 21 restrict their scope to the people who played the central role in vv. 1–14: Esau/Edom and Jacob. Verses 17 and 21 are allied through their mention of "Mount Zion," linking them equally to the address of those who have drunk the cup on "my holy mountain" in v. 16. Verses 19 and 20, on the other hand, with their specification of who will take possession of whom, connect singularly with v. 17's forecast of Jacob "taking possession" of others.

There is every reason to conclude that v. 17 was chosen as the counterpart to v. 16, even as it leaves behind the address to Israel as a group. Its contrast to v. 16 is well represented by the English adversative conjunction: "*But* on Mount Zion there shall be those that escape." The punishment forecast for the nations in repayment for their abuse of Israel (v. 16) turns naturally into a promise of escapees on Mount Zion, a term that recalls "my holy mountain," where Israel previously imbibed the LORD's potion (Ben Zvi, 1996a).

The surmise that v. 17 was matched to v. 16 is not necessarily the same as saying that it was formulated specifically for this passage. Although Joel 2:32 cites the words of Obadiah 17a as words "the LORD has said" – a revered oracle – we should not assume that Joel was quoting Obadiah directly. Theoretically, the author of Obadiah 17 might have used a previously existing oracle. Nevertheless, v. 17 is linked to the larger context of the book by its phrase "the house of Jacob," which alludes to the contrast between Esau and Jacob earlier in the book, although without naming Esau as "those who dispossessed" Jacob. That identification awaits v. 18, where "the house of Jacob/Joseph" will destroy "the house of Esau," who (in contrast to the house of Jacob) will have no survivor. The lack of survivors befits not only the image of a fire consuming fuel, but also the promise of v. 16 that the nations "shall be as though they had never been."

Verse 18 lacks a bond with its two preceding verses, since it moves beyond "the house of Jacob," taking possession of those who dispossessed it to annihilation of them, while it narrows the identification of those they will attack from the nations as a whole to "the house of Esau." More significantly, it offers a curious tension with v. 21, which has Jacob's survivors going "up to Mount Zion to rule Mount Esau." Because the verb translated "rule" always takes as its direct object a people rather than a territory, v. 21 presupposes that Edom will not be depopulated, despite v. 18 (Wolff, 1986).

The upshot of these observations is that vv. 15–18 and 21 are more composite than any other section of the book, betraying a scribe who utilized diverse traditions to compose the conclusion to the book (Lescow, 1999). Even at that, we have to reckon with two later supplements in vv. 19–20, the first of which keys in on the verb "take possession of" in v. 17, which appears again in v. 19, where it is translated "shall possess" (Weimar, 1985). Verse 19 answers the question *which* territories these survivors will possess, while v. 20 elaborates on this by speaking specifically of "the exiles of the Israelites" and "the exiles of Jerusalem," thereby designating which groups *returning from exile* will have control over which territories (Wolff, 1986).

Finally, the tension between the expectations for Edom voiced in vv. 18 and 21 might hint at alternative endings for the book, provided by different scribes. The phrase "for the LORD has spoken," at the end of v. 18, provides a fitting ending to a prophetic speech (Ben Zvi, 1996a). However, v. 21 may have been added after vv. 19–20 had been inserted, so as to soften the imagery concerning Israel's treatment of Edom, subsuming Jacob's "rule over Mount Esau" to the proclamation that "the kingdom will be the LORD's."

Not surprisingly, the different character of vv. 15a and 16–21 from vv. 1–14, together with their complex makeup, has raised the question whether all of these verses might have been added to a book that once concluded with v. 15b (Barton, 2001). The most prominent prompt for this hypothesis is the focus on an attack on the nations, whereas previously Edom was the focus. Equally, the fact that this attack stands under the warning "for the day of the LORD is near" – a phrase found in identical form in Isaiah 13:6; Joel 1:15, 3:14; and Zephaniah 1:7 – introduces a new motif in the book. Even though this phrase echoes Zephaniah 1:7, the qualification of this as a day "against all the nations" more closely aligns it with Joel, since only in Joel 3:14 is "the day of the LORD" explicitly linked with an assault on the nations, following a promise of deliverance for "everyone who calls on the name of the LORD" (Joel 2:32). The association of deliverance for those in Jerusalem at the same moment the nations undergo "the day of the LORD" forms a link between vv. 15a and 16–18 and the book of Joel, hinting that they come from similar scribal circles, but different from those that produced vv. 1–14 and 15b and one whose harsh prospects for Edom evidently provoked the modification voiced in v. 21.

Summary

The books of Joel and Obadiah reflect scribes utilizing earlier traditions to form what can be called literary works in a stronger sense than was true of any of the first four books we studied, inasmuch as reuse of earlier traditions defines each book. How are we to conceive of such scribes?

Although some scholars attempt to link all passages that share strong sentiments against the nations into an "editorial layer" that sought to unify the Twelve (for example, Nogalski, 1993b; Schart, 1998), such "layers" are difficult to prove, especially given the difficulties with concluding that these twelve works were blended to form a single book. Moreover, given what we know about the activity of scribes, it is more likely that the injection of this theme into Obadiah was the work of scribes who sought to place the forecast of an attack on Edom within a larger assault on the nations of the sort the book of Joel anticipates. In other words, it was a matter of scribes influenced by other books. And in fact, by adding vv. 15a and 16–17 and connecting with them v. 18, they interwove the theme of the LORD's reprisals on the nations with Jacob's reprisals on Esau. In this context, the assertion of a military assault on Edom acquires new significance by its inclusion in "the day of the Lᴏʀᴅ," directed against all the nations.

Notes

1. The verse citations follow English translations. The Hebrew Bible divides Joel into four chapters, with chapters 1–2 corresponding to 1:1–2:27 in English, chapter 3 equivalent to 2:28–32, and chapter 4 matching 3:1–21.
2. Wöhrle (2006a) argues that Joel contains a foundational layer declaring a drought as the onset of the day of the Lᴏʀᴅ (1:1–3, 8–20; 2:1–2a,c, 3, 6, 10, 15–17), followed by a report of deliverance from it (2:21–24, 26a). To this was added a layer describing a locust infestation, coupled with a motif of foreign armies and their defeat (1:4–7; 2:2b, 4–5, 7–9, 11, 14, 18–20, 25, 26b–18; 3:1–3, 9–17). (Chapter 2 vv. 12–14, 28–32, and chapter 3 vv. 4–8, 18–21, are still later expansions.) In my opinion, his argument assigns phrases to different layers too woodenly.
3. The contention that chapter 3 presents "an **eschatological** or early-apocalyptic understanding of salvation" that exceeds the hope for a mere restoration of goods in 2:18–27 (Beck, 2005, 192; my translation) fails to allow for varied hopes for an improved future in eschatology (see the text box "What Is Eschatology?", p. 56). What is more, the threat of warriors incomparable to any previously known (2:3–11) already raises the imagery of chapters 1–2 above the mundane.
4. The only hint of deficiency comes in the exhortation to "return to me with all your heart" by rending "your hearts and not your clothing" (vv. 12–13), although this is less an accusation than a call to thoroughgoing piety (Coggins, 2003). In fact, the verb "return" (*shub*) "does not necessarily imply guilt" (Crenshaw, 1995, 41) and can even be used of the Lᴏʀᴅ resuming his commitment to his people (Zech 1:3, 8:3; Mal 3:7).
5. Beck argues that "everyone who calls on the name of the Lᴏʀᴅ" (2:32) implies a distinction between those who experience deliverance and those who do not, thereby distinguishing 2:32 from 2:23–27 and from chapter 3, where all the people find deliverance (Beck, 2005, 182). However, the point of 2:32 is not a differentiation between the saved and the damned but a statement of the prerequisite for deliverance. As Beck himself points out, the phrase "call on the name of the Lᴏʀᴅ" assumes a **cultic** context (Beck, 2005, 186), making it parallel to the convocation urged in 2:15–17 and presumed as held in vv. 18–27.
6. "*In* Mount Zion" and "*on* Mount Zion" reflect the same Hebrew preposition. The only difference between Joel 2:32 and Obadiah 17 is the expansion "and in Jerusalem" in Joel.
7. Another problem with taking a locust plague as the real cause of calamity is the Lᴏʀᴅ's vow in 2:25 to repay them for "the *years*" that the locusts had eaten, since locust plagues are of shorter duration (Wöhrle, 2006a).
8. There are, of course, passages that describe locusts destroying vines and vineyards (e.g., Amos 4:9). In Joel, however, the "nation" is described as attacking "my land … my vine … my fig tree," not "your vineyards" and "your fig trees."
9. Many who argue that 2:28–3:21 were added to the book late to give it an eschatological theme also contend that the day of the Lᴏʀᴅ sayings were added at the same time to chapter 2's description of an invading army (e.g., Duhm, 1901). However, Wöhrle (2006a) has convincingly argued on literary grounds that the day of the Lᴏʀᴅ sayings are primary and were expanded by the description of the army, making the eschatological bent of the chapter fundamental to it. Even if this suggests that the borrowing from Isaiah 13 represents a secondary editorial layer (rather than a mere combination of traditions, as Bergler (1988) posits), it tells us nothing about when it was added or why.

10. The impact of locust hordes should not be underestimated. They can mass in swarms of over one billion, in a band covering 10 square miles (Brodsky, 1990).

11. The only other plague whose singularity is stressed is the hail said to have been "the heaviest hail to fall that has ever fallen in Egypt from the day it was founded until now" (Exod 9:18, 24). But while the hail was unprecedented, a comparable hailstorm is not ruled out for the future.

12. Biblical narratives often assume that mandated actions are carried out, but do not report that. Thus, for example, after Jeremiah's opponent Hananiah broke the yoke Jeremiah wore, the Lord commanded Jeremiah to tell him that he had replaced the "wooden bars" with "iron bars" under which the nations would serve Nebuchadnezzar (Jer 28:13–14). Although Jeremiah's words to Hananiah, reported in vv. 15–16, are not those prescribed in vv. 13–14, it would be inapt for a reader to suppose that Jeremiah failed to deliver the words mandated or that the words attributed to him in vv. 15–16 were not divinely authorized. The author leaves it to the reader to assume that all that Jeremiah did in this passage conformed to divine instructions.

13. This characterization finds its home in Exodus 34:6 and will be utilized again in Jonah 4:2 (see pp. 84–86). Most likely, Jonah borrowed the phrases from Joel, rather than the other way around (see pp. 127–128).

14. Attempts to construct profiles for Joel and Obadiah have focused on similarities between their books' oracles and **liturgies** used at worship sites, leading to identifications of them as prophets working at cultic sites (Coggins, 1982; Wolff, 1986) or simply as prophets who used patterns of speech employed in worship (Barton, 2001).

15. Indeed, the books of Chronicles portray prophets as authors and even historians (1 Chr 29:29; 2 Chr 9:29, 12:15, 21:12).

16. Although it is possible to read the Hebrew verbs as prohibiting a future action ("do not gloat over your brother on the day of his misfortune") (Bartlett, 1982), the stipulated actions to be avoided seem too specific for mere potentialities (Barton, 2001), while the clause translated "you too were like one of them" (v. 11) is difficult to construe as a warning.

17. I have modified the NRSV to align it more closely with the Hebrew, despite the occasional ambiguity this creates.

18. Nogalski's detection of influence from Amos 9 on the structure of Obadiah 1–9 and 15–21 (Nogalski, 1993b) is rightly resisted by Lescow (1999). Even if the structure of five conditional clauses and the use of "from there" is similar to the structure of clauses in Amos 9:2–4 (on which too much weight is placed equally by Wolff, 1986), the passage in Amos accents the fruitlessness of flight, whereas Obadiah uses this structure to speak of the certain debasement of Edom's pride (Lescow, 1999).

19. Classifying this phrase as an editorial link makes better sense than Wolff's identification of it as a **gloss** on v. 8 (Wolff, 1986). Glosses are supplied to clarify something obscure, while this phrase seems less specific than v. 8 but is similar to the verbal links supplied to join statements.

7

The Books of Nahum and Habakkuk

Nahum

> ### In the pages to come ...
>
> Nahum's unapologetic delight in the destruction of Nineveh strikes us as sadistic, for good reason. Nevertheless, perceiving how the book has been shaped to portray Nineveh's fall as the LORD's attack on his enemy clarifies how this fascination with Nineveh's destruction came to be integrated into prophetic literature. The description of the **theophany** in 1:2–8 and its exposition in the comments of 1:9–2:2 provide a lens through which to read the ghoulish mocking of Nineveh's fate in the remainder of the book.

Nahum's **superscription** provides two designations of the book's contents: "an **oracle** concerning Nineveh" and "the vision of Nahum of Elkosh." While "oracle" and "vision" are synonyms for divine communication, their joint use in a superscription is unique to Nahum.[1] Just as unique is its introduction of "the *book* of the vision of Nahum of Elkosh," for the specification that Nahum's "vision" is preserved *in writing* identifies its form, not just its contents.[2] This is the only prophetic book that identifies itself as a document.

Given that superscriptions for other prophetic books begin with "the word of the LORD which came to" or "the vision of," followed by the prophet's name, the identification of this book's topic, "an oracle concerning Nineveh," was likely sufficiently well established that the phrase "the *writing* of the vision of Nahum of Elkosh" had to be appended to it to align the composition with other **scrolls** bearing the name of a prophet.[3] If the superscriptions to the prophetic books generally evince having been

Prophetic Literature: From Oracles to Books, First Edition. Ronald L. Troxel.
© 2012 Ronald L. Troxel. Published 2012 by Blackwell Publishing Ltd.

supplied in the latter stages of editing (see above, p. 13), then the superscription to Nahum reflects that process in a special way.

Of "Authenticity" and "Integrity"

The terms "authenticity" and "integrity" often show up in discussions about the origins of a book's oracles (see, for example, Redditt, 2008; Weigl, 2001). "Authenticity" means to affirm that the oracles originated with the prophet named in the superscription. Asserting a work's "integrity" claims that its oracles are original rather than added later. Regrettably, these terms import misleading value judgments (who would want to judge an oracle as "inauthentic" or a book as lacking "integrity"?). Given what we know about ancient **scribes'** tendencies to incorporate new material into works they received, the view of authorship invoked by the term "authenticity" is more at home in the printing press era than when these books were written. The question is not authenticity, but what we can reconstruct about how these texts were composed.

In this light, it is difficult to know what to make of the name Nahum, even though it was common enough in the seventh century BCE (Spronk, 1997). The fact that "Elkosh" is mentioned only here in the Bible and that the site (assuming that it designates a place rather than a group called "the Elkoshites") has yet to be identified are not sufficient reasons to posit that "Nahum of Elkosh" is fictitious. It is likely the name of an actual prophet, whether he uttered the book's oracles or not (compare the book of Jonah's appropriation of "Jonah son of Amittai" from 2 Kings 14:25). In the end, it is inconsequential whether a prophet named Nahum spoke these oracles, since (as with Joel and Obadiah) we lack any details about him that might cast light on the book.

The Composition of Nahum: More than Meets the Eye

At the heart of the book are vivid descriptions of Nineveh attacked and laid waste (2:3–12, 3:1–4), the LORD's verbal assaults on that city (2:13, 3:5–7), mockery of its presumption of invincibility (3:8–17), and a taunt of Assyria's king (3:18–19). Much of the language accords with formulaic threats used in curses (parallel to modern "sanctions") for breach of treaties in documents from the **ancient Near East** (see Cathcart, 1973). It is these passages in the book's second half that are most directly related to the heading "An oracle concerning Nineveh."

Prior to these stands a less integrated set of verses. Chapter 1 vv. 2–8 portray the LORD as a conquering warrior, a stock image for deities throughout the ancient Near East (compare Ps 24:8; Hab 3:2–15); vv. 9–11 rebuke those plotting against the LORD; vv. 12–13 convey reassurance to Judah of release from bondage; v. 14 threatens annihilation for an unidentified addressee; v. 15 announces to Judah the good news that the wicked have been subjugated, after which 2:1 warns of a "shatterer" about to beset the addressee, and 2:2 proclaims that the Lord has restored "the majesty of Jacob and Israel." In short, while 2:3–3:19 consistently focus on Nineveh, 1:2–2:2 have shifting and often vague referents.

Despite this, it is possible to trace a progression of thought. The Lord's irresistible prowess (1:2–6) carries a twofold significance: protection for those taking refuge in him and punishment for his foes (1:7–8). This belief is made concrete in the declaration of deliverance for Judah and destruction for Nineveh (1:9–2:2), whose fall is detailed in gloating descriptions of suffering and gore (2:3–3:19) (Becking, 1996). Understanding how the book of Nahum was composed requires accounting for the combination of these themes.

While 3:8's reference to the Assyrians' capture of the Egyptian capital of Thebes in 663 BCE marks the earliest possible date for the book, the latest possible date for its composition is elusive. Some maintain that the book reflects the work of a single prophet in the middle of the seventh century BCE (Roberts, 1991) or a scribe of that era who composed a politically subversive tract (Spronk, 1997). Others place its composition closer to the fall of Nineveh in 612 BCE (Sweeney, 1992) or consider it to have been produced over a lengthy period extending well beyond Nineveh's fall (Lescow, 1995; Seybold, 1989).

Despite the vivid descriptions of Nineveh's distress in 2:3–12 and 3:1–4 that might suggest that its author was familiar with the city's collapse, other passages still anticipate that event (2:13, 3:5–7). The taunt of Nineveh for its presumption of invincibility (3:8–13) rings truer if its fall still lies in the future and, given that it is based on a parallel to Thebe's fall (v. 8), it would have carried the greatest weight if uttered before Thebes regained its independence (by 616 BCE) (Roberts, 1991). At the same time, it presupposes an era when Nineveh's succumbing like Thebes was imaginable (Nogalski, 1993b). Accordingly, it likely originated during the decline of the empire after the death of Assyria's last great king, Ashurbanipal (627), followed soon by the revolt of Babylon in 625. It was then that the sharp images of Nineveh's demise in chapters 2–3 became thinkable. Nevertheless, this benchmark cannot be used to date the book in isolation from other features.

For instance, while 3:8–13 speak of the city's destruction as yet future, 3:18–19 address Assyria's king as though he and his people have *already* suffered the destruction of their empire. Equally instructive are passages that reflect other prophetic books. For instance, the similarity between Nahum 1:15 and Isaiah 52:7 is noteworthy:

Nahum 1:15	Isaiah 52:7
Look!	How beautiful
On the mountains are the feet of one who proclaims good news, who announces peace! Celebrate your festivals, O Judah, fulfill your vows, for never again shall the worthless pass through you; they are utterly cut off.	*on the mountains are the feet of one who proclaims good news, who announces peace,* who brings good news, who announces salvation, who says to Zion, "Your God reigns."

The words in italics are identical in Hebrew and are the only instances of this phraseology in the Bible. Although some have argued that Nahum derived this language from the Jerusalem **cult** (Gray, 1961), or that Isaiah 52:7 draws its language from Nahum (Becking, 1996; Sommer, 1998; Sweeney, 1992), more likely Nahum 1:15 borrows from Isaiah 52:7 (Jeremias, 1970), both because its associated command to "celebrate your festivals" fearlessly assumes that Nineveh has already fallen and because the reassurance "for never again shall the worthless pass through you" bears a striking similarity (in Hebrew) to Isaiah 52:1b: "for never again shall enter you the uncircumcised and unclean" (Coggins, 1982).[4] Given that Isaiah 52 stands in a section within that book composed toward the end of the Judean **exile** in Babylon, Nahum 1:15 was likely penned much later than other parts of the book. These signals that Nahum's components come from widely varied times suggest that the process of composing the book was as complex as in the other books we have explored. This inference will be borne out by noting the marks of composition in the book's two major sections, beginning with 2:3–3:19, where we find the vivid descriptions of Nineveh's fall.

Marks of Composition in 2:3–3:19

Key to perceiving the structure of this section are the similar divine addresses to Nineveh in 2:13 and 3:5:

Nahum 2:13
See, I am against you, says the LORD of hosts, and I will burn your chariots in smoke, and the sword shall devour your young lions; I will cut off your prey from the earth, and the voice of your messengers shall be heard no more.

Nahum 3:5
See, I am against you, says the LORD of hosts, and I will lift up your skirts over your face; and I will let nations look on your nakedness and kingdoms on your shame.

These are the only marked divine speeches amid the descriptions of violence and devastation. 2:13 is written in prose (in contrast to the poetry that surrounds it) and takes up terms from its context: the pledge that "the sword shall devour your young lions" plays off the lament of Nineveh's demise as "the cave of young lions" (2:11), while the cutting off of "prey" echoes v. 12's assertion that the lion has provided prey for his cave. At the same time, the threat to "burn your chariots" recalls Nineveh's chariots that raced through the streets in v. 4. Taken together, these considerations suggest that 2:13 has been formulated as a transition from the description of Nineveh's collapse in 2:10–12 to the mock lament of the city that commences in 3:1 (Nogalski, 1993b).

Similarly, 3:5–7 stand out in their context. Chapter 3 v. 1 laments the death of a city characterized by bloodshed, deceit, and plunder, vv. 2–3 announce the comeuppance she will receive for her crimes, and v. 4 describes her as a prostitute, implying that Nineveh's fate is the consequence of her misdeeds. Even though the punishments stipulated in vv. 5–7 befit the crime of prostitution (compare Jer 13:26–27), they shift to address the city. Correspondingly, those verses cease lamenting Nineveh to proclaim judgment on it. And while the verses following vv. 5–7 taunt Nineveh for its presumption and its vulnerability, they do not employ the type of violent language ascribed to the LORD in vv. 5–7. The other place in the book where we find such vicious images is the poem about the divine warrior, in 1:2–8. These distinctive features of vv. 5–7 suggest that a scribe insinuated this speech into the lament to specify the LORD as the agent of the city's destruction, just as he did by supplying 2:13 (Lescow, 1995). As in 2:13, he picked up motifs from the preceding verse (in this case, prostitution) to formulate this judgment speech.

Marks of Composition in 1:2–2:2

What we have seen in chapters 2–3 is minor compared with the complexities in chapter 1, beginning with its poem of the LORD as divine warrior. Nineteenth-century scholars recognized in it the features of an **acrostic poem** (see text box). Despite early attempts to reconstruct a poem utilizing the entire alphabet and running through 2:2 (Gunkel, 1893), most scholars today perceive the acrostic ending in 1:8, having used not quite half the alphabet. The question, then, is how vv. 9–15 relate to this poem.

1:2–8:   An Acrostic Poem

An acrostic poem is built on the order of the letters in the alphabet, as in this inelegant but original composition of mine:

> **A**lthough the man looked smart,
>   his words were rather tart.
> **B**efore he even spoke,
>   you knew he would blow smoke.
> **C**riminals give kinder looks
>   than that man's verbal hooks.

While acrostic poems elsewhere in the Bible utilize all the letters of the alphabet, this one uses only the first 11.[5] Using the letters of the English alphabet down the left-hand side to reflect the Hebrew acrostic, the following translation (my own) shows the structure of Nahum 1:2–8:

A	2: A jealous and avenging God is the LORD,
	the LORD is avenging and wrathful;
	the LORD takes vengeance on his adversaries
	and rages against his enemies.
	3: The LORD is slow to anger but great in power,
	and the LORD will by no means clear the guilty.
B	His way is in whirlwind and storm,
	and the clouds are the dust of his feet.
C	4: He rebukes the sea and makes it dry,
	and he dries up all the rivers;
D	Bashan and Carmel wither,
	and the bloom of Lebanon fades.
E	5: The mountains quake before him,
	and the hills melt;

F and the earth heaves before him,
    the world and all who live in it.

G 6: When faced with his indignation, who can stand?
    Who can endure the heat of his anger?

H His wrath is poured out like fire,
    and by him the rocks are broken in pieces.

I   7: The LORD is good,
    a stronghold in a day of trouble;

J   he knows those who take refuge in him,
    8: even in a rushing flood.

K He will make a full end of his adversaries,[6]
    and will pursue his enemies into darkness.

Recognition of this passage as an acrostic came late because copyists' errors and additions obscured it at three points, although the corruptions are easily recognized and corrected.[7] While some scholars argue that the need to accept these changes undermines the proposal's likelihood (Floyd, 1994),[8] the salient question is whether "the recurrence of so many successive letters of the alphabet at regular intervals" is a matter of chance rather than design (Pinker, 2006, 99). The case for the acrostic is compelling enough that it has become the consensus.

Verse 9 presents problems because it admits more than one translation. Besides the NRSV's "Why do you plot against the LORD?" it is possible to translate it "What would you plot against the LORD?" (Floyd, 1994)[9] or "What do you think about the LORD?" (Sweeney, 1992) or even "Whatever you plot against the LORD [he will bring to an end]" (Becking, 1996; De Vries, 1966). A choice among these must be based on broader relationships between vv. 2–8 and 9–10.

Verse 9 leaves off describing the divine warrior to address a group (the form of the Hebrew verb translated "plot" addresses "you men"). What is more, v. 11 breaks rank with the verses preceding it, since the pronoun "you" is equivalent to "you woman," assuming (but not naming) a different addressee than v. 9. And yet both v. 9 and v. 11 contain vocabulary ties with the verses that precede them. The phrase "he will make an end" in v. 9 echoes the end of v. 8, while the Hebrew verb meaning "plot" in v. 11 is identical with "plot" or "think" in v. 9. Indeed, these words appear only in these verses in Nahum. Verses 9–11 most likely comment on the preceding poem (Christensen, 1987; De Vries, 1966; Sweeney, 1992), but what sort of comment do they make?

That question is bound up with the curious change of addressees introduced in v. 9. Not only does v. 9 address a group of men and v. 11 suddenly speak to a lone female figure, but vv. 12–13 continue to address that woman, while speaking about the actions and destruction of a group ("*they* will be cut off") and talking of the woman's oppression by a male ("I will break off *his* yoke from you"). And then, just as abruptly, v. 14 launches a threat against an unspecified male ("Your [individual male] name shall be perpetuated no longer"), following which comes the announcement to Judah that "the wicked" will never again invade her (1:15). Chapter 2 v. 1, by contrast, alerts a (lone) female that "a shatterer has come up against you" and urges preparation for battle, while v. 2 explains that announcement as having to do with the LORD "restoring the majesty of Jacob … and the majesty of Israel" in the wake of ravagers. In sum, by contrast to the readily identifiable actor in 1:2–8, 1:9–2:2 offer dizzying shifts from one addressee to another, giving an impression that they are a disorderly collection. Nevertheless, the fluctuating addressees follow discernible patterns.

Beginning with the observation that the men addressed in vv. 9 and 14 are threatened with disaster, while the woman addressed in vv. 12–13 is promised deliverance (Becking, 1996), a pattern becomes evident in 1:14 (peril for a male) and 1:15 (good news for a woman) (Sweeney, 1992). In retrospect, the woman addressed in vv. 12–13 is most likely Judah, while the men of vv. 9 and 14 are the Assyrians. Using this foothold, the ambiguous individual woman addressed in 1:11 ("From you one has gone out who plots evil against the LORD, one who counsels wickedness") is also Judah (Floyd, 2002). What is more, the fact that the word translated "wickedness" (*beliyya'al*) appears in v. 11 and again only in v. 15's promise of the removal of all "the wicked" (*beliyya'al*) suggests that the one "who counsels wickedness" but has departed from "you" (Judah) is the same foe, Assyria, retreating after an unsuccessful assault on Jerusalem (Sweeney, 1992). The outlier in this scheme is 2:1's warning to a female to prepare for an onslaught, since this does not conform to the pattern of the female being promised deliverance. And in fact, this warning is explained in 2:2 as having to do with deliverance for Judah, suggesting that the "you" addressed is Nineveh, as proves to be the case in subsequent verses (2:13; 3:5–7, 8–17) (Sweeney, 1992).

The translation of v. 9 that befits these observations is, therefore, "Whatever you plot against the LORD he will bring to an end," addressed to Assyria. The anomalies of these verses are best comprehended by recognizing that each component was probably extracted from an earlier setting (Roberts, 1991), much as we saw literary units created by the editorial arrangement of oracles in Amos, Hosea, and Micah.

Not only is the arrangement of 1:9–2:2 intelligible in this light, but it matches the themes of the acrostic poem, which unfolds as follows. Chapter 1 vv. 2–3a stress the LORD's propensity to execute wrath against his adversaries, while vv. 3b–5 depict his wrath trained on features of the world, leading to the rhetorical question "Who can stand before his indignation?" (v. 6). Verses 7–8a adduce a corollary: he proves a shelter during distress for those who take refuge in him. The poem concludes by restating the thesis of vv. 2–3: there is no escape for his enemies, whom he will annihilate (v. 8b). In effect, the alternation of punishment and deliverance for the addressees in 1:9–2:2 is a series of riffs on this theme.

Summary

Nahum's structure as a book that declares Nineveh's downfall as the outworking of the LORD's vow to punish the wicked and deliver those who trust in him is a literary creation. The book provides abundant evidence of scribal shaping, whether by the insertion of divine addresses to Nineveh in 2:13 and 3:5–7 or the complex construction of 1:2–2:2. And the prefixing of the acrostic poem about the attack of the divine warrior and the insertion of addresses by the LORD to Nineveh in 2:13 and 3:5–7 create ways for the (ancient) reader to absorb the bloodthirsty anticipation of that city's fall.

Habakkuk

In the pages to come ...

The book of Habakkuk represents a distinctive type of prophetic writing: one that seeks to make sense of an older oracle. The rise of the vicious Chaldeans has unnerved the prophet, who questions how their appearance fulfills an oracle when their actions call into question the LORD's reputation for upholding justice. The chief issues in studying this book are whether chapters 1–2 carry a dialogue between the prophet and the LORD and whether chapter 3 was part of the book from the outset.

The book's superscription classifies it as an "oracle" and labels Habakkuk a prophet. His name appears again in the superscription that introduces chapter 3 as "a prayer of the prophet Habakkuk." The moniker "prophet" is the sole description of him, leaving us again with a name and nothing more.

Attempts to date the book regularly take as their benchmark the LORD's trumpeting of his new deed: "I am rousing the Chaldeans, that fierce and impetuous nation" (1:6).[10] The announcement of this as novel suggests that this oracle presupposes the sack of Nineveh in 612 and probably also the Chaldeans' defeat of Egypt at Carchemish in 605 BCE. The lengthy complaint about Babylonian power in 1:12–17 and the mock laments of 2:6–19 appear to reflect an even more direct experience of Babylonian power, probably in the wake of Judah's first revolt against Babylon, in 600 BCE (Cleaver-Bartholomew, 2003; Roberts, 1991).

The arrangement of materials in this book has frequently been characterized as a dialogue between the prophet and the LORD (chapters 1–2), capped by a prayer (chapter 3). The perception of a dialogue, however, has come under suspicion, while the relationship of chapter 3 to chapters 1–2 has long been a matter of debate.

Habakkuk 1–2: A Dialogue?

The perception that the first two chapters are structured as a dialogue between the prophet and the LORD continues to enjoy supporters (Andersen, 2001; Roberts, 1991), who sketch its course as follows. The LORD responds to the prophet's initial complaint about social ills (1:2–4) by pointing to his rousing of the Chaldeans (1:5–11), an answer the prophet protests because of the Chaldeans' reputation for cruelty and arrogance (1:12–17). Having stated his case, the prophet awaits a divine response, which he receives in the form of a "vision" that contrasts the "proud" and the "righteous," whose fates will be determined by their behavior (2:1–5). Chapter 2 concludes with a series of five mock laments of the wicked (2:6–19) and a proclamation that "the LORD is in his holy temple; let all the earth keep silence before him!" (v. 20).

Although there remains widespread agreement on the identification of the boundaries between these literary units, there are problems with reading chapters 1–2 as a dialogue. While 1:2–4 lodges complaints against the LORD, 1:5–11 fails to acknowledge those, nor does it fit the form of divine responses to laments, which typically offer reassurance that the LORD will bring deliverance (Floyd, 2002). Moreover, the pronoun "you" in vv. 5–11 consistently addresses a group (in Hebrew) rather than an individual, such as Habakkuk.

Chapter 2 v. 2, on the other hand, explicitly introduces a divine response to the prophet, who has resolved to "stand at my watchpost, and station myself on the rampart … to see what he will say to me, and what he will answer concerning my complaint" (2:1). "Standing at my watchpost" adopts the figure of a sentinel, responsible to note any threat on the horizon and deliver a timely warning, an image adopted also by Hosea (9:8), Jeremiah (6:17), and Ezekiel (3:16–21, 33:1–9). The precise action "standing at my watchpost" denotes is undefined,[11] but apparently involves putting oneself in a state or location to receive an oracle (Sweeney, 1991b). By contrast, 1:5–11 provide no transition between the prophet's complaint and the LORD's (alleged) response, calling into question whether 1:5–11 address the complaint and highlighting 2:1 as the start of a new unit (Floyd, 2002).

There is also a problem of logical progression within chapter 1. Verses 12–17 seem to take up where vv. 2–4 left off, as if the complaint had gone unaddressed. Verses 5–11 do not acknowledge Habakkuk's accusation that the LORD is implicated in the violence he allows, and the LORD's satisfaction at imposing a force he acknowledges wreaks violence (v. 9) makes an odd response to the prophet's complaint about serial violence in v. 2 (Floyd, 1991). What is more, if the LORD's response to charges of inaction in the face of violence (v. 2) is to send more violence (v. 9), berating the LORD for not acting is a curious rejoinder (v. 13) (Cleaver-Bartholomew, 2003).

Similarly, the prophet's question whether the oppressor will be allowed to continue unchecked (v. 17) parallels his lament "How long shall I cry for help?" (v. 2), implying that Habakkuk has found no response to his complaint (Cleaver-Bartholomew, 2003). The accusation lodged in 1:2–4 is simply played out more fully in 1:12–17. If there is any advance from the initial complaint, it consists only in reminding the LORD that toleration of violence demeans his character (Floyd, 1991).

This does not lead inevitably to the conclusion that 1:2–4, 5–11, and 12–17 are three independent units, for vocabulary links between them signal that the chapter is a literary whole (Floyd, 1991). For instance, the noun "violence" is featured in the initial complaint (vv. 2–3), as well as in the description of the Chaldeans (v. 9). The paired verbs "see" and "look" are used in all three units: the prophet complains that the LORD "[makes] me *see* wrongdoing and *look* at trouble" (v. 3); the LORD calls on all to "*look* at the nations and *see*" what he is doing (v. 5); and the prophet reminds the LORD that "your eyes are too pure to *see* evil, and you cannot *look on* [NRSV: behold] wrongdoing" (v. 13; my italics in each citation). Similarly, the term "justice" occurs in all three units: the prophet complains that "justice never prevails" (v. 4); the LORD observes that the Chaldeans' "justice and dignity proceed from themselves" (v. 7); and the prophet exclaims, "O LORD, you have appointed him for justice [NRSV: judgment]" (v. 12).[12]

Structurally, "the wicked" and "the righteous" are set off against each other in both v. 4 and v. 13. Coupled with the observation that vv. 12–17 seem to continue the complaint of vv. 2–4, as if vv. 5–11 had not intervened, this suggests that the two complaints are more closely associated with each other than either is with vv. 5–11.

The objection most often raised to seeing these complaints as allied is that "the wicked" and "the righteous" in vv. 2–4 and vv. 12–17 are not the same groups. While lament of "violence" and "strife" in vv. 2–3 are general enough to apply to many circumstances, v. 4's complaint that "the law becomes slack and justice never prevails" is widely seen to refer to injustice within Judah, with "the wicked" and "the righteous" forming two groups. By contrast, vv. 12–17 links to the Chaldeans the complaint that "the wicked swallows the one more righteous than he" (v. 13). However, under the assumption that chapter 1 is a dialogue, this raises even more pointedly the question why the LORD's response to complaints of "violence" is to replace one set of wicked with another. Moreover, if in vv. 12–17 "the wicked" are the Chaldeans, and "the one more righteous than he" stands for Judah, then we are left with the question what happened to the original complaint about social injustice (Sweeney, 1991b). Given the similar questions about unimpeded wickedness in v. 2's "how long?" and v. 17's "is he then to *keep on* emptying his net?", the two complaints are likely allied. On the other hand, if we identify "the wicked" in *both* v. 4 and v. 13 with the Chaldeans, then it is unclear why, under the assumption that this is a dialogue, the Chaldeans are touted as the corrective to the situation decried in vv. 2–4 (Sweeney, 1991b). These problems can be resolved, however, under an alternative reading of chapters 1–2.

Chapter 1:   Complaints about an Oracle

Given the vocabulary links among the three units of chapter 1, the impulse to seek a literary relationship between them seems justified. In fact, it is possible to understand both laments as motivated by the rise of the new world power the LORD highlights in vv. 5–11, with the violence and disorder of the first lament describing the impact of these events on the local level, while vv. 12–17 apply the questions about divine justice raised in vv. 2–4 to the international stage (Floyd, 1991).

The complaint that "the law becomes numb" and "justice never goes forth" (v. 4; my translation) is specified as the *result* of "violence," "wrongdoing," and "trouble" (v. 3), even as the perversion of "justice" is portrayed as a *consequence* of "the wicked" oppressing "the righteous" (v. 4). The wicked pervert "law" and "justice," which likely do not refer to a specific legal code. Indeed, "law" can be used of divine pronouncements (compare Isa 2:3 and 51:4), so that the "numbing" of "the law" and the failure of "justice" could refer to a perversion of the divine word embodied in the Chaldeans' violence against Judah (vv. 5–11). In this reading, vv. 2–4 complains about an oracle (vv. 5–11) gone awry, prompting the prophet to accuse the LORD of causing him to "see wrong-doing and look at trouble" (v. 3).

Floyd (1991) has drawn attention to a passage in Jeremiah (15:10–18) that quotes an oracle (vv. 13–14) preserved elsewhere in the book (17:3b–4) but that is now situated in the midst of a lament (15:10, 15–18). The oracle is preceded by the prophet's summary of his commission, using laments about his work found elsewhere in the book (15:11–12). Differences between the oracle in 17:3–4 and the way the prophet presents it in 15:13–14 suggest that Jeremiah's complaint is that, while the oracle's threat of an attack has proved true, the forecast "I will make you serve your enemies in a land that you do not know" (15:14) has not come true, leaving him vulnerable to being discredited as a prophet (Floyd, 1991).

The similar structure of Habakkuk 1:2–17 – an oracle bounded by complaints – suggests that the failure of "law" and "justice" in vv. 2–4 does not refer to a corrupt legal system but to a perceived problem with the oracle of vv. 5–11 (Cleaver-Bartholomew, 2003). The LORD touts rousing the Chaldeans as an astounding deed without a contemporary parallel, while candidly admitting their brutality and arrogance. (However one resolves the knotty problems v. 11 presents, it likely does not carry the sort of condemnation of the Chaldeans that the NRSV suggests: see the text box.) The problems incurred by living through the fulfillment of this oracle are the subject of vv. 2–4 and, even more intensely, vv. 12–17.

The Ambiguous Hebrew of 1:11

Bible translators often face quandaries about the meaning of a verse. While v. 11 presents special problems, the NRSV's rendition of the phrase "their own might is their god" is untenable, since condemnation of making strength "one's god" would have been unintelligible in the ancient Near East, where valor and success in battle evidenced the *support* of one's deity. A better translation might be "this one [devotes] his might to his god," offered as a criticism of the LORD's commissioning of the Chaldeans as a people indebted to their own gods.

Moreover, while the verb translated "transgress" (*'abar*) can bear that meaning, when it does it typically specifies what is transgressed (such as a commandment). A different verb (*pasha*) is used for "transgress" when no object is specified. Following the phrase "they sweep by," it is more natural for *'abar* to mean "pass by," as it often does. And although "become guilty" makes sense to modern readers, it is a perplexing use of the Hebrew verb, which designates cultic sins rather than "war crimes" of the sort implied here (Andersen, 2001). In fact, the same Hebrew consonants can be read as "and I was astonished," leading one scholar to render the first half of the verse as the prophet's report of the end of receiving the oracle: "Then the spirit passed on, it departed, and I was astonished" (Roberts, 1991).

The concluding lament of the chapter picks up where the first left off, making more explicit the troubles vv. 2–4 cited. As noted earlier, the second half of v. 12 reminds the LORD that he has "appointed them for justice [NRSV: judgment]," which is ironic in light of his earlier complaint that their violence has perverted "justice" (v. 4). Verse 13 elevates this complaint to charge the LORD's tacit endorsement of injustice: if it is true (as believed) that the LORD cannot look on wrongdoing, then how can the LORD tolerate the abuse of the righteous by the wicked? In this light, it is possible to take "the wicked" and "the righteous" of both v. 4 and v. 13 as referring to the Chaldeans and Judah, respectively (Sweeney, 1991b).

Chapter 1, therefore, is a carefully constructed complaint about the actions of the Chaldeans, against the background of the oracle recalled in vv. 5–11. The question has become "how long" the LORD will tolerate what is obviously a violation of his standards of justice. The question posed is whether the oracle has become perverted by the way it has been fulfilled in violence against Judah (Cleaver-Bartholomew, 2003).

Chapter 2

Although 2:1 begins a new unit that announces the prophet's resolve to wait for a divine word and conveys his report of its arrival, the recognition that chapter 1 questions the validity of the earlier oracle makes it reasonable to expect that 2:1–5 will address that complaint.

The prophet's resolve to position himself to receive an oracle (v. 1) is followed by an explicit report of the LORD's response (v. 2). This response is intended for widespread publication, via a town crier who carries the announcement through the streets. Although the command to "write the *vision*" might suggest some sort of visionary experience, we must recall that "vision" can designate a prophetic message generally, relieving us of a (vain) search for a vision report.

While the command to "make [the vision] plain on tablets" has been taken as insistence on writing legibly, recent scholarship has illuminated the rare verb translated "make plain" as meaning something closer to English "promulgate," to "invest with legal force through public reading" (Schaper, 2007). The role of the town crier evoked in v. 2 (see above, p. 7) fits with this, since such a figure in ancient Mesopotamia served as a "legal witness confirming a protocol" (Schaper, 2009, 144). Correlatively, v. 3's description of the vision as "a *witness* to the decisive moment[13] that does not lie" (my translation) employs vocabulary used elsewhere to describe trustworthy witnesses (Prov 6:19; 12:17; 14:5, 25; 19:5, 9).[14] The notion of legal statements being promulgated by writing and then proclaimed is exampled elsewhere in the Bible (compare Exod 24:4–8 and Isa 8:1–2).

The certification of the vision through a legal process provides an apt response to questions about the validity of the oracle of 1:5–11. The "vision" the prophet is to transcribe and promulgate is no new revelation, but that very oracle. Thus, the second half of v. 3 exhorts correlatively, "If it delays, wait for it; for it will surely come without lingering."[15]

Verse 4 advocates faithfulness to the vision by contrasting the behavior of the arrogant with that of the righteous. While the verse presents numerous problems (on which, see Emerton, 1977), what seems apparent is that its first half draws attention (note the command "see!") to the wicked person's lack of stability "in it," i.e., the vision (see the text box). By contrast, the righteous person "will live" with stability of a particular kind.

"Their *spirit* is not right in them" (v. 4)?

As was the case with the NRSV's "their own might is their god" in 1:11, this rendering seems more heavily influenced by modern ideas than the likely meaning of the phrases in their ancient context.[16] The word translated "spirit" (*nephesh*) does not designate an immaterial element separable from the body, but denotes either one's appetite or one's whole person (Andersen, 2001), making "his person" a more accurate (if awkward) English equivalent. Additionally, in light of v. 3's focus on the trustworthiness of the vision, the pronoun in the phrase "in *it*" (NRSV: "in them") likely refers to the vision (Janzen, 1980). The proclamation of v. 4, then, is: "Take note of the proud, whose person is not directed straight [i.e., steadfast] in it [the vision]."

Despite the traditional rendering, "by his faith," the Hebrew noun *'emunah*, does not mean "trust," but comes closer to "steadfastness" or "faithfulness" (see Andersen, 2001). Accordingly, the statement "the righteous shall live by his steadfastness" most likely has to do with trusting firmly in the oracle. For even though 1:5–11 forecasts the rise of the Chaldeans as conquerors, it frankly recognizes their character. After all, chapter 1's complaints are not that this power has failed to rise, but that its viciousness demands rebuke. Given that 2:1–4 provide the only response to that protest, and given that the complaint concerns "how long" the LORD will permit Chaldean oppression to endure, the divine response accepts the premise of Chaldean wickedness and seeks to address it. The call to steadfast trust in the vision assumes that its complete fulfillment *will* redress Chaldean abuses, a reassurance made more explicitly in the verses that follow.

The word "moreover" at the start of v. 5 links the remainder of the chapter to vv. 1–4 (Lescow, 1995). Verse 5 turns from the trustworthiness of the oracle and a definition of the righteous to speak of the wealthy and arrogant, who have insatiable greed (like Sheol, the place of the dead) and amass peoples and nations for themselves. This editorial transition shifts the address to the fate of the Chaldeans, which is extended by v. 6's taunt by "all of these" (NRSV: "everyone"), a reference back to the nations and peoples of v. 5.[17]

The remainder of the chapter contains a series of mock laments, the first four beginning with "alas" (vv. 6b, 9, 12, 15), while the final one opens with a statement deriding idols (v. 18) before uttering "alas" regarding their worshippers (v. 19). Correlative to the different placement of the "alas" statement in vv. 18–19 is a change of topic. Whereas the first four laments pinpoint social crimes (stealing others' property, securing one's house at others' expense, building "a town by bloodshed," and debauchery toward one's neighbor) that are then applied to an unnamed evildoer on the international plane, vv. 18–19 highlight a fault (idolatry) that is especially applicable to Babylon. In contrast to these idols, stresses v. 20, "the LORD is in his holy temple," requiring all the earth to "keep silence before him."

The Composition of Chapters 1–2:   The Big Picture

The implication of this reading of chapters 1–2 is that 1:2–17 has been composed as a literary unit rather than a collage. Even if vv. 15–17 should prove to be an added riff on the image of people being "like the fish of the sea" (v. 14a), as Nogalski (1993b) conjectures,[18] chapter 1 is a literary whole.[19] In fact, the complex structure of the chapter suggests that, whether or not it was ever delivered orally, it was composed in writing.

As for chapter 2, after vv. 1–4 address a failure to trust steadfastly the oracle of 1:5–11, v. 5 reprises the image of a rapacious conqueror from 1:15–17. That image is elaborated in the woes of vv. 6b–19, pronouncing judgment on the wicked Chaldeans. Even if the hypothesis that these woes were originally directed against a Judean audience and only later rewritten to address Babylon (Jeremias, 1970) has merit, two features suggest that this set of woes has been shaped specifically for this passage (Roberts, 1991).

First, the link created by the rhetorical question of v. 6a ("Will not these all [a reference back to the 'nations' and 'peoples'] take up a taunt against him and mocking riddles about him and say …"; my translation) is awkward in Hebrew, and "these all" is imprecise (Andersen, 2001). It (along with v. 5) constitutes an editorial transition to the woes that follow.[20]

Second, while the first four woes (vv. 6b–17) rail against generalized rapaciousness of the sort described in chapter 1, the final woe (vv. 18–19) focuses on a religious symbol (an "idol"/"cast image") commonplace in the land of Israel (compare Judg 17:1–4), but curiously described here. It is said to be worthless, in so far as it is a "teacher of lies" (v. 18), suggesting that it is used as a means of **divination** (Roberts, 1991). Its ineffectiveness for that purpose is stressed by characterizing it as "an idol that cannot speak" or teach (v. 19). While the use of stone and wood as images for gods was native to Israel (compare Jer 2:27), the critique of idols plated with gold and silver but lacking life is a stock denigration of Babylonian idolatry in prophecy of the Babylonian era (compare Jer 10:2–4; Isa 40:19–20), suggesting that Babylon is the target of this harangue. The function of vv. 18–19 at the end of the woes is to highlight the flaw lying behind all Chaldean crimes: worship of gods other than the LORD (Sweeney, 1991b), much as 1:11 culminates in the exclamation "this one [devotes] his might to his god" (my translation).

The final verse of chapter 2 is a "call to worship" of the sort we encountered in Zeph 1:7 (see above, p. 75). By providing a counterpoint to the harangue against idols, it constitutes a capstone to 2:6–19 and a transition to the prayer that follows (Watts, 1996).

The Composition of Chapter 3

Another lively debate concerns the relationship of chapters 1–2 to chapter 3, the only explicitly marked **liturgical** unit in the prophets.[21] The superscription to this chapter identifies it as a "prayer" and describes it as "according to *shigionoth*," a word found also in the superscription to Psalm 7 ("a *shiggaion* of David") and probably a technical term for a lament (Kraus, 1988). Correspondingly, at the end of the poem we find instructions for performance: "To the leader: with stringed instruments" (Hab 3:19). These components parallel those in the superscription to Psalm 6: "To the leader: with stringed instruments; according to the Sheminith. A Psalm of David." Their demarcation of chapter 3 from chapters 1–2 raises questions about the prayer's relationship to "the oracle that the prophet Habakkuk saw" (1:1). Discussion of this issue raises the question whether it was an original part of the book or a later supplement (Dangl, 2001), beginning with the question whether the prayer is a whole or composite (Seybold, 1991). One can dissect the features of prayer in vv. 2 and 16–19 from the theophany of vv. 3–15,[22] the latter of which utilizes ancient motifs with Canaanite and Babylonian roots (Avishur, 1994; Herrmann, 2001). Nevertheless, it is reasonable to posit that a single author composed this psalm, incorporating traditional materials (Roberts, 1991; Watts, 1996).

Discussions of the demarcation of chapter 3 from chapters 1–2 have included suggestions that this prayer was used as a liturgical piece before its incorporation into the book (Nogalski, 1993b), regardless of whether Habakkuk's name was original to the heading. Thematic and formal parallels between this prayer and chapters 1–2 have been cited to argue that the prayer is original to the book. For instance, reference to an enemy invasion, anticipation of the LORD's deliverance, and a vision of a theophany correlate with themes in chapters 1–2 (Sweeney, 1991b). In terms of form, the prayer that surrounds the theophany (vv. 2, 16–19) fits the genre of lament (Dangl, 2001), a form prominent in 1:2–4, 12–17.

What is more, the poem never surrenders the tension that drives the book: a crisis for which the promise of the LORD's help of Israel has yet to materialize. Rather than following the theophany with an expression of thanksgiving based on a fresh experience of deliverance, the concluding lines quietly await calamity to befall the enemy (v. 16), even as they express confidence in the LORD and his strength (vv. 17–19). By hearing the "Habakkuk" who raised questions about divine justice speak so expectantly of divine action, the audience is given a key to facing a dark night (Watts, 1996). In that sense, the attribution of this prayer to Habakkuk is not merely an expedient to make its attachment to the book plausible; it makes the prophet the example of the faithful devotee of the LORD (Watts, 1996) and his prayer provides a model for those facing threat.

In contrast to the questions about divine justice in chapter 1, reassertion of the validity of the oracle in 2:1–4, and assurance that a nation like the Chaldeans will ultimately succumb (2:5–19), chapter 3 (beginning with the summons of 2:20) introduces a **theocentric** perspective. If the first two chapters focus on the threat from the Chaldeans, this chapter invokes the image of the LORD as divine warrior; if the Chaldeans are consuming the earth, the earth is full of the LORD's praise (3:3); though the Chaldeans' horses are terrifying (1:8), the LORD's horses have proved victorious over the mythic powers of the rivers and the sea (3:8, 15) (Watts, 1996).

The fact that the superscription and the final instructions mark this prayer for use in the cultic setting distinguish it from cultic material in other prophetic books, whose liturgical character must be inferred (as with Nahum 1:2–8 and Micah 7). The formal marking of chapter 3 as literature fit for the cult has led many to conclude that its author was a prophet who served at the temple or even that the entire book was constructed for use in the cult (Jeremias, 1970). Such a hypothesis draws too direct a correlation between the types of literature used and the author's social role, and thereby underestimates scribal sophistication in composing literature that imitates or draws on literary forms from diverse social settings (Watts, 1996, 223). Neither should we assume that 2:20–3:19 were always attached to chapters 1–2, any more than we would assume that the hymn of Nahum 1:2–8 was always prefixed to the book's mocking of Nineveh's plight. In both cases we likely have to do with liturgical pieces appropriated for their fitness in their literary contexts.

Summary

The likelihood, then, is that the book of Habakkuk was written in the wake of a Babylonian assault on Jerusalem, utilizing and reshaping earlier traditions to address not just the question of divine justice (Thompson, 1993), but even more so the question of whether all the implications of the old oracle would be realized. The answer, confessed in the concluding prayer, is that the LORD, whose power is renowned, will ultimately give the wicked Babylonians the comeuppance they deserve.

A curious feature of the Twelve is that the book of Nahum, with its delight in Assyria's downfall, and the book of Habakkuk, with its pressing questions about how the "god of justice" can allow the Babylonians' prosperity to continue, can stand in the same anthology as the book of Jonah, which lets one of these historic enemies off the hook. As we shall see in the next chapter, this story poses in a fresh way the question of divine justice.

Notes

1. The designation of it as "an oracle" parallels the superscriptions to oracles against foreign nations in Isaiah 13:1, 15:1, 17:1, 19:1, 22:1, and 23:1. Labeling it a "vision" recalls Isaiah 1:1 and Obadiah 1. Floyd's contention (2002) that the word translated "oracle" (*maśśā'*) defines the genre of Nahum is unpersuasive, since his inference of its meaning from 2 Kings 9:25–26 is flawed: it is not the interpretation of the oracle that is labeled a *maśśā'*, but the oracle itself.
2. Even if Isaiah 30:8 instructs Isaiah to "write it on a tablet with them, and in a text inscribe it" (my translation, reflecting the ambiguous identity of "it" in Hebrew) and Habakkuk 2:2 commands Habakkuk to "write the vision, make it plain on tablets," these commands apply to specific messages, not to a compendium of oracles.
3. Spronk contends that the Balaam inscription from Deir 'Alla speaks for the originality of the double title in Nahum 1:1, in so far as that text's title is compound ("Warnings from the Book of Balaam, the son of Beor. He was a seer of the gods"; Spronk, 1997). However, he glosses over differences, especially the fact that the second clause, as a clarification of Balaam's identity, could not have stood as an independent title, while the first component provides both a classification for the work and the name of the prophet.
4. Even if Isaiah 40–66 can split phrases from passages it borrows (Sommer, 1998), the distance between Isaiah 52:1 and v. 7 is greater than typical when Deutero-Isaiah uses split phrases.
5. The only other acrostic that may use only part of the alphabet is Psalm 9 (Christensen, 1975).
6. In agreement with the NRSV (and following the **Septuagint**) I read *beqamayw*, "his adversaries," for *meqomah*, "its place."
7. The three corruptions are: a letter *waw* ("and") erroneously placed before YHWH ("the Lord") in the "J" line; a scribe attempted to clarify the "G" line by prefixing the preposition "before" to the word "indignation"; most noticeably, it is necessary to replace the initial verb of the "D" line (which is identical with the final verb of that line) with a similarly formed one that begins with the requisite initial letter, under the assumption that a copyist replaced the less frequent verb with the more familiar one that stood at the line's end.
8. An objection to identifying this as an acrostic is that the second letter of the alphabet (v. 3b) is separated from the first (v. 2) by more lines than any of the others is separated from its neighboring letter (Floyd, 1994). The most likely explanation is that vv. 2–3a have been editorially expanded by reusing Exodus 34:6–7a (Nogalski, 1993b; van Leeuwen, 1993): "A jealous and avenging God is the Lord, the Lord is avenging and wrathful; the Lord takes vengeance on his adversaries and rages against his enemies, keeping steadfast love for the thousandth generation, forgiving iniquity and transgression and sin, yet by no means clearing the guilty." Nogalski (1993b) follows van Leeuwen (1993) in positing that this was added to help unify the Twelve. However, the substitution of "but great in power" for "and abounding in steadfast love," while omitting mention of forgiveness, underscores the assertion that "the Lord will by no means clear the guilty" rather than the Lord's propensity to forgive, as is the case in Joel and Jonah.

9. Floyd (1994) argues that the poem extends through v. 10, but disputes that it is an acrostic, arguing instead that its major structuring devices are the questions of vv. 6 and 9. The first asks the audience to infer a general principle from the description of the Lord in vv. 2–5: "Before his indignation who could stand?" (v. 6; my translation). The second asks the audience to draw an inference from the assertion of vv. 7–8 that the Lord watches over his devotees and punishes his foes: "What would you plot against the Lord?" (v. 9; my translation). In mounting this argument he must minimize the alphabetical order of the initial letter of some of these lines, overstate the obstacles to restoring other letters needed for an acrostic, and attribute greater significance to the questions of vv. 6 and 9 than seems sustainable. And, as Spronk (1998) notes, Floyd's reading depends on overriding a division between vv. 10 and 11 marked in the **MT**, at the same time that he argues to keep its wording.

10. These Chaldean Babylonians are immigrants that took over the old territory of Babylon, mentioned above, p. 57.

11. Whether the notion of a prophet positioning himself at his watchpost means that he enters an extraordinary frame of mind (see pp. 233–234) is uncertain.

12. The NRSV's translation ("you have marked them for judgment; and … have established them for punishment") presumes that vv. 12–17 respond to vv. 5–11. This runs contrary to the natural meaning of the Hebrew, as Andersen (2001) notes, at the same time that he argues that it must mean something along the lines of the NRSV's translation.

13. For the translation of *qets* with "decisive moment," see Janzen (1980, 66).

14. The word the NRSV translates with "it speaks" is likely a noun meaning "witness" (Andersen, 2001; Janzen, 1980).

15. While some contend that the Lord is the subject of these verbs (Andersen, 2001), the fact that v. 3a seeks to rehabilitate the trustworthiness of the oracle suggests that the "vision" is the subject.

16. The fact that Habakkuk 2:4 is quoted in early Christian literature, in the form found in the **LXX** ("The one who is righteous will live by faith," Rom 1:17; Gal 3:11; Heb 10:38), has had a strong effect on preserving that translation.

17. While Lescow (1995) identifies "moreover" alone as the transition and considers the remainder of the verse as the first woe, the woes are introduced in v. 6b with "Shall not everyone taunt such people and, with mocking riddles, say about them …." Verse 5's "treacherous" picks up vocabulary that appears elsewhere in the book only at 1:13, leading into the description of the Chaldeans as voracious conquerors, similar to the theme in the remainder of v. 5.

18. In latching upon the image of the peoples as fish, vv. 15–17 leave behind the second half of v. 14, which likens them to "crawling things that have no ruler."

19. Excluded by this construal of chapter 1 are the reconstructions of Albertz (2003a), Jeremias (1970), Lescow (1995), and Seybold (1991).

20. Andersen (2001) concedes that "the connections of this half-verse are not obvious" and concludes that it forms a transition in the same voice as the "reader" in v. 2.

21. While Micah 7 is composed of liturgical traditions, and hymnic lines appear in other prophets (such as Amos), only Habakkuk 3 is explicitly marked as a liturgical composition.

22. Even within the theophany one can detect components, inasmuch as vv. 3–7 describe the Lord's approach in third-person language, while vv. 8–15 address the Lord (Sweeney, 1991b).

8

The Books of Jonah and Haggai

Jonah

> ### In the pages to come ...
>
> Like Habakkuk, the book of Jonah attributes to its prophet an extended prayer (chapter 2) and has him protesting the failure of an **oracle**. However, unlike Habakkuk or any other prophet, Jonah runs from his commission. And when he does take it up, his hearers repent, and the LORD rescinds his threat, Jonah finds that outcome unacceptable. Most uniquely, the book offers a *narrative* about a prophet, in which he utters but one oracle (3:4b). The pressing questions are, what sort of prophetic book this is, why was it composed, and how?

Jonah 1:1 is an **incipit**, initiating a narrative by reporting Jonah's receipt of "the word of the LORD." Jonah is instructed to call the people of Nineveh, the Assyrian capital, to repentance. Although he tries to escape this mandate by boarding a seagoing ship heading west,[1] his treachery is exposed during a storm at sea, he winds up overboard, and is swallowed by a great fish provided by the LORD (chapter 1). Jonah prays, and the fish spews him onto dry land (chapter 2). This time he goes to Nineveh, where he announces impending judgment. The Ninevites repent, and the LORD relents (chapter 3). It takes Jonah's anger over a shriveled plant to expose his bigotry (chapter 4).

Prophetic Literature: From Oracles to Books, First Edition. Ronald L. Troxel.
© 2012 Ronald L. Troxel. Published 2012 by Blackwell Publishing Ltd.

The Narrative's Warp and Woof

The narrative never loses sight of Jonah as he reacts to the LORD's dealings with him and with Nineveh (Wolff, 1986). Nevertheless, it is less his activity that proves decisive in chapters 1 and 3 than the actions of non-Israelites. In chapter 1 it is the non-Israelite sailors who, despite their scruples and fears, heed Jonah's claim that throwing him into the sea will calm it (1:11–14). In chapter 3 it is the citizens of Nineveh who, having heard Jonah's forecast of calamity in 40 days, repent in hopes that "God may relent and change his mind" (3:9).

Jonah merely seems to be the chief actor. Before the sailors eventually follow Jonah's advice and throw him overboard, they try other measures to steady the ship and then seek absolution from the deity before sending a man to his death (1:14). When Jonah finally enters Nineveh, he utters the tersest of oracles, fulfilling the divine command in letter only, leaving the Ninevites to infer how to escape impending doom. And upon leaving the city, he erects a shelter as a spectator's perch to await the city's destruction, but where, instead, he becomes the target of a divine rebuke. Jonah proves at best only a reluctant participant in the book's action; more often he is the object of it.

Equally, Jonah's character is the antitype of a prophet. When the storm arises, the sailors spontaneously invoke their gods to save them, but must prompt Jonah to call on his god (1:5–6). When Jonah matter-of-factly informs them that the storm is due to his flight "from the presence of the LORD," the sailors are shocked at his audacity (1:10). Similarly, the king of Nineveh, upon hearing Jonah's curt warning, orders that his people repent of their wickedness, whereas it took a ride in a fish's belly for Jonah to obey the LORD's command. At the same time that Nineveh's king orders elaborate rites of penance on the off-chance that God might change his mind (3:7–9), Jonah sets up shop on a hill overlooking the city on the off-chance that judgment might yet fall (4:5). And while the sailors and the Ninevites do everything thinkable to escape death at God's hands, Jonah pleads with the LORD to kill him (4:3).

This portrayal of Jonah is not just demeaning: it is comical (Burrows, 1970). Jonah's attempt to flee "from the presence of the LORD" by ship is ironic, given his claim to worship "the God of heaven, who made the sea and the dry land" (1:9). The deity who "made the sea" would have no trouble finding a person attempting to escape by that route (Burrows, 1970). And once the LORD orchestrates the sudden sprouting and then death of a plant, his question whether Jonah is right to be angry about the plant sets up Jonah for ridicule by contrasting his anger about the plant with the LORD's concern for the people and animals of Nineveh (4:7–11).

These features raise questions about whether the book offers a historical report, as is often assumed. Although it employs well-known place names – such as Joppa, Nineveh, and Tarshish – and "Jonah son of Amittai" is a prophet mentioned in 2 Kings 14:25, facets of the book undermine the impression of historicity.

The picture of Nineveh in this story ill fits the time of Jonah son of Amittai referred to by 2 Kings 14:25 (mid-eighth century BCE) since Nineveh did not become a major city until its elevation to serve as the sole capital of Assyria after 700 BCE (McKenzie, 2005). Indeed, the fact that the narrator feels compelled to tell his audience, in an aside, "Now Nineveh was an exceedingly large city, a three days' walk across," assumes that the audience was unfamiliar with a Nineveh of these dimensions – and for good reason, since Nineveh was never this large, even if one included the settlements outside its walls (Burrows, 1970). The inference that the story is set in a fabled Nineveh is confirmed by the report that Nineveh's king issued a decree along with his nobles (3:7), at variance with what we know of Assyrian royal practices (kings issued their own decrees) but in accord with protocols in the Persian empire, long after Nineveh's destruction (Wolff, 1986).[2] Likewise, the Ninevites' repentance rites that have their animals fasting and donning sackcloth (3:8) lampoons the Persians' use of animals in mourning rituals, at least according to Herodotus' reports of their army shaving their horses in an act of grief (Wolff, 1986). Thus, while the book uses familiar place names and narrates events in chronological order, it contains hints that it is not historiography but a story meant to do something other than report events: but what? Unraveling that question requires investigating what we can detect about the way the book was composed.

Consistency: The Hobgoblin of Small Narrators?

Despite the artistry evident in this story, conflicts in how the narrative unfolds reveal the story to be less coherent than it appears. Consider, for example, the different reasons given for sparing the Ninevites. Once the people repented, "God saw what they did … [and] changed his mind about the calamity that he had said he would bring upon them" (3:10). This implies that the people's repentance spurred the LORD to relent. However, a different motive for the LORD's reversal surfaces in Jonah's complaint "Is not this what I said while I was still in my own country? That is why I fled to Tarshish at the beginning; for I knew that you are a gracious God and merciful, slow to anger, and abounding in steadfast love, and that you change your mind about calamity" (4:2; my translation).[3] Jonah's description of the LORD's character takes up the words of Exodus 34:6–7, which we encountered in Micah 7:18, Joel 2:13, and Nahum 1:3. Of those passages, Joel 2:13 is virtually identical to Jonah 4:2 (see the text box): "Return to the LORD, your God, for he is *gracious and merciful, slow to anger*, and *abounding in steadfast love*, and *changes* [his] *mind about calamity*" (my translation). Jonah's charge that God is merciful and has a reputation for changing his mind about calamity identifies this – *not* fear that the people of Nineveh would repent – as that which gave him pause "while I was still in my own country."

Jonah 4:2 and Joel 2:13

Of the four passages in the prophets that utilize Exodus 34:6 ("The LORD, the LORD, a God merciful and gracious, slow to anger, and abounding in steadfast love and faithfulness"), Jonah 4:2 mirrors it most closely. However, it is not the only passage from Exodus that finds an echo in this book.

The report of 3:10 – "And God changed his mind about the calamity that he had said he would bring upon them" – closely parallels the LORD's response to Moses' appeal on behalf of the people after their worship of the golden calf: "And the LORD changed his mind about the calamity that he said he would bring upon his people" (Exod 32:14; my translation). No other passage matches Exodus 32:14 like Jonah 3:10,[4] whose substitution of "God" for "the LORD" is due to the use of "God" throughout Jonah 3:5–9 (Wolff, 1986). What is more, the king's speculation that "God may turn and change his mind, and turn from his fierce anger" (3:9; my translation) is close to Moses' petition in Exodus 32:12 (Bergler, 1988): "Turn from your fierce anger and change your mind about the calamity to your people" (my translation). Jonah 3:9–10 relies on Exodus 32.

The case of 4:2 is more complex, since its close accord with Exodus 34:6 vanishes with "and changing his mind about the calamity" rather than using Exodus's "and faithfulness." Moreover, Joel 2:13 shares this deviation. In the end, it seems more likely that Jonah relies on Joel than the other way around (Müller, 2008). Whereas Jonah cites the assertion of the LORD's willingness to change his mind due to mercy as a well-known confession, Joel simply offers this as a reason to take his counsel to return to the LORD (Schart, 1998).[5] Not only that, but by qualifying this proclamation with the caution that his relenting is but a possibility, Joel 2:14 leaves uncertain the proposition that Jonah takes as a guarantee, turning it against the LORD as an accusation. Even though Jonah places the uncertainty voiced in Joel 2:14 in the mouth of Nineveh's king (Jonah 3:9), it does not serve to hedge divine mercy, but expresses uncertainty over the actions of an unknown deity. Seen through that lens, Jonah more likely takes up phrases from Joel to ridicule a confession viewed as a guarantee of mercy for Israel but not for others (Schart, 1998).[6]

While one might counter that 4:2 assumes the preceding narrative, so that Jonah's words must be read as assuming that Ninevite repentance would be the trigger for the LORD changing his mind (Jeremias, 2004), the LORD's final words to Jonah justify the prophet's fears: "And should I, for my part, not take pity on Nineveh,[7] that great city, in which there are more than a hundred and twenty thousand persons who do not know their right hand from their left, and many animals?" (4:11; my translation). The LORD attributes his decision to relent to his pity for clueless people and animals rather than to Nineveh's repentance (Cooper, 1993).[8] Thus, it becomes apparent that the author "can shift about in his application of different kinds of theological tenets" (Wolff, 1986, 87).

This sort of flexibility is equally apparent in the varied ways the book portrays foreigners. In the midst of the storm at sea, the sailors "each cried to his god" (1:5), implying that they worship various deities. And yet, they move from fear caused by a storm (v. 5) to being "even more afraid" when Jonah tells them that he is a lapsed worshipper of "the LORD, the God of heaven " (v. 9), to offering a prayer to the LORD (v. 14), and finally, to fearing the LORD "even more," offering sacrifices and making vows to him (v. 16). In the course of the narrative these foreign sailors are transformed from devotees of their gods to worshippers of the LORD (Jeremias, 2004).

The story of the Ninevites, by contrast, says nothing of them worshiping the LORD. They only "turn from their evil ways and from the violence that is in their hands" (3:8). In fact, whereas the sailors, in their growing fear of the LORD, are the antitype to Jonah in chapter 1, in chapter 3 it is the Ninevite king who fills the gap Jonah leaves by calling on the people to repent (Jeremias, 2004). Moreover, it is he who utters the words drawn from Exodus 32:12: "God may turn and change his mind, and he may turn from his fierce anger" (v. 9).[9] Nevertheless, there is no indication that the king or the people become the Lord's devotees. Once again the author works with a flexible set of tenets rather than imposing a consistent theological perspective.

Other incongruities occur, such as the variations in divine names, especially in chapter 4 (see the text box). An especially stubborn problem is the position of 4:5 in the narrative: "Then Jonah went out of the city and sat down east of the city, and made a booth for himself there. He sat under it in the shade, waiting to see what would become of the city." How does this follow naturally from the argument between Jonah and the Lord in 4:2–4, in which Jonah admits having known in advance that the Lord would relent from judging the Ninevites? Why set up camp outside the city, waiting to see what would happen, if Jonah knows the outcome? Many have suggested that a copyist erroneously transferred this statement here from just after 3:4, where Jonah completed his proclamation. There are, however, better explanations for the place of 4:5.

The Problem of the Divine Names

Chapter 1 uses divine names in a meaningful pattern. The proper name "Lord" occurs in the interactions between Jonah and the Lord (vv. 1–4), while the generic term "god" is used in the report that each sailor called on "the name of his god," as well as the captain's exhortation of Jonah to call on "his god" (vv. 5–6). The sailors learn the name of Jonah's god for the first time when he informs them that he worships "the Lord, the God of heaven" (v. 9), after which the narrator reports that Jonah had informed the sailors that he was fleeing "from the presence of the Lord" (v. 10). The sailors themselves subsequently use "the Lord" in v. 14, and appropriately so, since their appeal is to the god Jonah says caused the storm. The ensuing calm motivates them to offer sacrifices and pledge vows to the Lord, who has stilled the seas (v. 16). In v. 17 the narrator reports that the Lord appoints a fish to rescue Jonah, just as earlier he spoke of the Lord "hurl[ing] up a great wind" (v. 4). At the outset of chapter 2, Jonah "prayed to the Lord his God" (2:1), after which "the Lord spoke to the fish" (2:10).[10] Similarly, the narrator uses the **Tetragrammaton** in his reports that "the word of the Lord came to Jonah a second time" (3:1) and that "Jonah set out and went to Nineveh, according to the word of the Lord" (3:3). After that, however, it vanishes from chapter 3.

In 3:5 the narrator says that "the people of Nineveh believed God." Given that this is the narrator's report, and given that he does not say "believed their gods," it is not clear why he shies away from saying "the Lord."[11] Equally difficult to understand is why the narrator reports the outcome of the Ninevites' repentance with the words "When *God* saw what they did, how they turned from their evil ways, *God* changed his mind about the calamity" (3:10; my italics), especially since in 4:2 he will report that Jonah "prayed to the Lord." And matters become even more confusing later in chapter 4. Why should 4:9 recite that "*God* said to Jonah, 'Is it right for you to be angry about the bush?'" but v. 10 report, "Then the *Lord* said, 'You are concerned about the bush ...'"?[12] Here any sensible rationale in the vacillation of names vanishes.

One might argue that Jonah's action is no more unreasonable than his attempt to flee the presence of the God who made sea and dry land. More likely, however, the narrator reports Jonah setting up camp outside the city at that point because it sets the scene for the action of vv. 6–11, even though it logically precedes not only 3:5–10 but also Jonah's dialogue with the Lord in 4:2–4 (Lohfink, 1961).

Parallel to this is the conflict between the statement that Jonah "made a booth for himself" and "sat under it in the shade" (4:5b) and the following report, that "the Lord God appointed a bush, and made it come up over Jonah, to give shade over his head, to save him from his discomfort" (4:6). If Jonah was sitting in the shade of a booth, why was it necessary to provide him with a plant for shade?

Similar is the odd sequence from the report that, having heard Jonah's message, "the people of Nineveh believed God; they proclaimed a fast, and everyone, great and small, put on sackcloth" (3:5) and the decree of the king of Nineveh and his nobles that "no human being or animal, no herd or flock, shall taste anything" but "shall be covered with sackcloth" (3:6–7). The duplicate proclamation of a fast, like the provision of unneeded shade, suggests that the narrator was not supremely interested in a tightly ordered narrative (Lohfink, 1961).

Applying this observation to the broader narrative, the book of Jonah falls into discrete units. Setting aside chapter 2 momentarily, it is noteworthy that chapter 3 opens much like chapter 1:

> 1:1 Now the word of the Lord came to Jonah son of Amittai, saying, 2a: "Go at once to Nineveh, that great city, and cry out against it …."

> 3:1 The word of the Lord came to Jonah a second time, saying, 2: "Get up, go to Nineveh, that great city, and proclaim to it the message that I tell you."

The phrase "a second time" in 3:1 effects a restart, as if the entire act of rebellion had vanished. Of course, this is not true in the end, since Jonah's argument in 4:2 explains why he fled at the beginning. Nevertheless, 3:1–2 distinguish chapter 3 from what precedes. Similarly, chapter 1 reaches a fitting conclusion with the report of the Lord appointing a large fish to swallow Jonah. With that, the sailors are left behind, never to reappear. In the same way, the role of the fish ends with the report that "it spewed Jonah out upon the dry land" (2:10).

While the actions of the Ninevites are capped by the report that "when God saw what they did … God changed his mind about the calamity" (3:10), Jonah's objection rests on that decision proving "very displeasing to Jonah" (4:1). Thus, 3:10 brings to an end a scene in a particular place, and the next action in a specified place begins only in 4:5, with 4:1–4 constituting a dialogue "offstage."

Not only is the narrative of Jonah segmented, but it seems constructed of narrative plots that have been joined. For example, the story of Jonah's plight in chapter 4 is reminiscent of Elijah sitting under "a solitary broom tree" and wishing to die (1 Kings 19:3–4) (Wolff, 1986). Similarly, the odd juxtaposition of the reports that Jonah built a booth for shade (4:5) and the Lord's appointment of a bush to provide shade (4:6) betrays the use of two narrative templates: one in which the prophet provides his own shelter, and another story about a protective bush whose destruction serves as a means of teaching the prophet a lesson (Wolff, 1986).

Despite hints that different narrative motifs have been intertwined, attempts to identify sources the author used have proved unsatisfactory, since the individual episodes cannot stand on their own as complete stories (Sasson, 1990).[13] Moreover, there are terms that run through the book as a whole, such as the language of the LORD "appointing" incidents and objects (1:17; 4:6, 7, 8). As already noted, Jonah's statement "That is why I fled to Tarshish at the beginning" in 4:2 looks back to chapter 1, while "The word of the LORD came to Jonah *a second time*" (3:1) presupposes 1:1. Accordingly, whatever earlier narratives the book of Jonah presupposes, they have been woven into a single story (Sasson, 1990). Nevertheless, whatever the author aimed at creating, it was not a historical report.

The Curious Case of Chapter 2

Chapter 2 forms a special case within the book. Although this prayer shows points of contact with the story of Jonah 1, careful reading shows that they are not as precise as is often assumed. Even though the speaker calls on the LORD "out of the belly of Sheol" (2:2, reminiscent of "from the belly of the fish" in v. 1), talks of being "cast into the deep, into the heart of the seas" (2:3), and recalls that "weeds were wrapped around my head" (2:5), the prayer reflects an experience of drowning, a motif frequently used in the Psalms as a metaphor for death (for example, Psalm 69) (Sasson, 1990). If we are to integrate chapter 2 with the larger story, it must be seen as Jonah's thanksgiving for being rescued by the fish. Even then, the speaker differs from the belligerent prophet of the rest of the book, since while the Jonah of chapter 1 tries to flee "the presence of the LORD" (vv. 2, 4, 10), this speaker laments, "I am *driven away* from your sight" (2:4). If we should posit that this reflects Jonah's change of heart, we must deal with the fact that he subsequently repeats his objections to the divine commission (4:2), which suggests that he has not changed his views. And in fact, the prayer contains no explicit expressions of contrition or repentance.

Accordingly, there are good reasons to suspect that a prayer utilized in worship was pressed into service for this book, as we have witnessed on other occasions (for instance, Nah 1:2–8; Hab 3). Chapter 2 vv. 1–2a seeks to integrate the prayer within the narrative by assuming the location at sea begun in chapter 1 and linking the "belly of the fish" with "the belly of Sheol" (2:2). It also establishes a motif of Jonah addressing the LORD by referring to an otherwise unreported prayer of distress (2:2) prior to this one (about which chapter 1 is silent), thereby anticipating Jonah's renewed address of the LORD in 4:2–3 (Lichtert, 2005). Whatever its origin, chapter 2 has been carefully woven into the narrative.

What Is the Book of Jonah?

These observations about the book and its composition raise the question of what sort of book this is. While it is unique among the prophetic books, its distinctions should not be overstated. Even though it is a narrative, we saw a subtle narrative framework in Joel and will find a pronounced narrative structure in Haggai. And even if it focuses on the deeds and experiences of a prophet, other books have biographical stories. Moreover, Jonah approximates (on some level) the narratives about prophets in Samuel through Kings, placing it under the rubric of "prophetic literature."

On the other hand, its comparability to the stories of prophets in Samuel and Kings breaks down when we note that Jonah is not a hero, but an anti-hero (Burrows, 1970). Moreover, whereas the other prophetic books are filled with prophetic oracles, this book contains but one, succinct address (3:4b). And whereas other books might ask the audience to imagine the application of prophetic words to their day (for example, Joel) or even commend contemplation of them to the wise (Hos 14:9), the book of Jonah, with its final question hanging unanswered, seems to entice its readers and hearers to ponder the LORD's query for themselves.

What conclusion does the book expect its readers to draw? A common reading is that the story pits a deity whose capacity for forgiveness is boundless against a person whose spirit is too restricted to accept the implications of that for others (Wolff, 1986). However, that sort of theoretical discussion would not require the backdrop of ancient Nineveh, "that great city" (1:2).

Equally common are claims that the book seeks to counter the harsh views of books like Nahum by affirming the LORD's compassion for even a city like Nineveh (Allen, 1976) or, more generally, for non-Jews, whatever their origins (Burrows, 1970). The force of this argument is blunted, however, since the book was composed long after Nineveh's fall in 612 BCE, thereby allowing the reader the satisfaction of knowing that, no matter what reprieve Nineveh won in Jonah's day, it ultimately succumbed to divine judgment.

The fact that the audience would have known full well Nineveh's fate prompts the suggestion that the LORD's relenting is not the pivotal issue, but precisely the audience's knowledge that Nineveh fell. Perhaps the point is divine sovereignty: "he is not only free to love whom he will, Jew or Gentile, but also perfectly free to change his mind on such matters, even those which concern the fate of 120,000 people and their animals" (Bolin, 1995).

This interpretation has been given an especially sharp point by positing that the book's final verse should be construed as an assertion rather than a question: "As for me, I have no compassion for Nineveh," which is to say, "their repentance means nothing to him, and he has kept his real reason for sparing them (if, indeed, he had one) to himself" (Cooper, 1993, 158). Although this translation is grammatically possible, it is unlikely, for the comment that Nineveh is inhabited by numerous people and animals (4:11) loses its force if the LORD holds no concern for the city, especially since that description of the city is placed in contrast to the plant that Jonah did nothing to raise, implying that the LORD has an investment in Nineveh's people and animals (Ben Zvi, 2009).

So what, then, are we to make of Jonah, particularly as a prophetic book? First, the fact that its author and audience were aware of Nineveh's downfall is significant, but not crucial. In fact, the knowledge that Nineveh would ultimately fall to divine judgment might enhance the point: *even* a city like Nineveh, destined for destruction, could find mercy in the LORD's sight.

Second, the spotlighted characteristic of the city is its wickedness, not its foreign population or, for that matter, its role as Israel's foe. Thus, beyond even the question of the city's destiny is the notion that the LORD could reverse his plan to destroy such an extremely wicked city.

Third, we should likely see the book's pivotal issue as the revelation of the LORD's character in his responses to the Ninevites and Jonah. When, in 4:2, Jonah discloses his reason for fleeing in the first place, it has to do with the LORD's character. Even if the king of Nineveh was uncertain that repentance would win a reprieve (3:9), Jonah knew from the outset that the LORD would relent.

In this light, the book's meaning might well revolve around the two scenes in which Jonah protests the LORD's actions by asking for death. In the first, it is having witnessed the LORD doing exactly what Jonah knew he would that causes him to request execution, in response to which the LORD asks, "Is it right for you to be angry?" (4:3–4). In the second scene, it is the LORD's destruction of the plant (rather than Nineveh) that makes Jonah wish for death, after which the LORD again questions whether Jonah's anger is justified (4:8–9). This time the LORD specifies the reason for Jonah's anger: "Is it right for you to be angry *about the bush*?" And in contrast to the earlier question, which Jonah never answered, here Jonah replies, "Yes, angry enough to die" (4:9). What follows is not just a contrast between Jonah's relationship to the bush and the LORD's relationship to Nineveh, but a teasing out of what was left unstated earlier, when Jonah believed that his anger – over Nineveh being spared – was worth dying for.

The point of the LORD's final question seems to be that, just as Jonah's anger over the plant's destruction had little to support it, so his anger over the LORD's failure to destroy Nineveh is unreasonable. Although the LORD does not reveal to Jonah why he destroyed the plant, he does account for why he refrained from destroying Nineveh: its people and animals that he had made. Jonah was rightly convinced that the LORD would change his mind about overthrowing Nineveh, but he was wrong to see this as some sort of failure of principle. The LORD is quite willing to destroy something like a plant, but is reticent to destroy people and animals,[14] even if the reader knows that he will subsequently do so in the case of Nineveh. It is not simply that the LORD is sovereign and can do what he wants, but that he is concerned for his creatures, so that refraining from judgment for their sakes, even if only temporarily, is self-justifying.

By definition, Jonah is prophetic literature, inasmuch as it features a prophet through whom and with whom the LORD communicates. Similarly to Hosea 1:2–9, which is introduced by "When the LORD first spoke *through* Hosea, the LORD said to Hosea" and then narrates events in which the prophet has a minimal role, the book of Jonah uses the prophet as a vehicle for a divine message independently of anything the prophet himself says. The book is prophetic in function as much as form.

Haggai

In the pages to come …

Like Jonah, the book of Haggai narrates interactions between the prophet and those around him. However, whereas Jonah was a full-blown narrative, Haggai is composed of mini-narratives initiated by incipits that assign each scene a distinct date. The book is artfully structured, so that even the passage most often considered out of sync with its context proves, upon further study, to fit well within its sequence of stories.

Haggai 1:1 is an incipit, introducing an oracle addressed to the prophet, which it dates to a specific month and day, much like each successive incipit in the book (1:15; 2:1, 10, 18, 20).[15] Three of these (1:1, 15, and 2:10, each introducing a new unit) locate the month within the second year of the reign of the Persian king Darius, around 20 years after Judean **exiles** began returning from Babylon.[16] The arrangement of these scenes in chronological order provides the framework for the book of Haggai.

The Narratives of Haggai

Chapter 1 v. 1 introduces a scene in which the word of the Lord "came by the prophet Haggai to Zerubbabel ... and Joshua," after which v. 2 states in oracle form, "Thus says the Lord of hosts: These people say the time has not yet come to rebuild the Lord's house." The peculiarity of this private oracle to Zerubbabel and Joshua is shown by the fresh introduction in v. 3, "And the word of the Lord came by the prophet Haggai, saying," leading to a rebuff of the people's assertion: "Is it a time for you yourselves to live in your paneled houses, while this house lies in ruins?" This odd shift from an oracle informing Zerubbabel and Joshua of the people's opinion to one addressed to the people interweaves "the date and setting, the cast of characters, and the initial dramatic conflict and sets them before the readers/hearers" (Kessler, 2008, 10).

Narration is even more marked in v. 12, which reports the people's response to Haggai's oracle, and in v. 14, which states that "the Lord stirred up the spirit" of Zerubbabel, Joshua, and the people to rebuild the temple. More striking, however, is the statement sandwiched between these, in v. 13: "Then Haggai, the messenger of the Lord, spoke to the people with the Lord's message, saying, I am with you, says the Lord." Here Haggai's oracle is reported as part of a larger narrative rather than on its own, as oracles have been in other prophetic books.

A similar structure appears in 2:10–19. The date formula (v. 10) casts this as a report of the word of the Lord addressed to Haggai, and v. 11 attests a divine command for the prophet to "ask the priests for a ruling." However, with the report of the priests' answer at the end of v. 12, the unit slips into narrative mode, with Haggai posing a new question to the priests, to which they respond in v. 13. Verses 14–19 then resume the form of an oracle, introduced simply with "Haggai then said." The interweaving of narrative and oracles is again noteworthy.

The narrator's artistry is equally apparent from symmetries between units. Two features of the first (1:1–14) and third (2:10–19) units create a mirror effect (Assis, 2006). First, the enumeration of the losses suffered (1:7) is matched by a retrospect on those losses (2:16–17) before contrasting the circumstances the people now enjoy (2:18–19). Second, twice in the first unit the prophet exhorts the people, "Consider how you have fared" (1:5, 7), which is matched by three exhortations to "consider" how they now fare in 2:15 and 18.

At the same time, the second (2:1–9) and fourth (2:20–23) units share the motif of divine disruption of human affairs, both times expressed as "shaking the heavens and the earth" (2:6, 21) that affects primarily the nations, whose treasuries will be emptied (2:7) or their kingdoms overthrown (v. 22) (Assis, 2008). Such disruption emphasizes the LORD's role in Jerusalem's future, without which it and its temple would remain insignificant. Thus, the mirroring of features between narrative units attests an interest in coordinating these mini-narratives.

Statements sprinkled throughout the book certify that these are oracles by the frequent use of the **messenger formula** and "says the LORD" (1:2, 5, 7, 8, 9, 13; 2:4, 6, 7, 8, 9, 11, 14, 17, 23). However, because these occur in narrative comments rather than the prophet's speech, the emphasis on the prophet delivering divine speech is due to the scribal author (Floyd, 1995). In fact, the prophet's words are sometimes intertwined with a narrative about their origin. For example, 1:13, following a report that the people obeyed Haggai's words, says, "Then Haggai, the messenger of the LORD, spoke to the people with the LORD's message, saying, 'I am with you, says the LORD.'" Verse 14 then reports the LORD "stirring up" the people to rebuild the temple. The issue is not merely that Haggai's speech is encased in narrative, but that Haggai's role as "the messenger of the LORD" is specified by the narrator. Verse 12 describes the people obeying "the voice of the LORD their God, and the words of the prophet Haggai, as the LORD their God had sent him," thereby equating Haggai's words with "the voice of the LORD." In the wake of that, v. 13's introduction of an oracle of salvation with "then Haggai, the messenger of the LORD, spoke to the people with the LORD's message" conveys the narrator's stress on Haggai as the LORD's spokesman.[17]

Therefore, in considering the narrative units, not only are we faced with the fact that a written report of an oracle is never a transcript, but also with a narrator lobbying for the authority of the prophet. Haggai's words have not just been set within an "editorial framework" (Mason, 1977; Tollington, 1993), for the editorial framework creates Haggai's role in the book's narratives.

Another evidence of the narrator's hand is the focus on Zerubbabel, the governor, and Joshua, the high priest. Already 1:1 specifies them as the primary addressees: "the word of the LORD came by the prophet Haggai to Zerubbabel son of Shealtiel, governor of Judah, and to Joshua son of Jehozadak, the high priest." Despite v. 2 reporting to them the people's (errant) belief that the time has not come to rebuild the temple, the oracle introduced in v. 3 does not exhort Zerubbabel and Joshua to rouse the people for that task, but addresses the people themselves (vv. 4–11). The next mention of Zerubbabel and Joshua has them obeying the prophet's words, *along with* "the remnant of the people" (v. 12), even as their spirits are stirred *along with* those of "the remnant of the people" (v. 14). Despite vv. 1–2 singling out Zerubbabel and Joshua, the ensuing verses give them no leadership role.

This does not mean that Haggai himself showed no interest in them. There is no reason to doubt that Haggai spoke words to Zerubbabel along the lines portrayed in 2:20–23 (see the text box). Indeed, what is striking about that section is that it is addressed solely to Zerubbabel, the only passage where Joshua is not mentioned, whereas Joshua never appears without Zerubbabel.

Especially noteworthy is 2:2–9, which opens with the LORD commanding the prophet to speak "to Zerubbabel … and to Joshua son of Jehozadak … and to the remnant of the people."[21] The question "who is left among you that saw this house in its former glory" (v. 3) is addressed to everyone, as are the subsequent exhortation to take courage (vv. 4–5) and the allied promise that the new temple will have greater

The Role of Zerubbabel (2:20–23)

Throughout the book, Zerubbabel is called "governor of Judah," a title whose precise meaning in this period is unclear (Redditt, 1995) but likely does not imply that Judah was self-governed (Boda, 2003b). Chapter 2 vv. 20–23 emphasizes that Zerubbabel will be elevated when the LORD overthrows kingdoms and armies. But what does this mean?

The crucial statement is "(I will) make you like a signet ring, for I have chosen you" (v. 23). The closest modern comparison to a signet ring might be the instrument used to affix a seal to a document, representing the authority of the government. A signet ring was inscribed with words (written as a mirror image) that identified whatever bore its impression as authorized by or belonging to the person whose stamp was affixed. The promise to make Zerubbabel "like a signet ring" suggests that he will, in similar fashion, bear the LORD's authority.

Two other passages in the Bible associate an individual with a signet, the most important of which, for this discussion, is Jeremiah 22:24–25,[18] addressed to King Coniah (an abbreviated form of Jehoiachin, the last descendant of David to sit on the throne before Jerusalem's fall): "As I live, says the LORD, even if King Coniah son of Jehoiakim of Judah were the signet ring on my right hand, even from there I would tear you off and give you into the hands of those who seek your life." Jehoiachin is so objectionable that even if he represented divine authority, the LORD would send him into exile. How much more so is the LORD willing to cast him aside, given that he does not.

That Haggai should apply the image of a signet ring to Zerubbabel is hardly coincidental,[19] given that Zerubbabel's descent from Shealtiel placed him within David's line (1 Chr 3:17–19).[20] Although Zerubbabel's role is merely implied (Kessler, 2008) and is set in the unspecified future, the oracle's expectation of the nations' overthrow makes the imagery anticipate an elevation of Zerubbabel's status and, with it, Judah's position.

splendor than the old one (vv. 6–9). The curiosity is the way Joshua is addressed, in contrast to Zerubbabel. Every other place Zerubbabel is mentioned, his name is accompanied by either "son of Shealtiel" (1:12, 2:23) or "governor of Judah" (2:21) or both (1:1, 14; 2:2). Here is he addressed simply as "Zerubbabel." By contrast, Joshua is addressed under his full title, which never varies in the book: "Joshua son of Jehozadak, the high priest" (1:1, 12, 14; 2:2, 4). Accordingly, 2:4's exhortation at an earlier stage was likely directed simply to "Zerubbabel … and all you people of the land" (Tollington, 1993). The consistently lengthy identification of Joshua in the book, over against the various ways of identifying Zerubbabel, suggests that the inclusion of Joshua is attributable to the book's narrator. This interest in pairing Zerubbabel and Joshua as equals is a feature also of Zechariah 1–8, which is one reason why many have suggested that the editor of those chapters was the same one who gave shape to Haggai (Boda, 2003b).

A Dislocated Passage?

Some have detected a flaw in the book's structure. The Lord's initial complaint is that the people are delaying completion of the temple, the consequence of which is a failure of crops (1:5–11). By month's end, the people have resumed work on the temple (1:12–14), in response to which the Lord vows to restore abundance (2:15–19). In the meantime, however, 2:11–14 speaks as though the Lord remains displeased, but about a different issue. The questions posed to the priests about the transfer of ritual impurity from one object to another (2:12–13) serve as the basis for the Lord's declaration that "every work" of "this people" and "this nation" is permeated with impurity (2:14). This abrupt shift has spurred suggestions that these words have become misplaced and belong with the accusations of chapter 1. It is possible, however, to make sense of them in their setting, based on consideration of what constitutes this "uncleanness."

"Uncleanness" is used here as the antonym to "holy," neither of which has moral overtones.[22] The fact that both are defined according to contact between something holy (consecrated meat) or unclean (a person defiled by contact with a corpse) and "bread, or stew, or wine, or oil, or any kind of food" (2:12) assumes that holiness and impurity are contagious. And the fact that Haggai asks priests for their verdict in this matter confirms that this contagion has to do with **cultic** matters. Given that the declaration of holiness or impurity has to do with qualifying or being disqualified to appear at the deity's shrine, the people's "uncleanness" has something to do with the temple precincts.

The prophet's first question concerns whether the named foods can be infected with holiness, to which the priests reply in the negative (2:12). On the other hand, his follow-up question receives the answer that the same foods can be infected with uncleanness (2:13). Some scholars have argued that this addresses the problem of Jews fraternizing with the citizens of Samaria, saying that such contact renders Jews unclean rather than transferring their holiness to the Samaritans (Assis, 2006). However, this requires us to assume social interaction between Jews and Samaritans not mentioned in Haggai.

Just as important are the concluding statements of v. 14: "and so with every work of their hands; and what they offer there is unclean." The Hebrew verb translated "offer" connotes an act of sacrifice, in which light the adverb "there" implies the temple (the focus of vv. 3–9 and 15–19). In this light, "every work of their hands" refers to their actions at the altar (Meyers and Meyers, 1987; Petersen, 1984). The questions about what makes food holy or unholy in vv. 12–13 suggest that the issue is an offering *becoming* unclean through association. And given the context's focus on the temple, it is likely the uncleanness of the altar that contaminates the sacrifices (Petersen, 1984). But why should the altar be unclean and how can it be cleansed? Answering this question requires a closer look at the dates that punctuate the book.

Chapter 1 spans the time from the first day of the sixth month to its twenty-fourth day, when work began on the temple (as underscored in 1:15). Chapter 2 v. 1 introduces a scene around a month later (the twenty-first day of the seventh month) when construction had progressed enough that the people were disappointed at the size and quality of the building (2:3).[23] Chapter 2 v. 10 dates the remainder of the chapter's events to the twenty-fourth day of the ninth month, a date reinforced by "from this day on" in vv. 15 and 18, and specified as the date for v. 20's oracle regarding Zerubbabel.

The key event of the twenty-fourth day of the ninth month that will reverse the people's impoverishment is the placing of "stone upon stone" (2:15) and laying "the foundation of the LORD's temple" (2:18). Research on procedures for rebuilding temples in the **ancient Near East** has clarified these acts as a ceremony in which a stone from the old temple was set in place and prayers of consecration offered (Meyers and Meyers, 1987).[24] Even though it is likely that an altar was already in service at the old temple site, it would have been purified at the celebration of the new temple's foundation (Petersen, 1984), an action the people have recently executed. In fact, already the prophet can call on the people to consider the effects of their actions in dedicating the temple, since there "remains seed in the barn" (as a store of food) and the fig tree, pomegranate, and olive tree once again produce their fruits (v. 19). Given that the harvest recently concluded, an early repayment of the people's undertaking was already evident (Meyers and Meyers, 1987). In concert with this, the uncleanness that had attached to the people's sacrifices (complained about in vv. 11–14) had vanished.

The book presents a sensible series of events, whether or not an eyewitness would have certified its details accurate. It opens with the prophet castigating the people over their delay in rebuilding the temple,[25] on which he blames the current failure of crops and economic hardships (1:2–11). The narrative of 1:12–15 depicts the people's immediate action, highlighting the participation of their governor and high priest. Chapter 2 vv. 1–9 portrays conditions nearly a month later, when the inferior construction of the building (compared to the first temple) had dispirited some, in response to which the prophet announced that this edifice was not the sum total of the project, inasmuch as its full adornment would come with the LORD's diversion to it of the nations' wealth, so that "the latter splendor of this house shall be greater than the former" (v. 9).

The final set of events is set nearly two months later, at the consecration rites for the new temple, at which time the prophet declares an end to the "uncleanness" that has afflicted the people's sacrifices (and, by extension, their standing before the LORD), releasing them from the sufferings of the past, as has become evident from the recent harvest (2:10–19).[26] The final oracle of the book (2:20–23), dated to the same day, projects further into the future an even more striking upheaval that will result in a change of status for Zerubbabel. Thus, the book presents a sensible story line "in which the prophetic revelation of messages from Yahweh constitutes the main narrative action, not a collection of prophetic speeches to which editorial additions have been added" (Floyd, 1995, 479).[27]

Summary

The book of Haggai is neither modern historiography nor a loose collection of oracles. It is an artfully structured set of narratives that place oracles in the context of interactions between the prophet, the people, and their leaders. We can classify it as a "prophetic history" (Floyd, 1995), if we define that as a work concerned with the deliverance of the LORD's word through a prophet, the response of the people to it, and the outcome. Its portrayal of the cooperation of the governor and high priest serves the ideological aim of depicting a prophet as the supreme mediator of divine guidance, including his role in designating the LORD's choice of a new ruler, in this case, Zerubbabel.

Notes

1. The location of Tarshish (1:3) has been long debated, with the most frequently proposed site being in Spain. The phrase "ships of Tarshish" appears in several passages as the epitome of a seagoing vessel (e.g., 1 Kings 10:22; Isa 2:16, 23:1, 60:9; Ezek 27:25). Accordingly, the point of Jonah's flight to Tarshish seems to be an escape to the furthest point away from Judah (and Nineveh) one could find.
2. This is similar to what one might find in a novel about the struggles to fashion a constitution for the United States in the late eighteenth century that describes political intrigues as fights between Republicans and Democrats, even though those parties formed only in the nineteenth century.
3. The NRSV's "*ready to* relent from punishing" injects a notion not in the Hebrew (*weni-cham 'al ra 'ah*), making 4:2 easier to harmonize with 3:10 at the cost of accuracy.
4. The relationship of v. 10 to the Ninevites' repentance mirrors Jeremiah 18:7–8 (which itself has affinities to Exodus 32:14): "[7:] At one moment I may declare concerning a nation or a kingdom, that I will pluck up and break down and destroy it, [8:] but if that nation, concerning which I have spoken, turns from its evil, I will change my mind about the calamity that I purposed to bring on it" (my translation). Nevertheless, Jonah 4:2 shows a stronger resemblance in wording to Exodus 32:14.
5. Compare Jeremias's incredulity that the expansion of Exodus 34:6. around the theme of the LORD changing his mind, would occur for the first time in a book that concerned the nations rather than Israel (Jeremias, 2007).
6. Other arguments that Jonah was dependent upon Joel are less convincing. For instance, Wolff's contention that "Jonah shows a developing reflection about the function of the judgment saying directed against the nations which is still unknown in Joel" (Wolff, 1986, 77) questionably assumes that Joel is primarily interested in the status of the nations rather than the question of divine behavior per se.
7. The NRSV's "be concerned about" is too weak. Better is its translation of the same phrase in Jeremiah 21:7 ("he shall not pity them") and Ezekiel 16:5 ("No eye pitied you").
8. We have seen this sort of decision to relent without preconditions in Hosea 11:8–9. Compare also 2 Kings 14:26–27, where the LORD is said to deliver Israel through the wicked Jeroboam ben Joash simply because he "saw that the distress of Israel was very bitter; there was no one left, bond or free, and no one to help Israel" and because he "had not said that he would blot out the name of Israel from under heaven." In neither case are the people said to have turned from their wickedness; the focus is on the LORD's unconditional compassion, as it is in Jonah 4.
9. Verse 9 carries a significant change from earlier references to "God" in vv. 5 and 8 by using the definite article, providing the nuance, "the *true* God" (Jeremias, 2004).
10. I will leave aside the use of names for God in the prayer of chapter 2, which was likely not written by the author of the narrative.
11. Too wooden are attempts to find order in the use of the divine names by saying that "God" is used when speaking of non-Israelites in relationship to the LORD, unless they have been informed of the divine name (e.g., Goldstein, 2007). Why the *narrator* should have felt constrained by this convention is unclear.

12. Goldstein's argument (2007, 82) that "Elohim emerges to convey the concern God has for the Ninevites" not only sifts the matter too finely, but is undermined when *the* LORD speaks on behalf of the Ninevites again in vv. 10–11.

13. Equally unsatisfactory is Krüger's (1991) isolation of a core narrative that allows him to identify two layers of supplements. While his method allows him to get rid of problems like the juxtaposition of 4:5 and 4:6, it does so by ignoring the ways narratives can include side stories.

14. As Ben Zvi (2009) notes, the book assumes a hierarchy of humans and animals over plants.

15. The phrase "King Darius" shows an acceptance of Persian rule, in contrast to Ezekiel 1:2, which calibrates dates to "the exile of King Jehoiachin," the deposed Davidic king (Tuell, 2000). At the same time, omitting the nationality of the king (against typical practice: "Cyrus, the king of Persia," "Sennacherib, king of Assyria") accords with **superscriptions** to other prophetic books (Kessler, 2008). As Kessler adds, this does not mean that Persian domination was unproblematic for the book of Haggai, as is evident from 2:20–23.

16. The only introductory formula lacking that year marker is 2:20–23, although v. 20 states that "the word of the LORD came *a second time* to Haggai on the twenty-fourth day of the month," a reference back to v. 10's formula, "the twenty-fourth day of the ninth month, in the second year of Darius."

17. I dispute Tollington's (1993) inference that the frequent use of "LORD of hosts" within the oracles (even though it also occurs in the narrative) makes it likely that this usage (otherwise distinctive to Isaiah, Zechariah, and Malachi) goes back to the prophet himself.

18. The other passage is Ezekiel 28:12, which laments the king of Tyre's fall from being "the signet of perfection, full of wisdom and perfect in beauty." Despite its ambiguities, the imagery implies the king's close connection with the divine world (Tollington, 1993).

19. The fact that he qualifies the image by terming him "*like* a signet ring" maintains the distinction between the image and reality implied in "*even if* he *were* the signet ring on my right hand."

20. The problems of this genealogy (making Zerubbabel the son of Pedaiah, son of Shealtiel) have been widely discussed (see Tollington, 1993, 133 n. 4). The problem with taking the genealogy of 1 Chronicles 3 at face value becomes apparent from the fact that v. 16 lists Zedekiah as Jehoiachin's son (compare 2 Chr 36:10), in contrast to the report of 2 Kings 24:17 that "the king of Babylon made Mattaniah, Jehoiachin's uncle, king in his place, and changed his name to Zedekiah."

21. As Japhet (2004) argues, the book of Haggai provides no foundation for the inference, adopted by some (such as Wolff, 1988), that "remnant" refers strictly to those who have returned from exile. Rather, it includes those who remained in the land after the Babylonian assault.

22. This interpretation seems to be assumed by Mason (1982, 144), who speaks of the people as "having no capacity for self-regeneration." It is not the people who are called impure, but "every work of their hands" (v. 14) (Petersen, 1984).

23. This stage could reasonably have been reached in a month, since the burning of the temple by the Babylonians (2 Kings 25:9) would have affected only the timber, not the stonework (Redditt, 1995). And significantly, Haggai 1:8 commands the people to "go to the hills and bring wood and build the house." Given that the first temple was built with wood cut from the famed cedars of Lebanon (1 Kings 5:6), the substitution of wood culled from the surrounding hills would have made a visibly inferior building.

24. The fact that this ceremony is placed after the beginning of construction is not the problem Tollington (1999) suggests, as pointed out by Meyers and Meyers (1987) and Petersen (1984).

25. Their protest "the time has not yet come to rebuild the LORD's house" (v. 2) is less likely an expression of religious scruples than a complaint of inconvenience (Kessler, 2002).
26. Even though the prophet emphasizes what will take place "from this day on" (2:18), his words point to the palpable results of their work to this point (the restoration of crops) alongside promises of benefits yet to come (Meyers and Meyers, 1987).
27. While the dates in Haggai appear comparable to the dates that structure the book of Ezekiel, they are much more integral to the meaning of this book (Tuell, 2000).

9
Zechariah 1–8

In the pages to come …

We have studied books composed of distinguishable units that, nevertheless, shared enough themes and motifs to allow us to view the book as a unity (for example, Amos 1–3, 4–6, 7–9). Zechariah, by contrast, comprises two starkly different sections (chapters 1–8 and 9–14). Because they constitute independent units, we will treat them as separate works.

Chapters 1–8 begin with a narrative in which Zechariah's audience acknowledges their ancestors' failure to listen to their prophets (1:1–6), a theme that will be picked up again in chapters 7–8. In between stand 1:7–6:15, containing visions interspersed with **oracles**. And yet, there are indications that these chapters were fashioned to form a whole.

The profound differences between chapters 1–8 and 9–14 (see the text box below) justify treating them as distinct compositions. Chapters 1–8 have features reminiscent of Haggai. Like Haggai 1:1, Zechariah 1:1 is an **incipit** dating an oracle to the second year of Darius's reign, the same year to which Haggai assigns each of its scenes. Zechariah 1:7 and 7:1 also date materials to the reign of Darius, thereby placing the oracles and visions of Zechariah 1–8 in the same era as Haggai's narratives. Equally similar to Haggai, chapters 1–8 advocate rebuilding the temple (1:16, 4:9, 6:12–15) and pair Zerubbabel (4:6–10) and Joshua (3:1–9) as leaders (6:13). These parallels suggest that Zechariah 1–8 is somehow allied with Haggai. However, differences between Zechariah 1–8 and Haggai are equally evident.

Although the date given in Zechariah 1:1 falls within the range of dates specified in Haggai's incipits, the date in 1:7 is two months after the latest in Haggai, while the date in 7:1 falls two years later. Moreover, the contents of Zechariah 1–8 are not as

Zechariah 1–8 vs. 9–14

The distinctions between Zechariah 1–8 and 9–14 are pronounced. First, while chapters 1–8 specify three dates during the rule of Darius, chapters 9–12 make no mention of Darius or the Persians. Second, chapters 9–14 lack date formulas and are divided into two sections, each headed by the **superscription** "An oracle. The word of the LORD against/concerning" (9:1, 12:1). Third, Zerubbabel and Joshua, who feature prominently in chapters 1–8, vanish in chapters 9–14, along with the name "Zechariah" and the topic of rebuilding the temple. Fourth, gone are the bizarre images in visions interpreted by an angel that were central to chapters 1–8. Such differences support treating these sections as separate literary works.

closely linked to the dates as the narratives of Haggai's are to the dates of its incipits. Whereas Haggai's narratives presuppose the passing of time signaled by the progression of dates in the incipits, the visions and oracles of Zechariah 1–8 do not require passage of time. What is more, the assignment of all the visions and oracles of 1:7–6:15 to a single day is artificial. Consequently, Zechariah's date formulas (1:1, 1:7, and 7:1) serve as little more than formal divisions between literary subunits.

Striking thematic differences also distinguish Zechariah 1–8 from Haggai. First, while Haggai focuses on building the temple, Zechariah's visions and oracles range across many issues related to re-establishing and ordering Jerusalem's society (Petersen, 1984). Second, whereas Haggai highlights the people's present failures, he does not recall the crimes and calamities of Judah before the **exile** the way Zechariah does (1:2–6; 7:7, 11–14; 8:14) (Kessler, 2008). In accord with this, while Haggai emphasizes the people's unified and prompt obedience to the prophet, Zechariah's admonitions (5:2–4, 7:9–10, 8:16–17) anticipate disobedience (Kessler, 2008). Finally, while the book of Haggai is a series of narratives, aside from two retrospects on the ancestors' failures (1:2–4, 7:11–14), Zechariah's only hint of narrative is the report in 1:6: "So they repented and said, 'The LORD of hosts has dealt with us according to our ways and deeds, just as he planned to do.'" Central to Zechariah 1–8 are eight visions, elucidated by oracles and dialogues with an angel who assists Zechariah.

We will explore the composition of Zechariah 1–8 before reconsidering its similarities to the book of Haggai. Its chapters divide into three units, each introduced by a superscription (1:1–6, 1:7–6:15, 7:1–8:23) and being distinct in content: 1:1–6 and 7:1–8:23 bear only oracles, whereas the central unit is a thicket of vision reports and oracles. Given the dominant role of visions in the book, we will begin with them.

1:7–6:15: Visions and Oracles

The Vision Reports

Visions have fallen on hard times in the modern era. It is not just psychoanalytic dream theory that diminished their stature, but rationalism generally.[1] More recently, many neuropsychologists have attributed religious experiences to material processes (for example, Pinker, 2002). Whatever the merits of such hypotheses, the problem for the study of religion is that they do not accord with people's experience of themselves (Merkur, 2005). The social role of parapsychological phenomena, as studied by anthropologists, has affected understandings of prophecy (Wilson, 1980), including vision reports (Niditch, 1986). Because claims to have had visions abound and are given credence in literature from the ancient world (Rowland, Gibbons, and Dobroruka, 2006), their social functions and literary representations must be taken seriously.

Just as written reports of oracles recast what has been spoken, so a report of a vision is not identical with the prophet's experience but mediates it to the reader or hearer (Tuell, 1996). Not only have we no direct access to the visionary's experience (Tiemeyer, 2008), but the report is formatted as written communication, cast in terms the audience can comprehend. These reports, as attempts at communication, are the object of this study.

For instance, the first vision's image of horses forming a patrol, which returns the report "the whole earth remains at peace" (1:9–10), reflects a notion of divine reconnaissance much like that of a ruler who sends out scouts (compare 6:1–8).[2] Despite being set at night in a secluded glen populated by an unspecified number of horses and riders (1:10), the scene is otherwise composed of ordinary features: horses of typical colors, myrtle trees, and horsemen (Petersen, 1984). The prophet's question "What are these, my Lord?" (v. 9) is not about what sorts of being he sees but (judging from the angel's reply) what role they play. Even though this vision turns out to be about members of the divine realm, the scene's features are commonplace.

Likewise, the images of four horns and four blacksmiths (1:18, 20) and of a man with a measuring line (2:1) would have been familiar in the prophet's world. And even when the vision modifies accustomed images in unusual ways – as with the elaborate lampstand of chapter 4 or the flying **scroll** of chapter 5 – there is no need to define the images themselves, even if their functions require explanation (Tollington, 1993).

Thus, the man with the measuring line (2:1–5) is a divinely appointed surveyor whose role is defined by the forecast that "Jerusalem shall be inhabited like villages without walls" (2:4), making his services useless: Jerusalem will be too populated to have fixed boundaries. The appended comment "I will be a wall of fire all around it, says the LORD, and I will be the glory within it" (2:5) likely presumes the audience's knowledge of the unwalled city of the Persian kings, Pasargadae, surrounding which were fire altars representing the presence of the god Ahura Mazda (Petersen, 1984).

Nevertheless, fundamental to Zechariah's visions is an other-worldly scene, in which the prophet becomes a participant. The prophet's reliance on an angel to explain the meaning of his visions (especially in chapter 4) is in striking contrast to other prophets, whose visions either are self-interpreting (as in Am 7:1–6) or are explained by the LORD himself (see, for instance, Am 7:7–8, 8:1–2; Jer 1:11–16). While the prophet asks his angelic guide to explain the horses in the first vision (1:9), it is the man mounted on the red horse who identifies them as the LORD's patrol (1:10). That man (now identified as "the angel of the LORD") receives the patrol's report that the world is at peace (1:11), following which he lodges a complaint with the LORD about a delay in showing mercy to Jerusalem and Judah (1:12). Because the prophet's question to his guiding angel is answered by the rider in the glen, the prophet does not simply view the scene, but participates in it (Tollington, 1993).

The prophet's participation is even more prominent in the third vision, which begins with his report "I looked up and saw a man with a measuring line in his hand" (2:1). This time he addresses the man directly, asking where he is headed, and the man names Jerusalem as his destination (2:2). Only then does "the angel who talked with me" step in, although simply to receive a command from another angel to inform the surveyor that Jerusalem will lack walls.

It is noteworthy, however, that the LORD does not interact with the prophet. While the LORD responds to an angel (1:13) and his name is invoked in rebuffing attacks on Joshua (3:2), he remains aloof (contrast 1 Kings 22:19–22 and Isa 6),[3] likely parallel to the Judeans' dealings with the Persian ruler through bureaucratic channels (Meyers and Meyers, 1987). The prophet is defined by his interactions within these scenes of the **divine council** (see the text box), much as Jeremiah identifies a legitimate prophet as one who has "stood in the council of the LORD, so as to see and hear his word" (Jer 23:18) (Tollington, 1993).

The Divine Council

Throughout the **ancient Near East**, deities are portrayed as forming a council, headed by the chief god. In the Bible, this motif appears in 1 Kings 22:19–22, where the prophet Micaiah reports seeing "the LORD sitting on his throne, with all the host of heaven standing beside him to the right and to the left of him" (v. 19). After asking for a strategy to entice Ahab to enter an ill-fated battle, the LORD fields various suggestions, ultimately approving the plan of a spirit offering to mislead Ahab through his prophets.

The setting of the divine council is presupposed again in Isaiah 6, where the prophet overhears the deliberations in the divine council ("Whom shall I send, and who will go for *us*?" v. 8) and volunteers his services. It is equally the setting assumed in Job 1, where "the heavenly beings" present themselves before the LORD (v. 6).

In Zechariah the setting of the divine council lies behind the initial vision (1:8–13) and the contest with Satan over Joshua (3:1–10).[4]

When the prophet requires an explanation of what he sees, as in chapter 4's vision of the golden lampstand, the angel does not decode every feature in the vision but isolates elements, ascribing to them otherwise imperceptible meanings (Tollington, 1993). For instance, when the prophet inquires about the lampstand ("What are these?" v. 4), the angel spotlights the seven lamps, identifying them as "the eyes of the LORD, which range through the whole earth" (4:10b).[5] The prophet's next question is more specific: "what are these two olive trees on the right and the left of the lampstand?" (v. 11), which the angel eventually identifies as "the two anointed ones who stand by the Lord of the whole earth" (v. 14).[6] In each case a facet of the vision is isolated and its interpretation surpasses what the prophet could have inferred.

At the same time, the prophet's powers of perception vary. While chapter 4 highlights his lack of understanding through the angel's question "Do you not know what these are?" (4:5, 13), elsewhere his perception is keen. In 5:1–2 he not only identifies the flying scroll but also gives its dimensions, following which the angel volunteers its significance, without being asked and without chiding the prophet. Even in the first vision, once the horses are identified as "those whom the LORD has sent to patrol the earth" (1:10), the scene unfolds without the prophet voicing further perplexity.

Evidence we are about to uncover suggests that the oracles interspersed among these visions were supplied only after the vision reports were compiled in the earliest stage of forming 1:7–6:15.

The Interspersed Oracles

Most oracles stand at the end of visions, as in the case of the oracles following the first vision, which detail the "gracious and comforting words" the LORD spoke to Zechariah's angel (v. 13) in response to protests at the LORD's withholding of mercy from Jerusalem and Judah (v. 12). In vv. 14–15 the LORD attests his jealousy for Jerusalem and Zion, coupled with his anger against the nations for intensifying Jerusalem's distress. Surprisingly, however, the consequence of this jealousy and anger is not action against the nations, but a vow to show compassion in the rebuilding of the temple and Jerusalem (v. 16). Verse 17 extends this vow via a second oracle (with its own **messenger formula**), promising prosperity for the cities of Judah, reaffirming comfort for Zion, and pledging the LORD's renewed choice of Jerusalem.

Even if the references to the nations and Jerusalem pick up topics from the vision, this oracle stands as a virtual addendum to it, taking it in unanticipated directions. Chapter 1 v. 15 provides a sinister interpretation of the patrol's enigmatic report that "the whole world remains at peace" (v. 11). Although the verb "remains at peace" is neutral, the verb translated "are at ease" (v. 15) typically bears connotations of "complacency, insolence, and pride" (Wolters, 2008, 142). Thus, while the complaint about the report of the world at peace was that the LORD had withheld mercy during his 70 years of anger with Judah (the period Jeremiah had allotted for Babylon's rule: Jer 25:11–12, 29:10), this oracle places blame for Jerusalem's suffering on the nations in general and characterizes them as self-satisfied. Additionally, the promise that "my house shall be built in it" (v. 16) brings into play a theme that appears again only in describing Zerubbabel (4:9, 6:12–15), while the image of "a line ... stretched out over Jerusalem" anticipates the vision of a man holding a measuring line (2:1), and the vow that the LORD will "again choose Jerusalem" (v. 17) uses a phrase that will recur in 2:12.[7] Most likely, the oracles of vv. 14–17 were fashioned as a commentary on the vision of vv. 8–13, using motifs found elsewhere in the book.

Support for this perception comes from the oracles of 2:6–13, which comment on the three preceding visions (Tollington, 1993).[8] The command to escape from "the land of the north," further defined as "daughter Babylon" (vv. 6–7),[9] likely has in view Darius's campaign to subdue Babylon's revolt against Persia, reprisals described in the first vision as terrifying "the horns that have scattered Judah, Israel, and Jerusalem" (1:19) (Boda, 2005). Chapter 2 v. 9 suggests that this was uttered before the assault on Babylon and as an assurance that it would happen (Tollington, 1993). What is more, key phrases in vv. 6–7 show close ties to Isaiah and Jeremiah

(Boda, 2008). The title "daughter Babylon" (2:7), found only here in Zechariah, appears elsewhere in the prophets only in Isaiah 47:1 and Jeremiah 50:42 and 51:33, while "the land from the north" (2:6) recurs in Zechariah's second vision of horses sent out on patrol in 6:6, 8, but elsewhere only in Jeremiah 3:18, 6:22, 10:22, 16:15, 23:8, 31:8, 46:10, and 50:9.

The oracles of 2:10–12 shift the focus from Babylon to Zion, who is told to rejoice because of the LORD's plan to inhabit her. Whereas the oracles attached to the first vision interpreted the report of a peaceful world in terms of "nations that are at ease" that aggravated Israel's suffering (1:15), and the second vision pictures a plurality of nations to be punished for raising "their horns against the land of Judah to scatter its people" (1:21), 2:11 promises that "many nations shall join themselves to the LORD on that day, and shall be my people." The LORD's vengeance on the nations who afflicted Judah (2:6–9) abruptly and inexplicably gives way to many nations allying themselves with the LORD, using language found in Isaiah 14:1 and 56:3, 6, and Jeremiah 50:5.

Most striking in this series is 2:13: "Be silent, all people, before the LORD; for he has roused himself from his holy dwelling." While this resonates with the promise that the LORD will dwell in Zion's midst and with the anticipation that nations will attach themselves to him, it takes up the **liturgical** call we noted in Zephaniah 1:7 and (especially) Habakkuk 2:20. And as in the latter passage, this verse caps a series of oracles.

The accumulation of phrases drawn from other prophetic books makes it reasonable to conclude that vv. 6–12 are oracles appended in response to the visions, with v. 13 serving as its capstone (Tollington, 1993). While the oracles, together with the visions, are the fundamental building blocks of chapters 1–7, passages about Zerubbabel rebuilding the temple are also included as another distinguishable set of materials.

Joshua and Zerubbabel

Three visions ascribe to Joshua and Zerubbabel a shared leadership role, much as in the book of Haggai. Chapter 3 offers a scene of the divine council at which the high priest Joshua is defended by the angel of the LORD and cleansed of defilement. At the close stands an oracle (vv. 6–10) admonishing Joshua that,[10] if he maintains appropriate oversight of the temple, he will enjoy secure prerogatives as high priest.[11] Markedly distinct within this is v. 8, which shifts the focus from Joshua to "you and your colleagues who sit before you," described as "an omen of things to come."[12] Referring to men sitting "before you" shifts the scene from the divine council to an earthly setting (Tollington, 1993).[13] Moreover, once the verse identifies the omen as "my servant, the Branch," it leaves behind the consecration of Joshua to promise a figure whose role is intelligible only in the light 6:12–13, which are also addressed to Joshua:

> Thus says the LORD of hosts: Here is a man whose name is Branch: for he shall branch out in his place, and he shall build the temple of the LORD. It is he that shall build the temple of the LORD; he shall bear royal honor, and shall sit and rule on his throne. There shall be a priest by his throne, with peaceful understanding between the two of them.

Given the distinction between this "Branch" occupying his throne and the priest who stands beside him, and given that 4:9 asserts that Zerubbabel laid the temple's foundation and oversees its construction, the "Branch" in both 6:12–13 and 3:8 is clearly Zerubbabel.[14] But this renders peculiar the inclusion of him in chapter 3's vision, where it effectively undercuts the focus on Joshua's authority.

A similar diversion from Joshua to Zerubbabel appears in two other visions. Following the prophet's request for an explanation of the lampstand in 4:5 and the introduction of the angel's answer in v. 6a ("He said to me") stand two oracles. The first emphasizes the LORD's spirit as the effective power behind Zerubbabel, who is said to conquer a mountain, most likely an allusion to building the temple atop Mount Zion (vv. 6b–7). The second oracle speaks more explicitly of Zerubbabel's role in that task (vv. 8–10a). Then abruptly, in v. 10b, we find the body of the angel's answer that was introduced in v. 6a: 10b: "These seven are the eyes of the LORD, which range through the whole earth." Afterwards, the prophet asks about the identity of the two olive trees. In view of the lack of connection between vv. 6b–10a and the surrounding scene, while v. 10 provides the answer to the question raised in v. 6a, vv. 6b–10a must be reckoned a later insertion into the vision (Wöhrle, 2006a).

The other set of oracles concerning Zerubbabel that interrupts a passage about Joshua appears in a scene of Joshua being given a crown (6:9–11, 14). That scene is interrupted by an address to Joshua about the "Branch" (6:12–13). For a third time an editor injects into a vision about the elevation of Joshua a role for Zerubbabel, perhaps to countervail a notion of leadership in the temple focused on the high priest (Petersen, 1984; Tollington, 1993). These adjustments are at the expense of Joshua, who otherwise receives top billing.

1:7–6:15   in Review

In the end, the series of vision reports and oracles in Zechariah 1:7–6:15 has been created by intertwining oracles with the vision reports. While some oracles are integral to the visions, more often they seem to have been added secondarily, with the role of Zerubbabel as Joshua's equal being a special instance of such expansions.

Zechariah 7–8

Two features distinguish these chapters from 1:7–6:15. Most prominently, they contain only oracles. Moreover, while these chapters open with a date formula and a declaration that "the word of the LORD came to Zechariah" like 1:1 and 1:7, 7:1 is a superscription, not an incipit. It is followed by a report of representatives from Bethel arriving to ask the priests and prophets about whether to continue observing a fast in the fifth month, most likely in commemoration of the destruction of the temple (Petersen, 1984). Curiously, this question is not addressed until 8:18–19, which talk of converting fasts into "seasons of joy and gladness." But whereas 8:19 speaks of "fasts" in the fourth, fifth, seventh, and tenth months, the elders' question had to do with "mourning" and "practicing abstinence" in the fifth month. Thus, while 8:18–19 come closest to addressing the question of 7:2–3, they are not a precise match.

Nevertheless, the oracles intervening between 7:2–3 and 8:18–19 give an even less apt response.[15] Although the first oracle (vv. 4–7) addresses the theme of self-deprivation and lamenting about which Bethlehem's emissaries inquired, it questions whether the people's fasts have been truly devoted to the LORD (7:5), asking whether their "eating and drinking" were not self-interested actions (7:6). Rather than expressly apply these critiques to the activities mentioned by the emissaries, however, v. 7 cites such questions as characteristic of the prophets active "when Jerusalem was inhabited and in prosperity." The oracle of vv. 9–10 summarizes the sorts of ethical admonitions spoken by those prophets and then vv. 11–14 recall the people's failure to listen and the resultant judgment that befell them.

Perplexingly, 8:1 introduces a series of oracles that speak as though warnings against repeating the ancestors' errors have been rendered unnecessary by the LORD's determination to deliver Jerusalem. Using language found in 1:14, the LORD professes his jealousy for Jerusalem, which will be shown in his renewed habitation of Jerusalem (as in 1:16, 2:11), which will be restored to its status as the "faithful city" and again be filled with young and old (8:2–5). He buttresses this promise with a vow that, however impossible this seems to humans, he can accomplish what he sets out to do, restoring his scattered people and renewing his relationship with them (8:6–8).

Verse 9 launches a divine exhortation of those who recently heard "these words from the mouths of the prophets who were present when the foundation was laid for the rebuilding of the temple." The words are consonant with what we found in Haggai (1:7–11, 2:15–19): before the foundation was laid, provisions for humans and animals were meager, and security was lacking; but now there will be "a sowing of peace; the vine shall yield its fruit, the ground shall give its produce, and the skies shall give their dew; and I will cause the remnant of this people to possess all these things" (8:12).

The oracle that follows again looks to the past, but solely as a foil for the LORD's new acts: "Just as I purposed to bring disaster upon you, when your ancestors provoked me to wrath, and I did not relent, says the LORD of hosts, so again I have purposed in these days to do good to Jerusalem and to the house of Judah; do not be afraid" (vv. 14–15). Coupled with this is an admonition to speak truth, render justice, refrain from plotting evil, and refuse to swear false oaths, "for all these are things that I hate, says the LORD" (vv. 16–17). Nevertheless, this admonition is not a matter of stipulating preconditions for the LORD to act.

It is only at this point that we find a response to the emissaries' question about the mourning of the fifth month, and it follows suit with what has been promised (vv. 18–19). If these verses address the original question of 7:3, they expand its scope and subvert its thrust by transforming all fasts into feasts (Boda, 2003a). Moreover, while the brunt of vv. 18–19 is this promise of celebration, it concludes with the command to "love truth and peace," echoing v. 16's insistence on "speaking *truth* to one another" and rendering judgments that "make room for *peace*." Whoever postponed the answer to the question of 7:3 recalibrated it for its new context.[16] It certainly reinforces the perception that the challenge to the sincerity of the people's fasts in 7:5 was not originally linked to the question of 7:3. The order to transmute fasting into celebration hardly seems an apt follow-up to questions about whether the motives behind fasting have been sincere. And of course, v. 7's reminder that this question of sincerity was the sort of charge earlier prophets lodged raises an issue that sidetracks from the pressing question of Bethlehem's emissaries.

Verses 8–14 also look back on the prophets of old and the people's failure to heed them. Not only does their summary of themes common to earlier prophets leave behind the topic of fasting, but it introduces its words in the third person: "The word of the LORD came *to Zechariah*" (7:8). While this matches the pattern of the third-person style of the date formula in 7:1, other nearby formulas use the first person, "the word of the LORD came *to me*" (7:4; 8:1, 18). Moreover, each of those uses the title "LORD of Hosts" rather than simply "LORD." These two differences likely mark 7:8–14 as originally independent of 7:4–7, in the same way that 7:4–7 are not the original response to the men from Bethel.

In order to address fully the role of chapters 7–8, we need to explore 1:1–6.

Zechariah 1:1–6

After 1:1 reports the word of the LORD coming to Zechariah, v. 2 addresses a group: "The LORD was very angry with your [group's] ancestors." After v. 3 abruptly commands an individual to speak to this group ("And you [sir] shall say to *them*"; my translation[17]), v. 3b resumes addressing the group with a call to repent, reinforced by v. 4's notice that the ancestors refused to heed their prophets' calls to repent. Verse 5 poses rhetorical questions stressing that the ancestors and their prophets have been long gone, while v. 6a asserts that the LORD's "words and statutes" overtook them, implying that the same "words and statutes" could also overtake the addressees, in accord with which v. 6b reports that they repented (see the text box).

The report that the addressees repented, positioned at the outset of the book, paves the way for the LORD's vow to return to his people in compassion (1:16), avenge his wrath on the nations who have harmed them (1:15, 21), re-establish the temple (1:16) and its high priest (3:2–5), and remove their iniquity (5:5–11). Accordingly, the LORD contrasts his new purpose to "do good to Jerusalem" with his imposition of disaster "when your ancestors provoked me to wrath" (8:14).

Who Repented?

Verse 6 presents a conundrum. Even though its report "And [NRSV: So] they repented and said, 'The LORD of hosts has dealt with us according to our ways and deeds, just as he planned to do'" seems to presume "your ancestors" as the subject, this creates a conflict with v. 4's report that the ancestors did not turn from their evil ways and deeds. Accordingly, we should probably understand this as a report that the prophet's contemporaries heeded his call not to behave as their ancestors had done (Meyers and Meyers, 1987). Their return amounted to admitting that the calamitous events of the past were justified acts of divine wrath.

Chapter 1 vv. 1–6 provide several hints about their origins. While the "words and statutes" that were "commanded" and "overtook" the ancestors (v. 6) is a peculiar way of referring to the prophets' appeals to repent, it is strikingly similar to Deuteronomy 28:15, 45, which warn of curses "overtaking" the people if they refuse to follow all the "commands and decrees" that the LORD had "commanded" them

(Tollington, 1993). Equally striking is the reference to "my servants the prophets" (v. 6), a phrase we have noted previously is most at home in 2 Kings and Jeremiah (see above, p. 48). These features suggest that 1:1–6 were fashioned as an introduction to the book by someone familiar with the theme of the failure of the ancestors in chapters 7–8 and phrases from elsewhere in Israel's literature.

The Composition of Zechariah 1–8

Despite themes that run throughout these chapters, it is not possible to conclude that these three collections come from a single hand. First, we have seen that oracles accompanying the visions sometimes reinterpret the images against their grain, suggesting that 1:7–6:15 contains various reflections on the meaning(s) of the visions.

Second, we have seen that 1:1–6 is an amalgam of materials, the pinnacle of which is its report that the people responded as their ancestors should have, thereby averting divine wrath and positioning themselves for the benefits to be announced in the visions and the oracles. The report of v. 6 is the only narrative (outside a vision report) in chapters 1–8 and, to that degree, makes it akin to the narrative reports in Haggai.

Third, the correlation between the retrospective view on the ancestors and the "former prophets" in the narrative of 1:1–6 and in the oracles of the final two chapters (7:7, 11–14; 8:14) – in contrast with the absence of that theme in 1:7–6:15 – argues that the first and third units are a matched set forming a frame around the visions. What is more, even as chapters 7–8 reprise themes enunciated in 1:7–6:15, they show ties to the book of Haggai. Most prominently, the way 8:10–12 contrasts the paltry conditions the people endured before laying the temple's foundation with the abundance following that event echoes Haggai 1:6–11 and 2:18–19. Moreover, only in 7:3 and 8:9 within the book is the temple referred to as "the house of the LORD," a phrase found in Haggai 1:2, 14. Equally significant is the phrase "the remnant of this people," which appears only in 8:6, 11, 12, bearing the same sense as in Haggai 1:12, 14, and 2:2, where it designates the community as a whole, whether they remained in the land or were sent into exile (Japhet, 2004).

Other links to Haggai appear in the larger structure of Zechariah 1–8. The initial narrative, the vision reports, and chapters 7–8 are introduced by date formulas similar to those in Haggai. Especially striking is that 1:7–6:13 is headed by a single date formula, as if the prophet received these visions in one day.[18] More likely, however, the date formula of 1:7 (in the third person, in contrast to the first-person report that follows) was prefixed to the vision reports at the same time that 1:1–6 and chapters 7–8 were placed around it.

The implication of these observations is that the book as we have it is shaped to link it with Haggai. That hypothesis gains support from the observation that Joshua appears in Haggai only in the company of Zerubbabel, who is addressed individually only in Haggai 2:20–23. In Zechariah 1–8, by contrast, the figure of central importance is Joshua, and Zerubbabel has been penciled in. The reciprocal touching up of the books to deal with both men suggests, if not a common **scribe**, at least imitation of Haggai by the scribe who shaped Zechariah 1–8.

The conundrum is identifying the purpose of this link between the two works. Despite suggestions that this dovetailing meant to support the new temple (Meyers and

Meyers, 1987), the topic of rebuilding the temple is a minor motif in Zechariah (Boda, 2003c). Whereas Haggai demands repentance for the delay in building the temple, in Zechariah 1:1–6 the confession required of the people is that the LORD's wrath was justified by their ancestors' misdeeds. While Zechariah 1:16 promises the temple's rebuilding, the only other appearances of that theme are in the materials inserted about Zerubbabel (4:9–10, 6:12–13). And even when Zechariah 8:9 addresses those who had been present when the foundation of the new temple was laid, that event is not the focus it is in Haggai (contrast the general "before *those days*" in 8:10 with the precise "from *this day* on" in Haggai 2:15, 18; my italics). As Wöhrle (2006b) notes, in Zechariah "the rebuilding of the temple has no value for its own sake."

However, given Zechariah 8's adoption of Haggai's division between conditions before the start of temple reconstruction and conditions afterwards, it is likely that the editor who fitted 1:1–6 and chapters 7–8 around the visions and supplied the date formulas sought to correlate his book with the book of Haggai, even if his date formulas frustrate ascribing the editing of both books to the same person (see text box). In fact, the dates suggest that the scribal editor of Zechariah 1–8 intended it to be a *supplement* to Haggai.

The Date Formulas in Haggai and Zechariah 1–8

The similar date formulas in the two books also carry important differences. Only in Haggai are the key date formulas accompanied by a specification of those to whom the oracle is addressed (1:1–2, 2:1–2). Second, Zechariah's dates uniquely utilize the Babylonian names for the months (1:7, 7:1) (Wöhrle, 2006b). Third, the formulas in Haggai describe the word of the LORD coming "*by* [the hand of]" the prophet (1:1, 2:1; compare 1:3), while those in Zechariah report the word coming "*to*" him (1:1, 7; 7:1).[19] These differences make it unlikely that the same editor supplied the date formulas in both books.

While all the dates in Haggai and Zechariah are set within the reign of Darius, only two of them overlap: the initial date of Zechariah (the eighth month, in the second year of Darius) falls after the dates of Haggai 1:1, 15, and 2:1 (the sixth and seventh months) but before the crucial twenty-fourth day of the ninth month, when the temple was consecrated (Haggai 2:10, 18, 20). This provides a subtle corrective to the sequence of events in Haggai, inasmuch as it makes the people's contrition over the sins of the past precede the consecration of the temple (Wöhrle, 2006b). In keeping with this, the lessons taught by the ancestors' failure to heed the prophets (7:4–14) make clear the behaviors the people must adopt to avoid the same fate as their ancestors (8:14–17).

Summary

Zechariah 1–8 was formed by the expansion of a set of visions with oracles that interpret them, the whole of which was placed within a frame that set the visions and their oracles within a broader range of concerns, especially the need for the people to shun the errors of their ancestors, whose disobedience to the prophets led them to perdition. The scribe who gave these materials their overall structure linked them closely with the book of Haggai.

Notes

1. Even William James argued for the value of mystical experiences on utilitarian grounds: "The supernaturalism and optimism to which they may persuade us may, interpreted in one way or another, be after all the truest insights into the meaning of this life" (James, 1958, 328).

2. The Persians used horses as "the normal means of transport and therefore Zechariah may have become used to seeing messengers or officials on horseback" (Tollington, 1993, 103).

3. A seeming exception to this is 1:20–21, where the prophet speaks of the Lord showing him four blacksmiths and answering his question about what the blacksmiths will do. Nevertheless, following on vv. 19, where the heavenly guide answers the prophet's question, v. 21 likely has in view the angel providing the answer.

4. As Tollington (1993) points out, the Satan of this scene is not equivalent to the figure of a proponent of evil, but comes closer to the Satan of Job 1–2, who serves as a type of prosecuting attorney within the divine council.

5. This likely plays off the ancient Near Eastern idiom of "the eye(s) of the king" to denote the king's spies, even though the same phrase is used in 2 Chr 16:9 with the positive connotation of the Lord benevolently watching over his people (Petersen, 1984).

6. The next time the prophet raises the question, he is more specific: "what are these two olive trees on the right and the left of the lampstand?" (v. 11), which the angel subsequently identifies as "the two anointed ones who stand by the Lord of the whole earth" (v. 14). Curiously, before the angel can give his answer, the prophet poses the question again, adding details not part of the original vision: "What are these two *branches* of the olive trees, which *pour out the oil through the two golden pipes*?" (v. 12). Not only is this question launched before the first is answered (v. 14), but it never receives a response. There is good reason, then, to conclude that it was inserted by a scribe, even if its motivation is unclear (Petersen, 1984).

7. Admittedly, in this case it is also possible that 2:12 has taken over the phrase from 1:17.

8. For example, even though vv. 6–9 have thematic links to the *second* vision (1:18–21), they are appended to the *third* vision.

9. Verse 7's call to escape "to Zion" could also be translated "Escape, Zion, you who live with daughter Babylon" (Petersen, 1984; Redditt, 1995). However, given that Zion designates a city and its inhabitants in 1:14, 17; 2:10; 8:2, 3, the first translation is preferable.

10. This oracle appears integral to the vision, inasmuch as it is introduced by "he admonished" (NRSV's "assured" misrepresents the semantics), whereas later expansions settle for a more banal verb like "he said."

11. Chapter 3 v. 9 speaks of an engraved stone "with seven facets" entrusted to him, in connection with which the Lord "will remove the guilt of this land in a single day." This stone likely designates the engraved plate that Exodus 28:36–38 specifies as part of the high priest's headdress (Petersen, 1984; but compare Meyers and Meyers, 1987). Because v. 9 does not directly address Joshua, questions have arisen about whether it is an original component of this scene (Wöhrle, 2006a).

12. The NRSV's "they are an omen of things to come" suggests a string of events, whereas only one is specified: the Branch.

13. Boda's contention that this is technical terminology for those under another's authority is unconvincing (Boda, 2001 n. 28). The passages he cites concern people living communally under a prophet (2 Kings 4:38, 6:1) or assembling before a prophet (Ezek 33:31).

14. Wöhrle's contention that the "Branch" of 3:8 assumes a priestly figure conflicts with his admission that the "Branch" of 6:12–13 denotes Zerubbabel (Wöhrle, 2006a, 336, 344). Isaiah 11:1 and Jeremiah 23:5 refer to a new Davidic ruler as "branch."

15. These oracles are demarcated by the clauses "Then the word of the LORD of hosts came to me" (7:4); "The word of the LORD came to Zechariah, saying" (7:8); "The word of the LORD of hosts came to me, saying" (8:1). The last heading actually introduces a series of oracles, each introduced by "Thus says the LORD (of hosts)" (8:2, 3, 4, 6, 7, 9, 14).

16. The final unit of these chapters, 8:20–23, expands the vision of a new, ideal era for Jerusalem, forecasting a conversion of the nations to entreat the LORD in Jerusalem, reprising a theme introduced in 2:11.

17. The NRSV's "*Therefore*, say to them" glosses over the problem for the English reader, who might easily assume that "your fathers" is addressed to the prophet.

18. This impression has spurred scholarly debate about whether such a scenario is plausible (Petersen, 1984, 111–112).

19. Admittedly, Haggai 2:20 reports that the word of the LORD came "*to* Haggai," and Zechariah 7:7, 12 assert that the LORD communicated "by [the hand of] the former prophets." Nevertheless, the formulas designating a *new* date of divine communication follow the patterns noted.

10

Zechariah 9–14, the Book of Malachi, and the Twelve

Zechariah 9–14

In the pages to come ...

Chapters 9–14 are so different in content and topic from chapters 1–8 as to constitute a virtual appendix, or really two appendices: 9–11 and 12–14, each having its own **superscription** composed of "An **oracle**. The word of the LORD against/concerning ...." Despite this common feature, chapters 12–14 are distinguished from 9–11 in their pervasive use of "on that day," a phrase that occurs 17 times in chapters 12–14 (12:3, 4, 6, 8 (twice), 9, 11; 13:1, 2, 4; 14:4, 6, 8, 9, 13, 20, 21), but just three times in chapters 1–8 (2:11, 3:10, 6:10) and twice in chapters 9–11 (9:16, 11:11). The referents in both 9–11 and 12–14 are frustratingly difficult to pin down, since their metaphors, such as "the cornerstone" and "the tent peg" (10:4), which designate figures evidently obvious to the author and his audience, defy decoding. Such problems thwart inferring the origins or settings of these chapters.

While chapters 9–14 contain no reference to earlier prophets of the sort that appears in 1:4–6 and 7:7, 12, their language and images often echo other prophetic books. For instance, 9:1–4 pronounce judgment on Damascus, then Hamath to its north and west, and finally Tyre and Sidon, on the Mediterranean coast. The final verdict on Tyre is:

> But now, the LORD will strip it of its possessions
> and hurl its wealth into the sea,
> and it shall be devoured by fire.

(v. 4)

Prophetic Literature: From Oracles to Books, First Edition. Ronald L. Troxel.
© 2012 Ronald L. Troxel. Published 2012 by Blackwell Publishing Ltd.

The ensuing verses describe the effects on the Philistine cities, including Gaza and Ekron:

> The king shall perish from Gaza;
> Ashkelon shall be uninhabited;
> a mongrel people shall settle in Ashdod,
> and I will make an end of the pride of Philistia.
>
> (vv. 5–6)

The similarity of these verses to Amos's oracles against the nations is striking. Amos 1 begins with words against Damascus (vv. 3–5), the Philistine cities (vv. 6–8), and Tyre (vv. 9–10). More significantly, Zechariah 9:4's pronouncement regarding Tyre, "and it shall be devoured by fire," echoes Amos's verdict, "So I will send a fire on the wall of Tyre, fire that shall devour its strongholds" (Am 1:10). Since the idiom "eaten by fire" is frequent in the Bible, this, by itself, is not evidence of a link. However, the subsequent pronouncements, "the king shall perish from Gaza" and "Ashkelon shall be uninhabited," recall Amos 1:8: "I will cut off the inhabitants from Ashdod, and the one who holds the scepter from Ashkelon." Following a pattern common in the reuse of passages (see above, p. 53 n. 13), Zechariah 9:4 reverses the order of Amos 1:8, applying depopulation to Ashkelon and the loss of a king to Ashdod (Mason, 1973).

A striking resemblance to Ezekiel is apparent in statements about Tyre in 9:2–4:

> [1: The word of the Lord is against …]
> 2: Tyre and Sidon, though they are very wise.
> 3: Tyre has built itself a rampart,
>   and heaped up silver like dust,
>   and gold like the dirt of the streets.
> 4: But now, the Lord will strip it of its possessions
>   and hurl its wealth into the sea,
>   and it shall be devoured by fire.

Similarities are apparent in the address of the king of Tyre in Ezekiel 28:3–5:

> 3: You are indeed *wiser* than Daniel;
>   no secret is hidden from you;
> 4: by your *wisdom* and your understanding
>   *you have amassed wealth* for yourself,
>   and *have gathered gold and silver*
>   into your treasuries.
> 5: By your great *wisdom* in trade
>   you have *increased your wealth*,
>   and your heart has become proud in your wealth.

The themes of Tyre's great wisdom in securing wealth and yet finding itself and its wealth vulnerable are key points of resemblance, encouraging the perception that the first verses of Zechariah 9 are formulated with language borrowed from both Amos and Ezekiel, even though it does not quote them precisely (Mason, 1973).

Such perceptions, however, prompt the question whether these similarities were intended by the author or are merely associations we draw. The cumulative and persistent pattern of resemblances in chapters 9–14 has persuaded many that Zechariah 9–14 drew directly upon other prophetic books (Meyers and Meyers, 1993).[1] It is important to note, however, that the reuse of material does not require (or even anticipate) that the audience will recognize it. Such reuse may, in fact, constitute a sort of "loaded vocabulary" that other **scribes** might recognize, without the broader audience doing so (Floyd, 2003b).

Even if we conclude that such reuse is a prominent factor in how these chapters were composed, other issues are more resistant to resolution, such as the obscurity of the figures referred to. Although language in the book of Joel often seems detached from concrete events (recall the ominous anonymous enemy of chapter 2 or the "Valley of Jehoshaphat" in 3:2, 12), its images are familiar enough that we can make sense of most scenes. In Zechariah 9–14, by contrast, images that seem to have been clear to the author are enigmatic for us. For example, while "shepherds" are used as a metaphor for rulers in 10:3, 11:3–17, and 13:7 (an image likely drawn from Jeremiah 23 and Ezekiel 34), identifying which specific social roles these "shepherds" filled (prophets, priests, governors?) is difficult,[2] and it is not clear that the image consistently represents the same type of leader (Petersen, 1995).

Equally remarkable are differences in how the same topic is treated in these chapters. For instance, 9:13 and 10:6 anticipate that the south (Judah) and the north (Ephraim/Joseph) will be a united body, while in 11:14 the prophet executes a **sign act** effecting their dissolution. Similarly, according to 9:7 the Philistines will become "like a clan in Judah," and in 9:10 the anticipated ruler will "command peace to the nations," but in 9:13 the LORD says he will wield Judah and Ephraim "like a warrior's sword" against Greece, while in 11:10 the prophet enacts the annulment of "the covenant that I had made with all the peoples." Correlatively, whereas in 9:10 the ideal king is to demilitarize Judah and Ephraim, in 9:15 the same groups will devour their foes and "drink their blood like wine." And while sometimes the only problem the people are said to have is that they suffer under the rule of unjust shepherds who will be removed and their place taken by new leaders (10:3–7), elsewhere the "shepherd" is to be struck so that the sheep scatter, with two-thirds of them perishing and the other third being refined through "the fire" (13:7–9). Such a varied treatment of themes suggests that materials in these chapters come from diverse sources.

The Composition of Chapters 9–14

Consistent with this evidence of diversity, well-defined boundaries are apparent between units in chapters 9–11. For example, 9:9 breaks with the previous eight verses by addressing Zion directly (v. 8 referred to Judah indirectly with "them"). Then, after 9:9–17 address Zion under the figure of an individual woman, 10:1–2 address a group.[3] And while 10:2 concludes with a lament that "the people wander like sheep, they suffer for lack of a shepherd," in v. 3 that simile gives way to an expression of anger against "the shepherds," owing to the LORD's care for "his flock, the house of Judah." Accordingly, the unit that begins with v. 3 is associated with the sheep/shepherd simile of v. 2 on the **catchword** principle. When that unit concludes in v. 12, 11:1–3 summons Lebanon and Bashan to yield to destruction with lamentation. The remainder of the chapter contains a sign act, with the prophet assuming the role of "the shepherd of the flock doomed to slaughter" (11:7), annulling "the covenant … with all the peoples" (11:10) and dissolving the bond between Judah and Israel. Despite the frequent appearance of the shepherd metaphor in chapters 9–11, its use spans obviously disconnected oracles.

Boundaries between components of chapters 12–14 are harder to detect, given the use of "on that day" as a transition from one statement to the next. More precisely, following a hymn that extols the LORD as creator (12:1), the LORD declares that Jerusalem will be "a cup of reeling for all the surrounding peoples."[4] Verse 3 then introduces a series of statements (through 13:1) about what will happen "on that day," the effect of which is to characterize "that day" through a string of simultaneous events (Petersen, 1995).

Some statements introduced with "on that day" are likely later additions, such as 12:6–7, which grant the clans of Judah equal standing with Jerusalem in a passage that otherwise mentions Judah only in relation to Jerusalem (vv. 2b, 4b) (Redditt, 1995). Likewise, 13:1's assertion that a fountain will open in Jerusalem to cleanse its inhabitants (and "the house of David") of sin appears out of the blue, inasmuch as there has been no mention of Jerusalem's guilt.

The statements castigating prophets in 13:2–6, which have been judged by many scholars as announcing the end of prophecy, are introduced with "says the LORD of hosts," which means that they are themselves prophetic speech.[5] The description of such prophets speaking "lies in the name of the LORD" (v. 3) and associated with idolatry (v. 2) suggests that these verses have in view prophets considered illicit, much like Micah 3:5–7 condemns prophets as a group for shameless profiteering, even though the speaker regards himself as speaking on the LORD's behalf (Mic 3:8). The anticipation that these prophets will be ashamed of their profession is more radical than Micah's forecast that they will fail to receive oracles,[6] but the description of them putting on "the hairy mantle *in order to deceive*" (Zech 13:4) is little different than Micah's characterization of *all* prophets as shams, despite claiming that he spoke the LORD's word.

Although 13:7–9 have frequently been characterized as the misplaced sequel to 11:4–17, these verses are not a sign act like 11:4–17, and thus are distinct, despite also utilizing the theme of the wayward shepherd. Most likely, they form a transition to chapter 14 that utilizes the image of the wicked shepherd as a link back to chapters 9–11 (Nogalski, 2003). Its fractions of two-thirds of the population perishing and one-third surviving are likely indebted to Ezekiel's sign act of a threefold fate for Jerusalem's citizens (Ezek 5:1–4) (Mason, 1973), here pressed into service to foreshadow the decimation of Jerusalem's population in 14:2.

Even if the images of 13:9–11 are difficult to pin down, their foes are specific: Aram, Tyre and Sidon, Philistia, and certain wicked "shepherds." These foes' comeuppance is near: Judah and Israel are the LORD's weapons poised to strike the "sons of Greece" (9:13); the LORD's anger burns against "shepherds" who mistreat his people (10:3); destruction lies at the doorsteps of Lebanon and Bashan (11:1–3). In chapters 12–14, by contrast, the foes are the nations in general (12:2–3), whom the

LORD himself will attack (14:3–4) in an era when there will be neither cold nor frost, and daylight will be constant (14:6–7), with prodigious streams flowing from Jerusalem to water the surrounding territories (14:8). The "this-worldly" scene in chapters 9–11 is replaced by a fantastical new era forecast for "that day" (Petersen, 1995).

As the last three examples in the preceding paragraph hint, chapter 14 describes conditions that outstrip even chapters 12–13. The first verse announces the coming of "a day for the LORD," as a prelude to which v. 2 graphically describes Jerusalem's defeat. In contrast to chapter 12, where the LORD fortifies Jerusalem to repel attacks, here he spurs the attack by mustering the nations. Verses 3–5 envision the LORD's arrival, accompanied by his "holy ones," to do battle with Jerusalem's enemies under ideal conditions (vv. 6–8). His victory will establish his dominion over the earth (v. 9) and secure Jerusalem's exaltation (vv. 10–11). The LORD will impose plagues on Jerusalem's foes (vv. 12–15), and the nations will worship him owing to that threat (vv. 16–19). Jerusalem will be so holy that even its everyday cooking pots can be used for sacrifice (vv. 20–21). In short, chapter 14 focuses on Jerusalem, for whose sake the world will be refashioned to render the city impervious to attack or corruption (De Vries, 1995).

Here again the use of "on that day" links components, which (however) have a different relationship to each other than those in chapters 12–13. First, whereas chapters 12–13 occasionally strayed from central themes to elaborate (say) the relationship of "the clans of Judah" to Jerusalem or to posit the purging of illicit practices "from the land" (13:2–6), all the components of chapter 14 highlight features of "a day for the LORD" related to the status of Jerusalem. The chapter is tightly focused.

Second, whereas the montage of chapters 12–13 is formed of components that modify each other, the components of chapter 14 are connected like building blocks. Thus, vv. 4–5 leave behind the reference to the LORD's campaign against the nations (v. 3) to depict a **theophany** whose effects include people fleeing "as you fled from the earthquake in the days of King Uzziah of Judah," rather than turning the effects of the theophany on the nations of v. 3. Correlatively, vv. 6–7 underscore the unique features of "that day" already broached in vv. 4–5 with an unusual climatic report (no cold, accompanied by continuous daylight), while v. 8 embellishes the image of a stream flowing out from Jerusalem (compare Joel 3:18; Ezek 47:1–12), and v. 9 taps into images of the LORD's enthronement as ruler of the world (compare Psalm 97). Thus, whereas in chapters 12–13 the phrase "on that day" blends conflicting images together, in chapter 14 it links a series of images in a chain (Petersen, 1995).

Summary

The important observations of this survey are, first, that chapters 9–14 reuse passages from other biblical books. Second, chapters 12–14 are distinguished from 9–11 by their frequent use of "on that day" and by their more radical images. Third, while chapters 12–14 are placed under a single heading, chapter 14 is distinguished by the way it uses "on that day" to merge images into a scenario regarding the future of

Jerusalem. We must, however, postpone some additional observations about these chapters until we have explored Malachi's connections to Zechariah.

Malachi

> ### *In the pages to come …*
>
> Like Zechariah 9–11 and 12–14, the book of Malachi bears a superscription that begins "An Oracle. The word of the LORD." And like Zechariah 12:1, Malachi 1:1 directs its oracle to Israel, suggesting some sort of a link between the appendices to Zechariah 1–8 and the book of Malachi. At the same time, this book has features that distinguish it from Zechariah 9–14 and the rest of the prophetic books.
>
> Each of Malachi's six literary units includes an assertion, followed by a question and a response. However, this hint of a regular structure to the book's units can be deceiving, since the six units that make up the book show distinctive wrinkles, some of which point to the work of editors. This point notwithstanding, the recurring pattern of assertion, question, and response points to the book's composition as a literary work.
>
> Just as significantly, the epilogue of 4:4–6 is a late appendix that points readers beyond the literary boundaries of the latter prophets to the **Torah** and the former prophets.

The similarity of Malachi's superscription to Zechariah 9:1 and 12:1 is broken by its designation of a particular prophet uttering the oracle: "An Oracle. The word of the LORD to Israel by [Hebrew: through the hand of] Malachi." This name presents a puzzle, for it does not follow the typical pattern of Israelite names, which contain a form of a divine name (for example, Abijah, "the LORD is father"; Isaiah, "the LORD saves"; Ezekiel, "God seizes"). By contrast, Malachi (*mal'achi*) means "my messenger." Although one can point to Ethni, "my gift" (1 Chr 6:41) and Beeri, "my well" (Hos 1:1) as possible parallels, Beeri may designate the clan to which Hosea's father belonged ("Beerithite"), while Ethni is likely an abbreviated form of the name Ethniyah, "gift of the LORD." We must also consider that "my messenger" would be a peculiar name to choose for a child. Taking it as a shortened form of "messenger of the LORD" (*mal'achiyah*) raises even more questions about why parents would select this name for their child (Redditt, 1995).

The word *malachi* appears in 3:1: "See, I am sending *my messenger (mal'achi)* to prepare the way before me." A common suggestion is that an editor, wanting to attach a name to an otherwise anonymous book, adopted the word *mal'achi* from 3:1 and added "by the hand of." However, it is also possible (as will be argued below) that the author may have reticently referred to himself as "my messenger" in 3:1 and assumed that title for himself in 1:1. This hypothesis has implications for the relationship of this book to Zechariah 9–11 and 12–14 that will be teased out later, once we gain a sense of the book.

Malachi: A Book of Questions and Answers

The key issue for understanding this book is its structure. Even a casual reading shows that it contains a recurring pattern of assertions, questions, and rebuttals. In 1:2 the LORD asserts his love for Israel, but complains that they have voiced skepticism by asking, "How have you loved us?" In response he provides evidence of his love for Jacob's descendants, as proved by his disdain for Edom. Given the similarly structured exchanges in the following chapters, the book is commonly perceived as a chain of disputes between the LORD (or the prophet) and various groups within Judah.

The adequacy of this description has been questioned, however, since the nature of the exchanges varies. For example, 2:10–16 begins with rhetorical questions affirming that all Jews have the same God as father, so that breaking faith with each other profanes "the covenant of our ancestors" (vv. 10–11). While vv. 12–16 present many problems (see the text box "I hate divorce" below), they voice no objection to the accusations. The only question raised is why the LORD no longer accepts their offerings, which the prophet answers by pointing to the LORD as witness of the breached relationship with the "wife of your youth" (v. 14). To this degree, then, this unit varies from the overall pattern.

Accordingly, Malachi's exchanges are difficult to epitomize in a single description. Characterizations of them as a series of questions and answers (Fischer, 1972), as dialogues about the Torah (Lescow, 1990), as staged disputes with an imaginary opponent (Petersen, 1995), or as a series of speeches (Floyd, 2000)[7] suppress their diversity. Fundamental to these units is their engagement of the audience through a caricature of their beliefs or actions (Fischer, 1972; Redditt, 1995),[8] in response to which the audience voices perplexity (1:2, 6, 7; 2:17; 3:7, 8). Whether their perplexity is confrontational (so Petersen, 1995) is not always clear, but the prophet's responses typically focus on persuading them of his original claim.[9] This instructional tack is a distinguishing mark of Malachi (Glazier-McDonald, 1987c).

In the first unit (1:2–5) the people question the claim that the LORD loves them, in response to which the LORD asks them to consider his treatment of Edom. Drawing on the theme of kinship between Jacob and Esau that we saw Obadiah utilize, the LORD asserts that he has loved Jacob and hated Esau's children, Edom (vv. 2b–3a), whom he has destroyed and will continue to repress (vv. 3b–5). As morally objectionable to us as this supposed evidence of the LORD's love for Judah might be, the book of Obadiah's invective toward Edom attests that this would likely have carried weight with the audience.

The second and longest unit (1:6–2:9) is directed to the priests, who are accused of disrespecting the LORD by offering second-class animals (the lame and the sick). In this case, an extended harangue of the priests issues in a threat that he will disgrace them in front of the people because they have failed to live up to "my covenant with Levi," who revered the LORD and gave the people "true instruction" (2:4–7).

The third unit (2:10–16) opens with rhetorical questions that underscore the unity of all Jews, since they have "one father" and "one God created us," so that faithlessness to one another profanes "the covenant of our ancestors" (v. 10). The ensuing discourse offers multiple problems for interpreters, not least of which is how to translate vv. 15 and 16 (see the text box "I hate divorce"). A crucial debate concerns whether talk of marrying "the daughter of a foreign god" and betraying "the wife of your youth" in vv. 11–14 is a metaphor for Israel's infidelity to the LORD – as suggested by "Judah has been faithless," coupled with **cultic** language of "abomination" and "profaning" the sanctuary (v. 11) – or if it speaks concretely of divorcing a Jewish wife to marry a non-Jew, as suggested by talk of the LORD standing as "witness between you and the wife of your youth" (v. 14) (Glazier-McDonald, 1987a). The decision hangs, to a significant degree, on how one understands "the daughter of a foreign god" (v. 11).

A good argument can be mounted that this phrase refers to worship of a foreign goddess (goddesses are typically the daughters of a male deity; Shields, 1999). In that light, one could read the passage as an attack on religious infidelity. However, "daughter of a foreign god" could also refer to a woman devotee of a foreign deity who has become the wife of a Jewish man, displacing his Jewish "wife of your youth" (v. 14). In that case the passage condemns actual divorce. Or perhaps the ambiguity of the phrase "daughter of a foreign god" is deliberate, stressing that such foreign women are worshippers of foreign goddesses, so that Jewish men who marry them wind up committing apostasy (Glazier-McDonald, 1987a). It is also possible to give both options their due by viewing vv. 11–12 as attacking worship of a foreign goddess and vv. 13–16 as addressing literal divorce as a second stage in the discourse, introduced by "and this you do as well" (v. 13) (Shields, 1999).[10] In any case, this is the only unit in which a question from the audience appears but late in the discourse (v. 14). Moreover, it does not ask for clarification of the charges but only for an explanation of why the LORD does not accept their sacrifices.

"I hate divorce"

The common translation of v. 16, "I hate divorce," represents one solution to a problematic Hebrew phrase that actually does not identify the speaker as "I." Hewing closer to the Hebrew is: "'For the one who hates and divorces,' says the LORD God of Israel, 'covers his garment with violence'" (Shields, 1999). In other words, the man who divorces based on hatred commits an act so heinous that it is apparent to all, not least of all to the LORD.

Verse 15 contains other ambiguities that the NRSV again resolves for its readers. Literally translated, it reads, "And did not one make, and a remnant of spirit/breath belongs to him? And what does the one seek: godly seed [or, And why does the one seek godly seed?]. Be on guard in your spirit, and with the wife of your youth do not deal falsely." The NRSV's expansion of "one" into "one God" is possible ("one God" actually appears in v. 10), even if this would be the only time "one," by itself, served as a divine title (Shields, 1999). While the NRSV's "both flesh and spirit are his" is possible, it requires a slight change of the word translated "remnant." The NRSV's solutions to the verse's ambiguities are among the many that have been offered, although none has gained a consensus.

The frustrating sum of these problems is that they have found no simple solution. For discussion of these issues, see Glazier-McDonald (1987a) and Shields (1999).

The claim of the fourth unit, 2:17–3:6,[11] is that the people have "wearied the LORD with your words," a charge for which they ask an explanation. The prophet faults them for asserting that "all who do evil are good in the sight of the LORD," which is more likely a caricature of their cynicism than a direct quotation; the question "Where is the God of justice?" likely comes closer to the explicit complaint (2:17). The LORD's response is his announcement that he is sending "my messenger" (3:1) to "purify the descendants of Levi" (3:3) so that they might present pure offerings (3:3–4), at which time the LORD will impose judgment on those who commit serious crimes and fail to fear him (3:5). The LORD has not changed his stance toward justice; it is simply that – as Israel knows from experience – he does not destroy the wicked instantaneously (3:6). Divine justice has not failed.

The fifth unit (3:7–12) begins by reminding the people of their long-standing disobedience, but quickly moves to the appeal "Return to me, and I will return to you, says the LORD of hosts," to which the people respond with the query "How shall we return?" (3:7). Their fault (and thus, what needs modification) is that they are robbing the LORD, a charge prompting further perplexity: "How are we robbing you?" (3:8). The prophet isolates their crime as withholding their "tithes and offerings," needed to support the temple. If they mend this fault, the LORD will reverse their crop failures, giving them a prosperity that will make the nations take note.

The sixth unit (3:13–4:3) accuses the people of having "spoken harsh words" (3:13) against the LORD, a charge that perplexes them. The detailing of the charge seems another caricature of their attitude rather than a direct quotation: "It is vain to serve God. What do we profit by keeping his command .... Now we count the arrogant happy; evildoers not only prosper, but when they put God to the test they escape" (vv. 14–15). Whereas the fourth unit addressed their skepticism about divine justice by proclaiming the certainty of divine judgment, the sixth unit begins its response by reporting, "Then those who revered the LORD spoke with one another. The LORD took note and listened, and a book of remembrance was written before him of those who revered the LORD and thought on his name" (v. 16). This is followed by a vow to claim the pious as "my special possession," sparing them "on the day when I act" (v. 17). Only then does the passage address an audience, promising that the distinction between the righteous and the wicked will again become evident when the LORD destroys the wicked and rewards the righteous, who will "tread down the wicked" like ashes beneath their feet (4:1–3).

The concluding verses of the book (4:4–5) address a group, but in an entirely different vein, urging them to remember "the teaching of my servant Moses" and presaging the arrival of Elijah as an advance man, to prepare people for the day of the LORD.

Having identified these components of the book, what can we detect about its composition?

The Composition of Malachi

To what degree these dialogues reflect actual verbal exchanges is beyond knowing. However, the stylized shaping of all six units as interactions, with the people's words reported by the prophet ("And you say") and responses limited to asking "how" an assertion is true, does not seem to reflect the back-and-forth of an actual conversation, but smacks of a literary conceit (Glazier-McDonald, 1987c; Nogalski, 1993b). Accordingly, the question is not when these exchanges occurred, but how they were composed as literature.

Some have suggested that a core of passages (specifically, 1:2–2:9 and 3:6–12) was expanded (Bosshard and Kratz, 1990), while others posit that an editor merged a writing that criticized priests (1:6–2:9, 2:13–16) with another addressed to the people (1:2–5, originally followed by 3:6–7, but also including 2:17–3:1a, 5, 8–12, 13–15), to which he prefixed a superscription and supplemented the whole with other materials (Redditt, 1995). Other scholars regard the core units as composite themselves, arguing (for example) that 1:8b–10 were added as commentary on 1:8a, since they deviate from the issue of priests presenting inferior offerings, while vv. 11–14 are a further addition because they shift from addressing priests (Utzschneider, 1992).

The prime assumption in each of these reconstructions is that features that distinguish adjacent units from each other reflect different layers in the construction of the book, since one would expect an author to maintain a style of composition. Thus, categorizing passages according to whether they address the priests or the people, whether they hold out the possibility of turning curse into blessing or anticipate a day of judgment, and whether they deal with people as groups or individuals, are offered as the foundation for judging the book composite. Whether these are valid criteria must be answered by looking at individual cases.

First, the peculiar twists in 2:17–3:5 offer convincing evidence of editorial expansion. Following the people's complaint that "all who do evil" seem to win divine approval (2:17), it is strange that "the messenger of the covenant" (3:1) purifies "*the descendants of Levi*" until they present offerings to the Lord "in righteousness" (3:3), making "the offering of Judah and Jerusalem" acceptable once again (3:4). While that accords with the theme of priestly malpractice in 1:6–2:9, it is irrelevant to the complaint about "all who do evil" (2:17). That complaint receives a response only in 3:5's reassurance that apparent absence of "the God of justice" (2:17) will be resolved by his arrival to judge the full spectrum of evildoers: "sorcerers … adulterers … those who swear falsely … those who oppress the hired workers in their wages, the widow and the orphan … those who thrust aside the alien, and do not fear me" (Malchow, 1984). Chapter 3 vv. 1b–4 inexplicably interrupts this theme.

A related problem is identifying the players denoted by "my messenger" (see the text box), "the Lord," and "the messenger of the covenant" in 3:1. On the one hand, even though "Lord" translates the standard Hebrew word for "lord" (rather than the **Tetragrammaton**), the fact that this figure is to come to "his temple" suggests that it designates the deity. Since the people had asked, "Where is the God of justice?", the designation of "the Lord" as the "one whom you seek" is fitting (Malchow, 1984). The Lord's pledge of judgment for the wicked (v. 5) is the natural sequel to the announced coming of "the Lord" to his temple in v. 1a.[12]

In that light, it is doubtful that "my messenger" (v. 1a) and "the messenger of the covenant" (v. 1b) refer to the same person. While the parallel phrases "the Lord whom you seek" and "the messenger … in whom you delight" might suggest that they are the same person (so Glazier-McDonald, 1987c), nowhere else is the Lord called a "messenger" (Malchow, 1984). The "messenger of the covenant" who purifies "the descendants of Levi" is likely a later interpretation of "my messenger" of

The Identity of "my Messenger"

Various identities have been suggested for the "messenger" of 3:1a, the most plausible of which are a heavenly figure or (even more likely) a prophet. If it is the latter, "my messenger" might designate the prophetic voice in this book (compare "Haggai, the messenger of the LORD," in Haggai 1:13), sent to right the ways of the people before the LORD's arrival (Malchow, 1984). In fact, this identification might well explain how *mal'achi* is designated as the one by whom the word of the LORD comes in 1:1. In that case, it would less likely be a later insertion to provide a name for this prophet than a title the author used for himself.

3:1a, in light of the failure of the Levites to maintain "the covenant with Levi" in 2:4–9. Similarly, the modifier "in whom you delight" mirrors "whom you seek" in 3:1a. This wording creates a literary seam (comparable to a tailor's seam) to attach vv. 1b–4 to v. 1a, so as to connect the idea of a messenger with the Levites (Petersen, 1995). This messenger accomplishes the purification of "the descendants of Levi," enabling them to offer acceptable sacrifices on behalf of the people. By contrast, the role of "my messenger (*mal'achi*)" in v. 1a is to "prepare the way before me," that is, prior to the LORD's appearance in his temple for judgment. The intrusion of different themes via vv. 1b–4 marks it as a secondary insertion.

On the other hand, the hypotheses that 1:2–5 became dislocated from their original position, directly before 3:6–7 (Redditt, 1995), or have been supplied as a fresh introduction (Bosshard and Kratz, 1990) are unlikely. On the one hand, the address of "the descendants of Jacob" in 3:6 is more similar to "the tents of Jacob" in 2:12 than to the contrast between Esau and Jacob in 1:2. On the other hand, the evidence Bosshard and Kratz (1990) cite to show that 1:2–5 expounds 1:6–2:3 and 3:6–12 are the word "great" in 1:4 and 11, and the word "return" in 1:4 and 3:7, 12, each of which is too commonplace to support the argument.

Equally improbable is the claim that 1:8b–10 and 11–14 are expansions within 1:6–14 (Utzschneider, 1992). First, responding to the priests' question about how they were polluting the LORD's altar (v. 7) by citing their offering of blind, lame, or sick animals (v. 8a) suggests that this was a practice openly accepted among temple priests. The rhetorical questions of v. 8a ("… is that not wrong?") seek, therefore, to highlight the offense to the LORD this entails, while v. 8b's question of whether their governor would be happy with such second-rate offerings aims at leaving beyond doubt the slight their behavior carries. Verse 9 makes clear that responsibility for correcting this offense lies with the priests, while v. 10 underscores the severity of the offense by wishing that some courageous priest would take steps to stop all sacrifice.

Although it is possible that vv. 11–14 were added later, nothing marks them as an intrusion of the sort we found in 3:1b–4. Least of all can this judgment be based on the observation that v. 14 assails an individual who reneges on a vow by offering a blemished animal instead of continuing the address of priests (Utzschneider, 1992), since the verdict on whether an animal was acceptable was rendered by the priests (Lev 27:11–12) (Petersen, 1995). Just as significantly, the emphasis on the LORD's name as revered throughout the world in vv. 11 and 14 resumes the complaint of dishonoring the LORD that v. 6 raised but v. 7 left behind for the concrete problem of second-rate sacrifices. Verses 11–14 clarify how these problems are intertwined and are, then, integral to 1:6–14.

Suggestions that the book once ended with 3:6–12 rest on isolating 3:13–4:3 as unique within the book. Chapter 3 v. 13 charges, "You have spoken harsh words against me," followed by a question of how this is true. Verses 14–15 explain the charge as relating to the people's suspicions that evildoers fare better than those who keep the LORD's command. Verses 16–17 report a conversation among "those who revered the LORD," with the LORD taking note of their reverence by writing their names in a "book of remembrance," promising to spare them when he acts, enabling them to "see the difference between the righteous and the wicked" (v. 18), with the righteous triumphing and trampling the wicked (4:1–3).

Even though this unit follows the familiar pattern of posing a charge that is questioned by the people, the detailing of the crime results in no proposal of how to mend the fault. Instead we find a report about the response of the upright. Not only is this the only narrative report in the book, but it designates the upright by a title not found elsewhere: "those who revered the LORD." As distinct as this unit is within the book, each of Malachi's scenes are literary constructions and most have unique wrinkles, leaving us unable to rule out that the scribal author shaped this final discourse to depict an impasse that called for a more explicit statement of judgment and reward than was given in 3:5 (Petersen, 1995).

So, What Did They Say?

A vexing question is what "those who revered the LORD" said to one another (3:16) that distinguished them in the LORD's eyes from those who voiced skepticism about divine justice (vv. 14–15). Glazier-McDonald (1987c) posits that the conversation among "those who revered the LORD" involved a change of heart about their own words that the LORD just criticized (3:13). However, it is not clear that "those who revered the LORD" is the same group guilty of speaking "harsh words" against the LORD. And given that are we told nothing of their discussion, their topic could just as easily have been the illicit complaints of vv. 14–15. The LORD's affirmation that a distinction "between one who serves God and one who does not serve him" will become evident (v. 18) responds to the complaint, but without identifying who voiced it. In the end, we are not given enough information to answer the questions of what the righteous are assumed to have said to each other or who the scoffers were presumed to be.

In the final analysis, then, the book of Malachi resists, for the most part, attempts to isolate passages provided by later **scribes**. While 3:1b–4 provides clear evidence that such expansions occurred, and there is little reason to doubt that other expansions are present, most arguments made for specific instances are problematic. There is, however, another set of verses that show themselves the product of editing on a broader plane.

Malachi's Appendix (4:4–6)

There is little doubt that the book's concluding verses, 4:4–6, were affixed as an appendix at a late stage, inasmuch as they look away from issues affecting Judean society and point to other bodies of literature. Chapter 4 v. 4 directs the audience to "remember the teaching of my servant Moses, the statutes and ordinances that I commanded him at Horeb for all Israel." Nowhere else in Malachi are the legal codes of Moses commended. The dominant language has been living in fidelity to various "covenants," whether that with Levi (2:4–9), that of "the ancestors" (2:10), or that of maintaining allegiance to a "wife by covenant" (2:14). Moreover, even though 3:7 accuses the people of having "turned aside from my statutes," the phrase "the statutes and the ordinances" in 4:4 is terminology that appears elsewhere only in Deuteronomy 4:5, 8, 14, while the specification that these were commanded "at Horeb" utilizes the name for the divine mountain that is typical of Deuteronomy (Deut 4:10, 5:2, 9:8, 18:16, 29:1).[13] Additionally, the giving of these to "all Israel" accords with Deuteronomy's accent on "all Israel."[14] The inference that this phraseology derives from Deuteronomy is confirmed by the fact that "the teaching (*torah*) of Moses" is a phrase used in Joshua through 2 Kings in reference to Deuteronomy (Josh 8:31, 32; 23:6; 1 Kings 2:3; 2 Kings 14:6, 23:25) and is found in no other book among the latter prophets.[15]

The LORD's vow to "send to you the prophet Elijah before the great and terrible day of the LORD comes" (v. 5) takes up the language of 3:1 ("I am sending my messenger to prepare the way before me"), identifying "my messenger" with the revered prophet Elijah (1 Kings 17–2 Kings 2).[16] Meanwhile, the phrase "before the great and terrible day of the LORD comes" is a precise quotation of Joel 2:31b ("The sun shall be turned to darkness, and the moon to blood, *before the great and terrible day of the LORD comes*") (Petersen, 1995).[17] Although the reason for identifying Elijah's role as turning "the hearts of parents to their children and the hearts of children to their parents" is inscrutable, the idea that doing so will exempt the land from a "curse" answers the question "who can endure the day of his coming?" (3:2) (Petersen, 1995). Needless to say, the fact that 4:4–6 interprets 3:2 presupposes that 3:1b–4 already stood in the book known to this editor.

All three of these final verses look beyond the bounds of the book of Malachi, commending attention to the Torah (at least the book of Deuteronomy) and appealing to a key figure in the former prophets who is mentioned by name in the latter prophets only here. Even if v. 4 and vv. 5–6 were appended separately, together they imply that the Torah, the former prophets, and the latter prophets should be considered together (Blenkinsopp, 1977). The natural inference is that this appendix would have been added once Malachi stood at the end of a collection of prophetic books, considered subordinate to the Torah. That conclusion raises the question of how Malachi relates to the books that precede it.

Malachi, Zechariah, and the Twelve

The similarity between the superscriptions of Zechariah 9:1, 12:1, and Malachi 1:1 has prompted discussion of the interrelationship of these three bodies of literature. Some have posited that a limited set of passages in what we call Malachi were originally supplements to Zechariah rather than an independent book. Thus, some perceive that Malachi 1:2–2:9 and 3:6–12 (perhaps also 2:13–16) were appended to Zechariah 1–8, and only later was Zechariah 9–14 (with the superscription of 9:1) inserted, after which a superscription was interpolated into Zechariah 12:1a and another supplied for Malachi (Bosshard and Kratz, 1990; Steck, 1991). Under this hypothesis, Malachi became a distinct book only at a very late stage.

Some sort of association with Zechariah 1–8 is evident from comparison of "Return to me, and I will return to you, says the LORD of hosts" in Malachi 3:7 with "Return to me, says the LORD of hosts, and I will return to you, says the LORD of hosts" in Zechariah 1:3, especially since the failure of the ancestors is mentioned in the context of each (Mal 3:7; Zech 1:4). Likewise, Malachi 3:10–12 promises a bounty of crops as a reward for bringing the full tithe of crops into the temple, just as Zechariah 8:9–12 promises bountiful crops now that the people have begun rebuilding the temple.

However, there are also significant links between Malachi and Zechariah 9–14 (Schart, 2003). One of the more intriguing is the use of "one" in Malachi 2:15: "Did not one make [her]? … And what does the one desire?" (my translation). Verse 10 has already asked, "Has not one God created us?" There is a similarity between this use of "one" and that in Zechariah 14:9: "And the LORD will become king over all the earth; on that day the LORD will be one and his name one." This use of "one" recalls the *shema'*: "Hear, O Israel: The LORD is our God, the LORD is one" (Deut 6:4; my translation). While its use of "one" has been much debated, among the most plausible solutions is that given by the NRSV: "Hear, O Israel: The LORD is our God, the LORD *alone*" (my italics). This underscores the claim that "the LORD is our God" by stressing that he is the *only* god for Israel (compare Exodus 20:3, "You shall have no other gods before me").

It appears that Zechariah 14:9 interprets Deuteronomy's confession in the same way. The assertion that "his name" will be "one" equally reflects the thought of Deuteronomy, which uses "name" as a stand-in for the LORD himself. Coupled with the assertion that "the LORD will become king over all the earth," the verse asserts that the LORD alone will serve as "king over all the earth" (Meyers and Meyers, 1993), implying a denial of not only other human rulers but also other deities (Mason, 1973). Malachi 2:15 may reflect a similar use of "one," anticipated by 2:10, whose stipulation of "one God" and "one father" (compare Deut 32:6) is the grounds for decrying unfaithfulness "to one another, profaning the covenant of our ancestors." These verses tease out an implication of the confession that "the LORD is one" (Deut 6:4): because Jews have only one father, one God, they are inseparably joined together.

Only in Zechariah 14:9 and Malachi 2:10, 15, within the latter prophets do we find such reflection on this confession. It is unlikely that Zechariah 14:9 depends on Malachi 2:10, 15, since its statement about the LORD's "oneness" is more like Deuteronomy 6:4 (suggesting that it works from that confession), while Malachi's application of the LORD's oneness to relationships among his people seems an inference from such reasoning.

Although this does not necessarily mean that Malachi 2 was reliant on Zechariah 14:9, we should note a curious relationship between these verses. Zechariah 14:9's assertion that "the LORD will become king over all the earth" is echoed in the forecast of 14:16 that "all who survive of the nations that have come against Jerusalem shall go up year after year to worship the King, the LORD of hosts." Given that this kingship is exercised over nations said to worship the LORD, the claim of Malachi 1:14, "I am a great King … and my name is reverenced among the nations," is noteworthy, since only in these passages in Zechariah and Malachi is the LORD called "king" (Meyers and Meyers, 1993).

The most likely explanation of the relationship between Haggai, Zechariah, and Malachi is that the editor of Zechariah affected ties to Haggai, while the editors responsible for Zechariah 9–14 and Malachi created further lines of continuity between the various accretions, including the formulation of an entire book (Malachi) as an extension of themes drawn from Zechariah.

Other scholars have built on such observations to suggest that Malachi reflects not only Zechariah but also earlier books, serving as a capstone to the Twelve. This is based especially on perceptions that Malachi's core units rely on the book of Hosea (Bosshard and Kratz, 1990; Nogalski, 1993b; Steck, 1991). For instance, the use of the "son–father" relationship to posit an appropriate level of respect in Malachi 1:6 is compared to the LORD speaking of Israel as his "son" in Hosea 11:1, since that passage also professes the LORD's "love" for Israel (compare Mal 1:2) and v. 2 speaks of offer ing incense, like Malachi 1:11. However, given the scattered distribution of those words in Hosea 11 and that they are used in quite different statements than in Malachi 1 (for example, Hosea 11:2 complains of Israel offering incense to idols, while Malachi 1:11 points to incense offerings to the LORD), these associations are convincing only if one wishes to find links. None of them approaches the level of shared language we have noted between Malachi and Zechariah. While Malachi shows clear ties to Zechariah, there are no solid ties to Hosea and no indication that Malachi was written specifically to serve as a cap to a **"Book of the Twelve."**

A Retrospect on 12 Prophetic Books

The 12 books we have studied show different types of scribal editing. The formation of Hosea and Amos appears to have begun in the last quarter of the eighth century, with the Hosea traditions already exerting an influence on the shaping of Amos, whereas the Amos traditions appear to have affected the book of Hosea only through scribal expansions. Both books show efforts to corral received oracle traditions into collections, but also to correlate the message of one book with the other. While discrete oracles provided the building blocks, these books are not simple compendiums, for they use literary structures (such as Amos's five visions) to represent their prophet's message.

The book of Micah likewise presents oracles arranged in a sequence to convey an impression of a prophetic message, with the aid of themes and language borrowed from elsewhere, such as the talk of idols and a harlot's wages drawn from Hosea, and the disparaging of chariots and horses that is native to Amos. The book evinces a large-scale inclusion of oracles that ill fit Micah's day and are capped with verses anticipating Israel's purification, together with the subjugation of the nations. The book also expands the use of hymnic materials that appeared as fragments in Amos, with Micah 7 built exclusively from such material, as will happen again in Habakkuk 3 and Jonah 2.

The superscription to Zephaniah places its prophet in the era of Josiah, although its earliest oracles more likely reflect the reign of Josiah's son Jehoiakim. Unifying the book is the pronounced theme of "the day of the LORD," around which are gathered discrete oracles, including ones adopted from other books. However, that theme reaches its zenith in Joel, built largely of material drawn from other books. Because Joel offers a lightly sketched narrative about earlier events and their outcome to provide guidance to future generations about how to survive the day of the LORD, it looks past any particular place and time, thereby marking itself as literary prophecy from its inception.

Equally marked as literary prophecy is the book of Obadiah, at whose center stands a list of allegations against Edom. While these charges seem to have originated after the Babylonian sack of Jerusalem in 587 BCE, they are set amid traditions utilized also in Jeremiah 49 and later expansions, forming a work that constitutes a bitter denunciation of Edom on a par with Nahum's invective against Nineveh.

The book of Jonah evidences scribal development of the genre of a story about a prophet (as in Amos 7:10–17) into a full-blown narrative about a prophet and his engagement with his mission. Although the book of Haggai is not focused on the figure of the prophet, it also builds on narratives more than oracles, even if to a lesser degree than Jonah.

Despite these evidences of prophetic books that betray marked literary origins, only the book of Nahum touts its written form: "the *writing* of the vision of Nahum of Elkosh." There is good reason to surmise that this is a late appendage to the superscription, "an oracle concerning Nineveh," thereby evincing scribal interest in assigning prophetic namesakes to such books.

The forging of Zechariah 1–8 as a sequel to Haggai, and the composition of Zechariah 9–14 and Malachi as a set of subjoined oracles further exemplifies the ways scribes undertook the development of prophetic books as literature.

What this review makes evident is that prophetic books are not primarily oracle repositories. They are literary works composed by many contributing scribes. Even though each book is ascribed to a particular prophet, they are prominently literary improvisations on oracles and stories that mean to convey an outworking of the LORD's word to and will with Israel. These books give us every reason to infer that scribes who transmitted and shaped them considered their contributions on the same level as the oracles that inspired the earliest developments of each book. It is the evidence of that belief that compels us to take account of their role in bequeathing us these works.

Notes

1. A potentially significant corollary to the reuse of material from other prophetic books is the relatively infrequent use of "thus says the LORD" (19 times in 1–8, but then again only in 11:4) and "says the LORD" (13 times in 1–8, twice in 9–11, five times in 12–14), suggesting that the sense of prophetic authority in these chapters derives primarily from reuse of earlier prophetic oracles, much as we observed in Joel (Jeremias, 2002).
2. For a summary of attempts to resolve this problem see Foster (2007).
3. Despite the fact that 9:14–17 switch to speaking of those the LORD protects as "them" and "they," it is plausible that these verses are part of the unit begun in v. 9 (Petersen, 1995).

4. The second half of v. 2 presents quandaries and syntactical ambiguities that cannot be addressed here.

5. Whether v. 2b is integral to the attack on idolatry in 2a or is a supplement is immaterial, since "and also" (*wegam*) links the removal of prophets with the elimination of idols, especially given that their removal entails the expurgation of "the unclean spirit."

6. The "shame" that befalls the seers and diviners in Micah 3:7 includes the lack of revelation and, thus, designates a loss of face, whereas the shame spoken of in Zechariah 13:4 is internal, in so far as they divest themselves of (or make excuses for) any mark of being prophets (vv. 5–6).

7. Floyd (2000) recognizes 1:2–5 as a true disputation and divides the remainder of the book into four speeches (1:6–2:9, 2:10–16, 2:17–3:12, and 3:13–4:6).

8. As Glazier-McDonald (1987c) observes, given the uniform style of the book's discourses, they do not report actual dialogues between a prophet and the people, even if they might reflect such debates within the community. The book offers a stylized literary consideration of the issues (Petersen, 1995).

9. This applies even to the prophet's assertion that his addressees will see, when the LORD acts, "the difference between the righteous and the wicked" (3:18), since his point is to bring reassurance to "those who revered the LORD," for whom such a distinction seems to have been obscured. Chapter 3 vv. 1–5 presents peculiar problems that will be considered below.

10. It is not necessary to view "and this you do as well" as a mark of secondary material, as do Bosshard and Kratz (1990), who consider vv. 10–12 a later expansion, or Lescow (1990), who regards vv. 11b–13a ("And this you do as well") as secondary.

11. Even though 3.6 has typically been considered the start of the next unit, the conjunction "for" typically connects a statement closely to what precedes it (1:11, 14; 2:7, 11, 16; 3:2, 12; 4:3), and it likely signals a connection here. The LORD's assertion that he does not change could be understood as denying the insinuation of 2:17 that "the God of justice" has ceded ground to the wicked. The response to the people's complaint is not simply that the LORD will act, but also that his delay in acting is not a sign that he has changed character.

12. Glazier-McDonald's defense of vv. 1b–4 as original to their context because "they flow directly out of the previous section, 2:10–16" (Glazier-McDonald, 1987b, 96) does not account for v. 17, which changed the topic to the question of **theodicy** more generally. This is the question answered in v. 5, marking vv. 1b–4 as intrusive.

13. Although the name Horeb appears also in Exodus 3:1, 17:6, and 33:6, only in the last of these does it refer specifically to the mountain around which Israel camped, otherwise called "Sinai" throughout Exodus, Leviticus, and Numbers, or simply "the mountain of God" in Exodus 18:5 and 24:13. "Sinai" appears in Deuteronomy only in the hymn of Moses (33:2).

14. This phrase appears in Exodus 18:25 and Numbers 16:34, but 14 times in Deuteronomy.

15. While it is true that the term "instruction" (*torah*) is found in Malachi 2:6–9 (Glazier-McDonald, 1987c), there it concerns the "instruction" priests render (compare Hag 2:11), something very different than is designated by the phrase the "instruction of Moses."

16. It is possible that Elijah's reputation as having "ascended in a whirlwind to heaven" (2 Kings 2:11) had something to do with his identification with this divine messenger (Petersen, 1995), much as Enoch's being taken by God (in lieu of a report of his death; Gen 5:24) made him a natural vehicle for divine communication in apocalypses of the second temple period.

17. While Glazier-McDonald (1987c) contends that this verse simply uses common phraseology for speaking about "the day of the LORD," it is the identity of this entire phrase with Joel 2:31b that favors the inference that it quotes that passage. Given that 3:2 is part of a secondary insertion, this phrase most likely draws on Joel (Wöhrle, 2006a).

11

The Book of Isaiah

> *In the pages to come …*
>
> The book of Isaiah provides our first exposure to a large prophetic book. While each of the larger books has its own characteristics, the processes of composition and editing we observed in the shorter books will be apparent in them as well.
>
> This book has been built by expanding traditions that doubtless trace back to Isaiah, even if those have become enshrouded in layers of expansions. Although this situation is hardly novel in the prophetic books, what this longer book will show us is a more elaborate compositional process that yielded not only larger units, but also greater complexity. That complexity justifies devoting two chapters to Isaiah, which will also serve as an introduction to issues that will appear in Jeremiah and Ezekiel.

The Structural Signals of Isaiah

The place to begin exploring this book is with the **superscriptions** and **incipits** that signal new units. Chapter 1 v. 1 is reminiscent of the superscriptions in Hosea, Joel, Micah, and Zephaniah:

> The vision of Isaiah son of Amoz, which he saw concerning Judah and Jerusalem in the days of Uzziah, Jotham, Ahaz, and Hezekiah, kings of Judah. (Isa 1:1)

Surprisingly, we find a similar superscription at the start of chapter 2:

> The word that Isaiah son of Amoz saw concerning Judah and Jerusalem. (Isa 2:1)

Prophetic Literature: From Oracles to Books, First Edition. Ronald L. Troxel.
© 2012 Ronald L. Troxel. Published 2012 by Blackwell Publishing Ltd.

The prime differences between these superscriptions are the phrases "the vision of Isaiah ... which he saw ...," followed by the names of Judah's kings (1:1), versus the simple heading "the word that Isaiah ... saw" (2:1).

A new superscription stands at the outset of chapter 13: "The **oracle** concerning Babylon that Isaiah son of Amoz saw." Briefer ones appear in 14:28 ("In the year that King Ahaz died this oracle came"), 15:1 ("An oracle concerning Moab"), 17:1 ("An oracle concerning Damascus"), and 19:1 ("An oracle concerning Egypt"), the final superscription in the book.

We also encounter incipits in Isaiah, beginning with 6:1: "In the year that King Uzziah died, I saw the LORD sitting on a throne, high and lofty; and the hem of his robe filled the temple." The story of Isaiah's confrontation with Ahaz (7:1–17) begins with a summary of events relevant to the story: "In the days of Ahaz son of Jotham son of Uzziah, king of Judah, King Rezin of Aram and King Pekah son of Remaliah of Israel went up to attack Jerusalem, but could not mount an attack against it" (7:1). Similarly, 20:1 reports, "In the year that the commander-in-chief, who was sent by King Sargon of Assyria, came to Ashdod and fought against it and took it ...." Each of these incipits initiates a narrative.

The most extensive narrative is chapters 36–39, which focus on Isaiah's activity in two crises during King Hezekiah's reign. Chapter 36 v. 1 introduces a military threat with the report "In the fourteenth year of King Hezekiah, King Sennacherib of Assyria came up against all the fortified cities of Judah and captured them." The remainder of the story concerns the appeal of an Assyrian military official to Jerusalemites not to listen to Hezekiah's claims that the LORD would save them, in response to which Isaiah delivers an oracle promising that the king of Assyria would not set foot in Jerusalem. The story concludes with reports of the Assyrian army's defeat and of King Sennacherib's assassination by his sons (37:36–38).

The second crisis, connected to the previous story by "in those days" (38:1), concerns a mortal illness that befell Hezekiah, with Isaiah admonishing him to put his house in order in preparation for his death. However, Hezekiah's appeal to the LORD for an extension of his life, on the basis of his piety, was successful in gaining for him an additional 15 years, in the wake of which Hezekiah offered a prayer of thanksgiving (38:9–20).

The events of chapter 39 are set in the same period as the story of chapter 38: "At that time King Merodach-baladan son of Baladan of Babylon sent envoys with letters and a present to Hezekiah, for he heard that he had been sick and had recovered." Isaiah takes Hezekiah to task for showing the Babylonian envoys his entire treasure, which the prophet says will, in a later era, be carried off to Babylon.[1] After chapter 39 there are no more narratives in the book.

Other passages use literary forms that mark them as distinct units. For example, chapter 12 is a hymn rejoicing in the LORD's salvation (vv. 1–4, 5–6), just as hymnic passages appeared in the minor prophets (Nah 1:2–8; Hab 3; Jon 2).

Chapter 13 introduces an oracle against Babylon that extends through 14:23, before yielding to oracles against Assyria (14:24–27), Philistia (14:28–31), Moab (chapters 15–16), Damascus (17), Cush (18), and Egypt (19). Collections of oracles against foreign nations occur also in Jeremiah 46–51 and Ezekiel 25–32, reflecting a common impulse among these larger prophetic books.[2]

Another literary form in Isaiah that recurs in Jeremiah and Ezekiel is a first-person narrative of the prophet receiving a call to his task. None of the minor prophets present a narrative of the sort we find in Isaiah 6:1–13, Jeremiah 1:4–19, and Ezekiel 1:1–3:15. Quite conspicuously, however, Isaiah's commissioning narrative stands some distance into the book (chapter 6), while those in Jeremiah and Ezekiel stand at the outset. Exploring why that is the case will touch on several important issues and, thus, provide a good introduction to the complex process of how this book was shaped. Before taking up that issue, however, we must note a shift chapters 40–66 introduce from the historical backdrop assumed in most of chapters 1–39.

The Change of Setting Assumed in Chapters 40–66

The first 39 chapters are punctuated by references to events and people in the eighth century BCE. They repeatedly mention the Assyrians, who gained control of the countries along the Mediterranean by the mid-eighth century and dominated the region until 622 BCE. They also refer to kings who ruled Judah in the latter half of the eighth century. Thus, 6:1 refers to "the year that King Uzziah died," leaving the throne to his son Ahaz (7:1, 14:28), who was succeeded by his son Hezekiah, featured in the narrative of chapters 36–39. Isaiah 7:1–6 deals with the intrigues of the Syro-Ephraimite crisis that we encountered in the book of Hosea (see above, pp. 23–24). Thus, chapters 1–39 commonly assume the backdrop of the late eighth century BCE.

By contrast, chapters 40–66 lack allusions to that era and mention by name a ruler of a century and a half later: Cyrus, king of Persia, whom the LORD calls "my shepherd" (44:28) and "my anointed" (45:1), who "shall build my city and set my **exiles** free" (45:13). The backdrop for this is the decree Cyrus issued after conquering Babylon in 539 BCE, permitting those exiled in Babylon to return to Jerusalem. As natural as it has traditionally proved for readers to assume that these references are simply elements of Isaiah's predictions for the distant future, there are substantial marks that the author of chapters 40–66 actually lived and wrote in the middle of the sixth century, 150 years after Isaiah.

The supposition that Isaiah spoke these words to his contemporaries falters on two grounds. First, chapters 40–66 never mention the name of Isaiah, unlike chapters 1–39, where his name appears fairly frequently. Whereas Jeremiah is mentioned by name throughout that book and Ezekiel consistently identifies himself as the speaker, the name Isaiah does not appear after chapter 39, and only rarely does a prophetic voice in chapters 40–66 speak in the first person (Berges, 1998).

Second, the references to Cyrus in Isaiah 44:28 and 45:1 assume that the audience will recognize his name. Isaiah could not have spoken of Cyrus so matter-of-factly, any more than a hypothetical prophet in Philadelphia, Pennsylvania, in the late 1700s could have said, "Thus says the LORD of my servant, Lincoln, who will free the slaves," and presumed his audience would recognize the name.[3]

Arguing that Isaiah imagined his true audience as the Judean exiles of the sixth century BCE, for whom he spoke *as if* he lived in their day (Oswalt, 1986), would make Isaiah anomalous as a prophet.[4] Throughout the **ancient Near East**, prophets spoke on behalf of a deity to their contemporaries, addressing issues of their day. Even on the occasions Isaiah speaks of preserving his words for the future (Isa 8:16, 30:8), they are words he has addressed to his contemporaries and they have rejected, not ones tailored to an audience living in different circumstances.

Arguing that Isaiah spoke *as if* he lived a century and a half later would also subvert his pattern of distinguishing what he says about the future from statements about the present. For example, in 1:21–26, after lamenting the current corrupt state of Jerusalem, he forecasts a purge of the city's wicked, after which its purity will be restored. He does not blur the boundaries between the present and the future by speaking as if the city were already cleansed of wickedness.

By contrast, the voice in chapters 40 through 55 *assumes* (rather than forecasts) the destruction of Jerusalem and the exile of its citizens. Whereas 1:21–26 still await hardship for Jerusalem, 40:2 reassures Jerusalem "that her penalty *is* paid, that she *has* received from the LORD's hand double for all her sins." Similarly, Zion's lament over being forgotten by the LORD (49:14) receives a reassurance that her "waste and desolate places" will be restored and she will swell with children born when she was "bereaved and barren, exiled and put away" (49:19–21). This reflects, rather than predicts, circumstances in the mid-sixth century BCE, when a prophet encouraged his fellow exiles to anticipate a return to Jerusalem.

The theme of the return of the LORD's people by a newly constructed highway through the wilderness stands at the outset of these chapters (40:3–11) and is subsequently reprised (43:14–21, 49:8–12) and matched by promises that the LORD will restore the people to their land (43:5–7, 51:11). Isaiah 48:20 clearly identifies where the addressees live: "Go out from Babylon, flee from Chaldea, declare this with a shout of joy, proclaim it, send it forth to the end of the earth; say, 'The LORD has redeemed his servant Jacob!'"

Finally, chapters 40–66 reflect a different attitude toward the monarchy than appeared in chapters 1–39. While the early chapters decry Jerusalem's current rulers (1:21, 26; 7:13), they entertain expectations for a new, upright ruler (9:6–7; 11:1–3, 10; 16:4b–5). Chapter 16 v. 5 furnishes a typical example, promising that, after the invaders have left, "then a throne shall be established in steadfast love in the tent of David, and on it shall sit in faithfulness a ruler who seeks justice and is swift to do what is right." By contrast, the only king chapters 40–66 mention is the LORD (41:21, 43:15, 44:6). And when the LORD promises those who listen to him "an everlasting covenant, my steadfast, sure love for David" (55:3), this promise – far from pledging a new king from David's line – effectively transfers the LORD's "steadfast, sure love for David" to those who listen to him. Expectation of a new Davidic king vanishes in chapters 40–66.

The argument I have sketched to this point has simplified matters in the interest of clarity. But in the interest of accuracy, we must note that the era assumed in chapters 40–66 makes occasional appearances already in chapters 1–39.[5] Most prominently, the first of the oracles against the nations (chapters 13–14) speaks of Babylon as plundered by the Medes and the Persians (13:17–22), and 21:9 depicts messengers announcing Babylon's fall, even though neither Babylon nor Persia was a factor in Isaiah's day. Additionally, Isaiah 11:11–16 describes the LORD repatriating the remnant of his people via a "highway from Assyria," and a divinely provided highway and streams in the desert appear in chapter 35.

Consequently, while there is a clear distinction between the era of Isaiah's activity and circumstances presumed and addressed elsewhere in the book, the dividing line is not always as clear-cut as a division between 1–39 and 40–66. The explanation for this overlap is sufficiently complex to consume both this chapter and the next. That we should find a complex process of editing in Isaiah comes as no surprise, however, given what we have witnessed in the minor prophets.

Two Marked Expansions of an Oracle

As confirmation that the same sorts of expansion exist in Isaiah that we saw in the Twelve, we can isolate two obvious expansions of an oracle in Isaiah 16. Chapters 15–16 contain a series of oracles and mock laments for Moab, one of Israel's neighbors on the east side of the Dead Sea. Through 16:12, these are written as poetry. Then, unexpectedly, in 16:13–14 we find prose statements that refer to the preceding oracle as an old tradition:

> This was the word that the LORD spoke concerning Moab *in the past*. But *now* the LORD says, In three years, like the years of a hired worker, the glory of Moab will be brought into contempt, in spite of all its great multitude; and those who survive will be very few and feeble. (my italics)

Since the bulk of 15:1–16:12 spoke of Moab's defeat as already accomplished (a style not infrequent in oracles against foreign nations, as we saw in Nahum), the abrupt assertion that Edom's downfall still lies in the future is remarkable. Even more strikingly, the hope that this oracle will prove true within three years implies that the difficulty that Moab's continued existence creates for this oracle will be resolved soon. Finally, the description of the oracle as "this … *word* … that the LORD *spoke*" (16:13; my italics) uses phraseology not found elsewhere in the oracles against the nations,[6] but is common in chapters 1–9 and 20–39.[7] These observations confirm that 16:13–14 are a **scribe**'s attempt to reinvigorate the oracle to speak of Moab's fate in his day (Jenkins, 1989).

This is not the only case of updating in chapter 16. Especially conspicuous is 16:5's reference to a throne "in the tent of David." While 15:1–9 offers a coherent lament over the destruction of Moab, and the call to bewail Moab's fate in 16:6–7 leads naturally to the lament uttered in vv. 8–11, wedged between those sections stands a peculiar call to "send lambs to the ruler of the land," equated with "the mount of daughter Zion." This command likely concerns paying tribute, much as 2 Kings 3:4 speaks of the Moabite king Mesha paying tribute to Jehoram in the form of rams (Kaiser, 1974). Verses 3–4a stipulate the appeal that should accompany this tribute, requesting that "the outcasts of Moab" might receive shelter and protection.[8] Curiously, this appeal is addressed to a woman (as indicated by the Hebrew pronouns), even though the refugees have been instructed to address their appeal to "the ruler of the land." Since cities are regularly depicted and addressed as women (compare 1:27's reference to Zion as "her"), the "ruler of the land" to be addressed is likely the city of Zion.

Then we come upon vv. 4b–5:

> When the oppressor is no more, and destruction has ceased, and marauders have vanished from the land, then a throne shall be established in steadfast love in the tent of David, and on it shall sit in faithfulness a ruler who seeks justice and is swift to do what is right.

Because these words foresee a time when the disappearance of oppressors and marauders will clear the way for a ruler, they assume that such a ruler is impossible in the present; there is no king in Zion.[9] Moreover, the characterization of the anticipated ruler has little to do with the appeal the Moabites are advised to offer. Rather, the description of a ruler who seeks justice and hastens to do what is right is more indebted to the earlier forecast of a child who will establish the throne of David "with justice and with righteousness" (9:7). Most likely, 16:4b–5, which pick up the terms "land" and "ruler" from v. 1, are a scribal addition that seeks to specify what ruler in the city of Zion will receive this appeal (Kaiser, 1974).

Clearly, then, Isaiah was expanded through the same sort of expansions we witnessed in the Twelve. However, we need not wait for chapter 16 to find this. Already in a passage central to the early chapters of the book stand indications that scribal editors shaped and reshaped Isaiah's words. Devoting the remainder of this chapter to this passage will provide a snapshot of how the book of Isaiah arose.

Isaiah 6:1–8:18:   An Isaiah Memoir?

Chapter 6 v. 1 through chapter 8 v. 18 are widely considered among the earliest traditions about Isaiah's work. They present a mixture of narrative and oracles that seem to report key incidents early in the prophet's work. At the least, they are the core of the book's first large section, chapters 1–12.

Early in the twentieth century Isaiah 6:1–8:18 became dubbed Isaiah's "memoir," recounting his address of a national crisis.[10] It begins with Isaiah's report of being in the divine presence and overhearing the LORD ask whom he should send, leading Isaiah to volunteer his services. The remainder of the chapter summarizes the commission he received. Chapter 7 reports Isaiah's encounter with King Ahaz, as he oversaw preparations to repel Syria and Ephraim's attempt to replace him with a ruler more congenial to their plans for revolt against Assyria. Despite Isaiah's assurances that the LORD would not allow that plot to succeed, Ahaz resisted Isaiah's call to trust in the LORD, in the wake of which Isaiah appended to the promise of deliverance an ominous forecast of calamity, in the form of an Assyrian attack. Chapter 8 opens with a promise of escape from the clutches of Syria and Ephraim, but turns quickly to renewed forecasts of an Assyrian assault, in repayment for the people's unwillingness to trust the LORD. After Isaiah recounts a warning he received at the outset of his work, not to join the people's failure to trust the LORD, he calls for "the testimony" and "the teaching" (v. 16) to be preserved among his disciples, while he awaits the LORD, who hides "his face from the house of Jacob" (v. 17).

Chapter 8 v. 18 forms a natural end to this so-called memoir, with 8:19–9:7 constituting an appendix whose announcement of liberation from foreign domination through the birth and rule of an upright Davidic king seems to reflect chapter 7's forecast of the birth of Immanuel (Barthel, 1997).

It is easy to see why this portrayal of the prophet's activities during a crisis proved intriguing in an era when scholarship focused on reconstructing the person of the prophet. Above all, if there was a passage that seemed useful for recovering the words of Isaiah, it seemed to be here. In recent decades, however, this hypothesis has been subjected to criticisms that have also touched on the relationship between this book and the prophet Isaiah. Because these verses have regularly been considered part of the book's core material, and given the implications of debates about whether or to what degree its oracles go back to Isaiah, we will give detailed attention to this unit as representative of questions about the origins and development of chapters 1–39.

Problems with the "Memoir" Hypothesis

A major obstacle for the proposal that these chapters constitute the prophet's memoir is that chapter 7, a narrative told in the third person, breaks with the first-person reports of chapters 6 and 8. To overcome this, some have argued that the third-person pronouns in chapter 7 are corruptions of original first-person forms. Thus, instead of "Then the LORD said to Isaiah" in 7:3, we should read, "Then the LORD said to me"; rather than "Again the LORD spoke to Ahaz" in 7:10, we should read, "Again the LORD spoke to me"; and in place of "Then Isaiah said" in 7:13, we should adopt "Then I said."[11] While one might be able to justify those conjectures if all other features of chapter 7 showed it integral to chapters 6–8, other observations reveal that it is a foreign body.

On the one hand, chapters 6 and 8 show close connections with each other that simultaneously distinguish them from chapter 7 (Becker, 1997). First, while chapter 7 portrays an encounter between the prophet and the king, chapters 6 and 8 report exchanges strictly between the prophet and the LORD. Second, the disparaging phrase "this people" appears in 6:9–10 and 8:6, 11–12, but never in chapter 7. Third, 8:11–15, with its reference back to what the LORD instructed the prophet "while his hand was strong upon me," and 8:16–18, with its resolve to "wait for the LORD, who is hiding his face from the house of Jacob," strongly point back to chapter 6's report of Isaiah's commission.

On the other hand, similarities between chapters 7 and 8 suggest that one served as the template for the other. First, both 7:14–16 and 8:3–4 concern the birth of a child whose name portends disaster for Damascus and Samaria. However, on the heels of this good news comes an announcement of calamity for Judah (7:17 and 8:6–8). That these motifs, in the same sequence, should figure in both chapters is noteworthy (Becker, 1997).

Second, chapters 7 and 8 contain identical phrases: "for before the child knows" in 7:16 and 8:4; "the LORD again spoke to" in 7:10 and 8:5; and the introduction of a judgment speech in 7:5 and 8:6 with a Hebrew phrase meaning "because" that appears only twice elsewhere in the book (3:16, 29:13) (Becker, 1997). These literary peculiarities raise strong suspicions, therefore, that chapters 6–8 are not simply a diary or memoir written by the prophet.

The place to begin considering their composition is with chapter 7, which explicit markers divide into seven sections. Verses 1–9 narrate Isaiah's attempt to reassure King Ahaz in the face of the threat from Syria and Israel. Verse 10 introduces a second phase of his speech (vv. 10–17), in which Ahaz is commanded to ask a "sign" from the LORD, which he refuses to do. Therefore, Isaiah gives the LORD's own sign to the king, although it is a confusing sign, embodying both a promise of deliverance and the specter of a calamity so severe that it can only be compared to the traumatic secession of the northern tribes from the state they formed with Judah under David (vv. 10–17). Subjoined to those exchanges are four brief addresses, each introduced by "On that day" (vv. 18–19, 20, 21–22, 23–25).

A Threat to the Dynasty: 7:1–9

Chapter 7 v. 1 sets events in the distant past ("in the days of Ahaz") and takes care to trace his lineage beyond his father (Jotham) to his grandfather (Uzziah). These features suggest that 7:1 means to join this narrative closely to chapter 6, which was set "in the year that King Uzziah died" (6:1) (Barthel, 1997; Becker, 1997). However, two features suggest that this segue is not native to chapter 7. First, there is a curious break between v. 1 and the situation reported in v. 2, for v. 1 not only reports Rezin and Pekah's attempt against Jerusalem but also that they "could *not* mount an attack against it."[12] And yet, v. 2's report of Ahaz's consternation draws the reader back from the outcome to place her/him in the midst of Ahaz's anxiety over Jerusalem's fate during the crisis. The central question of the succeeding verses will be whether Ahaz will show faith. To that degree, v. 1's report of the failure of the attempt is beside the point, while v. 2 alone could reasonably introduce the narrative of vv. 3–9 (Barthel, 1997).

A second feature that tells against v. 1 as native to chapter 7's narrative is its difference in language from vv. 2–9. Whereas v. 1 speaks of "Israel" and uses the name Pekah, vv. 2–9 speak of "Ephraim" and "the son of Remaliah" (Barthel, 1997). This distinction drives us to consider, in turn, the close similarity of v. 1 to 2 Kings 16:5 (my translations):

Isaiah 7:1	2 Kings 16:5
In the days of Ahaz son of Jotham son of Uzziah, king of Judah, King Rezin of Aram and King Pekah son of Remaliah of Israel came up to wage war against Jerusalem, but could not prevail against it.	Then King Rezin of Aram and King Pekah son of Remaliah of Israel came up to wage war against Jerusalem; they besieged Ahaz but could not prevail against him.

Notably, Isaiah 7:1 uses the same wording as 2 Kings 16:5 to identify the northern king: "Pekah son of Remaliah." Given the uniqueness of this phrase within Isaiah 7, this agreement signals that the author adopted v. 1 from 2 Kings 16 (Barthel, 1997).

Even more striking is the temporal clause in Isaiah 7:1 that sets the threat to Jerusalem in the reign of Ahaz and provides his ancestry for two generations. The closest parallel in 2 Kings 16 is its first verse: "In the seventeenth year of Pekah son of Remaliah, King Ahaz son of Jotham of Judah began to reign." However, this comparison highlights the distinctive extension of Ahaz's pedigree, "son of Uzziah," in Isaiah 7:1, making it reminiscent of the report of Uzziah's death in 6:1 and reinforcing the perception that 7:1 means to link chapter 7 closely with chapter 6. If this is the case, we must consider how vv. 2–9 fit with this.

The reassurance that these two nations carry no weight (they are but "smoldering stumps of firebrands," v. 4) is matched by the reminder that these kingdoms are headed by cities ruled by two men, neither of whom the author calls "king" (Beuken, 2003). More importantly, the reader is left to supply the phrases "the head of Judah is Jerusalem, and the head of Jerusalem is its Davidic king" (Berges, 1998; Wildberger, 1991). This tacit affirmation offers Ahaz reassurance in the face of a coalition (v. 7), as ancient Near Eastern prophets commonly afforded kings facing such a threat (see de Jong, 2007; Wildberger, 1991).

What stands out as extraordinary in this passage, however, is the final sentence of v. 9: "If you are not firm, you will not be made firm" (my translation). This play on words likely alludes to Nathan's promise to David in 2 Samuel 7:16: "Your house and your kingdom shall be *made firm* [NRSV: sure] forever before me; your throne shall be established forever." Isaiah's demand is that Ahaz show the kind of "firmness" that the promise of a house "made firm" presupposes.

There are, however, a couple of peculiarities in this wording. First, this challenge to a king facing a crisis is unusual, in that it makes the reassurance equivocal. The interpretation of the name prescribed for Isaiah's child in 8:3 (Maher-shalal-hash-baz) embodies an unconditional promise of relief: "before the child knows how to call 'My father' or 'My mother,' the wealth of Damascus and the spoil of Samaria will be carried away by the king of Assyria" (8:4). And when 8:5–7 forecast an invasion by the Assyrians, it is due to the rejection by "this people" of "the waters of Shiloah that flow gently" (a reference to a stream running beneath Jerusalem), a metaphor for Jerusalem's resources that the people have rejected in favor of foreigners (Barthel, 1997). The fault is not the king's lack of faith, but the people's infidelity; nor is the dynasty's future directly threatened.

In this light, what might seem like a minor observation about 7:9b proves significant. Because Hebrew verbs and pronouns differentiate between "you" addressed to an individual and "you" addressed to a group, it is remarkable that, although the words addressed to Ahaz in 7:4–5 address him as an individual, the challenge of v. 9b speaks to a group: "If you all do not stand firm in faith, the lot of you shall not stand at all" (my translation). What is more, v. 11 resumes addressing an individual, and Ahaz's response, in v. 12, is phrased in the first person singular, "I" (rather than "we"). Verses 13–14 then return to addressing a group: "the house of David," a phrase that appears elsewhere in the passage.

Its first occurrence was in v. 2: "When it was reported to the house of David that Aram had exerted pressure on Ephraim, his heart and the heart of his people shook the way the trees of the forest do before the wind" (my translation). Contrary to vv. 9b and 13–14, "the house of David" is referenced by "*his* heart and the heart of *his* people." And in what follows the reassurance is addressed to Ahaz as an individual – appropriately enough, since the plot aims at removing him in favor of another ruler (vv. 5–6). But this, again, creates tension with the subsequent addresses to Ahaz as if he were a group when the threat is aimed at the Davidic dynasty. Nowhere is this more apparent than in v. 9b, whose play on "be made firm" and its address of a group shows that the Davidic house as a whole is in view. In short, at the core of vv. 2–9 stands an oracle reassuring Ahaz personally of deliverance in the face of the Syro-Ephraimite threat that has been subsequently overlaid with criticism of the royal house for a failure of faith.

The second stage of this encounter – introduced formally with the phrase "Again the Lord spoke to Ahaz, saying" (v. 10) – bears out this perception. The king's refusal to ask for a sign is portrayed as a mark of disobedience not simply by an individual ruler (the pronouns in vv. 11–12 address an individual), but by "the house of David" (the pronouns in vv. 13–14 signal that a group is addressed). Correspondingly, when impending calamity is announced in v. 17, it is directed not just against Ahaz and the people, but also against "your ancestral house" (i.e., the Davidic line), so that Ahaz becomes representative of the dynasty (Barthel, 1997; Becker, 1997).

The Sign of 7:10–17

The real conundrum in vv. 10–17 concerns the sign given to Ahaz. Discussion long centered on the meaning of the Hebrew word *'almah*, traditionally translated "virgin." It is now widely recognized that the use of this and related words in various Semitic languages favors a translation more along the lines of "young woman" (Wildberger, 1991). Thus, the character of neither the woman nor the child is central, but the name assigned the child and its explanation.

The announcement of a birth follows the pattern of other announcements of upcoming births in the Bible. Especially helpful comparisons are Genesis 16:11–12 and 17:19, where the name of the child is integral to the announcement: "Now you have conceived and shall bear a son; you shall call him Ishmael, for the LORD has given heed to your affliction" (Gen 16:11); "your wife Sarah shall bear you a son, and you shall name him Isaac" (Gen 17:19). In the first case, the name assigned the child is rooted in the narrative: "Ishmael" means "God hears." And even though the second passage does not explain the name Isaac (Yitschaq), later we learn that there is a rationale for its choice, when Sarah exclaims, "God has brought laughter for me; everyone who hears will laugh [*yitschaq*] with me" (21:6).[13] These announcements shed light on Isaiah 7:14–16, in which the name Immanuel likewise derives from the narrative.

First, however, we must note that v. 15, with its forecast of what the child will eat "by the time he knows how to refuse the evil and choose the good," is likely a scribal expansion, based on v. 16 and v. 22, taking the first step toward focusing on the character of the child himself (Barthel, 1997; Becker, 1997; Beuken, 2003; de Jong, 2007). Verse 16 is the original explanation of why the child is to be named Immanuel: relief from the threat from the Syro-Ephraimite alliance will occur "before the child knows how to refuse the evil and choose the good." This seems to mark a point early in the child's development, much as in 8:4 Damascus and Samaria will already have been plundered "before the child knows how to call 'My father' or 'My mother.'" The ability to "refuse the evil and choose the good" likely denotes discrimination between what is appealing and what is not, rather than moral sensitivity (Wildberger, 1991).[14] Before the child develops this capacity, the threat will have vanished, verifying the prophet's assignment of the name Immanuel, "God is with us" (Beuken, 2003). The "sign" reinforces v. 7's forecast of the coalition's failure.

While the sign does not hinge on identifying the mother or the child, their identity is implied by the structure and grammar of the passage. The use of the definite article ("*the* young woman") in the course of a conversation with Ahaz makes it likely that this refers to a woman evident to both the prophet and the king (Joüon and Muraoka, 2006, section 137 n.), while the need to reassure Ahaz in the face of a coalition set on dethroning him makes the sign more likely for the near term than the distant future. Because such announcements of upcoming births elsewhere are directed to a parent of the child rather than a third party, Immanuel is likely a son to be born to Ahaz and his queen (Barthel, 1997; Becker, 1997; Wildberger, 1991).

At the same time that this sign is announced to Ahaz, it is given to "the house of David" as a whole (recall the plural pronouns of vv. 13–14). And like the oracle of vv. 2–9a, it turns out to be mixed news: relief in the short term, but calamity in the long term. In fact, v. 9b, which shifts from an unconditional promise to demanding a choice, sets the scene for vv. 11–12, where Ahaz refuses to exercise the sort of firmness the prophet requires. As a result, the sign's promise of deliverance in the near term yields quickly to a forecast of disaster: "The Lord will bring on you and on your people and on your ancestral house such days as have not come since the day that Ephraim departed from Judah – the king of Assyria" (v. 17). The phrase "the king of Assyria" is widely recognized as a **gloss**, identifying for the reader what constitutes a trauma on the scale of the northern tribes' secession from the union with Judah following Solomon's reign (Wildberger, 1991).[15] In view is the assault on Jerusalem by Sennacherib's armies in 701 BCE, after Hezekiah made a bid for independence from Assyria.

The abrupt change from promises of deliverance to a forecast of disaster implies an ironic twist to "Immanuel," in which the Lord's presence is no longer good news (compare 8:8) (Barthel, 1997). While we cannot explore vv. 18–25, these supplements (each beginning with "on that day") envision harsh conditions after this calamity (Becker, 1997; Beuken, 2003).

Taken as a whole, chapter 7 recasts oracles that, in their earliest setting, proclaimed relief from distress, turning them into a criticism of "the house of David" for its failure to remain firm.[16] Within the setting of chapters 6 through 8, this becomes a fulfillment of the commission given the prophet at the outset (6:9–10): his words will not simply fall on deaf ears, but will engender disobedience (Becker, 1997).

Chapter 7, between 6 and 8

On the broader plane, however, we need to ask how chapter 7 fits within 6:1–8:18, since chapters 6 and 8 are closely associated. Chief among their common features is the use of the phrase "this people." Its first two occurrences in the book are in chapter 6 (vv. 9–10), and then it appears three times in chapter 8 (vv. 6, 11, 12). Thereafter it occurs only in 9:16 and chapters 28 (vv. 11, 14) and 29 (vv. 13, 14), which are widely considered part of the other major repository of early Isaiah traditions: chapters 28–33 (Stansell, 2006; Wildberger, 1997). Those chapters underwent a lengthy process of editing similar to chapters 1–12 (de Jong, 2007; Kratz, 2010).

The first occurrences of "this people" tell us little about whom it designates, since the commands to "say to this people" (6:9) and "make the mind of this people dull" (6:10) do not betray their identity. By contrast, in 8:6 "this people" is faced with an attack by Assyrian forces because they have "refused the waters of Shiloah that flow gently, and take delight in Rezin and the son of Remaliah."[17] The final two appearances of "this people" are in back-to-back verses and, once more, bear a disparaging tone: "For the Lord spoke thus to me while his hand was strong upon me, and warned me not to walk in the way of this people, saying: Do not call conspiracy all that this people calls conspiracy, and do not fear what it fears, or be in dread." This is consistent with the use of the phrase in its five remaining occurrences in the book. In 9:16 it refers to those who, according to 9:13, did not "seek the Lord of hosts." In 28:11 "this people" has refused to listen to the Lord's commands, after which v. 14 addresses the "scoffers who rule this people in Jerusalem." Shortly thereafter, "this people" is charged with skin-deep piety, because of which it will be treated in shocking ways (29:13–14). Given the consistently negative use of the phrase in each of its other occurrences,[18] it seems safe to assume that it carries negative tones in 6:9–10, as well.

Chapter 8 is key to understanding this negative assessment of the people. The disparagement of "this people" for rejecting "the waters of Shiloah that flow gently" in favor of Rezin and Pekah (v. 6) uses "the waters of Shiloah" metaphorically for the benefits of Zion (Barthel, 1997). Rejection of Zion is not just (implicitly) treason against its king, but a failure to trust in the Lord, while a favorable disposal toward Rezin and Pekah suggests that "this people" may have entertained the hope that the coalition would free them from Assyrian rule (Barthel, 1997; Beuken, 2003). Such faulty judgment will bring upon them an overwhelming substitute for the quiet "waters of Shiloah": "the mighty flood waters of the River, the king of Assyria and all his glory" (v. 7).

Consistently with this, "the way of this people" that the prophet was admonished to avoid from the outset (vv. 11–12) involved something the people branded a "conspiracy," in place of which one must treat the Lord as holy and fear him (v. 13).[19] The intimation of v. 6 that "this people" favors Rezin and Pekah undermines supposing that this conspiracy is simply Rezin and Pekah's plot against Ahaz.[20] Moreover, the term "conspiracy" (*qesher*) is used uniformly elsewhere for a coup by once-loyal subjects (Barthel, 1997; Beuken, 2003), and neither Syria nor Israel could be considered once loyal to Ahaz or Judah. The demand not to label conspiracy "*all* [or *everything*] that this people calls conspiracy" suggests that not a single event is in view, but a range of suspicions and rumors rife among the people (Barthel, 1997), all of which are considered at odds with trust in the Lord.

A significant feature not evident in translation is that, while the prophet begins by reporting the Lord's warning "not to walk in the way of this people" (v. 11), the words he recounts are addressed to a group: "None of you must call conspiracy all that this people calls conspiracy, and none of you must fear what it fears, or be in dread; but the Lord of hosts, him you all shall regard as holy; let him be your shared fear, and let him be your common dread" (my translation). These verses apply the prophet's message to all who differentiate themselves from "this people" by correctly evaluating events, recognizing that the Lord can impose true fear and terror, and who find in events evidence of the Lord's actions (Barthel, 1997; de Jong, 2007).[21] This is likely the same audience that 8:1–2 anticipate will receive the prophet's testimony and those the prophet describes as preserving his teaching in v. 16 (Barthel, 1997; Beuken, 2003).

Integral to this admonition is the claim that those who do not treat the Lord as holy will experience the danger he embodies, whether as threatening holiness or as a rock one stumbles over.[22] Noteworthy is against whom this danger is directed: "for both houses of Israel … for the inhabitants of Jerusalem." In contrast to the use of "this people" in vv. 6, 11, and 12 to designate Judeans (Beuken, 2003), v. 14 forecasts calamity for "*both* houses of Israel": northern and southern kingdoms. Such a declaration of calamity for both north and south likely assumes Judah's destruction by Babylon (Becker, 1997; de Jong, 2007).[23] In fact, in the context of chapter 8, this anticipation of destruction is noteworthy.

Chapter 8 vv. 1–4 presume a setting during the Syro-Ephraimite threat, and the details given about the witnesses and the mention of "the prophetess" give a sense of believability to the story. In particular, the names of the witnesses suggest high officials in Jerusalem, while the woman he calls "the prophetess" was likely among the female prophets serving in Jerusalem (Blenkinsopp, 2000).[24] Her involvement in the story seems parallel to those of the witnesses: as a prophetess in the Jerusalem palace or the temple, she would have been a public figure, so that her giving birth to the child could offer another mark of the veracity of Isaiah's claim to have forecast the fall of Syria and Israel through two acts involving "Maher-shalal-hash-baz" (Williamson, 2010). The inscribing of these words on a "large tablet" and the attaching of witnesses' names suggests this is a public announcement that not only verifies Isaiah as their source, but also attests that he predicted Assyria's plunder of these two states (Barthel, 1997).

However, the order of the narration is peculiar. Even if one accepts that Isaiah was instructed (in 8:3) to name the child with the same phrase he inscribed on a large tablet (8:1), that phrase is explained only with the naming of the child, even though the inscription would have required a similar explanation. The report of Isaiah creating a public record of his words in the face of the Syro-Ephraimite crisis was, curiously, placed first, out of logical order, probably because it provided an apt introduction to a passage that culminates in him entrusting his teaching to his disciples, using as a metaphor terms for creating a document: "bind" and "seal" (v. 16) (Carr, 2005).[25]

Reports related to the Syro-Ephraimite crisis (8:1–4) are quickly – and without any perceptible connection – followed by a forecast of calamity for Judah at the hands of the Assyrian army. It is in that context that the castigation of "this people" appears, while the statement that the LORD will prove a danger "for both houses of Israel" hints at a still-later perspective: one that can unite the fall of the north and the south, just as in 7:14. The parallels between chapters 7 and 8 reveal that they have been shaped to depict allied responses to the prophet's message: chapter 7 shows that the king is under the spell of Isaiah's words that are (according to chapter 6) destined to engender stubbornness, and chapter 8 shows the people having fallen under the same spell (Blenkinsopp, 2000).

In this light, we can return to chapter 6's disdainful references to "this people" as those whom Isaiah's words prevent from hearing and seeing (6:9–10). This passage, similar to chapters 7 and 8, is placed in a specific historical context: "the year that King Uzziah died" (around 740 BCE), prior to the Syro-Ephraimite crisis.

The prophet describes seeing the LORD, in royal robes, sitting on such a gigantic throne that only "the hem of his robe" was visible, and it "*filled* the temple" (v. 1). The description of being in the divine presence is enhanced by a report of winged creatures ("Seraphs") flying around the LORD, antiphonally proclaiming his glory. Once the prophet's mouth has been cleansed of impurity, he overhears the LORD's question "Whom shall I send, and who will go for us?" (v. 8), and volunteers his services. The scene is similar to 1 Kings 22:13–28, where the prophet Micaiah accounts for his prediction of disaster for King Ahab in battle – at variance with the chorus of prophets supporting the proposed campaign – by reporting a vision in which he sees the LORD seated on a throne, with all "the host of heaven" attending him. When the LORD asks, "Who will entice Ahab, so that he may go up and fall at Ramoth-gilead?", he receives a flurry of proposals from these attendants and commissions the one who proposes to be "a lying spirit in the mouth of all his prophets" (1 Kings 22:22).

Both Isaiah 6 and 1 Kings 22 assume the setting of the **divine council**, where deliberations are held and the divine king's decree is issued. It is such a scene that explains the question "Whom shall I send, and who will go for us?" (Isa 6:8), in response to which the prophet volunteers. And like the proposal to mislead King Ahab by prophets, the task given to Isaiah is to impose on his hearers a stubborn resistance to the right path. Accordingly, the purpose of this report is not to legitimize the prophet's authority or to characterize his message, but to account for the rejection of his words as having been decreed in advance (Barthel, 1997).

The significant difference between Isaiah 6 and 1 Kings 22 is that Isaiah is not a member of the divine council. His recognition that he, "a man of unclean lips" living "among a people of unclean lips," is imperiled by the divine presence is tailored to this scene. The cleansing of his lips is not preparation for speaking as a prophet (contrast Jer 1:9), but anticipates his speaking up in the divine council, where he, as a (garden variety) human, does not belong.

The culmination of this narrative is Isaiah's commission, with its peculiar consignment of "this people" to hard-heartedness (vv. 9–10). No other prophet is saddled with this prospect from the outset, prompting Isaiah to ask, "How long, O Lord?" (v. 11). As the ensuing verses show, this should not be understood as a question of how long Isaiah must work, but how long "this people" will remain under this spell. The answer is that their stubbornness will continue until it produces its full effect: until cities are devoid of inhabitants and "the land is utterly desolate," with everyone sent away (vv. 11–12). Just how extensive this emptying will be is clarified by v. 13's simile: just as one would destroy a stump left after the felling of a tree, so the LORD will destroy anyone still left in the land. In short, the prophet's word will have its full effect in the complete depopulation of the land.[26]

In keeping with this, those referred to as "this people" are clearly of the same stripe as those chapter 8 describes as having placed themselves in peril of judgment. In fact, both chapter 7 and chapter 8 play out the effects of Isaiah's commission, so that 6:1–8:18 present later reflection on Isaiah's work (Barthel, 1997; de Jong, 2007).

And yet, as integrated as chapter 6 seems to be, it bears marks of expansions. Verses 12–13b constitute a late expansion, since v. 12 switches from divine speech to third-person speech about the LORD's actions and introduces the notion of an exile, going beyond a devastation of the land (Barthel, 1997; Wildberger, 1991; Williamson, 1994).[27] The depopulation of the land reflects the events of 587 BCE.

Despite the similarities between chapters 7 and 8 and the way that both chapters flesh out Isaiah's commission to impose "deafness" and "blindness," the common use of "this people" in chapters 6 and 8, and their common formulation as first-person reports, lead to the conclusion that chapter 7 is the interloper – that it has been constructed using chapter 8 as a template and has been inserted in order to demonstrate the failure of the monarchy, alongside that of the people, even though chapter 6 speaks only of "this people" and does not single out the monarchy. But of course, as we have seen, chapter 7 seems also to be built upon a tradition that Isaiah uttered reassurances to Ahaz in the midst of the crisis. To this base have been added criticisms of the Davidic house as a whole for their failure of faith.

Throughout 6:1–8:18, then, we find narratives that show the marks of multiple contributors. The ostensible setting is the period of the Syro-Ephraimite crisis. And some of the oracles in chapters 7 and 8 probably reflect Isaiah's assurances to Ahaz in the midst of that crisis. However, these chapters also show signs of being stretched to address the Assyrian attack on Judah in 701 BCE, some 30 years after the crisis. Even more strikingly, there are indications of editing by someone aware of the fall of Jerusalem and the exile of its most prominent citizens in 587 BCE. Consequently, the composition of the whole narrative is more complex than the setting during the Syro-Ephraimite crisis suggests.

The Setting of 6:1–9:7 within the Book

We can learn more about this unit and its role in the book if we take brief note of two features of its context. First is the recurrent refrain "For all this his anger has not turned away, and his hand is stretched out still." Its five occurrences are curiously located. The first is in 5:25, just preceding chapter 6, while the remaining four appear in close sequence in 9:12, 17, 21, and 10:4. Since the first and second occurrences form a frame around 6:1–9:7 (the second concludes a unit that begins in 9:8), it is safe to assume that 8:19–9:7 had already been added as appendages to 6:1–8:18 before this frame was added. We need to consider their contents before we can explain why and how this section was composed.

Chapter 8 vv. 19–20 utter a curse on anyone who consults the dead for "teaching and instruction" rather than (implicitly) consulting the "teaching and instruction" Isaiah left with his disciples (8:16). The fate of those who do so will be frustration and futility: "They will turn their faces upward, or they will look to the earth, but will see only distress and darkness, the gloom of anguish; and they will be thrust into thick darkness" (8:21–22). It is in contrast to this that those in the northern reaches of Israel's former territory will find gloom replaced by the light of liberation (9:1–5). This theme is then wedded with an announcement of a new, upright king (9:6–7). The similarity of phrasing to 7:14, 16, and 8:3–4 suggests that this unit forms an epilogue that took shape in the late decades of the seventh century BCE, when Assyria's power began to wane and Judah came under the rule of Josiah, a ruler that 2 Kings 22–23 hail as unparalleled (Beuken, 2003; de Jong, 2007).

However, this epilogue also finds a tie with the words immediately before 6:1. When 8:22 says that if those seeking information from the dead "will look to the earth," they will see "only distress and darkness," it echoes 5:30's final clauses: "And if one look to the earth [NRSV: land] – only darkness and distress; and the light grows dark with clouds." This statement follows oddly on the description of an army on the march in 5:27–30a, but, paired with 8:22, it creates a set of brackets around 6:1–8:18 (Berges, 1998).

Returning to the repeated refrain about the LORD's outstretched arm, its first occurrence (5:25) stands just before the summons of the army and the description of it on the march (5:26–30a), constituting a cap to six laments (each introduced by "ah!") in 5:8–10, 11–17, 18–19, 20, 21, 22–25. Curiously, we find a seventh lament (introduced by "ah!") in 10:1–4a, culminating in the final reference to the LORD's outstretched arm in 10:4b.[28] Accordingly, the frame around 6:1–9:7 consists of seven laments (six before, one following) and the fivefold refrain (once before, four following), while 5:30 and 8:17 are inner brackets that speak of looking to the earth and finding only gloom and doom (Beuken, 2003).

Summary

The implication of these observations is that chapters 5–12 are composed of concentric rings emanating from 6:1–8:18, with the theme of darkness on the land (5:30, 8:22) forming brackets around it, its next outer layer being the fivefold refrain about the

Lord's outstretched arm (5:25; 9:12, 17, 21; 10:4), and the outermost bookends created by the series of seven laments (5:8–10, 11–17, 18–19, 20, 21, 22; 10:1–4) (Berges, 1998; Beuken, 2003). But of course, even 6:1–8:18 has its own set of concentric circles, since 6:1–13 and 8:1–18 are spoken by the prophet about his communication with the deity, while chapter 7 presents a story about the interactions between the prophet and the king. And yet, even that description is too simple, since 6:1–8:18 shows its own expansions that betray settings from the Syro-Ephraimite crisis, to the Assyrian assault of Jerusalem in 701, to the city's fall in 587.

Like all the other books we have studied, Isaiah provides no transparent access to the prophet's words. It is a literary work whose pieces have been fitted together and modified. While we have already seen that chapters 1–39 were shaped by scribal editors long after the prophet's era, the web of interrelations between his day and those who expanded the traditions will be revealed as even more complex in exploring chapters 40–66.

Notes

1. This narrative shows a close relationship with 2 Kings 18:13–20:19, just as Jeremiah 52 parallels 2 Kings 24:18–25:30.
2. The closest parallel in the minor prophets is Amos 1–2, although that collection serves the rhetorical purpose of portraying Israel as being as vulnerable to judgment as the surrounding nations.
3. This – rather than a supposed prejudice against prophets making predictions (Oswalt, 1998; Young, 1972) – is what makes the forecast of Cyrus as deliverer problematic. Neither do the book's silence about any author besides Isaiah nor the assertion of chapters 40–66 that the Lord foretold Cyrus's rise require one to "accept the evidence as given and adopt the conclusion" (Oswalt, 1998, 192; compare Vasholz, 1980). The Lord's claims to have forecast Cyrus's actions (such as 44:7) never specify when he made those forecasts. The frequent expansions of prophetic books by anonymous editors that we have witnessed debunk the assumption that everything in a book is from the prophet named at its beginning.
4. Oswalt (1986, 26) contends that this is not as unexampled as is claimed, since Ezekiel 37–48, Daniel 7–11, and Zechariah 8–13 do the same. The only real parallel here is Daniel 7–11, which claim to be visions that apply to an age much later than Daniel's (8:26; 12:4, 9). However, Daniel is apocalyptic literature, a genre that frequently claims to reveal events beyond the visionary's day. Ezekiel 37–48 envisions a new era and organization for Jerusalem, but does not address those living in that era. The same is true of Zechariah 8–13, which (as we have seen) presents its own problems.
5. This is offered as an objection to distinguishing between chapters 1–39 and 40–55 and 56–66 (Oswalt, 1998; Young, 1972). However, shared features in 1–39, 40–55, and 56–66 need not imply that they originate with one author.
6. "Thus says the Lord" (*nĕ 'um yhwh*) appears in 14:22, 23; 17:3, 6. However, this formula is distinct from the designation of an oracle as a *word* (*dabar*) that the Lord *spoke* (*dibber*).
7. Isa 1:2, 10, 20; 2:1; 7:10; 8:5; 9:8; 20:2; 21:17; 22:25; 25:8; 28:13, 14; 30:12; 31:2, 4; 37:22; 38:4; 39:5, 6.
8. The comparison of "the daughters of Moab" to "fluttering birds" in v. 2 is likely an expansion meant to characterize the helplessness of Moab's survivors (Wildberger, 1997).
9. Chapter 16 vv. 1–5, as a whole, lack a parallel in Jeremiah 48, which otherwise shows signs of having borrowed from Isaiah 15–16 (Beuken, 2007; Jenkins, 1989).

10. The earliest delineation of the "memoir" hypothesis was offered by Karl Budde in 1928, who called this unit a "book in the book" (Budde, 1928, p. v). However, already in 1922 Bernhard Duhm had identified 6:1–9:6 as a composition traceable to Isaiah, although without labeling it a "memoir" (Reventlow, 1987).

11. Both Budde and Duhm proposed these **emendations**, which became a staple of the "memoir" hypothesis (Reventlow, 1987).

12. The Hebrew phrase "they could not attack it" (*yakol* + *hillachem*), appears in Numbers 22:11, 1 Samuel 17:9, and Jeremiah 1:19, 15:20, with the sense "to prevail in battle." In Isaiah 7:1 the phrase likely refers to the failure of the assault.

13. This is not even to mention the number of times that laughter plays a role in the narratives surrounding the forecast of Isaac's birth (Gen 17:17; 18:12, 13, 15). The choice of a name due to its meaning is commonplace (compare Gen 25:26, 30; 29:32, 34).

14. The word translated "evil" can be used for something useless or displeasing (for example, Gen 41:20, 27 (NRSV: "*ugly* cows"); Jer 24:2, 3, 8 (NRSV: "*bad* figs")), while "good" can designate something pleasing or useful (Gen 2:9, 3:6 (NRSV: "good for food"); 2 Kings 2:19 (NRSV: "a good location")).

15. This surmise is supported by the awkward syntax of the Hebrew phrase introduced with *'et*, a word frequent in glosses (Fishbane, 1985).

16. This hypothesis has profound implications for understanding the historical Isaiah, since it suggests that he, like prophets throughout the ancient Near East, proclaimed oracles supporting the royal house (de Jong, 2007; Köckert, Becker, and Barthel, 2003; Williamson, 2004).

17. This translation differs from the NRSV, which says that they "melt in fear before Rezin and the son of Remaliah." This difference is rooted in the uncertain meaning of the Hebrew word *meśoś*. The NRSV extrapolates its translation by reading this as equivalent to *mesos* (a difference in which Hebrew "s" is read), in which case it would mean "a *melting* with Rezin and the son of Remaliah." However, it is also possible to read *meśoś* as "rejoicing" and, thus, "take delight" (Barthel, 1997).

18. Outside Isaiah, the phrase occurs most frequently in Jeremiah (31 times), Numbers (16 times), and Exodus (10 times), uniformly in contexts where the people are characterized as disloyal and stubborn (de Jong, 2007).

19. The terms of vv. 12–13 are carefully paired: "conspiracy … fear … dread," "regard as holy … fear … dread." While some have conjectured that v. 13 originally read "regard as a conspiracy" rather than "regard as holy" (a scribal change to avoid applying an objectionable notion to the deity) (Wildberger, 1991), it seems more likely that "regard as holy" (composed from the Hebrew letters *q-d-sh*) contrasts with "conspiracy" (*q-sh-r*) as a deliberate play on the forms of the words, given the strong visual similarity between the letters *d* and *r* in Hebrew.

20. Even if 7:2 reports that not only Ahaz was terrified, but also "the heart of his people shook" in the face of the threat, nowhere else in chapter 7 is "his people's" reaction to the threat mentioned.

21. While some have understood the people's cry of "conspiracy" as their characterization of Isaiah's own words (so de Jong, 2007), that identification is not clear from the text.

22. The translation "He will become a sanctuary" can spur a misperception, if it makes one think of a refuge. The Hebrew *miqdash* designates a holy site or holy items. Given that the phrase "and he shall become" introduces a chain of nouns that define the LORD as a menace, and given that holiness was regarded as a dangerous commodity in Israel (as in 6:5), most likely the point of this phrase is that those who refuse to acknowledge the LORD as holy will encounter his holiness as a harmful force (Barthel, 1997; Beuken, 2003).

23. Less likely is Wildberger's suggestion (1991, 360) that Isaiah explicitly places the two kingdoms together to deny Jerusalemites the right "to stand by as merely an observer of

the tragedy of the Northern Kingdom and stay untouched." This would deviate from the focus of this passage on the cultural and political winds within Jerusalem, over against which he posits the need to hold the correct attitude toward the LORD.

24. Isaiah's relationship to this "prophetess" is not explicitly stated, although most readers assume that she was his wife.

25. Williamson's argument (1994) that the language of 8:16–18 can only refer to a document demands that metaphors must be marked, when they seldom are.

26. The concluding statement of v. 13, "The holy seed is its stump," betrays itself as a scribal addition for two reasons (Barthel, 1997). First, it isolates the "stump" as a topic for comment, whereas it originally served as part of a simile (compare: "The Virginia defense sliced through the Georgia offense like a hot knife through butter; the knife is the linebacker"). Second, the notion that the stump constitutes "the holy seed" suggests that it has a positive function, which undercuts the reason the stump was used in the first part of the verse: to highlight the completeness of the destruction.

27. Barthel (1997) and Becker (1997) argue that the core is 6:1–8, to which vv. 9–13 were later added. However, it is difficult to find a satisfactory explanation for the existence of vv. 1–8 without vv. 9–11.

28. This series of woes plays out the meaning of the charge at the end of 5:1–7 that Israel has disappointed the LORD's expectation of righteousness, producing only bloodshed and cries of distress (Beuken, 2003).

12

The Book of Isaiah (Continued)

In the pages to come …

The previous chapter left several questions unanswered: (1) If chapters 40–55 were written long after Isaiah's day, why are they included in the book? (2) How are the **oracles** against Babylon in chapters 13–14 and the announcement of its fall in 21:9 related to allusions to Babylon's defeat in chapters 40–66? (3) What role do chapters 36–39, which closely parallel 2 Kings 18:13–20:19, play in the book? In answering these questions, we will also detect differences between chapters 40–55 and 56–66 revealing that these are separate units, each of which has its own compositional history.

The Reuse of Oracles in Isaiah 40–55

In studying the Twelve, we observed the reuse of phrases and sentences from other books. The book of Isaiah also contains examples of reuse, as in 43:8's description of Israel: "Bring forth the people who are blind, yet have eyes, who are deaf, yet have ears!" This is in effect a hyperlink to Isaiah 6:9: "And he said, Go and say to this people: 'Keep listening, but do not comprehend; keep looking, but do not understand.'" Indeed, 43:8 is comprehensible only if the reader knows 6:9 (Nurmela, 2006). This allusion is followed by a closely related one.

After v. 9 summons the nations to appear alongside this blind and deaf people for a contest over whose gods are real, v. 10 addresses the people: "You are my witnesses, says the LORD, and my servant whom I have chosen, so that you may know and believe me and understand that I am he." The curse of 6:9 is reversed: the people

Prophetic Literature: From Oracles to Books, First Edition. Ronald L. Troxel.
© 2012 Ronald L. Troxel. Published 2012 by Blackwell Publishing Ltd.

made deaf and blind there, so as to be deprived of comprehension, will now know, believe, and understand (Sommer, 1998).

Similar to this reversal of an earlier oracle is the way 43:16–21 relativizes an earlier tradition:

> Thus says the LORD, who makes a way in the sea, a path in the mighty waters, who brings out chariot and horse, army and warrior; they lie down, they cannot rise, they are extinguished, quenched like a wick: Do not remember the former things, or consider the things of old. I am about to do a new thing; now it springs forth, do you not perceive it? I will make a way in the wilderness and rivers in the desert. The wild animals will honor me, the jackals and the ostriches; for I give water in the wilderness, rivers in the desert, to give drink to my chosen people, the people whom I formed for myself so that they might declare my praise.

The lengthy identification of the LORD by alluding to his acts in the Exodus (leading the people through the sea and destroying Pharaoh's army) provides the backdrop for the fresh promise of "water in the wilderness, rivers in the desert," recalling the LORD's provision of water during the people's journey (Exod 17:3–6) (Fishbane, 1985). And yet, Isaiah 43 does not simply equate the new "way in the wilderness" with the Exodus, but admonishes addressees *not* to "remember the former things, or consider the things of old" (v. 18). This seems an odd admonition after vv. 16–17 brought to mind the LORD's past deeds, suggesting that the order to forget the LORD's earlier acts does not require erasing them from one's memory (Tull Willey, 1997). Rather, v. 18 exhorts the audience to expect deliverance that will supersede the legendary Exodus.

While these two examples use allusion to reverse or relativize earlier traditions, others reinforce and reapply earlier oracles, as in 51:4–5:

> Listen to me, my people, and give heed to me, my nation; *for instruction will go out from* me, and *my justice* for a light to the peoples. I will bring near my deliverance swiftly, my salvation has gone out and my arms *will judge the peoples;* the coastlands wait for me, and for my arm they hope. (my translation)

The words in italics echo the italicized words in Isaiah 2:3–4 (Nurmela, 2006; Sommer, 1998):

> 3: Many peoples shall come and say, "Come, let us go up to the mountain of the LORD, to the house of the God of Jacob; that he may teach us his ways and that we may walk in his paths." *For out of* Zion *shall go forth instruction,* and the word of the LORD from Jerusalem. 4: He *shall judge* between *the nations,* and shall arbitrate for many *peoples;* they shall beat their swords into plowshares, and their spears into pruning hooks; nation shall not lift up sword against nation, neither shall they learn war any more. (my translation)

The major modification in 51:4–5 is that the LORD himself, rather than Jerusalem, becomes the source of the teaching, teasing out what is implicit in chapter 2's stress on Jerusalem as the seat from which the LORD instructs the nations. The words of Isaiah 2 are given fresh life in 51:4–5.

The Complexities of Allusion

Allusion involves "the simultaneous activation of two texts": the text containing the allusion and the text to which it alludes (Ben-Porat, 1976, 107). However, the degree to which the source text must be recognized by the reader varies. The allusion in Isaiah 43:16–17 requires that the entire Exodus story be activated in the reader's mind to make sense of the contrast between the "former things" and the "new thing" the LORD is doing. On the other hand, a reader could understand Isaiah 51:4–5 without activating or even knowing Isaiah 2:3–4.

But how do we identify allusion? Beyond recognizing words common to two texts, we must consider how distinctive the shared words are, the number of words shared, the degree to which the text before us presumes knowledge of the other text (as in 43:16–21), and how many other clear allusions occur nearby. Criteria for identifying allusions must be precise if we want a useful picture of how the author worked (Nurmela, 2006; Schultz, 1999).

Even when there are solid grounds to detect an allusion, we are left with the question of who borrowed from whom, or if they drew on a common source (such as we concluded in Obadiah's parallels to Jeremiah 49). The primary consideration in determining the source is whether a phrase is better integrated into one passage than the other (Nurmela, 2006) or whether one passage assumes familiarity with the broader context of the other (Leonard, 2008).

The Author and his Audience

The reuse of earlier texts engages the audience by alluding to traditions they know and respect (Tull Willey, 1997). An example comes from Isaiah 43:10: "Before me no god was formed, nor shall there be any after me." Mesopotamian traditions spoke of the formation of the gods, both as ethereal beings and as concrete images (Goldingay, 2006a). The initial lines of the Babylonian myth entitled Enuma Elish describe the origins of the world by prompting the audience to imagine a time when the accustomed features of the world did not exist:

> When on high the heaven had not been named, Firm ground below had not been called by name, Naught but primordial Apsu, their begetter, (And) Mummu-Tiamat, she who bore them all .... Then it was that the gods were formed within them. (Pritchard, 1969, 60–61)

The LORD's denial that any gods were formed before him repudiates the Mesopotamian deities, while the extension "nor shall there be any after me" resonates with the LORD's assertion "I, the LORD, am first, and will be with the last" in 41:4. The author engages his audience by denying the validity of a claim with which they would have been familiar.

This author's engagement of his audience is equally evident in arguments he mounts against idols. Already 40:19–20 lampoons idols as wooden images vulnerable to rotting and needing support to stand upright (compare 44:9–20). In such passages we can sense the prophet seeking to undermine the attraction of the Babylonian deities.

The author also alludes to laments over Jerusalem written shortly after the city's fall that are preserved in the biblical book of Lamentations (Hillers, 1992; Westermann, 1994). The fact that allusions to these laments appear in Isaiah 40–55 means not only that this literature was known in Babylon, but also that the author was forced to join what amounted to a dialogue between the **exiles** and those left in Judah (Newsom, 1992). A prime example is the reuse of Lamentations 4:15 in Isaiah 52:11:

> "Depart! Unclean!" people shouted at them; "Depart! Depart! Do not touch!" So they became fugitives and wanderers; it was said among the nations, "They shall stay here no longer."[1] (Lam 4:15)

> Depart, depart, go out from there! Touch no unclean thing; go out from the midst of it, purify yourselves, you who carry the vessels of the LORD. (Isa 52:11)

Lamentations 4:15's call to depart is directed to the prophets and priests that v. 13 described as having "shed the blood of the righteous in the midst of her" and v. 14 described as having "wandered through the streets, so defiled with blood that no one was able to touch their garments" (Westermann, 1994). Isaiah 52, by contrast, calls on the exiles to escape contamination from their surroundings, without acknowledging that the sorts of priests and prophets that Lamentations 4:5 labels "unclean" would surely have been among them. By modifying the call for the unclean to depart into a call to depart without touching any unclean thing, the author locates uncleanness in something other than the exiles, thereby rehabilitating their image (Newsom, 1992).

Such a rehabilitation is equally evident in the next verse's reuse of language about Israel's exodus from Egypt: "For you shall not go out *in haste*, and you shall not go in flight; for the LORD will go before you, and the God of Israel will be your rear guard" (Isa 52:12; my italics). The phrase translated "in haste" appears in only two other places (my translations):

> Thus shall you eat [the Passover]: with your loins girded, your sandals on your feet, and your staff in your hand; and you shall eat it *in haste*. (Exod 12:11)

> You shall not eat anything leavened with it. Seven days you shall eat with it unleavened bread (the bread of affliction), for *in haste* you escaped the land of Egypt. (Deut 16:3a)

This allusion, via "in haste," simultaneously links the returning exiles with those who entered Israel's land after the Exodus but accents the superiority of their return by asserting that their departure will *not* be in haste.

There are other ways that Isaiah 52 subtly reuses language from the Exodus story to describe the returning exiles. Verse 12's statement that "the LORD will go before you, and the God of Israel will be your rear guard" alludes to Exodus 14:19, and v. 11's address of those who "carry the vessels of the Lord" recalls Exodus 12:35's report that the Hebrews took from Egypt "jewelry of silver and gold" (McKenzie, 1967). By these allusions, also, the author casts the returning exiles as equivalent to the Israelites of yore.

This is not to say that he never criticizes the exiles. Isaiah 40:27 chides them for despairing of their God's attention: "Why do you say, O Jacob, and speak, O Israel, 'My way is hidden from the Lord, and my right is disregarded by my God'?" The complaint itself is characteristic of laments protesting one's plight, as in Psalm 44:24: "Why do you hide your face? Why do you forget our affliction and oppression?" (Westermann, 1969). Isaiah 40:27 rejects such complaints as unacceptable.

To address this lament, 40:28–31 uses a hymn of praise similar to those found in Psalms:

> The Lord is the everlasting God, the Creator of the ends of the earth. He does not faint or grow weary; his understanding is unsearchable. He gives power to the faint, and strengthens the powerless. Even youths will faint and be weary, and the young will fall exhausted; but those who wait for the Lord shall renew their strength, they shall mount up with wings like eagles, they shall run and not be weary, they shall walk and not faint.

The author's use of a hymn likely familiar to the audience counters laments the exiles had taken too deeply to heart (Westermann, 1969).[2]

Therefore, the author's reuse of traditions is not simply an artistic flare, but a centerpiece of his argument. He engages his audience through traditions they already know. But how broad were the traditions he used and what sort of work did he create by using them?

The Literary Character of Isaiah 40–55

In this brief span of 16 chapters, scholars have identified allusions to Genesis, Exodus, Numbers, Deuteronomy, Isaiah 1–39, Jeremiah, Ezekiel, Nahum, Zephaniah, Zechariah, Psalms, Proverbs, Job, Lamentations, Song of Songs, and Ruth (Nurmela, 2006; Sommer, 1998; Tull Willey, 1997). The most numerous allusions are to Isaiah 1–39 and to Psalms (Nurmela, 2006).[3]

Especially noteworthy is that the most commonly used divine title in chapters 1–39, "the Holy One of Israel" (occurring 12 times), appears 11 times in chapters 40–55 and twice more in chapters 56–66.[4] Given how sparsely this title appears outside Isaiah (2 Kings 19:22 (= Isa 37:23); Jer 50:29, 51:5; Ps 71:22, 78:41, 89:19), its concentration in this book is remarkable. At the same time, it is noteworthy that the themes associated with "the Holy One of Israel" differ in chapters 1–39 and 40–55. Whereas in chapters 1–39 "the Holy One of Israel" threatened Judah with destruction, in chapters 40–55 he promises return and restoration (Goldingay, 2006a).

Correlative to this shift are other features of chapters 40–55 that distinguish them from 1–39, such as their multiple allusions to the Exodus, to which only 11:15–16 is comparable in chapters 1–39 (and that is an editorial expansion, as we shall see shortly). Equally significant is the way 55:3 displaces the Davidic dynasty by transferring to the people promises given to David (see p. 175). Also distinctive to these chapters are the 12 times the LORD is referred to as "Redeemer," a title that never appears in chapters 1–39.[5] Such features signal that the author did not pattern himself solely after Isaiah but placed himself within the broad stream of Israel's traditions (Blenkinsopp, 2001).

Just as distinctively, even though the author adopts the language of a prophet – calling the addressees to hear (42:18; 44:1; 46:3, 12; 47:8; 48:1) and challenging them to respond (41:22, 42:23, 43:9, 44:8) – he delivers his message in writing. Even though all the prophetic books are literature, chapters 40–55 show an especially strong literary coherence (Blenkinsopp, 2001). The impression given is that "the collection has deliberately eradicated any indicators of the process of growth ... as if we were intended to see only the final pattern of arrangement" (Melugin, 1976, 175). Its artful arrangement is especially clear in the way chapters 41–48 and 49–54 are distinct sections bound together by the bookends of chapters 40 and 55.

Characteristics in chapters 41–48 and 49–54 distinguish them from each other. The addressee in 41–48 is Jacob or Israel, also called "my servant." By contrast, in 49–54 addresses to Zion alternate with speeches about or spoken by the servant: 49:1–13 (servant), 49:14–50:3 (Zion), 50:4–11 (servant), 51:1–8 (addressed to a group), 51:9–52:12 (Zion), 52:13–53:12 (servant), 54:1–7 (Zion) (Tull Willey, 1997).

Just as strikingly, only chapters 41–48 refer to the Persian ruler Cyrus, whether by name (44:28; 45:1, 13) or indirectly (for instance, 41:2–3, 25). Correspondingly, the summons of 48:20, "Go out from Babylon, flee from Chaldea," is the final reference to Babylon in the book, and the berating of idols and their makers likewise ceases after chapter 48.

These features that distinguish chapters 41–48 from 49–54 are complemented by the way that chapters 40 and 55 form brackets around them. Chapter 40 shows familiarity with features unique to chapters 49–54. For example, 40:1–8 commission a messenger to proclaim comfort to Zion,[6] after which Zion is commissioned as a "herald of good tidings" to announce the LORD's approach to "the cities of Judah." This focus on Zion, which vanishes in chapters 41–48, reappears in chapters 49–54, where she is promised that her children will return (49:19–21; 54:1–3), that her waste places will be rebuilt (51:3), and that she will become an architectural gem, impervious to attack (54:11–17). There are also strong thematic links between chapter 40 and chapter 55: the motif of a journey back to the land in 40:3–5 is echoed in 55:12–13, and the emphasis on the endurance of the divine word in 40:8 resurfaces in 55:10–11 (Blenkinsopp, 2001).

The literary characteristics of chapters 40–55 signal that they are a carefully constructed work, rather than a haphazard repository for oracles.

The Servant of the LORD

Passages in chapters 40–55 that focus on the servant have spurred much discussion. In contrast to the servant's identification with Jacob/Israel in chapters 41–48, he is depicted as an individual in chapters 49–55, as is already evident in 49:1: "The LORD called me before I was born, while I was in my mother's womb he named me." Although the servant seems equated with Israel in v. 3 ("And he said to me, 'You are my servant, Israel ...'"), this identification becomes muddied in vv. 5–6:

And now the LORD says, who formed me in the womb to be his servant, to bring Jacob back to him, and that Israel might be gathered to him, for I am honored in the sight of the LORD, and my God has become my strength – he says, "It is too light a thing that you should be my servant to raise up the tribes of Jacob and to restore the survivors of Israel; I will give you as a light to the nations, that my salvation may reach to the end of the earth."

While the servant speaks of having had a mission to Israel, he claims that his mission has been "upgraded" to bringing salvation to the nations. How do we account for this abrupt change in the servant's role?

First, we must note that the language of 49:1–6 resembles Jeremiah's recollection of the LORD's commission to him: "Before I formed you in the womb I knew you, and before you were born I consecrated you; I appointed you a prophet to the nations" (Jer 1:5) (Blenkinsopp, 1997). Like Jeremiah, the servant speaks of his pre-birth selection and of being assigned a mission to the nations.[7] The servant of Isaiah 49 seems fashioned after Jeremiah.

The servant of 49:1–6 also shows similarities to and differences from 42:1–4, the first poem about the LORD's servant:

Here is my servant, whom I uphold, my chosen, in whom my soul delights; I have put my spirit upon him; he will bring forth justice to the nations. He will not cry or lift up his voice, or make it heard in the street; a bruised reed he will not break, and a dimly burning wick he will not quench; he will faithfully bring forth justice. He will not grow faint or be crushed until he has established justice in the earth; and the coastlands wait for his teaching.

The theme of the LORD's choice of the servant is clear, even if it is not traced to a prenatal stage. Despite the fact that this servant is not given a strong voice, his mission includes propagating "justice in the earth." However, in 49:1–6 the servant's mission to the nations is described as plan B, since his mission "to raise up the tribes of Jacob and to restore the survivors of Israel" has proved too trifling. Accordingly, while he bears the name Israel, he can be distinguished from it, as if Israel were merely an honorific title for him. As this observation suggests, the images of the servant in chapters 40–55 are not easy to correlate.

At the start of the twentieth century, Bernhard Duhm (1901) isolated four passages about the servant (42:1–4, 49:1–6, 50:4–9, 52:13–53:12) that, he suggested, existed independently as a unit before a **scribe** distributed them throughout Isaiah 40–55. Since Duhm's day, there has been much discussion about whether the servant is an individual or a group, whether he was the prophet of this book or someone else, and what his role was in events of the era.

However, the fact that the LORD's servant is mentioned many times outside these four passages (such as 41:8–9, 42:19, 43:10) makes it difficult to argue that the four passages Duhm isolated originated outside the book (Haran, 1963). Moreover, the first of these passages, 42:1–4, is well integrated with its context (Blenkinsopp, 2001; Goldingay, 2006a). Even if a reasonable argument can be mounted that 52:11–12 once formed the conclusion to the section begun in chapter 49, to which the servant passage of 52:13–53:12 and the final address to Zion (chapter 54) were later appended (Blenkinsopp, 2001), this is different from hypothesizing that all four passages were composed together and inserted late.

The identity of the servant remains enigmatic. Indeed, the association of the servant with a solitary figure in chapters 49–54 may be related to the other changes characteristic of these chapters (Blenkinsopp, 1997).[8] In the end, it seems best to read these passages within their individual contexts, especially since, whatever their origins,[9] they most likely stand in their current contexts because they fit well there (Beuken, 1972). The question of whether the servant imagery means to speak of a single character is less pertinent than understanding how each passage speaks of its servant.

The Character of Isaiah 56–66

The book's final 11 chapters have a different character than chapters 40–55. Already 56:8 hints that circumstances differ from those assumed in 40–55: "Thus says the Lord God, who gathers the outcasts of Israel, I will gather others to them besides those already gathered."[10] Rather than anticipating a return, this assumes that exiles *have* returned and promises more will do so.

Correlative to this, while chapters 40–55 situate Judah among the nations, chapters 56–66 focus on life in Judah (Blenkinsopp, 2003). For instance, although the Lord continues to be described as Israel's "Redeemer," his appearance in Zion will be for "those in Jacob who turn from transgression" (59:20) rather than Israel as a whole. The Lord's refusal to destroy all Israel because his "servants" within it are like the sweet wine in the grapes that must be preserved rather than thrown out with the fleshy part (65:8) places the division between good and evil within Israel (Beuken, 1990). Accordingly, it is the upright who will inhabit the land and prosper, while the wicked will be deprived of anything good (65:9–15).[11] This discrimination between the pious and the wicked within Israel appears already in 56:1–2, where the reassurance "soon my salvation will come, and my deliverance be revealed" is voiced only for the one "who keeps the sabbath, not profaning it, and refrains from doing any evil." These chapters draw a bright line between the wicked and the upright *within* Israel.

The definition of the pious in these chapters is related to ritual observance, a topic absent from chapters 40–55. Chapter 56 v. 2 promises a blessing for the one "who keeps the Sabbath, not profaning it," a standard emphasized again in vv. 4 and 6. Similarly, 58:13–14 makes faithful observance of the Sabbath a prerequisite for enjoying the Lord's benefits, while 66:23 foresees all humanity coming to Jerusalem to worship "from new moon to new moon, and from sabbath to sabbath." Chapter 1 v. 13 is the only previous mention of the Sabbath, where it, alongside the new moon festival, was identified as abominable in the Lord's sight. Chapters 40–55 never mention the Sabbath, although 47:13 derides the new moon festival as an occasion for practicing divination. Accordingly, the elevation of the Sabbath and the new moon observance in chapters 56–66 is unexpected.

Equally remarkable is the way these chapters treat temple life as a realistic prospect. Even though chapters 40–55 (especially 49–55) have much to say about Zion the city, they never refer to the temple mount (Beuken, 1986). By contrast, in chapters 56–66 "my holy mountain" is the destination of those returning (56:7, 66:20) and the inheritance of those who take refuge in the Lord (57:13), making "'the holy mountain' … the focus of all salvation" (Beuken, 1986, 51). Already chapter 56 seeks to still qualms among eunuchs and foreigners over whether they will find a place in the temple. Eunuchs who practice piety are promised "in my house and within my walls, a monument and a name better than sons and daughters" (56:5), while foreigners who do the same are promised admission to the temple, since "my house shall be called a house of prayer for all peoples" (56:7).

Fears among "Eunuchs" and "Foreigners"

Upon a first reading, the fears expressed by eunuchs and foreigners in 56:3–7 might seem paranoid. However, grounds for the fears are evident in Deuteronomy 23:1's exclusion of men with mutilated genitalia from "the assembly of the LORD," and Deuteronomy 23:3's barring of Ammonites and Moabites from that assembly illustrates why foreigners might fear exclusion. In fact, Nehemiah 13:1–3 reports an interpretation of Deuteronomy 23:3 as a basis for excluding all foreigners from the temple. Therefore, the promise that eunuchs and foreigners who keep the Sabbath and hold fast to the covenant would be assured a place within the temple doubtless addresses real fears among these groups as restoring temple life was contemplated.

Correspondingly, while chapters 40–55 say nothing of bringing offerings to the temple – except to charge that Israel failed to do so (43:22–24)[12] – the topic makes a robust comeback in chapter 66, where v. 20 compares foreigners' return of the exiles to offerings brought to the temple:

> They shall bring all your kindred from all the nations as an offering to the LORD, on horses, and in chariots, and in litters, and on mules, and on dromedaries, to my holy mountain Jerusalem, says the LORD, just as the Israelites bring a grain offering in a clean vessel to the house of the LORD.

This is the outcome of the LORD's promise to send messengers "to the coastlands far away that have not heard of my fame or seen my glory" (66:19), and shortly afterwards we read, "all flesh shall come to worship before me, says the LORD" (66:23).

These distinctive features do not mean that chapters 56–66 form a coherent whole, however. Above all, features in chapters 60–62 mark them as a distinct core in chapters 56–66 (Blenkinsopp, 2003; Smith, 1995; Steck, 1989).[13] First, terms characteristic of chapters 60–62 are absent from 56–59 and 63–66. For example, "the Holy One of Israel," favored throughout chapters 1–55, appears only in 60:9 and 14, while the word "praise" (*tehillah*), which occurs five times in chapters 40–55, appears again only in 60:6, 18; 61:3, 11; and 62:7, even though it might have been expected in 65:17–25 and 66:7–14 (Smith, 1995). Conversely, whereas the **messenger formula** appears elsewhere in chapters 56–66, it is absent from 60–62.

Alongside these distinctions between chapters 60–62 and the surrounding chapters stand thematic differences: (1) while 60–62 concern relations between the nations and Jerusalem, 56–59 and 63–66 address issues within the community; (2) while

56–59 and 63–66 distinguish between the upright and the wicked within the community, 60–62 view the community as a whole, much like 40–55; (3) 56–59 and 63–66 specify religious and moral prerequisites for people to enjoy the coming salvation, a theme absent from 60–62; (4) Zion is addressed in 60–62, whereas 56–59 and 63–66 address the people, groups, or individuals; (5) rhetorical questions figure prominently in 56–59 and 63–66, investing them with the tenor of a dispute, while 60–62 simply proclaim salvation (Smith, 1995; Steck, 1989).

Thus, we must consider chapters 60–62 separately from 56–59 and 63–66, beginning with some observations about their relationship to 40–55. First, despite similarities to chapters 40–55 (like "the Holy One of Israel"), it seems improbable that 60–62 come from the same author, given that they assume a different setting and develop images uniquely (Steck, 1989). For example, while the summons to Jerusalem to "rise up" (60:1) is the same command directed to her in 51:17 and 52:2, there her rising up was to shake off the effects of drinking from the cup of the LORD's wrath (51:17) or the dust from her captivity (52:2). Chapter 60 v. 1, by contrast, calls on a triumphant city to arise in recognition that she is bathed in light that will draw the nations to her (Steck, 1989).

On the other hand, 60:4–16 contains five allusions to 40–55 – "the highest concentration of references to one and the same writing in Isa 40–66" (Nurmela, 2006, 106) – while 62:10–12 contains three allusions to 40–55 (Nurmela, 2006).[14] These demonstrate that, for this author, "prophecy is the outcome of reflection on earlier prophecies, principally those contained in 40–55" (Blenkinsopp, 2003, 242).

While there are allusions to chapters 40–55 in 56–59 and 63–66, as well, they take a different tack in reusing passages, as shown by the following comparison of how 62:10–11 and 57:14–15 take up the theme of the highway running through the wilderness.

> Go through, go through the gates, prepare the way for the people; build up, build up the highway, clear it of stones, lift up an ensign over the peoples. (62:10)

Given the context of chapter 62, "the gates" through which the addressees are to proceed are those of Zion, and the stated purpose is to "prepare the way for the people" and raise "an ensign over the peoples." More importantly, 62:10 alludes to Isaiah 40:3–4:

> In the wilderness *prepare the way* of the LORD, make straight in the desert a *highway* for our God. Every valley shall be lifted up, and every mountain and hill be made low; the uneven ground shall become level, and the rough places a plain.

Whereas the call to "prepare a way" in 40:3 seems addressed to members of the **divine council** (Cross, 1953), in 62:10 it commands those in Jerusalem to clear a path for those yet in exile (Westermann, 1969). Consistently with this, what is to be prepared is "the way for *the people*," in contrast to 40:3's "way of *the* LORD."

In the wake of this call, 62:11 takes up language from 40:9–10:

> The LORD has proclaimed to the end of the earth: Say to daughter Zion, "*See, your* salvation *comes; his reward is with him, and his recompense before him*." (62:11)

> Say to the cities of Judah, "Here is your God!" See, the Lord GOD *comes* with might, and his arm rules for him; *his reward is with him, and his recompense before him.* (40:9–10)

By contrast, when we turn to 57:14, its similarity to 40:3–4 remains clear, but it seems more directly dependent on 62:10:

> And one said,[15] "*Build up, build up,* prepare the way, *remove* every obstruction from my people's way." (57:14)

While both 62:10 and 57:14 share with 40:3 the summons "prepare the way," only the former two verses use the double command "build up, build up" and have in common the Hebrew verb that the NRSV translates "lift up" in 62:10 and "remove" in 57:14. However, 57:15 plays out the image of a highway quite differently than either 40:3–4 or 62:10:

> For thus says the high and lofty one who inhabits eternity, whose name is Holy: I dwell in the high and holy place, and also with those who are contrite and humble in spirit, to revive the spirit of the humble, and to revive the heart of the contrite.

Whereas those to be summoned and given a clear path in 62:10 are, as in 40:3, exiles, those for whom "the way" is prepared in 57:14 are the "humble and contrite in spirit," who enjoy association with the one "whose name is Holy" and dwells "in the high and holy place." By the time this was written, the literal "way" from Babylon to Zion was well traversed and no longer a concern, so that now "The way" is changed into a metaphor for the association of the Holy One with the pious, so that "my people" no longer embraces all Israel (Blenkinsopp, 2003). Thus, even though 57:14 is similar to 40:3, its vocabulary is more directly indebted to 62:10, even though its highway is devoted to a more restricted group.

While chapters 60–62 are distinct within 56–66, chapters 56–59 and 63–66 are not a unified whole. For example, 57:14–21 does not smoothly continue 57:1–13. Not only does talk of the upright enjoying close association with "the high and lofty one" in vv. 14–15 diverge from the harangue of a group said to weary themselves with wickedness in vv. 3–13, but in vv. 16–19 the LORD promises that he "will not continually accuse" (v. 16) and speaks of his anger as past, offering healing and comfort for those who "kept turning back to their own ways" (v. 17). Even if v. 13b prepares for these verses by offering promises to "whoever takes refuge in me," the LORD's sudden resolve, in vv. 17–18, to cease haranguing the wicked, without any mention that they have repented, is surprising. Additionally, v. 19's proclamation implies that this promise encompasses a large group: "Peace, peace, to the far and the near." Consequently, v. 20's comparison of the wicked to "the tossing sea that cannot keep still" is as unexpected as was the sudden resolve of vv. 14–19. Verse 21 places a cap on the chapter with the statement "'There is no peace,' says my God, 'for the wicked.'" Verses 20–21 resume castigating the wicked (last seen in vv. 1–13) in a way that sets off vv. 14–19 as distinct from its context.

Such abrupt shifts in chapters 56–59 and 63–66 signal that these chapters are a collage of material from different authors that have been arranged so that themes recur, without producing a unified whole. Nevertheless, it has become apparent that 56:1–8 and chapters 65–66 have been composed by a single hand as a frame around this section of the book (Stromberg, 2011).

Both 56:7 and 66:19–20 speak of the return of exiles to "my holy mountain." The reassurance to foreigners that they will find a place in the temple in 56:6–7 is matched by the implication of 66:21 that foreigners will have a role in temple life. It is also these two sections of the book that emphasize keeping the Sabbath (56:2, 4, 6; 66:23) and both designate those obedient to the Lord as his "servants" (56:6; 65:8–9, 13–15; 66:14). Accordingly, however diverse are the materials in chapters 56–66, they seem to have been deliberately framed as a unit.

The Relationship of Chapters 40–66 to 1–39

Many scholars in the first half of the twentieth century viewed chapters 40–66 as a late appendage to 1–39, whether by accident or because some scribe perceived thematic connections between them and joined them. One such link between these sections that has long perplexed scholars is the way that Isaiah 35 contains themes found otherwise only in chapters 40–66. For instance, 35:6 forecasts that "waters shall break forth in the wilderness, and streams in the desert" (compare 43:20), following which v. 8 posits, "A highway shall be there, and it shall be called the Holy Way; the unclean shall not travel on it, but it shall be for God's people; no traveler, not even fools, shall go astray." Although the qualification of this as "the Holy Way" is reminiscent of 57:14's association of the highway with "the contrite and humble," it is not the moral character of travelers that is key (even "fools" can tread it) but the description of the way as "holy." Given that the destination of those who tread it is Zion, approaching it "with singing" (v. 10), the highway is a processional path to the temple (Blenkinsopp, 2000).

On first glance, we might suspect that this image of a highway has borrowed from chapters 40–55, pointing to similarities between 35:4 and 40:10 (my translations):

> Say to those panicked at heart, "Be strong, do not fear! Behold, your God will come with vengeance, with terrible recompense he will come and save you." (35:4)

> Say to the cities of Judah, "Behold your God!" Take note that the Lord God comes as a mighty man, with his arm executing his rule. Observe that his reward is with him, and his earnings before him. (40:10)

Both passages proclaim, "Behold your God," coupled with an announcement that the Lord will bring deliverance (Steck, 1985). Equally important, however, are differences: whereas 40:9–10 alerts Zion of the Lord's approach at that moment, 35:4 promises the despondent that he will arrive for vengeance and salvation in the future (Rendtorff, 1993). Moreover, some vocabulary in 35:4 is more at home in chapters 56–66 than 40–55. The word "vengeance" (*naqam*) in 35:4 appears in 47:3, but then again only in 59:17, 61:2, and 63:4, while the term with which it is paired, "recompense" (*gemul*), does not appear in chapters 40–55 but occurs in 59:18 and 66:6 (as well as 3:11). Thus, the terms used in 35:4 seem more at home in chapters 56–66 than 40–55 (Blenkinsopp, 2000). On the other hand, the phrase translated "those who are panicked at heart" in 35:4 occurs in only one other place in the Bible, Isaiah 32:4 (Steck, 1985). Accordingly, the author of chapter 35 utilized language found throughout the book.

For these and other reasons, chapter 35 – along with chapter 34, which also uses language closer to chapters 56–66 than 40–55 (Blenkinsopp, 2000) – seems to have been integrated into the book as a conclusion to 1–33 that, at the same time, provided a bridge to later material in the developing book. This conclusion, however, raises the question of the role of chapters 36–39, since they abut 40–55 more directly.

Chapters 36–39

While chapters 36–39 closely follow 2 Kings 18:13–20:19,[16] they also show differences. Although some of these are due to the different processes of editing each book after the story was incorporated (Person, 1999), others are more significant for the story's role in Isaiah. For example, whereas in 2 Kings 20:8 Hezekiah responds to Isaiah's promise of a full recovery by requesting a sign that the LORD would heal him, in Isaiah 38:5–8 the prophet transitions from the promise of full recovery to giving a sign, without mentioning that Hezekiah requested it (Ackroyd, 1987). And whereas in 2 Kings the grant of the sign is the final scene in the narrative, in Isaiah 38 that is followed by a prayer Hezekiah utters after recovering (38:9–20).[17] Also noticeable is that 2 Kings's report of Hezekiah suing for terms of peace when Sennacherib began devastating Judah (2 Kings 18:14–16) is absent from Isaiah 36, which moves from the report of Sennacherib seizing Judah's cities (v. 1) to his demand that Hezekiah capitulate (v. 2, parallel to 2 Kings 18:17). As a consequence, Isaiah 36 contains no suggestion that Hezekiah succumbed to fear of an assault.

The relationship between Isaiah 36–39 and its parallel passage in 2 Kings has been much debated.[18] The weight of the evidence favors the hypothesis that the narrative was composed independently of either Kings or Isaiah (its features differ from other narratives in 2 Kings, but also from other passages in Isaiah), after which it was used first in 2 Kings and then adapted from there for Isaiah 36–39 (Wildberger, 1997; Williamson, 1994). The more important question is to what use this narrative was put in the book of Isaiah (Beuken, 2000).

A common suggestion is that Isaiah's forecast that one day "all that is in your house … shall be carried to Babylon" provides a transition to chapters 40–55, set in the Babylonian exile (Smelik, 1986). However, the forecast of Judah succumbing to Babylon applies only to the royal house, without any intimation of Jerusalem's destruction (Beuken, 2003). In fact, it comports better with the events of 598, when Babylon stripped the temple of its wealth and deported the king and his house (2 Kings 24:12–16) (Clements, 1984). Given that there are no substantive links between chapters 36–39 and 40–55 (Williamson, 1994), the case for these chapters forming a deliberate link to the second part of the book is weak.[19]

These chapters do, however, have striking connections to 7:1–9:7. Both narratives are set near "the conduit of the upper pool on the highway to the Fuller's Field" (7:3, 36:2); both concern threats to Jerusalem, in the face of which Isaiah tells each king, "Do not fear" (7:4, 37:6); both involve signs given to the king (7:11, 14; 37:30; 38:7); and both promise deliverance from the immediate threat while also foreseeing calamity. Finally, chapter 9's heralding of an ideal ruler concludes with "The zeal of the LORD of hosts will do this" (9:7), a phrase that appears again only in 37:32, following the sign to Hezekiah (Ackroyd, 1987).

At the same time, these chapters offer striking contrasts in the response of the kings to the threats facing them. Whereas Ahaz refuses Isaiah's command to ask for a sign (7:11–12), Hezekiah simply accepts the sign Isaiah gives, after which he offers thanksgiving for healing (38:9–20). Whereas 7:1–3 highlight Ahaz's fear in the face of an inconsequential threat, 36:1–2 portray the Assyrian threat as real and significant, yet Hezekiah does not waver. Even when Hezekiah is told that in the future the palace treasures will be carted off and some of his descendants will be taken away to become "eunuchs in the palace of the king of Babylon," his response is "The word of the LORD that you have spoken is good" (Ackroyd, 1987).[20] The contrast between Hezekiah and Ahaz is pointed and was likely a reason these chapters were inserted.

11:11–16 as a Late Expansion

Editorial attempts to unify different parts of the book are evident long before we reach chapters 34–39. Chapter 11 vv. 11–16 describe the LORD repatriating his people via a "highway from Assyria" (v. 16), echoing themes in chapters 40–66. Verses 11–12 describe the LORD gathering "the remnant that is left of his people" from their places of exile, while vv. 13–14 promise a healing of strife between Ephraim and Judah, with the two joining to subdue the Philistines, Edom, Moab, and Ammon. These verses assume that Israel's survivors are scattered among the nations and that they must be reunited to resume rule of their land. Still more striking is how vv. 15–16 describe their return:

> And the LORD will utterly destroy[21] the tongue of the sea of Egypt; and will wave his hand over the River with his scorching wind; and will split it into seven channels, and make a way to cross on foot; so there shall be a highway from Assyria for the remnant that is left of his people, as there was for Israel when they came up from the land of Egypt.

The notion of "a highway" to return from Assyria, much as Israel was led from Egypt, recalls the theme of Exodus, which is found nowhere else in the first half of the book but is prominent in chapters 40–66, where the image of drying up the sea to provide a path for the people appears (42:15, 44:27, 50:2, 51:10). Moreover, the term for "highway" (*mesillah*) in 11:16 is the same as that used to describe a path for the people's return from exile in 40:3 and 49:11 (Williamson, 1994).

Viewed in this context, v. 12 acquires heightened importance: "He will raise a signal for the nations, and will assemble the outcasts of Israel, and gather the dispersed of Judah from the four corners of the earth." Similar language was used in 5:26's preparation for the description of a dread army on the march: "He will *raise a signal* for a nation far away, and whistle for a people at the ends of the earth." Chapter 11 v. 12's talk of raising a signal for the nations involves a change in tone from 5:26, since the raised signal now summons the exiles to return, rather than calling an army to attack.

Equally significantly, however, the language of raising a signal to the nations to repatriate the people finds a parallel in 49:22: "Thus says the Lord GOD: I will soon lift up my hand to the nations, and raise my signal to the peoples; and they shall bring your sons in their bosom, and your daughters shall be carried on their shoulders."

Given the other links with themes distinctive to chapters 40–66 (the Exodus motif, the highway), 11:11–16 was probably inspired by 49:22 (Wildberger, 1991; Williamson, 1994). Indeed, talk of gathering both "the outcasts of Israel" and "the dispersed of Judah from the four corners of the earth" (v. 12) implies that all of Israel has experienced exile and is now poised for restoration (Beuken, 2003).

Therefore, the entire book of Isaiah holds material incorporated in the final stages of editing. Even though it is a stretch to argue that the book is a carefully structured whole, its successive expansions took into account parts of the book that existed before them, thereby creating a network of links across the book (Berges, 1998, 48).

The Beginning and the End

An important question in the study of the book is the relationship between its first chapter and its final two, for some have found here an attempt to set bookends around the entire collection. The pertinent observations begin with 1:1, which is nearly identical with 2:1:

> The vision of Isaiah son of Amoz, which he saw concerning Judah and Jerusalem in the days of Uzziah, Jotham, Ahaz, and Hezekiah, kings of Judah. (1:1)

> The word that Isaiah son of Amoz saw concerning Judah and Jerusalem. (2:1)

Since it is less likely that a scribe would supply 2:1 if 1:1 was already in place, 2:1 probably existed before 1:1 became the book's **superscription** (Blenkinsopp, 2000),[22] once chapter 1 was supplied as the book's introduction (Carr, 2006; Williamson, 1997b).

In what sense, however, does chapter 1 introduce the book? It certainly does not foreshadow its major themes (Carr, 2006). In fact, some of the issues it raises never appear again, such as the futility of upper-class religion in 1:10–17. The most we can conclude is that chapter 1 calls for repentance in preparation for reading the book (Carr, 2006).

Nevertheless, already in the middle of the twentieth century scholars began noticing links between chapters 1 and 66 (for example, only in 1:13 and 66:23 are "new moon" and "Sabbath" paired) (Liebrich, 1956). Once bonds between chapters 65 and 66 were recognized, the perceived links between chapters 1 and 65–66 were expanded (Liebrich, 1957).

Isaiah 65–66

Bonds between chapters 65 and 66 are visible in their similar themes. Chapter 65 is a divine speech about a "rebellious people" (v. 2) who spurned the LORD's call, "sacrificing in gardens and offering incense on bricks," sitting "inside tombs," lodging overnight "in secret places," and eating "swine's flesh" (65:3–4). Talk of eating swine's flesh occurs again in 66:17, the only other place in the Bible that phrase appears (Smith, 1995). Equally uniting chapters 65 and 66 is the LORD's indictment of those he plans to punish for not having answered when he called, committing evil instead (65:1–2 and 66:4).

Recent scholarship has drawn back from such expansive claims, noting that allusions to chapters 65–66 do not pervade chapter 1, but are restricted to vv. 29–31 (Williamson, 2006). Note the comparable words in italics:

> 29: For you shall be ashamed of the oaks in which you delighted; and you shall blush for *the gardens that you have chosen*. 30: For you shall be like an oak whose leaf withers, and like *a garden* without water. 31: The strong shall become like tinder, and their work like a spark; they and their work shall *burn together*, with *no one to quench them*. (1:29–31)

> 2: I held out my hands all day long to a rebellious people .... 3: a people who provoke me to my face continually, sacrificing *in gardens* and offering incense on bricks .... 12: ... but you did what was evil in my sight, *and chose* what I did not delight in. (65:2–12)

> And they shall go out and look at the dead bodies of the people who have rebelled against me; for their worm shall not die, *their fire shall not be quenched*, and they shall be an abhorrence to all flesh. (66:24)

Talk of gardens as a site for worship and of punishment by fire that will not be quenched suggests a connection with chapters 65–66.[23] Correlatively, 1:29–31 differ from the bulk of chapter 1, inasmuch as they decree inevitable punishment for apostates, whereas the call for repentance earlier in the chapter presupposes a potential escape from judgment (Carr, 2006). Features that connect 1:29–31 with chapters 65–66 but also differentiate them from the rest of chapter 1 suggest that these verses were likely tacked on as an ad hoc link to the end of the book, but are not an indication that chapter 1 as a whole was composed to correspond to the closing chapters (Williamson, 2006). Thus, once more it seems appropriate to speak of the book as exhibiting sporadic internal links showing that scribes were interested in establishing connections between its parts but not in creating a unified book.

Summary

The observations in the previous chapter and this one lead to the conclusion that the book of Isaiah was fashioned over centuries rather than within the labors of a single prophet, and by many hands rather than a single one. The variety of compositional and editorial devices we saw in the Twelve – from recasting and expanding on prophetic oracles, to reuse of passages from other prophetic books, to insertions of later material – are not only evident in Isaiah but are more prominent, as they will be again in the two large prophetic books that remain: Jeremiah and Ezekiel.

Notes

1. I have modified the NRSV's translation to "depart!" from "away!" to reflect that the same verb stands here as in Isaiah 52:11.
2. Verse 31's promise of renewed strength to "mount up with wings like eagles" finds a parallel in the description of the LORD's beneficence in Psalm 103:5: "who satisfies you with good as long as you live, so that your youth is renewed like the eagle's." The fact that

we cannot match the words of 40:28–31 with a particular Psalm is not surprising, given what we have noted about Nahum 1 and Habakkuk 3.

3. Although Sommer (1998) and Tull-Willey (1997) claim that the author appealed to Jeremiah more frequently than Isaiah 1–39, their identification of allusions rests on too scant a relationship between the presumed allusion and its source. See the text box "Quotations, Allusions, and Echoes" in Chapter Six.

4. Also notable is 43:15: "I am the LORD, your Holy One, the Creator of Israel, your King," which parallels 10:17's "The light of Israel will become a fire, and his Holy One a flame" and 29:23's "they will sanctify the Holy One of Jacob, and will stand in awe of the God of Israel."

5. "Redeemer" (*go'el*) is a word rooted in family law, designating the closest kin, who is obliged to deliver a family member from debt or to rescue property in danger of falling out of family control (see Lev 25:25–26, 47–55; Ruth 2:20, 3:9) (Blenkinsopp, 2001).

6. Like the NRSV, I accept the reading of 1QIsaᵃ (the most complete copy of Isaiah found among the **Dead Sea Scrolls**) and the **LXX** as superior to that of the **MT** in 40:6, "And *I said*, 'What shall I cry?'"

7. While it is true that the motif of appointment in the womb appears in royal texts from Mesopotamia and Egypt (Goldingay, 2006b), the correlation of this with a twin mission to Israel and the nations makes this passage more similar to Jeremiah 1:4–8.

8. The oft-voiced suggestion that the solitary servant represents the prophet behind the book (so for example, Goldingay, 2006b) is difficult to verify (Blenkinsopp, 2001).

9. Most recently, Nurmela (2006, 140) has argued that the absence from the servant poems of any allusion to other biblical passages, together with the absence of any allusion to the servant poems by chapters 56–66, "indicates that the Servant Songs were incorporated in the book of Isaiah at a later stage." However, as he earlier concedes (pp. 82–83), the fact that these passages comprise only 31 verses of the whole provides slender evidence for this inference.

10. Compare, for instance, 43:5's promise "I will bring your offspring from the east, and from the west I will gather you." Throughout chapters 40–55 this "gathering" remains but a promise.

11. As Beuken (1990) notes, with chapters 56–66 we find no more descriptions of the servant, with the focus turning to the LORD's servants (plural) – although the first instance of this group of servants appears in 54:17.

12. Sommer (1998) rightly considers this a charge concerning the people's prior life in the land.

13. Smith's argument (1995) that 63:1–6 are included has been refuted by Blenkinsopp (2003).

14. Chapter 60 vv. 4 and 9 allude to Isaiah 43:6 and 49:22–23; 60:9 alludes to 51:5 and 55:5; 60:10 alludes to 54:8; and 60:16 alludes to 49:26 (Nurmela, 2006).

15. The ancient **manuscripts** and translations preserve different understandings of the verb at the start of 57:14. 1QIsaᵃ reads, "and they said," similar to the **Septuagint**'s "and they will say," which is also what we find in the Syriac translation, the Peshitta. The (Latin) Vulgate reads, "and I will say," a translation that assumes the same Hebrew consonants found in the MT (*w'mr*), although the MT'S vowels take this as an impersonal report, which the NRSV translates in the passive voice and the future tense: "It shall be said." However, given that this introduces an earlier oracle, the verb should be cast in the past tense (Blenkinsopp, 2003).

16. While Jeremiah 52 also has a parallel in 2 Kings (24:18–25:30), there are three distinctions between its use of 2 Kings and that in Isaiah 36–39. First, Jeremiah 51's concluding words, "Thus far are the words of Jeremiah," set a firm boundary before the narrative. Second, Jeremiah 52 forms a bookend with Jeremiah 1:3's report that Jeremiah spoke

"until the end of the eleventh year of King Zedekiah son of Josiah of Judah, until the captivity of Jerusalem in the fifth month." By contrast, Isaiah 36–39 stands in the midst of the book. And whereas Jeremiah never appears in Jeremiah 52, Isaiah is a key actor in chapters 36–39 (Ackroyd, 1987; Wildberger, 1997).

17. Both Isaiah's prescription of a poultice and Hezekiah's request for a sign are added to the end of chapter 38 (vv. 21–22), apparently by later editors who felt obliged to include the parallel material from 2 Kings (Person, 1999; Wildberger, 2002).

18. Five explanations are possible: (1) the narrative is original to 2 Kings, from which it was borrowed for Isaiah 36–39; (2) the narrative is original to Isaiah and was borrowed by 2 Kings; (3) both depend on a common source; (4) an independent narrative was first used by Isaiah, from which it was borrowed by 2 Kings; (5) an independent narrative was first used by 2 Kings, whence it was appropriated by Isaiah.

19. They can be said, however, to form a tacit bridge. Given that Hezekiah models pious acceptance of the divine will with regard to Babylon, chapters 36–39 imply a path that leads from the Jerusalem of Isaiah's day to the era of Babylonian dominance assumed in chapters 40–55 (Beuken, 2007; Blenkinsopp, 2000).

20. The NRSV's translation of the final clause with "For he thought, 'There will be peace and security in my days'" gives a cynical cast to these words, which could just as easily be a simple statement: "And he declared, 'There will be peace and faithfulness in my days'" (Beuken, 2007).

21. The NRSV follows the MT here, but a preferable reading is "will dry up" (*wehecheriyb* in place of *wehechriym*).

22. This is not universally accepted. Peter Ackroyd's suggestion (1963) that 2:1 was inserted by someone who recognized that 2:2–5 parallels Micah 4:1–3 has been adopted by many, while Becker (1997) proposed that 2:1 was added after 1:27–31 were inserted, breaking the natural connection between 1:21–26 and 2:2–5.

23. Gardens as a place of worship occur only in these passages, while punishment by unquenchable fire is found again only in 34:9–10, a chapter whose connections with chapters 40–66 we have already noticed.

13

The Book of Jeremiah

In the pages to come …

The book of Jeremiah offers a complex interweaving of poetic **oracles**, biographical narratives, and prose speeches. At times, the cross-references of dates and events throughout the book function like hypertexts, evincing the complex process of the book's composition as much as giving it structure. While one can use such hypertexts to construct a literary unity for the book, it proves just as intriguing to use them to study the processes that produced this 52-chapter compendium. This effort is aided in Jeremiah by evidence from the **Septuagint** and some **manuscripts** among the **Dead Sea Scrolls** showing that editorial expansions of the oracles and narratives crystallized in successive editions of the book.

The book of Jeremiah contains large blocks of oracles, much like Isaiah, but it also offers extended narratives about the prophet, as well as complaints voiced by the prophet about his task, including accusations that the Lord hoodwinked him into his mission. The detailed reports about Jeremiah's actions and his reflections on his mission seem to give us unusual access to the prophet. They leave the impression that we are witnessing the prophet's life and work unfold, beginning with his report of receiving a call to serve as a prophet, then seeing him endure opposition for words that were (reasonably) viewed as treasonous, watching him face the last days of the city, and finally seeing him spirited away to Egypt, where he continued speaking as a prophet. Particularly in its central chapters (36–45), this book seems to come closer to presenting a running biography of a prophet than any other book. And through that narrative it also appears to offer more information about a prophet's use of writing than any other prophetic book.

Prophetic Literature: From Oracles to Books, First Edition. Ronald L. Troxel.
© 2012 Ronald L. Troxel. Published 2012 by Blackwell Publishing Ltd.

The Writing of Prophecy in Jeremiah

As noted in Chapter One, in some cases writing served as a means of conveying the prophet's voice. This is clear in the letter Jeremiah reportedly sent to Babylon to address those exiled in 597 BCE, when Babylon's armies quelled a revolt begun under King Jehoiakim, carting off many of Jerusalem's citizens into **exile**. Jeremiah's letter counters reassurances voiced by prophets living among the exiles that they would all soon return to Jerusalem (29:1–23). And in response to a letter sent to Jerusalem by the prophet Shemaiah, urging temple officials to silence Jeremiah, he consigns Shemaiah's household to annihilation (29:24–32). This exchange of letters amounts to a long-distance duel between prophets, parallel to Jeremiah's face-to-face confrontation of the Jerusalemite prophet Hananiah (chapter 28), whom Jeremiah condemned to death for leading the people to expect a speedy end to the crisis with Babylon.

Chapter 51 vv. 59–64 report Jeremiah sending another document to Babylon, on a different topic. Jeremiah is told to record all his oracles against Babylon on a **scroll** and send them there in the hands of a member of King Zedekiah's court, Seraiah. After reciting these oracles aloud upon his arrival, Seraiah is to utter a reminder to the LORD that "you yourself threatened to destroy this place" (v. 62), then tie a stone around the scroll and throw it into the Euphrates, announcing, "Thus shall Babylon sink, to rise no more, because of the disasters that I am bringing on her" (v. 64). Although Seraiah serves as Jeremiah's substitute voice, the words and actions prescribed for him make his actions a **sign act** performed on Jeremiah's behalf and launched directly against Babylon.

Chapter 30 vv. 1–2 attest a different use of writing as a substitute for the prophet's voice: "The word that came to Jeremiah from the LORD: 'Thus says the LORD, the God of Israel: Write in a book all the words that I have spoken to you.'" In this case, the recorded oracles forecast a day when "I will restore the fortunes of my people, Israel and Judah … and I will bring them back to the land that I gave to their ancestors" (v. 3). The remainder of the passage – through the end of chapter 31 – speaks of calamity having already befallen the people (see 30:5–7, 12–14) and anticipates its reversal. In the same way that Isaiah 30:8 commands making a record of oracles "so that it may be for the time to come as a witness forever" (compare Isa 8:16–20), so Jeremiah 30 carries oracles that will be understood only in the future (v. 24). Here the issue of comprehensibility does not relate to understanding what forecasts of restoration means, for these expectations are no different than prophets like Hananiah uttered (28:10–11) or, for that matter, than what Jeremiah said would happen at the end of Babylon's rule (29:10). What seems in view in declaring that the written oracles would be intelligible only in the future (NRSV: "in the latter days") is the comprehension of the grand sweep of what the LORD will have accomplished in punishing Israel and then redeeming her. The written record of oracles, as an extension of the prophet's voice and presence, will facilitate that.

In chapter 36, Jeremiah is again instructed to "take a scroll and write on it all the words that I have spoken to you against Israel and Judah" (v. 2), in hopes that the people of Judah will listen and "turn from their evil ways, so that I may forgive their iniquity and their sin" (v. 3). Thus, Jeremiah dictates to Baruch, the **scribe**, "all the words of the LORD that he had spoken to him" during his 23 years of work (v. 4).

Barred from visiting the temple himself, Jeremiah instructs Baruch to read the scroll aloud to the crowds assembled for a fast at the temple. An official who hears Baruch's reading consults with palace officials and then summons Baruch to bring the scroll and read it to them. Disturbed at what they have heard, they decide to read the words to the king, but first instruct Baruch to go into hiding with Jeremiah. Before dismissing Baruch, however, they have him verify that the words of the scroll came from Jeremiah's mouth (vv. 17–18), much as Mesopotamian officials sent a lock of the prophet's hair, a fingernail, or the hem of his/her garment along with a written report of the prophet's words to certify their authenticity (Huffmon, 2000; Moran, 1969). At each step in this story, the emphasis is on the scroll as an extension of the prophet's voice,[1] just as in the other examples we have reviewed. There is no reason to conceive of this as the prophet beginning to assemble a prophetic book of the sort we think of.

Nevertheless, it is noteworthy that while Jeremiah 36 portrays King Jehoiakim burning the scroll in a stove placed beside his throne to warm him during the winter, the chapter ends with a report that Jeremiah dictated to Baruch a new scroll, containing "all the words of the scroll that King Jehoiakim of Judah had burned in the fire; and many similar words were added to them" (v. 32). To this degree, Jeremiah 36 explicitly acknowledges growth of a written collection of oracles by the addition of "many similar words."

Correlatively, the book's several **superscriptions** and the distinguishing features of its literary units attest to the book's growth by expansion and adaptation over a lengthy period of copying and editing. In order to perceive the book's development, we will begin with signs of its structure.

The Structure of Jeremiah

Throughout the book we find dates stipulated, some of which recur in significant ways. For instance, the book's superscription (1:1–3) unfolds in two stages:

> 1: The words of Jeremiah son of Hilkiah, of the priests who were in Anathoth in the land of Benjamin, 2: to whom the word of the LORD came in the days of King Josiah son of Amon of Judah, in the thirteenth year of his reign. 3: It came also in the days of King Jehoiakim son of Josiah of Judah, and until the end of the eleventh year of King Zedekiah son of Josiah of Judah, until the captivity of Jerusalem in the fifth month.

Verse 3's initial "It came also" stipulates that Jeremiah's work continued after Josiah's reign, into the reigns of Judah's final two kings. Most significant in v. 2 is the specification of the year the prophet first received oracles: "in the thirteenth year of his reign." Despite apparently designating the year in which Jeremiah began his work, it is phrased as if it introduces a limited period of prophetic activity, much like Amos's superscription places him "two years before the earthquake."[2] By contrast, v. 3's statement "And it came also in the days of King Jehoiakim …" designates his activity *throughout* the reigns of two kings. This awkward coordination with v. 2 suggests that v. 3 is a supplement to make the superscription encompass the entire span of Jeremiah's work.

Reference to the thirteenth year of Josiah appears again in 25:3, where Jeremiah recalls for his audience a lengthy period of work: "For twenty-three years, from the thirteenth year of King Josiah son of Amon of Judah, to this day, the word of the LORD has come to me, and I have spoken persistently to you, but you have not listened." The first verse of the chapter sets this address "in the fourth year of King Jehoiakim son of Josiah of Judah" (25:1) (equivalent to 605 BCE), the first of the two kings mentioned in the expansion to the book's superscription (1:3).

This "fourth year of King Jehoiakim son of Josiah of Judah" figures again in chapter 36, where Jeremiah dictates his record of the LORD's words "against Israel and Judah and all the nations, from the day I spoke to you, from the days of Josiah until today" (v. 2). The same date is given as the occasion of Jeremiah's assurance to Baruch that he will survive Jerusalem's destruction (chapter 45). Three times, then, the "fourth year of King Jehoiakim" appears as a pivotal date in the book, just as the thirteenth year of Josiah twice serves as a starting point.

Equally noteworthy is that, corresponding to 1:3 specifying Jeremiah's receipt of the LORD's word "until the captivity of Jerusalem," the book concludes with an account of the fall of Jerusalem and its aftermath in chapter 52, a passage taken over from 2 Kings 24:18–25:30.[3] However, the final verse of chapter 51 explicitly marks the boundary between Jeremiah's oracles and the narrative of Jerusalem's fall by specifying, "Thus far are the words of Jeremiah" (51:64). Accordingly, chapter 52 seems to be an addition meant to serve as a bookend, corresponding to the claim of 1:3 that Jeremiah spoke until the fall of Jerusalem.

However, the impression that the book follows a straight course from "the thirteenth year of King Josiah" to Jerusalem's fall to the Babylonians is betrayed by chapters 42–44, which report oracles Jeremiah delivered *following* Jerusalem's fall, first in the environs of Judah and then after he had been spirited away to Egypt by Judean refugees. The last we hear of him, he is inveighing against Judean exiles there for offering sacrifices to foreign gods (chapter 44). This spurs suspicion that the 40-year period from 627 ("the thirteenth year of King Josiah") to 587 BCE – the ideal 40-year time span within the Bible – reflects nothing more than an editor counting backwards 40 years from Jerusalem's fall to create this framework (Aejmelaeus, 2002; Carroll, 1986).[4] This suggestion is supported equally by the difficulty of identifying anything in the book that reflects circumstances in the time of Josiah (Carroll, 1986; Holladay, 1989), notwithstanding the fact that 3:6 dates an oracle to Josiah's reign (see McKane, 1986, 68–69). The series of linked historical references in 1:2–3, 25:1–3, 45:1, and chapter 52 appears an attempt to impose on the book a kind of idealized chronology.

The editorial arrangement of the book involves other types of marker, as well. Not surprisingly, we find frequent introductions to oracles like that in 2:1, "The word of the LORD came to me, saying," but also superscriptions of the sort found in 7:1, "The word that came to Jeremiah from the LORD." Unfortunately, however, in chapters 2–20 such superscriptions so often lack a date as to leave open-ended the setting of the oracles they introduce (Carroll, 1986).

Recognizable literary forms mark some passages as distinct literary units. For instance, 1:4–19 constitutes a **call narrative**, a first-person report of a dialogue between the prophet and the LORD during which the prophet is summoned and commissioned. Chapter 2 v. 1 leaves behind the call narrative but continues the style of first-person report ("The word of the LORD came to me"), introducing the first of many oracle series, in the course of which Jeremiah expresses dismay at the circumstances Jerusalem faces (4:19, 8:18–23) and speaks of the personal toll his message exacts (6:10–11).

More pointed and distinctive, however, are his so-called laments, in which he complains about the hardships that his call has entailed (11:18–12:6, 15:10–21, 17:12–18, 18:18–23, 20:7–18).[5] In the most poignant of these, he blames the LORD directly for imposing this task upon him (12:1–4, 15:15–18) and receives a divine reprimand in response (12:5–6, 15:19–21). Such complaints by a prophet about the hardships of his call are unique to Jeremiah,[6] and his laments form distinct literary units in the book.[7]

Following these laments, we find collections of oracles against the royal house (21:1–23:8) and the prophets (23:9–40), while chapter 24 relates a vision of two baskets of figs: one good, representing those already in exile (after 597 BCE), and one rotten, representing those left in the land, who are destined for "sword, famine, and pestilence" (v. 10).

Equally distinctive are chapters 30–31, introduced as a written record of "all the words that I have spoken to you" (v. 2). However, these are not predictions of calamity of the sort Jeremiah recalls in 25:3–7 and summarizes in the scroll of chapter 36. Rather, 30:5–31:22 concentrate on reversals of fortune for Jacob/Israel, names that here refer to exiles from the northern kingdom.[8] Beginning with 31:23 his attention turns to Judah's exiles, and from there through the end of the chapter both "the house of Israel and the house of Judah" are promised revitalization. What distinguishes these chapters from the rest of the book is their undiluted expectation of salvation for Israel and Judah, while viewing their punishment as already enacted.

While the following chapters contain hope, they lack the recognition underlying chapters 30–31 that Jerusalem has been destroyed. Even though chapter 32 narrates Jeremiah's purchase from a cousin of a tract of land as a sign that "fields and vineyards shall again be bought in this land" (v. 15), what lends this action poignancy is that the purchase is made in the face of the siege of Jerusalem and the expectation of its fall. Similarly, the forecasts of restoration in chapter 33 are dated to Jeremiah's confinement to "the court of the guard" (v. 1) and, thus, before Jerusalem's fall.

Chapters 34–39 contain a series of speeches Jeremiah delivers to the palace, condemnations of Judean society, the story of the scroll dictated to Baruch, and reports of how Jeremiah fared during Jerusalem's death throes. Chapter 40 commences a set of narratives about what happened after Jerusalem's fall, among the most prominent of which is the account of Gedaliah's assassination in 40:7–41:18 (in which Jeremiah plays no role) and the subsequent story of survivors consulting Jeremiah about their proposed flight to Egypt. Even though Jeremiah asserts that the LORD opposes such flight, they spirit Jeremiah into Egypt with them as a hostage, and the succeeding chapters narrate his interactions with them there (chapters 42–44). At the end of this narrative, in chapter 45, we are transported back to the fourth year of Jehoiakim (the same year specified in 25:1 and 36:1) for a brief address by Jeremiah to the scribe Baruch, promising that his life will be preserved after Jerusalem's fall.

The book's largest and most clearly defined set of oracles is its collection of oracles against the nations, introduced in 46:1 with "The word of the LORD that came to the prophet Jeremiah concerning the nations." Oracles are then leveled against Egypt (46) the Philistines (47), Moab (48), Ammon (49:1–6), Edom (49:7–22), Damascus (49:23–27), Kedar (49:28–33), Elam (49:34–39), and Babylon (50:1–51:58), following which stands the report of Jeremiah writing down his oracles against Babylon and having them cast into the Euphrates river in a sign act (51:59–64a).

After 51:64b remarks, "Thus far are the words of Jeremiah," chapter 52 provides the narrative of Jerusalem's defeat by Babylon and its aftermath.

There are, then, structural markers in the book, consisting of dates, superscriptions for units of diverse oracles, laments, narratives, and oracles addressed to specific groups. These markers hint at some sort of process of composing the book, without providing a clear understanding of how that happened.

The Composition of the Book: (Not) As Easy As A, B, C

The Classic Explanation

Early attempts to explain the book's composition differentiated between its types of material. At the dawn of the twentieth century, Bernhard Duhm (1901) identified a set of poetic oracles attributable to Jeremiah, a prose biography of the prophet, and a large body of supplements in a style of speech much like Deuteronomy. Extending Duhm's thesis, Sigmund Mowinckel (1914) gave these divisions their classical statement, labeling them A, B, and C, respectively. The oracles he attributed to Jeremiah (labeled "A") included more than Duhm had identified, since Mowinckel accepted additional poetic oracles – and even some cast as prose – into this group. He identified this collection with the record Jeremiah dictated to Baruch in chapter 36.

The series of biographical reports Duhm had segregated, Mowinckel labeled "B." He initially ascribed these to an anonymous admirer of Jeremiah, but later attributed them to Baruch (Mowinckel, 1946).

Very different, in Mowinckel's estimation, was the material he labeled "C": a set of lengthy prose speeches that interpreted and elaborated on Jeremiah's oracles (the "A" material). He detected in this set of materials the influence of language and ideas in Deuteronomy and the **Deuteronomistic History**.[9] In his estimation, these "prose sermons" were interpretations of the genuine Jeremiah tradition that were eventually blended with them, often constituting prose renditions of older poetic oracles (Mowinckel, 1946).[10]

Jeremiah's address to the people in 25:1–14 is a prime example of such a prose sermon. The address is dated to "the fourth year of King Jehoiakim son of Josiah of Judah," the same year to which chapter 36 dates the dictation to Baruch and in which chapter 45 places Jeremiah's assurances to Baruch. At the outset (25:3), Jeremiah looks back over 23 years of proclamation that began in the thirteenth year of Josiah (recall 1:2). In this year (605 BCE) Egyptian forces were defeated by the Babylonian army at Carchemish, far to the north of Israel, opening the way for them to launch their conquest of territories along the Mediterranean (Carroll, 1986), thereby making concrete Jeremiah's warnings about a foe coming from the north (4:6; 6:1, 22; 10:22) (Aejmelaeus, 2002). In this prose sermon, Jeremiah recalls the people's refusal to respond to his calls to turn from their evil deeds and their worship of other gods, leading to his proclamation of a verdict against Judah.

Despite the explicit dating of Jeremiah's sermon to the fourth year of Jehoiakim, there is reason to conclude that it is a reformulation of oracles found elsewhere, woven together with phrases and ideas common to the other prose sermons. For instance, the diction "I have spoken persistently to you, but you have not listened"

(25:3) appears again only in 7:13 and 35:14; the expression "persistently sent you all his servants the prophets" (25:4) recurs in 7:25, 35:15, and 44:4; the summons "turn now, every one of you, from your evil way" (25:5) appears again in 35:15; the suggestion that the LORD will permit them to "remain upon the land that the LORD has given to you and your ancestors from of old and forever" (25:5) is found in 7:7; the prohibition of going "after other gods" (25:6) occurs again in 7:6 and 35:15, while the charge of "going after other gods," followed by the phrase "to serve them," appears again in 11:10, 13:10, and 35:15; the claim that their misdeeds will result in harm to them (25:7) is found again (albeit in a mirror form) only in 7:5–7.

These phrases create obvious lines of connection between 25:1–7 and the prose sermons in chapter 7 and 35:13–15, the last of which is most likely the source of much of the language used in chapter 25. For example, whereas the LORD's claim to have repeatedly sent "all my servants the prophets" (35:14) fits the context of the complaint

---

Jeremiah's "Seventy Years"

While the Jeremiah's specification of "seventy years" (25:11–12) has been interpreted variously (see the survey in Carroll, 1986, 493–495), the key expectation is that, at the end of this period, the nation from the north will be punished.

"Seventy years" appears also in 29:10, which counters other prophets' assurances of a quick return to Judah with the caution, "Only when Babylon's seventy years are completed will I … fulfill to you my promise and bring you back to this place." The precise time designated by "seventy years" is again obscure, but the end of Babylon's "seventy years" is to be the occasion of Judah's return. In contrast to chapter 25, 70 years is a timeline not for the destruction of Judah's foe, but for its own restoration to its land. During the interim, the people are to treat Babylon as home:

> 5: Build houses and live in them; plant gardens and eat what they produce. 6: Take wives and have sons and daughters; take wives for your sons, and give your daughters in marriage, that they may bear sons and daughters; multiply there, and do not decrease. 7: But seek the welfare of the city where I have sent you into exile, and pray to the LORD on its behalf, for in its welfare you will find your welfare.

Even if prayer for the welfare of the city is a means to ensure their own well-being, it is difficult to square this command with a view of Babylon as ripe for judgment, such as we find in chapters 50–51. Those chapters charge Babylon with arrogance and wrongdoing and forecast that the LORD will punish it as a sign that "Israel and Judah have not been forsaken" (51:5), out of "vengeance for his temple" (51:11) and in repayment for "all the wrong that they have done in Zion" (51:24).[12] The notion that Jeremiah saw Babylon as the appointed means of judgment and the place of exile to which Judah's expatriates should be loyal is difficult to correlate with expectation of Babylon's fall as punishment for its evils (McKane, 1996).[13] Passages that speak of Babylon's punishment are best understood as late additions, embodying grudges against Babylon for destroying Jerusalem and Judah.

about the people's persistent refusal to repent in 35:15, Jeremiah's assertion that "the LORD persistently sent you all his servants the prophets" in 25:4 follows peculiarly on his own claim to have "spoken persistently to you" for the last 23 years. That is, there is no logical role for other prophets in the context of Jeremiah's complaint about the people's failure to hear *his* words, suggesting that the reference to "all his servants the prophets" has been imported from chapter 35 (Aejmelaeus, 2002).[11]

It is equally important to notice that while some phrases in 25:1–7 are characteristic of the book of Jeremiah as a whole (such as, "speaking/sending persistently" (7:13, 25; 11:7; 25:3, 4; 29:19; 32:33; 35:14–15; 44:4)),[14] others more nearly reflect language used in Deuteronomy and the Deuteronomistic History. The phrase "his servants/my servants, the prophets" (v. 4) is found outside Jeremiah (7:25, 26:5, 29:19, 35:15, 44:4) primarily in 2 Kings (9:7; 17:13, 23; 21:10; 24:2), where it is used to claim that the LORD has sent fair warning through the prophets.[15] Similarly, the phrase "the land (*'adamah*) which you/the LORD gave to us/to the ancestors" appears in Jeremiah 16:15, 24:10, 25:5, and 35:15, but elsewhere largely in Deuteronomistic literature (Deut 26:10, 15; 1 Kings 8:34, 40; 9:7; 2 Kings 21:8).[16] The expression "go after other gods" (v. 6), followed by the phrase "to serve them," appears outside Jeremiah 11:10, 13:10, and 35:15 only in Deuteronomy 28:14 and Judges 2:19. Likewise, the expression "to provoke him/me with the work of your/their hands," found in Jeremiah 25:6–7, 32:30, and 44:8, appears elsewhere only in Deuteronomy 31:29, 1 Kings 16:7, and 2 Kings 22:17 (based on which it appears also in 2 Chr 34:25). As a result, scholars have detected in the prose sermons ("C" material) a strong kinship with Deuteronomy and the Deuteronomistic History.[17] An analysis of these prose sermons reveals that 11 percent of their phraseology is indebted to Deuteronomy and the Deuteronomistic History (Stulman, 1986). Adding to these the 8 percent of phrases frequently considered akin to Deuteronomistic language (such as "speaking/sending persistently"), the total of phrases considered to give C a Deuteronomistic aura amounts to 19 percent (Stulman, 1986).[18]

A More Nuanced Accounting

Further study of the language in the biographical narratives ("B" material) confirms their distinction from the prose sermons ("C"), but in a more nuanced way than Mowinckel perceived. On the one hand, the phrases that composed 19 percent of the phraseology in the prose sermons constitute only 6.3 percent of the phraseology in B (the biographical narratives), reinforcing the distinction between them (Williams, 1993). If, however, we concentrate on the speeches that are *embedded* in B, recognizing that "many of the narratives provide nothing more than the historical framework for a prose sermon" (Nicholson, 1970, 36), the percentage of distinctive phrases rises to 12.3 percent (Williams, 1993). Although the contrast between 19 percent of this phrasing in the prose sermons (C) and 12.3 percent of it in the speeches found in the biographical materials (B) remains sufficient to maintain that B and C are distinct from each other, their use of some of the same phraseology suggests that they are more closely related than Mowinckel perceived. How are we to account for this relationship?

Mowinckel's hypothesis (1946) was that B contained narratives that Baruch wrote about Jeremiah and appended to the prophet's oracles ("A"), while C was an independent set of prose sermons that later editors wove into the book. However, even if chapter 32 has Jeremiah engage Baruch in posting a deed of purchase for his cousin's property, and even if Baruch is the scribe to whom Jeremiah dictates a summary of his oracles in chapter 36, these provide no foundation "for viewing him as a creative writer, biographer or lifelong companion" of Jeremiah (Carroll, 1986, 45).[19] Neither is there any reason to assume that B's narratives were composed in close association with A's oracles. More likely, materials in both B and C were composed as elaborations on earlier oracles. Sermons in C frequently inspired the composition of additional sermons, as we noted in attributing many of chapter 25's phrases to chapter 35, itself a prose sermon (Aejmelaeus, 2002). Moreover, language from one passage – whether in prose or poetry – could trigger an expansion within its own context or elsewhere, whether in prose or poetry (McKane, 1986; Parke-Taylor, 2000).

A useful example of these complex developments is the way 39:1–3 presents an abbreviated description of the Babylonian sack of Jerusalem, anticipating chapter 52's story (see text box). Verses 1–2 are a clear condensation of Jeremiah 52:4–7a (McKane, 1996), while v. 3 has no parallel in chapter 52.[20] The strong resonance of vv. 1–2 with 52:4–7a gains even greater significance from the fact that vv. 1–2 interrupt what appears to have been an original connection between 38:28 and 39:3.

Jeremiah 39	Jeremiah 52
1: In the ninth year of King Zedekiah of Judah, in the tenth month, King Nebuchadrezzar of Babylon and all his army came against Jerusalem and besieged it. When Jerusalem was taken, 2: … in the eleventh year of Zedekiah, in the fourth month, on the ninth day of the month, a breach was made in the city. 3: And all the officials of the king of Babylon came and sat in the middle gate: Nergal-sharezer, Samgar- nebo, Sarsechim the Rabsaris, Nergal-sharezer the Rabmag, with all the rest of the officials of the king of Babylon.	4: And in the ninth year of his reign, in the tenth month, on the tenth day of the month, King Nebuchadrezzar of Babylon came with all his army against Jerusalem, and they laid siege to it; they built siegeworks against it all around. 5: So the city was besieged until the eleventh year of King Zedekiah. 6: On the ninth day of the fourth month the famine became so severe in the city that there was no food for the people of the land. 7: Then a breach was made in the city wall ….

Chapter 38 reports that Jeremiah was confined to the court of the guard during the siege of Jerusalem, capped with the statement "And Jeremiah remained in the court of the guard until the day that Jerusalem was taken" (v. 28), which is followed in Hebrew by the phrase "When Jerusalem was taken." But this phrase leads awkwardly into the report of 39:1 that "In the ninth year of King Zedekiah of Judah, in the tenth month, King Nebuchadrezzar of Babylon and all his army came against Jerusalem and besieged it."[21] (This difficult connection from 38:28 to 39:1 is why the NRSV postpones translating "When Jerusalem was taken" from 38:28 until the start of 39:3, where it makes better sense: "When Jerusalem was taken, all the officials of the king of Babylon came and sat in the middle gate ….") Most likely, vv. 1–2 were inserted at an early stage in editing as a hypertext between "when Jerusalem was taken" and the fuller report in chapter 52 (McKane, 1996). This sort of "triggering" of an expansion accords with the way that chapter 36 already describes the second edition of Jeremiah's scroll as expanded from the first.

Editions of the Book of Jeremiah

Evidence in Black-and-White

The inference that the book grew through successive editions spawned by these sorts of "triggered" expansions finds remarkable support from a comparison of the **Masoretic text** (MT) to the Septuagint (LXX), along with manuscripts among the Dead Sea Scrolls. Whereas the oracles against the nations (similar to those in Isaiah 13–23) occupy chapters 46–51 in the MT, in the LXX they stand in 25:14–31:44, the middle of the book.[22] But tellingly, that position proves a better fit for them than at the end of the book,[23] supporting the conclusion that editors had transferred them to the end of the book before the manuscripts of the MT were copied (McKane, 1986).

Differences in arrangement appear also within individual passages, such as in 10:3–10, where the LXX not only lacks vv. 6–8 but also positions the last half of v. 5 toward the end of the passage (see text box).[24] Although at one time scholars conjectured that the translator condensed and rearranged the text as suited him (see the overview in McKane, 1986, 217), the discovery of a manuscript in a cave near the site called Qumran, situated on the shores of the Dead Sea, undercuts this explanation. Even though the scroll (4QJer[b]) is fragmentary, it provides evidence that it also lacked vv. 6–8 and positioned the halves of v. 5 exactly like the LXX (Tov, 1992b).[25] Meanwhile, comparison of the LXX's translation of Jeremiah 43:2–10 and another manuscript from a cave near Qumran (4QJer[d]) again shows that the LXX's differences with the MT are attributable to a Hebrew text that diverged significantly from the MT (Tov, 1992b).[26]

Jeremiah 10:3–10

MT[27]	LXX
3: For the customs of the peoples are vain: a tree from the forest is cut down – the work of an artisan's hands with an ax; 4: with silver and gold it is adorned; with hammer and nails they secure it, and it will not totter.	3: For the customs of the peoples are vain: a tree from the grove is cut down – the work of an artisan and a molten image; 4: with silver and gold it is adorned; with nails and hammers they secure it, and it will not move.
5a: [The idols] are like scarecrows in a cucumber field: they cannot speak;	5a: Crafted silver it is; they will not go.
5b: they must be carried, for they cannot walk. Do not be afraid of them, for they cannot do harm, nor is it in them to give a benefit.	[5b stands at the end of this passage]

6: There is none like you, O LORD; you are great, and your name is great in might. 7: Who would not fear you, O King of the nations? For that is your due; among all the wise ones of the nations and in all their kingdoms there is no one like you. 8: They are both stupid and foolish; the instruction given by idols is [no better than] wood!	[vv. 6–8 are absent from the Septuagint]
9: Hammered silver is brought from Tarshish and gold from Uphaz, the produce of a craftsman and the handiwork of a refiner; blue and purple is their clothing – the work of skilled laborers, all of them.	Overlaid silver will come from Tarshish, gold of Mophas and the hand(iwork) of goldsmiths – all of them works of craftsmen. With blue and purple will they clothe them. 5b: Raised up, they will be carried, because they will not move. Do not fear them, because they cannot do harm, and good is not in them.

At the same time, two other fragmentary manuscripts of Jeremiah found in the same cave (4QJer[a] and 4QJer[c]) align more closely with the MT, and one of them (4QJer[a]) contains scribal corrections that draw it even closer to the MT (Tov, 1992a). The Hebrew texts found in cave 4 at Qumran show, therefore, that the MT is an expanded and reorganized version of what is found in the LXX, 4QJer[b] and 4QJer[d] (Stulman, 1986).[28] In essence, these manuscripts, along with the LXX, provide evidence of two different and successive editions of Jeremiah.

The basis for classifying the MT as a new edition of the book (rather than a set of sporadic expansions) comes from the types of addition that characterize it, as can be illustrated from 25:1–13 (see the text box). Some additions make explicit what an editor apparently considered implicit in this passage (Tov, 1985), as when the MT identifies "that nation" as Babylon (also called, more properly, "the Chaldeans"), headed by King Nebuchadnezzar (vv. 9, 12).[29] This identification, while apt in the context of the book, resolves the ambiguity of references to "the north" or "the tribes from the north" found not only here in the LXX but throughout the book (see, for example, 1:13–15; 4:6; 6:1, 22). Similarly, the MT's novel correlation of "the fourth year of Jehoiakim" with "the first year of Nebuchadrezzar, king of Babylon" (v. 1) illustrates the scribe's tendency to supply information to synchronize the event with affairs in Babylon.

More striking are reformulations of phrasing. On the one hand, whereas in vv. 3–4 the voice speaking in the first person in the LXX is the LORD (note "*my* servants the prophets"), in the MT the "I" is just as clearly the prophet, who refers to "the word of the LORD" that had come to him (note also, "And *the* LORD persistently sent to you all *his* servants the prophets"). Even more remarkably, whereas v. 11 in the LXX

Jeremiah 25:1–13

MT[30]	LXX
1: The word that came to Jeremiah concerning all the people of Judah in the fourth year of Jehoiakim, son of Josiah, king of Judah *(that was the first year of Nebuchadrezzar, king of Babylon)*,	1: The word that came to Jeremiah concerning all the people of Judah, in the fourth year of Jehoiakim son of Josiah king of Judah,
2: which the prophet Jeremiah spoke to all the people of Judah and to all the inhabitants of Jerusalem, saying, 3: "Since the thirteenth year of Josiah son of Amon, king of Judah, to this day – these twenty-three years – *the word of the LORD has come to me*, and I have spoken to you persistently, but you have not listened.	2: which he spoke to all the people of Judah and to the inhabitants of Jerusalem, saying, 3: "In the thirteenth year of Josiah son of Amon, king of Judah, to this day – twenty-three years – I have spoken to you persistently
4: *And the LORD* persistently sent to you all *his* servants the prophets, but you did not listen or incline your ear to hear	4: and I persistently sent to you my servants the prophets, but you did not listen or pay attention with your ears
5: their words, "Turn, each of you, from his evil way and from your evil deeds, and dwell upon the land that the LORD gave to you and your ancestors from of old and forever.	5: their words, "Turn, each of you, from his evil way and from your evil deeds, and you shall dwell upon the land that I gave to you and your ancestors from of old and forever.
6: And do not go after other gods to serve them and worship them, and do not provoke me to anger with the work of your hands. Then I will not harm you." 7: Yet you did not listen to me, says the LORD, and so you have provoked me with the work of your hands to your harm.	6: Do not go after other gods to serve them and worship them, in order not to provoke me to anger with the works of your hands so as to do evil." 7: Yet you did not listen to me.
8: Therefore, thus says the LORD of hosts, because you did not obey my words,	8: Therefore, thus says the Lord, because you did not believe my words,
9: behold, I am going to send and take all the tribes of the north, says the LORD – specifically, *King Nebuchadrezzar of Babylon, my servant* – and I will bring them against this land and its inhabitants, and against all these nations around, and I will destroy them and make them an appalling sight and hissing and everlasting wastelands.	9: behold, I am going to send and take a tribe from the north and I will bring them against this land and its inhabitants, and against all the nations around it, and I will devastate them, and make them a destruction and a hissing and an everlasting reproach.

<table>
<tr><td>

10: And I will destroy from them the sound of joy and the sound of gladness, the sound of the bridegroom and the sound of the bride, the sound of the millstones and the light of the lamp. 11: All this land shall become a ruin and a waste, and these nations shall serve *the king of Babylon* seventy years. 12: Once seventy years are finished, I will punish *the king of Babylon* and that nation for their iniquity – *the land of the Chaldeans* – says the Lord, and I will make it everlasting desolations. 13: And I will bring upon that land all my words that I have spoken against it, everything written in this book, which Jeremiah prophesied against all the nations.

</td><td>

10: And I will destroy from them the sound of joy and the sound of gladness, the sound of the bridegroom and the sound of the bride, the odor of myrrh and the light of the lamp. 11: And the whole land shall become a destruction, and they shall serve among the nations seventy years. 12: Once seventy years are completed, I will avenge that nation, says the Lord, and I shall make them an everlasting destruction. 13: And I will bring upon that land all my words that I have spoken against it, everything written in this book.
14: The things that Jeremiah prophesied against the nations: The things against Elam:

</td></tr>
</table>

forecasts that "they [the people of Judah] will serve among the nations seventy years," the MT rephrases this as "*these nations* shall serve *the king of Babylon* seventy years."

Stepping back to the broad plane of the entire book, these sorts of expansions found in the MT make a substantial impact on the language of the book's prose sermons (C). While occasionally the MT carries an expansion that uses language from Deuteronomy or the Deuteronomistic History (such as "you have provoked me with the work of your hands," in v. 7), more typically its phrases number among those scholars consider akin to Deuteronomistic diction, such as "persistently speaking" in the MT of 7:25 or "persistently sending" in 35:15. If we look at all of the phrases considered to give the prose sermons their Deuteronomistic flavor, 55 percent of those already found in the edition presupposed by the LXX are directly indebted to Deuteronomy or the Deuteronomistic History (Stulman, 1986). On the other hand, if we look at phrases that the MT adds to the prose sermons, only 21 percent of such phraseology are of that character (Stulman, 1986). What this means is that from the earliest accessible edition, the prose sermons had a distinctly Deuteronomistic character, while the scribes who expanded the prose sermons by the time the MT circulated were not as focused on the diction of Deuteronomy and the Deuteronomistic History as those who created the sermons (Stulman, 1986).

The Earliest Editions: What Do We Know?

One implication of this analysis is that scribes had different agendas. And given this evidence, together with chapter 36's portrait of the earliest surviving collection of Jeremiah's oracles as already new and expanded, there is reason to suppose that the book grew through expansion. While we can recover principles that seem to have guided those who helped shape the edition preserved in the MT (thanks to accessing the edition witnessed by the LXX), we have few clues about the layers of editing that preceded the LXX, 4QJer[b], and 4QJer[d]. Nevertheless, some expansions are detectable already in the edition attested in the LXX.

To cite but one example, circumstantial evidence can be found in 10:1–16. First, v. 11, which is present in the LXX, is written in Aramaic (a language akin to Hebrew) and stands aloof from its context by its introduction (also in Aramaic), "Thus shall you say to them ...." The words to be uttered might be a curse on foreign gods: "May the gods who did not make the heavens and the earth perish from the earth and from under the heavens" (Carroll, 1986). At the same time, this distinctive Aramaic statement (the only one in the book) effectively summarizes vv. 12–16, and especially v. 15's forecast that the idols shall perish (McKane, 1986). Both the rare use of Aramaic and the summary character of the verse indicate that v. 11 was an early expansion.[31]

Looking more specifically at vv. 12–16, these describe the LORD in a hymn, with vv. 12–13 and 16 declaring his distinction as creator of the world, while vv. 14–15 contrast with him idols as delusions that will perish. Although Jeremiah 2:26–28 condemns Israel's worship of Baal and other Canaanite deities,[32] the denigration of idols in 10:14–15 stands closer to the sort of polemics we saw in Isaiah 40:18–20, 44:9–20, and 46:5–7 (Parke-Taylor, 2000).[33] The only other place this type of polemic occurs in Jeremiah is 51:15–19, where the words of 10:12–16 have been taken up in the oracles against Babylon (Carroll, 1986; Parke-Taylor, 2000). The recognition that this polemic is otherwise unique within the book supports a perception that 10:14–15 were composed during the Babylonian exile rather than during Jeremiah's activity in Judah (Carroll, 1986).

In fact, 10:3–16 as a whole seems to tease out the admonition of v. 2: "Thus says the LORD: Do not learn the way of the nations, or be dismayed at the signs of the heavens; for the nations are dismayed at them." The reference to "the signs of the heavens" that dismay the nations has to do with the practice of astrology (common in Mesopotamia) that Israel is to shun. The branding of the customs of the peoples as "vain" (NRSV: "false") at the outset of v. 3 is of a different order than the prohibition against adopting astrology, inasmuch as it evaluates the *effectiveness* of the nations' practices rather than their legitimacy. Because the word translated "vain" (*hebel*) is frequently used as a disparaging term for foreign deities (as in Jeremiah 14:22, "Can any one among the *vanities* [= idols] of the nations give rain?"), this became a springboard for an attack on Babylonian idols as delusions (McKane, 1986). Thus, there is justifiable suspicion that 10:1–16 as a whole was teased out from v. 2.

These hints of the processes involved in editing the book suggest that new editions of the book arose via expansions that reflected scribes' intuitions of the book's meanings. Recognizing that prophetic books were the products of many scribes, therefore, is to say that they were the products of many hearts and minds.

Summary

The editorial processes evident in Jeremiah are similar to what we saw in the book of Isaiah. First, embedded within the book are oracles reflecting and elaborating on traditions about Jeremiah's proclamations. Whether or not they represent a summary composed at the prophet's direction, they constitute the foundational layer of the book.

Second, multiple layers of expansion in the book prevent us from identifying each stage of its development, let alone isolating what composed its earliest edition. Indeed, the story of chapter 36 cautions against pursuing such a goal, for it imagines the earliest edition to have been lost. We are left with a book that sketches a prophet at work, in words often enough patterned after the diction of Deuteronomy and the Deuteronomistic History. Much like the book of Isaiah, the prophet himself is less important than the characterization of him and his words fashioned by the book's scribes.

Finally, like the book of Isaiah, Jeremiah straddles the defeat and suffering of 587 BCE, offers a diagnosis of what caused it, and looks to a brighter future, when Israel would be restored and its wounds healed.

A prominent feature of this panoramic view is an extended set of oracles against the foreign nations that, at the earliest stage of editing we can detect (reflected in the LXX), stood in the heart of the book, much as in Isaiah. Even if we find occasional accusations against foreign nations in the minor prophets (such as in Amos 1–2, Nahum 2–3, and Joel 3), only in the major prophets do we find a lengthy series of oracles compiled as a unit and placed in the interior of the book. That feature appears again in the book of Ezekiel, where we will find further evidence of editorial activity in the arrangement and expansion of a prophetic book.

Notes

1. Schaper's attempt (2009) to fit this story into the mold of legal enactment that he (aptly) identifies in Habakkuk 2:2 conflicts with the emphasis on the scroll as a replacement for the prophet's voice. It should be noted that the technical verb for enactment that figured in Habakkuk 2:2 (*ba'er*) does not occur here.
2. Compare the precise date in the **incipits** to the initial oracles in Haggai 1:1, Zechariah 1:1, and Ezekiel 1:1, introducing individual oracles.
3. While Isaiah 36–39 is also borrowed from 2 Kings, in that case the prophet of the book was an actor in the story, whereas Jeremiah is mentioned nowhere in this chapter (McKane, 1996).
4. Holladay's attempt (following Hyatt) to deal with this problem by identifying the thirteenth year of Josiah as the date of Jeremiah's birth (Holladay, 1989) has been rigorously disputed (McKane, 1986).
5. The demarcations of these laments are debated. The divisions cited are those of Jacques Vermeylen, reported by Bernard Gosse (1999), who notes additional proposals.
6. Jonah protests the LORD's compassion on the Ninevites, not the hardships of his call.
7. While his complaints are phrased similarly to the laments that we noted in Isaiah 40–55, they are even closer to – and have likely been shaped by – laments in the book of Psalms (Gosse, 2004).
8. Chapter 30 v. 17's designation of Zion as the one who has experienced plunder likely reflects an alteration of the earlier reading, attested in the Septuagint's "our plunder" (probably reading Hebrew *tseydenu* rather than *tsiyon*).
9. The following list is from Stulman (1986): 3:6–13; 7:1–8:3; 11:1–14; 16:1–15; 17:19–27; 18:1–12; 19:2b–9, 11b–13; 21:1–10; 22:1–5; 25:1–14; 27:1–22; 29:1–32; 32:1–44; 33:1–26; 34:1–22; 35:1–19; 39:15–18; 44:1–14; 45:1–5.
10. Subsequent to Mowinckel, these prose sermons came to be seen less as a literary work than as the product of preaching, whether to exiles who had returned to Judah (Janssen, 1956) or to those still living in exile (Nicholson, 1970).
11. This remains true even if 35:13–15 are secondary to their context (Knights, 1995).

12. Compare 25:8–14, which manifest a similar turn and are, likewise, late additions.

13. Although Isaiah 10:5–19 condemns Assyria for overstepping its mission, no such motif appears in Jeremiah.

14. Its only other occurrence is in 2 Chronicles 36:15, which is likely dependent on Jeremiah (Parke-Taylor, 2000).

15. As we have seen, it occurs in the editorial addition of Amos 3:7, with the same emphasis. It appears in Zechariah 1:6, within the editorial addition that binds Zechariah with Haggai (see above, p. 151). It is an editorial supplement in Ezekiel 38:17, while its occurrences in Ezra 9:11 and Daniel 9:6, 10, are influenced by its usage in Kings and Jeremiah.

16. It is embedded in Amos 9:15, part of the editorial supplement to the book. Its appearance in 2 Chronicles 6:25, 31, and 7:20 is due to Chronicles' reliance on Kings. Ezekiel 28:25 is a variation on this phrase but not a precise match. The use of *'adamah* for "land" marks this as Deuteronomistic language, although the same phrase, "the land which the LORD gave our ancestors," using the more common word for "land," *'erets*, appears throughout the **Torah** (Genesis and Exodus once each; Leviticus three times; Numbers and Deuteronomy six times each) and the rest of the Bible, including Jeremiah 7:7 and 30:3.

17. Arguments that this phraseology is simply characteristic of the vernacular of Jeremiah's day (Weippert, 1973) have not withstood scrutiny. Even if Weippert (1973) justifiably protests labeling C "Deuteronomistic," without further ado, the similarities in language justify the perception that those who fashioned these sermons were influenced by Deuteronomy and the Deuteronomistic History (McKane, 1986).

18. Although the majority of scholars acknowledge a difference in phraseology used by A and C, some have argued that the amount of distinctive phraseology in C is not sufficiently different from B to justify dividing them (Bright, 1966; Holladay, 1960; Nicholson, 1970), or even that there is no substantial distinction between material in A and C (Holladay, 1989).

19. The question is not whether there was a historical figure named Baruch (on which, see Dearman, 1990), but whether the reports about him – especially those in chapters 43 and 45 – reflect the interest of scribal editors (Brueggemann, 1994). Baruch's role in chapter 43 and the divine promise spoken to him in chapter 45 are editorial embellishments that effectively make him Jeremiah's constant companion (Carroll, 1986). Dearman (1990) refers to a well-known seal impression in clay (a *bulla*) that bears Baruch's name, but it and another like it have proved forgeries (van der Toorn, 2007).

20. Verses 4–13 are absent from the LXX and have been added from chapter 52 to harmonize chapter 39 with that longer narrative, as indicated especially by the attempt of v. 13 to restore the connection with the actors of v. 3 (McKane, 1996). Compare Tov's examples (1985, 235–236) of the editor resuming the original narrative by repetition of the final phrases before the inserted material, in this case the list of officials given at the end of v. 3.

21. This phrase is not in the LXX, likely because it was absent from the translator's Hebrew text, owing to the similar ending of the final two phrases in v. 28: "until the day that *Jerusalem was taken*. When *Jerusalem was taken* ..." (McKane, 1996).

22. Accordingly, the verse and chapter numbers differ significantly between the MT and the LXX through the rest of the book. The order of these oracles also differs, the most significant variance being that the oracles against Babylon stand last in the MT (chapters 50–51), whereas they stand third in the nine-oracle sequence in the Septuagint. The evidence points to the LXX's unorganized string of oracles "as original and the arrangement of them in the MT as a secondary development of the tradition" (Carroll, 1986, 759), the major effect of which is to place "the ritual dismissal of Babylon as the last word of Jeremiah" (757).

23. See the parallel text of the MT and the LXX on pp. 219–220. Verse 13 dangles in the MT, but provides an appropriate segue to the oracles against the nations in the LXX, where its

final phrase ("which Jeremiah prophesied against all the nations") serves as a superscription: "The things that Jeremiah prophesied against the nations" (Tov, 1985). This also makes sense of the assertion that "I will bring on that land ... everything written in this book," in which "that land" is the "nation" mentioned in v. 12 (McKane, 1986). Finally, talk of the "cup of the wine of wrath" that the LORD forces on the nations through Jeremiah (25:15–31 in the MT) forms an apt epilogue to these oracles in the LXX, whereas it finds no fitting context in the MT (Tov, 1985).

24. The differences between the LXX and the MT at the start of v. 5, which is part of v. 9 in the LXX, likely reflect a different way of reading the initial Hebrew phrase (Holladay, 1986), as well as the LXX's interpretation of the verb translated "they cannot speak" in the light of its meaning in Aramaic (McKane, 1986).

25. Verses 6–7, found only in the MT, are similar to the **liturgical** material we have previously seen inserted in prophetic books. Verse 8 turns from addressing the LORD to denigrating both those who worship idols and the idols themselves.

26. 4QJer[b] is not identical to the Hebrew text from which the LXX was translated, but it stands closer to the LXX than it does to the MT (Tov, 1985).

27. The translations of both the MT and the LXX are mine.

28. Even if the LXX's shorter version occasionally reflects an accidental omission of words, the majority of differences reflect the MT's expansions (McKane, 1986).

29. Verse 9's designation of Nebuchadrezzar as "my servant" is remarkable, but is found again in the MT at 27:6 and 43:10, although in neither of those passages does the phrase appear in the LXX. The discussion of this becomes dense in considering 27:6, since both "my servant" and "to serve him" are found in manuscripts of the LXX. Most likely, however, based on the absence of any representation of the word in Codex Sinaiticus, the earliest Greek translation lacked an equivalent for it, as in 43:10 and 25:9 (see McKane, 1996, 688–689).

30. The translations of both the MT and the LXX are mine.

31. Daniel 2:4b–7:28 and Ezra 4:8–6:18, 7:12–26, are the only lengthy compositions in Aramaic in the Bible. The only other individual verse in Aramaic is Genesis 31:47, commonly considered a late addition to that book (Westermann, 1985).

32. This is indicated by the reference to addresses to a tree (common symbols of the Canaanite fertility goddesses) and a stone (a typical representation of Canaanite gods).

33. Whereas Jeremiah 1:16, 25:6–7, 32:30, and 44:8 speak of "the works of your hands" as offenses against the LORD, none of them defines these in terms of crafted idols of the sort lampooned in 10:12–16 (McKane, 1986), while 1:16, 25:6–7, and 44:8 link these "works of your hands" with "other gods," language that Deuteronomy uses to refer to illicit Canaanite deities (as in Deut 6:14, 7:4) and shows up frequently in Jeremiah (such as Jer 7:9, 18; 11:10).

14

The Book of Ezekiel

In the pages to come …

The book of Ezekiel offers the prophet's own account of his activities and of the **oracles** he delivered to his fellow **exiles** in Babylon. However, the structure of the book, the character of its reports, the instances of borrowing from other books, and the obvious expansions of its text indicate that it is a literary construct rather than a memoir. This conclusion is supported not only by incongruities in the book that signal later additions, but also by black-and-white evidence from a comparison of the **MT** with the **Septuagint** that reveals phrases added to the Hebrew text after it had been translated into Greek. Even though these processes of growth are of the same sort we saw evidenced in Jeremiah, the way they are carried out make Ezekiel unique, as do the book's distinctive concerns and themes.

In studying Jonah, we noted that it is the only book whose prophet has a mission to a people outside of Israel and Judah. With Ezekiel, we find the only prophet whose mission to his people takes place entirely outside the borders of the land: in Babylon, where he lives among those taken into **exile** with King Jehoiachin in 597 BCE (2 Kings 24:15), following the failed revolt initiated by Jehoiachin's father, Jehoiakim.[1]

In a peculiar twist, however, Ezekiel does not remain in Babylon, since twice he visits Jerusalem in extended visionary experiences. The first is in chapters 8–11, when he visits the Jerusalem temple to see the abominations occurring there that occasion divine judgment, whose start he witnesses. The second visit is reported in chapters 40–48, where Ezekiel is whisked away to Jerusalem in a vision to be shown the layout of the new temple and the assignment of land parcels surrounding it to each of Israel's 12 tribes. In the course of this visionary tour, he also receives instructions for the

Prophetic Literature: From Oracles to Books, First Edition. Ronald L. Troxel.
© 2012 Ronald L. Troxel. Published 2012 by Blackwell Publishing Ltd.

Prophetic Literature

behavior of priests and the right ordering of life under the rule of a prince. The brief vision reports we read in Amos, Zechariah, Isaiah, and Jeremiah cannot hold a candle to Ezekiel's extended out-of-the-body tours of Jerusalem.

Equally distinctive is the way that every report in the book – whether of visions, oracles, or encounters with others – is given by Ezekiel himself. Occasionally punctuating these reports is a series of dates, the study of which will help us begin to understand the book's composition.

The Structure of the Book

The consistent casting of the book as first-person reports is key to the book's appearance of unity. This appearance is enhanced by a series of dates, in chronological order, embedded in superscriptions that appear at irregular intervals (see the chart). We saw this device used in Haggai, where dates supplied a temporal structure for a narrative in which the prophet was both a character and a speaker. Dates also appeared in Zechariah 1–8, whose three **superscriptions** (1:1, 1:7, 7:1) were supplied as a ploy to link those chapters closely with the book of Haggai.

Key Superscription Dates in Ezekiel						
Passage	1:1–2	8:1	20:1	24:1	33:21	40:1
Date	5th year, 4th month	6th year, 6th month	7th year, 5th month	9th year, 10th month	12th year, 10th month	25th year, 1st month
Contents	**Call narrative**	Visionary tour of Jerusalem	Elders consult Ezekiel	Siege of Jerusalem begins	Messenger: "Jerusalem has fallen"	Visionary tour of Jerusalem

Among these dates, those in 1:1–3 present the greatest conundrum, since they include an odd mix of features:

1: In the thirtieth year, in the fourth month, on the fifth day of the month, as I was among the exiles by the river Chebar, the heavens were opened, and I saw visions of God.
2: On the fifth day of the month (it was the fifth year of the exile of King Jehoiachin),
3: the word of the LORD came to the priest Ezekiel son of Buzi, in the land of the Chaldeans by the river Chebar; and the hand of the LORD was on him there.

First, the phrase "the thirtieth year" raises the obvious question "Thirtieth year from what date?" Rather than answer that question, v. 2 provides a different way of dating the oracle: the fifth year of "the exile of King Jehoiachin," the Judean king deported to Babylon in 597 BCE. Although Jehoiachin is mentioned nowhere else in the book, the subsequent date formulas appear calculated from the year of his exile, since they fall in a reasonable sequence with the date cited in the formula of 33:21, "In the twelfth year *of our exile*" (my italics).[2]

Equally peculiar is v. 2's omission of the year and the month, naming only the day of the month, an anomaly among the book's date formulas. More notably, v. 3 switches from the first-person report initiated in v. 1 to speak *about* the prophet, the only exception to the first-person format in the book (v. 4 resumes the first-person report: "As I looked …").[3] Because v. 2 provides the temporal setting for v. 3, the two verses must be taken together. Given that vv. 2–3 redefine the date of v. 1 ("the thirtieth year") in terms of Jehoiachin's exile, given that they adopt a third-person perspective, and given that v. 2 supplies a pedigree for the prophet, most likely these verses were added by an editor interested in modifying the book's superscription so that it would accord with the formula used in other prophetic books (Zimmerli, 1979).[4]

The date of 1:1 presents its own problems, inasmuch as "the thirtieth year," if viewed in the sequence of dates in the book, would fall beyond the last one mentioned ("the twenty-fifth year" of 40:1), even though chapters 1–3 report Ezekiel's call, at the outset of his work. None of the attempts to account for this date have convinced the majority of scholars, although among the most appealing is that Ezekiel received this call in his thirtieth year, the same year that those of priestly descent (as was he) were to begin their service, according to Numbers 4:30.[5] However one explains "the thirtieth year," the editorial addition of "the fifth year of the exile of King Jehoiachin" suggests that the sequential dates in 8:1, 20:1, 24:1, and 33:21 are central to the literary structure of the book.

Evidence of editorial arrangement, by the use of such dates, becomes prominent in the oracles against the nations in 25:1–32:32. As in Isaiah and Jeremiah, the oracles against the nations are grouped together. However, in contrast to the orderly sequence of dates elsewhere in Ezekiel, the dates in these oracles appear in disarray (see the chart). The dates of the eleventh year (26:1, 30:20, 31:1) fall in sequence after that given in 24:1 (ninth year, tenth month) and precede the twelfth year, tenth month cited by 33:21. However, the date in 29:1 precedes even the one given in 26:1, that in 32:1 falls after the date in 33:21, and that in 29:17 is later than the date cited in 40:1 (twenty-fifth year, first month). Given this hodgepodge of dates, it appears that this collection is arranged differently than the rest of the book, using geography as its organizing principle.

Oracles against the Foreign Nations (Ezekiel 25–32)

	Nation/city	Date
Chapter 25	Ammon, Moab, Edom, the Philistines	None specified
Chapters 26–28	Tyre and Sidon	11th year (no month given)
29:1–16	Egypt	10th year, 10th month
29:17–30:19	Egypt	27th year, 1st month
30:20–26	Egypt	11th year, 1st month
31:1–18	Egypt	11th year, 3rd month
32:1–16	Egypt	12th year, 12th month
32:17–32	Egypt	12th year, 1st month

What is more, there is good reason to conclude that an editor cleared space for these oracles through a contrivance.[6] Chapter 24 v. 1 dates the beginning of the Babylonian siege of Jerusalem to "the ninth year, in the tenth month, on the tenth day of the month," and vv. 2–14 mark that day with an oracle about the inevitable fall of the city. The LORD then advises the prophet that his wife is about to die and instructs him not to mourn or weep when she does (24:15–18). Asked by the people about his refusal to mourn, Ezekiel tells them that his actions should serve as an example of how they are to behave when Jerusalem falls (24:19–24). The concluding verses of the chapter alert Ezekiel that, after the city's fall, he will be visited by a refugee from Jerusalem, at which time "your mouth shall be opened to the one who has escaped, and you shall speak and no longer be silent" (24:27). The impression this leaves is that Ezekiel will fall silent until word of Jerusalem's end arrives. The refugee's arrival is reported in 33:21, which bears a date three years after the events of chapter 24. The implied imposition of silence seems not to materialize, however, for it is in the intervening chapters that we find the oracles against the nations (25:1–32:32).

The explanation for this curiosity involves recognizing that the report of Ezekiel's release from silence in 33:22 is of a different sort than is implied by 24:27. In 33:22 Ezekiel reports, "the hand of the LORD had been upon me the evening before the fugitive came; but he had opened my mouth by the time the fugitive came to me in the morning; so my mouth was opened, and I was no longer unable to speak." According to this statement, his speechless state lasted less than a day, starting only "the evening before the fugitive came." The tension created by 24:27's implication that Ezekiel would be silent in the years before the announcement of Jerusalem's fall is a byproduct of an editor's scheme to create space for a collection of oracles against the nations between the announcement of the start of Jerusalem's siege and the report of its fall. By merging the image of Ezekiel's silent mourning for his wife (24:16–17) with an anticipation of the report of Ezekiel's release from silence when the messenger arrived (33:21–22), the editor has created a bridge between chapter 24 and 33:21, across the intervening oracles (Zimmerli, 1979). However, the frame around those oracles does not fit the picture those oracles give, inasmuch as 24:27 leads us to expect that the prophet will be silent.

This is not, however, the first time Ezekiel is silenced. The LORD has already imposed silence on him in 3:26–27 (my translation):

> And your tongue I will make stick to the roof of your mouth, so that you will be mute and will not harangue them, for they are a rebellious house. But when I speak with you, I will open your mouth and you will say to them, "Thus says the Lord GOD!" As for the one who hears, let him hear, and the one who does not, let him not, for they are a rebellious house.

Not surprisingly, many have noted the relationship between this report and Ezekiel's statement that "the LORD opened my mouth" by the time a refugee arrived from Jerusalem (33:22) (see, for example, Greenberg, 1997). A peculiarity of 33:22, however, is that Ezekiel gives *two* reports of the LORD opening his mouth: "Now, the hand of the LORD was upon me in the evening, before the refugee came, *and he opened my mouth* by the time he came to me in the morning. *And he opened my mouth*, and I was no longer mute" (my translation). The repeated phrase "and he opened my mouth" likely introduces a **gloss**: "and I was no longer mute," bespeaking a decisive release from silence. This is suggested by the fact that the verb "be mute" was used in connection with the LORD's forecast that he would make Ezekiel's tongue cling to the roof of his mouth ("and you shall be mute [NRSV: speechless]," 3:26). Read in light of 3:26, 33:22 ends Ezekiel's tongue-tied life.

The only other occurrence in Ezekiel of the verb "be mute" is in 24:27, the forecast that Ezekiel will "speak and no longer be mute [NRSV: silent]." The use of this word evidences the work of scribal editors in both 24:27 and 33:22. We can trace the progression of editing as beginning with the addition of "and he opened my mouth and I was no longer silent" to 33:22, coordinating it with 3:26. Subsequently, the conclusion of chapter 24 was expanded with the forecast of the opening of Ezekiel's mouth when the refugee arrived, ending his silence. Even though this addition erroneously implied that Ezekiel would be silent in the intervening period, it cleared space for inserting the oracles against the nations.

The insertion of these oracles creates three major sections within the book: chapters 1–24, 25:1–33:21, and 33:22–48:35. The oracles form a buffer between the portrayal of Ezekiel's work before the siege of Jerusalem began and his labors after its fall. Although it would be inaccurate to say that oracles promising deliverance appear only after Jerusalem falls, only five of the 15 doing so appear before that point, and one of those (11:16–21) is a reassurance of the LORD's watch over those already in exile, spoken in the face of disparaging remarks about them made by those left in Judah.[7] More significantly, all of these oracles, no matter where they stand, assume that a full devastation of Jerusalem and its people has already taken place and speak of deliverance undertaken without demanding that the people repent to merit it (Raitt, 1977).

Not only do oracles of deliverance appear more frequently in the book's latter chapters, but the book culminates in a vision in which Ezekiel is shown the plan for a new temple, at the center of the 12 tribes of Israel. The LORD's presence in the temple, at the center of this ideal layout, will guarantee the holiness whose earlier loss brought about the destruction of the land and its people (Greenberg, 1984). Accordingly, both in the quantity of speech about a new day for Israel and in overall tenor, chapters 34–48 represent a new phase in the book, in contrast to chapters 1–24. The oracles against the nations mark the divide between the two.

Literary Prophecy in Ezekiel

This overview of the structure of the book already reveals its composition as literary prophecy. Further consideration of its features confirms this, helping us understand its character.

A Book Hard to Swallow

The report of Ezekiel's call is much more graphic than that of Jeremiah, and not just because Ezekiel's commissioning takes place after the LORD swoops from the sky, enthroned on an elaborate heavenly vehicle.[8] Jeremiah's call narrative began with the simple report "Now the word of the LORD came to me saying" (1:4) and featured the

Lord's declaration that he had placed his words in the prophet's mouth (1:9), with no requirement that the prophet do anything to make that so. By contrast, Ezekiel's receipt of the "word of the Lord" is bizarrely concrete and requires the prophet's cooperation.

After the Lord commissions Ezekiel to deliver oracles to rebellious Israel (2:3–4), his first command to the prophet is that he open his mouth to eat what he sees (2:8). Ezekiel reports seeing an outstretched hand holding a **scroll** unrolled to reveal two features (2:9–10). First, it is "written on the front and on the back." Although no **manuscripts** have survived from ancient Israel to show us whether writing on both sides was a common practice,[9] the report of King Jehoiakim slicing off and burning Baruch's scroll of Jeremiah's words after each section had been read (Jer 36:22–23) suggests that it was written on but one side.[10] Additionally, the specification in Ezekiel 2:10 that the scroll had writing on both sides suggests that this feature was remarkable (there would be no reason to report this if it were common).

This description of a scroll full of writing must be considered with the report that written on it were "lamentation and mourning and woe" (2:10). This is less likely a summary of the scroll's contents than of the effects its words will have, causing the people to lament, mourn, and bewail their fate (Zimmerli, 1979). Much as Jeremiah identifies legitimate prophecy with forecasts of doom (Jer 28:8), this summary characterizes Ezekiel's prophecy as forecasts of disaster that will bring about grief.

The most significant feature of the scene of Ezekiel swallowing a scroll is that it portrays the divine word given the prophet as a full advance script of what he is to say. After Ezekiel eats it, the Lord commands him to speak, in phrasing most accurately represented with "you shall speak to them, *using my words*" (3:4). In sum, Ezekiel's task is to be "the mouthpiece of a book" (van der Toorn, 2007, 228). And notably, whereas Isaiah and Jeremiah speak of creating summaries of some of their oracles, Ezekiel never mentions producing such a document.[11] The only text he speaks of is the one he ingests and is told to recite. Despite this scene forming the master image of Ezekiel's mode of operation, a look at the descriptions of his actions and words leaves a different impression.

First, the book is cast as Ezekiel's reports of interactions that determine and shape his speech on specific occasions. This, however, undermines the image that all his words were prescribed in advance. For instance, in 14:1 he reports the arrival of Israel's elders to consult with him, in response to which the Lord commands him to berate them for their practice of idolatry. In 20:1 he reports the elders arriving for another consultation, causing the Lord to order him to rebuff their request for an oracle. Even though the words Ezekiel speaks on these occasions accord with the dour character of the book he eats in chapter 3 (a book full of "lamentation and woe," 2:10), in each case he reports his words as the Lord's ad hoc response to an overture by the elders. While this is what we are accustomed to finding in prophetic books, it is a quite different notion than Ezekiel reciting a text he ingested at his call.

The spontaneous character of the prophet's utterances becomes apparent, also, in his accounts of being transported within a vision to another location to witness scenes that affect his message. The first of these occurs in chapters 8–11, opening with Ezekiel's report of having been grasped by "a lock of my head" (v. 3) and transported to Jerusalem to view abominations plaguing the temple. At intervals in the tour

Ezekiel is asked, "Have you seen this, Son of Man?" (8:12, 15, 17). Finally, at the conclusion of his tour, Ezekiel sees the "glory of the LORD" exit the temple and depart to the east of the city (11:22–23), in advance of which he is instructed to pronounce condemnation on a group of men he witnesses standing at the east gate of the temple (11:1–12). Again, the prophet describes himself interacting with what he sees during his tour rather than executing a script. For the reader, this interaction creates Ezekiel's prophecy.

The same is true in the famous vision of chapter 37, where Ezekiel is transported to a valley full of bones and instructed to prophesy to them, so that they assemble into bodies and, finally, are given breath. Only at the end does the LORD reveal the vision's significance by quoting the people's lament that their "*bones* have been dried up" (v. 11). Curiously, however, while that lament explains why the vision features bones (rather than, say, sticks), vv. 12–14 extrapolate from the images of resuscitated corpses to command Ezekiel to announce to the exiles that the LORD will restore them to life and return them to their land (vv. 12–14). The image of disjointed bones is left to the early stage of the vision, while the outcome of the vision – corpses brought to life – is the springboard for what Ezekiel is to say.

This vision certainly does not fit with the "lamentation and mourning and woe" (2:10) said to characterize the book Ezekiel swallowed. What is more, the vision and its interpretation give Ezekiel an expanded role in addressing the exiles: the LORD's word through him will be the vehicle for reviving them and restoring them to their land, just as it brought about the reassembly and reviving of the disjointed bones in the vision.

The book presents, then, two different images of the origins of the prophet's words. At the outset Ezekiel describes his utterances as a script delivered in advance. But as the book unfolds, he reports receiving the divine word in the same way other prophets do. An analogy might be an account of a sporting event in which the winning coach is said to have constructed a playbook that scripted every play to be used, even though the coach himself admits, in post-game interviews, that plays he called were thwarted by the opponent, forcing him and his staff to make adjustments to their strategies. Just as our experience with sporting events undercuts believing that a playbook can be written that needs only execution, so the notion of a script given the prophet at his call strikes us as artificial, especially when the prophet tells of his work in a way that suggests he addressed new situations under freshly given divine direction.

Accordingly, the fact that Ezekiel engages situations with ad hoc messages, just as we saw Isaiah and Jeremiah doing, marks his description of devouring a script for his prophecies as an artifice, but a significant one. It reflects knowledge that prophets' words have come to be collected in scrolls, suggesting that this book was composed in the era when literary prophecy had become the norm.

A Book of Fancy

The contrast between this image at the outset and Ezekiel's reports hints that his ingestion of a scroll is a fanciful scene that tells us more about how its authors and editors viewed prophetic books than about the work of a particular prophet. "Fanciful" is also an apt adjective to describe other features in the book.

For instance, in 4:4–5 the prophet is ordered to lie on his left side, bearing the guilt of the house of Israel for 390 days,[12] one day for each year of Israel's guilt. It does not take a medical degree to recognize that depicting a person lying on his side for this long is fanciful, but no less so than the notion that one could consume a scroll. Given that several such actions attributed to Ezekiel are "physically impossible" (Wilson, 1980, 283), we must reckon that this book does not always provide a straightforward description of the prophet, but rather frequently presents imaginative scenarios to describe him and his message.

In part this is accomplished by pressing to an extreme metaphors found in other prophetic books (Zimmerli, 1979).[13] For example, Ezekiel's report of eating a scroll containing the LORD's words is an imaginative expansion of the image of the LORD placing his words in Jeremiah's mouth (Jer 1:9), while his description that the book tasted "as sweet as honey" (Ezek 3:3) goes a step beyond Jeremiah's metaphorical exclamation "Your words were found, and I ate them, and your words became to me a joy and the delight of my heart" (Jer 15:16).

To cite another example, Isaiah described the Assyrian king as a razor that would shave "the head and the hair of the feet, and it will take off the beard as well," using this as a metaphor for the coming destruction of Judah (Isa 7:20). In a virtual parody, Ezekiel receives a command to cut off the hair of his head and beard with a razor, and then divide it into three equal amounts (Ezek 5:1–2). One third of it he is to "burn in the fire inside the city," while striking another third "with the sword all around the city" and casting the final third to the wind (5:2). Although on the surface this might seem conceivable as an actual **sign act** (despite the impression of insanity it would have left on the observer), the scene contains a hint that it does not report actual actions by the prophet. The LORD's abrupt vow to pursue with a sword the hairs that Ezekiel throws into the air (5:2) imparts the bizarre image of the LORD sending a sword after the hairs themselves. While this makes sense in v. 12's interpretation of Ezekiel's action (just as 37:11–14 makes concrete the imagery of 37:1–10), the LORD's chasing after actual hairs with a sword is a bizarre turn, even for this sign act. Accordingly, this scene as a whole is better understood as a metaphor,[14] very much at home in a book constructed of fanciful, symbolic scenarios.

A Book of Borrowed Phrases

Equally in accord with the book as literary prophecy is the way it uses language borrowed from elsewhere in biblical literature. Particularly prominent is its reuse of phrases from Leviticus 17–26, chapters dubbed "the Holiness Code" owing to their concern over how Israel as a whole can be holy. Certain phrases from those chapters show up unmistakably in Ezekiel, such as Leviticus 26:22: "I will send against you wild animals and they will bereave you and cut off your cattle and decimate you, and your roads will be desolate" (my translation). Similar wording is evident in two passages in Ezekiel. In Ezekiel 5:17a the LORD threatens, "*I will send against you* famine and *wild animals, and they will bereave you*" (my translation). Even more striking is Ezekiel 14:15: "If I cause *wild animals* to pass through the land *and bereave* it, and it shall become *desolate* for lack of anyone passing through, owing to the wild animals …" (my translation). In effect, Ezekiel 14:15 clarifies the meaning of Leviticus

26:22, explaining that the desolation of the roads has to do with an absence of travelers because of wild animals that ravage the land (Lyons, 2009).

Another way Ezekiel shows dependence on the Holiness Code is by transforming its commands into assurances. Notice the close parallels in wording between Leviticus 18:4 and Ezekiel 11:20 and 36:27 (my translations):

> My decrees you shall perform and my statutes you shall keep by walking in them. I am the Lord your God. (Lev 18:14)

> [I will give them a new heart] that in my statutes they might walk and my decrees they might keep and perform them. And they will be my people, and I will be their God. (Ezek 11:20)

> My spirit I will place among you and will make it so that in my statutes you shall walk, and my decrees you will keep and perform. (Ezek 36:27)

Whereas Leviticus *commands* the people to keep the Lord's "decrees and statutes," Ezekiel uses the same language to *promise* that the Lord will program that obedience into the people (Lyons, 2009).

Ezekiel shows faint similarities with language elsewhere in the **Torah**, but its most pronounced parallels are with Leviticus 17–26 (Zimmerli, 1979), and those are sufficiently precise and extended to suggest that the book of Ezekiel utilized what we call the Holiness Code of Leviticus 17–26 (Lyons, 2009).

Equally evident is the heavy reliance of chapters 38–39, the oracles against Gog, on passages from other biblical books. Rather than draw on Leviticus 17–26,[15] these chapters reflect language from a variety of biblical books, as well as other passages within Ezekiel (Tooman, 2010). Their author has created a verbal collage from texts that focus on "the vindication of Israel and the ultimate fate of the nations" so as to deal with an issue he apparently saw unresolved by the book to that point: "the restoration of the proper world order" (Tooman, 2010, 80–81).

Accordingly, while the book of Ezekiel has often been treated under the assumption that it is a personal report of oracles the prophet spoke to the people, its *literary* character is prominent and needs explication (Davis, 1989).

The Literary Characterization of the Prophet

Even allowing for the book's fanciful images, Ezekiel's behavior strikes us as outside the range of normal human psychology. In this he is hardly unique among the prophets. 2 Kings 9:11, Jeremiah 29:26, and Hosea 9:7 contain casual references to Israel's prophets as "madmen." In the first of these, a military officer named Jehu, speaking with his fellow officers, attempts to deflect their questions about a prophet's visit to him by saying, "You know the sort and how they babble" (2 Kings 9:11). Given that the prophet had just privately anointed Jehu the new king, effecting a *coup d'état*, one can understand his desire to throw his companions off track. Even though they persist until they uncover the truth, his attempt to derail their question with this disparaging remark suggests something about the reputation of prophets. The other two characterizations of prophets as mad (Jer 29:26; Hos 9:7) attest the same reputation.

One can comprehend the reputation of prophets as madmen from stories about Israel's first king, Saul. Shortly after being anointed king by the prophet Samuel, Saul falls into a wild frenzy when he meets a band of prophets descending from a shrine (1 Sam 10:5–6, 10). Later, as he chases David, an overwhelming force of prophetic power again reduces him to a frenzied state, in which he strips off his clothing, lying incapacitated for a day (1 Sam 19:23–24). In both cases, the question of those observing him is "Is Saul also among the prophets?" (1 Sam 10:11, 19:24).

Such reports tally with the eleventh-century Egyptian story of Wen-Amun, a courtier who, while visiting Phoenicia, witnessed a young man attached to the king of Byblos fall under divine possession and deliver an oracle (Pritchard, 1969, 25–29). Likewise, the letters from **Mari** attribute oracles to prophet figures who fell into similar trances. It is easy to understand how such behavior could brand prophets as psychologically aberrant, even though such behavior could, paradoxically, convince people that the prophet was more in touch with the divine world than with that of humans (Wilson, 1980).

In Ezekiel, such experiences are frequent and are often introduced with "the hand of the Lord fell upon me" (1:3; 3:14, 22; 8:1; 33:22; 37:1; 40:1). This language is not novel to Ezekiel, since 2 Kings 3:15–16 reports Elisha's request for a musician, whose music brought "the hand of the Lord" upon him, so that Elisha delivered an oracle (2 Kings 3:15–16).[16] Nevertheless, this language is especially prominent in Ezekiel.

At the end of Ezekiel's first vision, he reports that "the hand of the Lord" was "strong" upon him, lifting him up and bearing him away (3:14), after which he sat stunned for seven days (3:15).[17] In 8:1 he reports that "the hand of the Lord" fell upon him, so that he envisioned a heavenly spirit seizing him "by a lock of the head" and transporting him, in midair, to Jerusalem (8:3). There he was shown abominable scenes in the temple precincts, saw judgment unleashed against the city, and witnessed the divine glory exiting the temple and leaving Jerusalem. At the end he reports, "the spirit lifted me up and brought me in a vision by the spirit of God into Chaldea, to the exiles" (11:24). The vision of the valley of dry bones also begins with the report "The hand of the Lord came upon me, and he brought me out by the spirit of the Lord and set me down in the middle of a valley" (37:1).[18]

In biblical prophetic literature we find only one other apparent mention of a prophet being transported. In 1 Kings 18, a servant of King Ahab of Israel on reconnaissance mission encounters Elijah in a field, after he has been in hiding, eluding the king's search parties. Not surprisingly, then, when Elijah instructs the servant to inform his king that he wants to talk with him, the servant responds, "Suppose I depart from you – and in the meantime the spirit of the Lord transports you somewhere I don't know – and I go to tell the king. When he does not find you, he will kill me!" (1 Kings 18:12; my translation). While previously the Lord sent Elijah to the Wadi Cherith (17:3) and then to Zarephath, near Sidon (17:9), neither of those were accounts of him being transported in the way Ezekiel claims. The servant's complaint about Elijah being "spirited" away before the king arrives is likely sarcasm, emphasizing his fear that taking the prophet at his word could cost him his life (Sweeney, 2007b); he requires some sort of guarantee that Elijah will not leave before he returns. By contrast, the portrayal of Ezekiel's transportation by the spirit under "the hand of the Lord" has a distinctively surreal cast to it.

That surreal cast is marked by one other feature: Ezekiel reports not simply what he hears and sees in the visions, but also his participation in them. Thus, in 2:8–3:3 he not only sees a scroll, but eats it. In chapter 37, after a tour of the dry bones, he prophesies to them, so that they form bodies, and then he prophesies to the wind, causing it to enliven the bodies; Ezekiel is the agent of the action. Whereas other prophets witness extraordinary scenes (Isaiah sees the LORD enthroned in chapter 6), are recipients of divine action (Isaiah's lips are touched with a coal), or speak during the vision (as does Isaiah), Ezekiel does not merely respond to what he sees; his actions are integral to or even drive the vision (McKeating, 1994). This distinctive role for Ezekiel marks him as a prominent character in the book, albeit not its protagonist.

The Book's Real Protagonist

A prominent literary device helps seduce the reader to accept these surreal images as the prophet's actual experiences: Ezekiel himself narrates each scene. While such first-person reports appear in other books (such as Isaiah 6, Jeremiah 1), they do not dominate the books the way those in Ezekiel do. We are repeatedly invited to accept these as Ezekiel's reports of his own experiences. And because the reader's sympathies naturally lie with the narrator of a text, we readily assume that such first-person speech originated with the prophet. Nevertheless, "there is no necessary connection between a feature of literary style (autobiographical discourse) and a certitude of unblemished historicity" (McKane, 1996, 894). Just because a report is in the first person does not preclude the possibility that it is a literary device.

What is more, calling these reports "autobiographical" is somewhat inaccurate, since they are first-person accounts not of the prophet's life, but of isolated incidents (Odell, 2000). As such, they are analogous to other first-person inscriptions from the **ancient Near East** in which a prominent figure (typically a king) speaks of his exploits (whether military or building) in service of the deity.[19] Such inscriptions were composed by **scribes** on behalf of their ruler and follow the literary conventions for royal reports (Van Seters, 1997).[20] There is no evidence in the ancient Near East of anything akin to our "journaling" about a day's events. Since the only parallel to the first-person reports common in Ezekiel is this scribal literary convention, it is highly doubtful that these are reports by the prophet himself.

In fact, despite these elaborate reports, Ezekiel is not the book's central character; the LORD is, as two features underscore. The first is the phrase "son of man," the moniker by which the LORD addresses the prophet 93 times in this book. While the phrase "son of X" can mean the direct descendant of a person ("Ezekiel, son of Buzi," in 1:3), it can also be used to classify a person, as in Genesis 5:32's report that "Noah was a son of five hundred years," meaning that he was 500 years old. Likewise, when Amos objects, "I am not a prophet, nor am I a son of a prophet" (Am 7:14; my translation), he is not denying that his father was a prophet, but underscoring his denial that he is to be understood as a prophet, a member of the prophetic guild, so to speak.[21] Similarly, the LORD's persistent address of Ezekiel as "son of man" is tantamount to calling him "you human." Even if this label is not inherently derogatory, its point is to accent Ezekiel's subjugation to the LORD (Haag, 1975).

Another indication that the LORD is the central character is the phrase "you/they will know that I am the LORD," which, in each of its 54 occurrences, specifies what witnesses will infer when the LORD acts, whether in judgment or deliverance.[22] Rather than designating merely intellectual comprehension, however, this recognition will affect Israel's character. This becomes clear from the correlation between this acknowledgment and the people's recognition of their shame, as conveyed in a passage like 20:42–44 (my translation):

> And you will know that I am the LORD when I bring you to the land of Israel, to the land I swore with an oath to give to your ancestors. And you will remember there your ways and all your deeds by which you defiled yourselves, and you will despise yourselves because of all the evils that you performed. And you will know that I am the LORD, when I deal with you for the sake of my name – not according to your evil ways and your corrupt deeds, O house of Israel, says the Lord GOD.

The notion that the people's acknowledgment of the LORD will be accompanied by recognition of their despicable actions, leading to self-deprecation, is characteristic of this book. Such recognition will be possible only after the LORD has restored Israel from exile, but it will not be incidental to its restoration. Indeed, "both knowledge of God and knowledge of self are crucial in Ezekiel's vision of a new human moral identity" (Lapsley, 2000, 144). Israel's recognition of the LORD will entail recognition of their previous refusal to acknowledge him. Such acknowledgment is the goal of Ezekiel's work, even if it will occur only in the future.

Two instances of a similar phrase underscore this, inasmuch as in them it is not the LORD who will be recognized, but Ezekiel's role: "and they shall know that a prophet has been among them" (2:5, 33:33). According to 2:5, this is true whether or not they listen, while 33:33 asserts that they will draw this inference only after calamity has befallen them. Most striking is the way this phrase refers to Ezekiel while treating him as though he were anonymous. That is to say, it is far removed from something like "and they will know that *you* were a prophet." The person of Ezekiel is irrelevant to what the people are forecast as saying: "and they shall know that *a prophet* has been among them." And like their recognition of the LORD, this acknowledgment will take place belatedly. For the present, Ezekiel will be treated "like a singer of love songs, one who has a beautiful voice and plays well on an instrument," since they will listen to him with delight but not obey (32:32).

In a way more pronounced than in any other prophetic book, the prophet is a tool, as becomes especially clear in the peculiar statements of 3:25–27 (my translation):

> As for you, human: behold, they will place cords on you and bind you with them, so that you do not go out among them, while your tongue I will make stick to the roof of your mouth, so that you will be mute and will not harangue them,[23] for they are a rebellious house. But when I speak with you, I will open your mouth and you will say to them, "Thus says the Lord GOD!" As for the one who hears, let him hear, and the one who does not, let him not, for they are a rebellious house.

Both images involve figurative speech. The first figure is decoded for us as the prophet being restricted to his home, and since the "them" among whom he does not walk is the same group that places cords on him, this seems to imply curbs put upon him by fellow exiles. On the other hand, the restriction of his speech – which is what the sticking of his tongue to the roof of his mouth seems to depict – is imposed by the

LORD and lifted only when the LORD gives him an oracle to speak. Since his oracles are subject to rejection by the people ("whether they listen or not," in 2:5), these are likely the messages of approaching judgment that Ezekiel is to proclaim (Greenberg, 1983). The prophet is not free to "harangue" at will; he will speak only when the LORD gives him words, and the only assured outcome will be that, some day in the future, "they will know that a prophet has been among them."

Thus, even though the book's reports are consistently phrased in the first person, Ezekiel stands conspicuously in the background, compared with prophets like Hosea, Amos, Micah, Isaiah, and Jeremiah. Despite the impression given by the first-person reports that these are the prophet's eyewitness testimony, the prophet's own character is largely reduced to a character of the book, whose real protagonist is the LORD.

Evidence of Continued Editing

As in the other books we have studied, the book of Ezekiel cannot be attributed to a single author or editor. Evidence of ongoing editing is evident from two directions. First, we can detect expansions to individual passages. Second, as with Jeremiah, the Septuagint reveals that phrases and even whole passages in the MT have been added.

Earlier we noted the fanciful command that Ezekiel lie on his side for 390 days (4:4–5). As fantastic as that project is, the command that follows it adds an equally bizarre stage: "And when you have finished these [390 days], lie down a second time, on your right side, and bear the guilt of the house of Judah for forty days; a day for each year I assign you" (4:6; my translation). This command presents two problems, aside from the obvious physical challenge. First, when v. 9 orders the prophet to make bread to eat during this ordeal, it specifies, "Throughout the days that you lie on your side – three hundred and ninety days – shall you eat it" (my translation). The mention of lying on one side and the period of 390 days accord with the command of vv. 4–5, but there is no mention of the second stint of 40 days lying on his other side.

Second, the command that he bear "the guilt of the house of Judah" for 40 days (v. 6), after 390 days on his first side to bear "the guilt of the house of Israel" (vv. 4–5), makes an unexpected distinction between the northern kingdom of Israel and the southern kingdom of Judah. Up to this point, "the house of Israel" has referred to the south and the north alike (3:1, 5, 7, 17; 4:3).[24] Evidently v. 6 was supplied by an editor who understood "the house of Israel" as designating only the north and, therefore, felt compelled to add a parallel period of bearing the guilt of the south (Zimmerli, 1979).

The command of v. 8 offers an additional oddity: "Take note that I place upon you cords, and you will not be able to turn from your one side to the other until you complete the days assigned for your siege" (my translation). However, Ezekiel's being bound in place makes it difficult to see how he would turn from one side to the other or bake bread, as v. 9 demands. These oddities suggest that v. 8 has been added in order to correlate this scene with the statement about Ezekiel's fellow exiles binding him with cords in 3:25, which uses the same word for "cords" as here (Zimmerli, 1979).

The Septuagint of Ezekiel provides concrete evidence of editorial expansions. Although the Septuagint is not as much shorter than the MT as was the case in Jeremiah – only around 4 to 5 percent shorter (Tov, 1986) – comparison to the MT reveals the same types of editorial expansion that we detected in the MT of Jeremiah, as well as similar variations in the arrangement of the book's contents (Mackie, 2010). And as was true for Jeremiah, research into these differences establishes that the MT is an expanded edition of the book (Tov, 1986). However, whereas the expansions in Jeremiah typically used language found elsewhere in that book, those in the MT of Ezekiel more often draw on writings outside the book (Mackie, 2010).

For example, the MT of Ezekiel 5:15 speaks of what will happen "when I execute against you judgments in anger and in wrath, and with enraged reproofs" (my translation). The Septuagint, however, lacks the phrase "in anger and in wrath." It seems to have been added to the book based on Deuteronomy 29:27 (my translation): "and the LORD uprooted them from their land *in anger and in wrath*" (the same phrase appears in Jeremiah 21:5) (Tov, 1986). Similarly, the MT of 3:1 reads, "Human, that which you find, eat: eat this scroll and go, speak to the house of Israel" (my translation). The phrase "that which you find, eat" is lacking from the Septuagint and is probably based on "your words were found, and I ate them" in Jeremiah 15:16 (Tov, 1986). As a final example, Ezekiel 36:11 in the MT reads, "and I will multiply upon you [Israel's mountains] humans and beasts, and they will be fruitful and multiply, and I will make you inhabited as formerly" (my translation). The Septuagint lacks "and they will be fruitful and multiply," language that has been adopted from Genesis 1:22, 28 (Stromberg, 2008).

Besides insertions of phrases from other biblical books, the Septuagint shows that the MT contains changes in the order of contents. For instance, this sequence of statements appears in Ezekiel 7:3–5a of the MT:

> 3: Now the end is upon you, and I will send my wrath against you and will judge you according to your ways and will repay to you all your abominations. 4: My eye will not spare you, I will have no pity. For your ways I will repay to you, and your abominations will be in your midst, and you will know that I am the LORD. 5a: Thus says the Lord GOD. (my translation)

This set of statements appears in the Septuagint, but positioned after the equivalent to v. 9 in the MT. Given that v. 5 in the MT concludes with phrases found nowhere in the Septuagint ("Disaster after disaster! See, it comes") and attempts to integrate the preceding verses within their (new) context, it is more likely that the order of verses in the MT reflects editing of the Hebrew text after the Septuagint was translated (Mackie, 2010).

One manuscript among the many used to reconstruct the history of the Septuagint has been especially telling. Papyrus 967 dates from the second century CE, but accords with other ancient witnesses to the text in lacking both 12:26–28 and 36:23c–38 (Scatolini Apóstolo, 2005). Still more strikingly, chapter 37 follows chapter 39 in Papyrus 967, standing just before Ezekiel's tour of the new temple layout and its features (Scatolini Apóstolo, 2005). This evidence suggests that rather significant rearrangements of material occurred in the continued editing of the book of Ezekiel, just as in the book of Jeremiah.

Parallel to the case of Jeremiah, the MT of Ezekiel reflects a late edition of the book. Needless to say, we have no way of knowing how many stages of editing preceded the Hebrew text used by the Septuagint.

Summary

The book of Ezekiel reflects the work of scribal editors who used the same tacks we have witnessed throughout our study. Its literary structure as a series of reports in largely chronological order, under the guise of first-person speech, is a seductive artifice. Whatever core of oracles derived from a prophet named Ezekiel, the book ironically eclipses him. In fact, the character of Ezekiel virtually evaporates as he reports the experiences that shaped his message. Above all, the book accents the importance of the prophetic message as divinely prescribed speech that leaves the prophet without a voice of his own. He speaks only when his tongue is loosed and his mouth is opened. It is in that mode that he steadfastly forecasts Jerusalem's inevitable fall, but, beyond that, foresees a new, hopeful future.

Notes

1. Jehoiakim died before the siege concluded (2 Kings 24:6), leaving Jehoiachin to surrender to the Babylonians (2 Kings 24:12).
2. The date formulas in 8:1, 20:1, and 24:1 do not provide a benchmark for their "sixth year," "seventh year," and "ninth year."
3. As Zimmerli (1979) observes, the only other third-person reference to Ezekiel comes in a divine address to the people (24:24), which is reported by Ezekiel himself (24:20).
4. This is preferable to Zimmerli's subsequent conjecture (1979, 113) that the date of v. 2 "must at one time have stood in the first verse," only subsequently to be replaced by the "thirtieth year." It is easier to understand why someone would attempt to correlate the obscure "thirtieth year" of v. 1 with "the fifth year of the exile," as well as supply a characterization of Ezekiel's vision as a receipt of "the word of the LORD," than to understand v. 1 as an expansion.
5. This speculation, cited by Zimmerli (1979), traces back to as early as Origen.
6. As Scatolini Apóstolo (2005, 354) observes, "Chapters 24 and 33 are so closely interrelated, that Ezek 25–32 can better be described as an excursus or an after-thought."
7. The oracle of deliverance in 16:59–63 scarcely fits the history of Israel's rebellion outlined in the preceding verses, marking it as secondary to its literary context (Clements, 1986), as is the case also with 17:22–24 and 28:25–26 (Raitt, 1977).
8. Although the details of this vision cannot be considered here, the overall image seems to be of a chariot throne that, like many thrones in the ancient Near East, depicts heavenly beings (here, the four "living creatures") supporting its occupant (see Greenberg, 1983, 55–57).
9. Papyrus documents in Egypt were written on both sides, but no papyrus fragments have survived from Israel, while scrolls made of animal skins were written on only one side until the first century CE (Haran, 1981; cited by Greenberg, 1983, 67). The Qumran scrolls are composed mainly of parchment (a form of leather) and were written on just one side.
10. The only other passage commonly regarded as having a scroll with writing on both sides is Zechariah 5:3, which describes the "flying scroll" bringing punishment for two groups: "everyone who steals shall be cut off according to the writing on one side, and everyone who swears falsely shall be cut off according to the writing on the other side" (NRSV). Despite the NRSV's translation, the Hebrew phraseology does not support the notion of two sides (Meyers and Meyers, 1987), even if the phrases are problematic (compare Petersen, 1984).

11. While in 43:11 Ezekiel is instructed to "write down" the plan of the new temple, this comes closer to preparing a blueprint than a written record (Zimmerli, 1983). The only other reference to Ezekiel writing is in 24:2, where – in the context of the announcement that the siege of Jerusalem has begun – he is commanded to "write down the name of this day, this very day."

12. The NRSV translates the phrase in v. 4 with "the *punishment* of the house of Israel." While the Hebrew word *'awon* can mean "punishment," the meaning "guilt" is also well established and fits this context better, since the 390 years of v. 5 less likely forecast a period of punishment than refer to the entire life of the people of Israel (Zimmerli, 1979), which Ezekiel characterizes as plagued by iniquity from the start (see, for example, 2:3–4).

13. Zimmerli (1979, 20) attributed this to "a prophet of particular sensitivity and dramatic power, for whom a metaphor could become a fully experienced event, however strange in itself this might be." Nevertheless, earlier he characterized such reports as showing such "a strongly stylized form" that "the underlying experience and action is often no longer clearly recoverable" (Zimmerli, 1979, 18). Accepting the latter conclusion, it is difficult to follow his attribution of exaggerated features to the prophet's personality. How could we know?

14. Even if one can agree with Zimmerli's (1979, 172) suspicions that the phrases "use it as a barber's razor" (5:1) and "when the days of the siege are completed" (5:2) are "interpretive glosses" (judging from their awkward fit in the Hebrew syntax), it is difficult to find similar grounds for excluding other phrases he suggests are additions that "project the interpretation back into the sign." His resolute elimination of every element that ill fits an imagined setting for the prophet begs the question whether this vignette began as a realistic report. It may well be that it is deliberately portrayed in surreal tones, like many of the prophet's other experiences.

15. The phrase "live securely," found in Leviticus 26:5, occurs in Ezekiel 38:8, 11, 14; 39:6, 26, but is not distinctive to Leviticus, since it appears throughout the Bible, including other passages in Ezekiel. Even though Ezekiel 39:27 shares with Leviticus 26:36 the phrase "the lands of your enemies," this hardly ranks as distinctive enough to signal direct borrowing (see Lyons, 2009, 184), and the same applies to "in the eyes of the nations," found in Leviticus 26:45 and Ezekiel 38:23 and 39:27 (the latter two are likely dependent on Ezekiel 36:23).

16. Language of "the hand of" a god being upon a person appears within both the Bible and other ancient Near Eastern texts to designate a "'disastrous manifestation of the supernatural power' especially as seen in sickness or plague" (Roberts, 1971, 249). The application of this phraseology to the behavior of prophets in Israel is understandable, given their reputation as "madmen": their behavior was likely perceived as akin to other pathological states (Roberts, 1971). A connection between the "hand of the LORD" and a prophet's reception of an oracle seems equally implied in Isaiah's report of what "the LORD said to me *when his hand was strong*" (my translation) (Isa 8:11), even though he gives no hint of what he experienced.

17. Not every report of the "hand of the LORD" coming upon him involves transport. In 3:22, where he claims that "the hand of the LORD was upon me," he reports being instructed to "rise up, go out into the valley." In 33:22 the coming of the "hand of the LORD" upon him simply leaves him speechless.

18. Although chapter 37 is not labeled a vision, its imaginative character marks it as something other than a report of a concrete scene, while the language of being "brought out *by the spirit of the LORD*" recalls his reference to a "spirit" that transported him in 3:14 and 8:3.

19. The best examples of extended uses of the first person are likely the accounts of Sinuhe the Shipwrecked Sailor and Wen-Amun, both of which are fictional *narratives* from Egypt (Hallo and Younger, 2003).

20. Odell (2000) contends that the book of Ezekiel follows the pattern of the Babylonian inscriptions of Esarhaddon.

21. Compare 2 Kings 6:1, where the NRSV's "the company of prophets" translates the phrase "the sons of the prophets." In that passage they form a band of prophets under Elijah's oversight (a different Hebrew word lies behind "the company of the prophets" in 1 Samuel 19:20).

22. Another 18 times it is expanded by an additional phrase, such as "you shall know that it is I, the LORD, who strike" (Ezek 7:9).

23. A more literal translation would be "you will not be to them a person who rebukes." The phrase translated "a person who rebukes" involves a verb (*mokiach*) used in Amos 5:10 for reproving others. In restricting Ezekiel's speech only to occasions when the LORD has spoken to him, the point seems to be that he will not come off as ceaselessly berating them.

24. As Greenberg (1983) points out, a similar use of these phrases occurs in 9:9: "The guilt of the house of Israel and Judah is exceedingly great." However, that is equally an anomaly in the book, spurring reasonable suspicions that the words "and Judah" were supplied by a scribe who added them to distinguish between the names "Israel" and "Judah" that are used indiscriminately in chapter 8 to refer to those in Jerusalem (Zimmerli, 1958).

Glossary

acrostic poem   A poem structured on the alphabet, with the initial letter of each line's first word being the next letter in alphabetical order after the first letter of the preceding line.

Akkadian   An ancient Semitic language that arose in ancient Mesopotamia and was used by both the Assyrians and the Babylonians.

ancient Near East   The territory in the sweep from the Persian Gulf north and westward, encompassing present day Saudi Arabia, Iraq and Iran, western Turkey, Syria, Lebanon, Israel, Jordan, and Egypt (see Map 1, "The Ancient Near East").

Book of the Twelve   The books of the minor prophets, especially when conceived of as edited into a literary unit distinct from the major prophets.

call narrative   A first-person account by a prophet of the divine summons and commissioning of a prophet.

catchword   A word shared by adjacent passages that links them and is the basis of their juxtaposition (e.g., Isa 1:7–9, 10–11, associated on the basis of "Sodom" and "Gomorrah").

codex   What we commonly call a "book": pages in the form of leaves, held together at a spine. Its predecessor was the **scroll**.

cognate   Having a familial linguistic relationship, as in the English word "night" and the German "Nacht."

cult (*adj.* **cultic**)   The societal institution responsible for carrying out worship, sacrifices, and the celebration of festivals.

Prophetic Literature: From Oracles to Books, First Edition. Ronald L. Troxel.
© 2012 Ronald L. Troxel. Published 2012 by Blackwell Publishing Ltd.

Dead Sea Scrolls   A large set of ancient **manuscripts** and manuscript fragments found in caves near the shores of the Dead Sea, mainly in 11 caves surrounding the ruins of the ancient site of Qumran. These manuscripts contain copies of biblical books, non-canonical literature common to Judaism, and **scrolls** distinct to the community that lived at Qumran.

Deuteronomistic   Motifs, ideas, and vocabulary associated with the whole **Deuteronomistic History**.

Deuteronomistic History   The books of Deuteronomy, Joshua, Judges, 1 and 2 Samuel, and 1 and 2 Kings, which tell and evaluate the story of Israel's life from Moses' valedictory speech to the fall of Jerusalem, measuring it particularly by standards derived from Deuteronomy.

divination   The use of learned methods to access information about the future, such as reading animal entrails, observing the stars, or noting other correlations between physical phenomena and events. While Deuteronomy 18 prohibits such practices, episodes in the Bible make it clear that such specialists were active in ancient Israel.

divine council   The depiction (common throughout the ancient Near East) of an assembly of divine beings, under the oversight of the supreme deity, collaborating to make decisions about the disposition of affairs in the world. The premier examples of this within the Bible are 1 Kings 22:19–22 and Psalm 82. Job 1–2 and Isaiah 6 likewise presuppose this scene.

doxology   A statement extolling the deity's virtues or deeds.

emendation   A change in the reading of the Hebrew based on **textual criticism**.

eschatology   A vision of a new era, introduced by God, that definitively realizes the loftiest divine and/or human ideals.

exile   The expatriation of citizens from (first) Israel in 722, at the hands of the Assyrians, and from Judah in 587, at the hands of the Babylonians.

gloss   A phrase or word added to clarify an obscure reference or term in the text.

graduated numerical saying   A literary device that specifies a certain number of phenomena, plus one more, as in Amos 1:3: "*For three* transgressions of Damascus, *and for four*, I will not revoke the punishment."

high place   A religious shrine common throughout Israel (considered illicit by the books of Kings).

hyperbole   Exaggeration for rhetorical effect.

incipit   A heading grammatically bound with what follows, inasmuch as it launches a narrative. Like the **superscription** it provides a name for the prophet featured in the narrative, especially as the speaker of its oracles.

implied audience   An inference about the type of audience a literary work addresses, based on the perspectives and views it assumes its readers possess.

implied author   The image of the author that arises from examining how the story is woven or rhetoric is used to shape the reader's understanding of the text.

intermediary   A person who practices **intermediation**.

intermediation   The abstract term for all practices by which a human mediates messages between the divine and human realms.

LXX   *See* Septuagint.

literary structure   The sequencing and organization of sentences and paragraphs that allows the reader to make sense of a work of literature.

liturgical   Anything used or fit for use in an assembly gathered for worship.

liturgy   A specified order or structure for components used in an assembly gathered for worship.

manuscript   A handwritten copy of an ancient text (from Latin "written by hand").

Mari   A city of the eighteenth century BCE, located on the Euphrates (see Map 1), where a set of official correspondence was found, including reports of oracles spoken by prophets.

Masoretic text (MT)   Any codex produced by the Masoretes, **scribes** of the early medieval period who produced copies of the Hebrew Bible that became the standard text used in worship and as a starting point for scholarly study. Often "Masoretic text" is used to refer to the codex Leningrad B19A, the oldest surviving copy of the entire Hebrew Bible.

messenger formula   "Thus says the LORD."

MT   *See* Masoretic text.

oracle   A speech presented as a message from a deity.

patriarchs   Israel's founding fathers, as described by the book of Genesis. They include Abraham, his son Isaac, Isaac's twin sons Esau and Jacob, and the 12 sons born to Jacob (Reuben, Simeon, Levi, Judah, Issachar, Zebulun, Gad, Asher, Dan, Naphtali, Joseph, and Benjamin).

pillar The sacred pillar (*matsebah*) was a common appurtenance of religious shrines, a stone of phallic shape that may have represented a male deity. Such pillars are considered natural religious symbols in the stories of the **patriarchs** in Genesis (e.g., Gen 28:18, 22), but are to be destroyed as foreign religious images, according to Israel's legal codes (e.g., Exod 23:24; Deut 7:5) and are associated with the despised **high places** in 1 and 2 Kings (e.g., 1 Kings 14:23; 2 Kings 18:4).

redaction criticism (Ger. *Redaktion*, "editing") The identification and analysis of features that mark a work or a passage as a composite of distinct traditions that have been melded together by a redactor (editor) to fashion a document.

scribe An individual who was trained in the use of writing, well versed in his culture's literature, and schooled to create documents for the state or individuals. Scribes copied, edited, and preserved the literary traditions of their society.

scroll Papyrus (or, less commonly, leather) pages stitched together to form a length of writing material that was wrapped around a spindle at both ends. To read the scroll, one would wind the material from one spindle to the other.

Septuagint (= LXX, "Seventy") A translation of the Hebrew Bible into Greek begun with the translation of the **Torah** in the third century BCE and completed piecemeal by the first century CE.

sign act An action carried out by a prophet (typically one mandated by the LORD) that conveys a message the people are to take to heart (e.g., Isaiah walking about Jerusalem naked to prefigure Egypt's humiliation when its people are led away captive to Assyria (Isa 20)).

superscription A heading grammatically separate from the body of the book, which provides a name for the prophet by whom the book's **oracles** were implicitly delivered and occasionally adds bibliographic information or specifies the era in which he worked. *Compare* incipit.

Tetragrammaton The four Hebrew letters (equivalent to YHWH) forming the personal name of Israel's god. The name came to be regarded as too sacred to pronounce.

textual criticism The art of evaluating differences in wording between **manuscripts** that have survived from as early as 200 BCE in order to recover the most likely wording for a passage.

theocentric Focused (centered) on God.

theodicy A defense of divine action, particularly in response to calamity (e.g., "Why did God allow this evil?").

theophany A description of a deity's arrival and appearance.

Torah A Hebrew word that came to be applied to the first five books of the Bible and gained, by association, the notion of "law." At root, however, it means "instruction," and it is still used in that sense in some of the prophets (e.g., Isa 1: 10; 5: 24; 8: 16; 30: 9–10; Hag 2: 11).

Ugaritic An ancient Semitic language, akin to Hebrew, attested in tablets found at the site of ancient Ugarit, on the coast of the Mediterranean, nearly 200 miles north of Israel. The majority of the texts found date to the fourteenth and thirteenth centuries BCE.

References

Ackroyd, P.R. (1963) A note on Isaiah 2:1. *Zeitschrift für die Alttestamentliche Wissenschaft*, 75, 320–321.

Ackroyd, P.R. (1987) Isaiah 36–39: structure and function, in *Studies in the Religious Tradition of the Old Testament* (ed. P.R. Ackroyd), SCM Press, London, pp. 105–120, 274–278.

Aejmelaeus, A. (2002) Jeremiah at the turning-point of history: the function of Jer. XXV 1–14 in the book of Jeremiah. *Vetus Testamentum*, 52, 459–482.

Albertz, R. (2002) Exile as purification: reconstructing the "Book of the Four," in *Thematic Threads in the Book of the Twelve* (eds P.L. Redditt and A. Schart), Walter de Gruyter, Berlin, pp. 232–251.

Albertz, R. (2003a) Exilische Heilsversicherung im Habakukbuch, in *Textarbeit: Studien zu Texten und ihrer Rezeption aus dem Alten Testament und der Umwelt Israels* (eds K. Kiesow and T. Meurer), Ugarit-Verlag, Münster, pp. 1–20.

Albertz, R. (2003b) *Israel in Exile: The History and Literature of the Sixth Century B.C.E.*, Society of Biblical Literature, Atlanta.

Allen, L.C. (1976) *The Books of Joel, Obadiah, Jonah and Micah*, W.B. Eerdmans, Grand Rapids, MI.

Alt, A. (1959) Hosea 5,8–6,6: Ein Krieg und seine Folgen in prophetischer Beleuchtung, in *Kleine Schriften zur Geschichte des Volkes Israel*, vol. 2 (ed. A. Alt), C.H. Beck, Munich, pp. 163–187.

Amit, Y. (2006) The role of prophecy and prophets in the chronicler's world, in *Prophets, Prophecy, and Prophetic Texts in Second Temple Judaism* (eds M.H. Floyd and R.D. Haak), T&T Clark, New York, pp. 80–101.

Andersen, F.I. (2001) *Habakkuk*, Doubleday, New York.

Andersen, F.I. and Freedman, D.N. (1980) *Hosea*, Doubleday, New York.

Andersen, F.I. and Freedman, D.N. (1989) *Amos*, Doubleday, New York.

Andersen, F.I. and Freedman, D.N. (2000) *Micah*, Doubleday, New York.

Assis, E. (2006) Haggai: structure and meaning. *Biblica*, 87, 531–541.

Assis, E. (2008) The temple in the book of Haggai. *Journal of Hebrew Scriptures*, 8. www.purl.org/jhs (accessed July 16, 2009).

Avishur, Y. (1994) Habakkuk 3, in *Studies in Hebrew and Ugaritic Psalms* (ed. Y. Avishur), Magnes Press, Jerusalem, pp. 111–205.

Barthel, J. (1997) *Prophetenwort und Geschichte: die Jesajaüberlieferung in Jes 6–8 und 28–31*, Mohr Siebeck, Tübingen.

Bartlett, J.R. (1982) Edom and the fall of Jerusalem, 587 B.C. *Palestine Exploration Quarterly*, 114, 13–24.

Barton, J. (1984) "The law and the prophets": who are the prophets? in *Prophets, Worship and Theodicy* (eds J. Barton, R. P. Carroll, and J. P. Fokkelman), Leiden, E.J. Brill, pp. 1–18.

Barton, J. (2001) *Joel and Obadiah: A Commentary*, Louisville, KY: Westminster/John Knox.

Barton, J. (2007) Biblical criticism and religious belief, in *The Nature of Biblical Criticism*, Louisville, KY: Westminster/John Knox, pp. 137–186.

Beck, M. (2005) *Der "Tag YHWHs" im Dodekapropheton: Studien im Spannungsfeld von Traditions- und Redaktionsgeschichte*, Berlin, Walter de Gruyter.

Beck, M. (2006) Das Dodekapropheton als Anthologie. *Zeitschrift für die Alttestamentliche Wissenschaft*, 118, 558–581.

Becker, U. (1997) *Jesaja: von der Botschaft zum Buch*, Vandenhoeck and Ruprecht, Göttingen.

Becker, U. (2004) Die Wiederentdeckung des Prophetenbuches. *Berliner Theologische Zeitschrift*, 21, 30–60.

Becking, B. (1996) Passion, power, protection: interpreting the God of Nahum, in *On Reading Prophetic Texts* (eds B. Becking and M. Dijkstra), E.J. Brill, Leiden, pp. 1–20.

Beentjes, P.C. (1982) Inverted quotations in the Bible: a neglected stylistic pattern. *Biblica*, 63, 506–523.

Ben-Porat, Z. (1976) The poetics of literary allusion. *Poetics and Theory of Literature*, 1, 105–128.

Ben Zvi, E. (1993) History and prophetic texts, in *History and Interpretation: Essays in Honour of John H. Hayes* (eds P. M. Graham, W. P. Brown, and J. K. Kuan), JSOT Press, Sheffield, pp. 106–120.

Ben Zvi, E. (1996a) *A Historical–Critical Study of the Book of Obadiah*, Walter de Gruyter, Berlin.

Ben Zvi, E. (1996b) Twelve prophetic books or "the Twelve": a few preliminary considerations, in *Forming Prophetic Literature* (eds J.W. Watts and P.R. House), Sheffield Academic Press, Sheffield, pp. 125–156.

Ben Zvi, E. (1997) The urban center of Jerusalem and the development of the literature of the Hebrew Bible, in *Urbanism in Antiquity: From Mesopotamia to Crete* (eds W.E. Aufrecht, N.A. Mirau, and S.W. Gauley), Sheffield Academic Press, Sheffield, pp. 194–209.

Ben Zvi, E. (1999) A Deuteronomistic redaction in/among "the Twelve"? A contribution from the standpoint of the books of Micah, Zephaniah and Obadiah, in *Those Elusive Deuteronomists* (eds L.S. Schearing and S.L. McKenzie), Sheffield Academic Press, Sheffield, pp. 232–261.

Ben Zvi, E. (2000a) Introduction: writings, speeches, and the prophetic books – setting an agenda, in *Writings and Speech in Israelite and Ancient Near Eastern Prophecy* (eds E. Ben Zvi and M.H. Floyd), Society of Biblical Literature, Atlanta, pp. 1–29.

Ben Zvi, E. (2000b) *Micah*, W.B. Eerdmans, Grand Rapids, MI.

Ben Zvi, E. (2003) The prophetic book: a key form of prophetic literature, in *The Changing Face of Form Criticism for the Twenty-First Century* (eds M. A. Sweeney and E. Ben Zvi), W.B. Eerdmans, Grand Rapids, MI, pp. 276–297.

Ben Zvi, E. (2005a) Josiah and the prophetic books: some observations, in *Good Kings and Bad Kings* (ed. L.L. Grabbe), T&T Clark, London, pp. 47–64.

Ben Zvi, E. (2005b) *Hosea*, W.B. Eerdmans, Grand Rapids, MI.

Ben Zvi, E. (2009) Jonah 4:11 and the metaprophetic character of the book of Jonah. *Journal of Hebrew Scriptures*, 9. www.purl.org/jhs (accessed July 21, 2009).

Berges, U. (1998) *Das Buch Jesaja: Komposition und Endgestalt*, Herder, Freiburg.

Bergler, S. (1988) *Joel als Schriftinterpret*, Peter Lang, Frankfurt.

Beuken, W.A.M. (1972) Mišpāt: the first servant song and its context. *Vetus Testamentum*, 22, 1–30.

Beuken, W.A.M. (1986) Isa 56:9–57:13: an example of the Isaianic legacy of Trito-Isaiah, in *Tradition and Re-interpretation in Jewish and Early Christian Literature* (eds J.W. van Henten, H.J. de Jonge, and P.T. van Rooden), E.J. Brill, Leiden, pp. 48–64.

Beuken, W.A.M. (1990) The main theme of Trito-Isaiah: "the servants of YHWH." *Journal for the Study of the Old Testament*, 47, 67–87.

Beuken, W.A.M. (2000) *Isaiah*, part 2, vol. 2: *Isaiah 28–39*, Peeters, Leuven.

Beuken, W.A.M. (2003) *Jesaja 1–12*, Herder, Freiburg.

Beuken, W.A.M. (2007) *Jesaja 13–27*, Herder, Freiburg.

Bin-Nun, S.R. (1968) Formulas from royal records of Israel and Judah. *Vetus Testamentum*, 18, 414–432.

Bird, P. (1989) "To play the harlot": an inquiry into an Old Testament metaphor, in *Gender and Difference in Ancient Israel* (ed. P.L. Day), Fortress Press, Minneapolis, pp. 75–94.

Blenkinsopp, J. (1977) *Prophecy and canon: a contribution to the study of Jewish origins*, University of Notre Dame Press, Notre Dame, IN.

Blenkinsopp, J. (1996) *A History of Prophecy in Israel*, rev. edn, Westminster/John Knox, Louisville, KY.

Blenkinsopp, J. (1997) The servant and the servants in Isaiah and the formation of the book, in *Writing and Reading the Book of Isaiah*, vol. 1, E.J. Brill, Leiden, pp. 155–175.

Blenkinsopp, J. (2000) *Isaiah 1–39*, Doubleday, New York.

Blenkinsopp, J. (2001) *Isaiah 40–55*, Doubleday, New York.

Blenkinsopp, J. (2003) *Isaiah 56–66*, Doubleday, New York.

Boda, M.J. (2001) Oil, crowns and thrones: prophet, priest and king in Zechariah 1:7–6:15. *Journal of Hebrew Scriptures*, 3. www.purl.org/jhs (accessed July 21, 2009).

Boda, M.J. (2003a) From fasts to feasts: the literary function of Zechariah 7–8. *Catholic Biblical Quarterly*, 65, 390–407.

Boda, M.J. (2003b) Majoring on the minors: recent research on Haggai and Zechariah. *Currents in Biblical Research*, 2, 33–68.

Boda, M.J. (2003c) Zechariah: master mason or penitential prophet? In *Yahwism after the Exile: Perspectives on Israelite Religion in the Persian Period* (eds R. Albertz and B. Becking), van Gorcum, Assen, pp. 49–69.

Boda, M.J. (2005) Terrifying the horns: Persia and Babylon in Zechariah 1:7–6:15. *Catholic Biblical Quarterly*, 67, 22–41.

Boda, M.J. (2008) Hoy, hoy: the prophetic origins of the Babylonian tradition in Zechariah 2:10–17, in *Tradition in Translation: Haggai and Zechariah 1–8 in the Trajectory of Hebrew Theology* (eds M.J. Boda and M.H. Floyd), T&T Clark, New York, pp. 171–190.

Bolin, T.M. (1995) "Should I not also pity Nineveh?" Divine freedom in the book of Jonah. *Journal for the Study of the Old Testament*, 67, 109–120.

Bosshard, E. and Kratz, R.G. (1990) Maleachi im Zwölfprophetenbuch. *Beiträge zur Namenforschung*, 52, 27–46.

Bright, J. (1966) The prophetic reminiscence: its place and function in the book of Jeremiah, in *Biblical Essays: Proceedings of the Ninth Meeting of Die Ou-Testamentiese Werkgemeenskap in Suid-Afrika*, Baker and Taylor, Potchefstroom, pp. 11–30.

Brodsky, H. (1990) An enormous horde arrayed for battle. *Bible Review*, 6 (4), 32–39.

Brueggemann, W. (1994) The "Baruch connection": reflections on Jer 43:1–7. *Journal of Biblical Literature*, 113, 405–420.

Budde, K. (1928) *Jesaja's Erleben: eine gemeinverständliche Auslegung der Denkschrift des Propheten (Kap. 6,1–9,6)*, Klotz, Gotha.

Burrows, M. (1970) The literary category of the book of Jonah, in *Translating and Understanding the Old Testament: Essays in Honor of Herbert Gordon May* (eds H.T. Frank and W.L. Reed), Abingdon Press, Nashville, pp. 80–107.

Carr, D.M. (2005) *Writing on the Tablet of the Heart*, Oxford University Press, New York.

Carr, D.M. (2006) Reading Isaiah from beginning (Isaiah 1) to end (Isaiah 65–66): multiple modern possibilities, in *New Visions of Isaiah* (eds R.F. Melugin and M.A. Sweeney), Society of Biblical Literature, Atlanta, pp. 188–218.

Carroll, R.P. (1986) *Jeremiah*, Westminster, Philadelphia.

Cassuto, U. (1973) The sequence and arrangement of the biblical sections (trans. I. Abrahams), in *Biblical and Oriental Studies*, vol. 1 (ed. U. Cassuto), Magnes Press, Jerusalem, pp. 1–6.

Cathcart, K.J. (1973) Treaty-curses and the book of Nahum. *Catholic Biblical Quarterly*, 35, 179–187.

Chaney, M.L. (2004) Accusing whom of what? Hosea's rhetoric of promiscuity, in *Distant Voices Drawing Near* (ed. H.E. Hearon), Liturgical Press, Collegeville, MN, pp. 97–115.

Childs, B.S. (1979) *Introduction to the Old Testament as Scripture*, Fortress Press, Philadelphia.

Christensen, D.L. (1975) Acrostic of Nahum reconsidered. *Zeitschrift für die Alttestamentliche Wissenschaft*, 87, 17–30.

Christensen, D.L. (1984) Zephaniah 2:4–15: a theological basis for Josiah's program of political expansion. *Catholic Biblical Quarterly*, 46, 669–82.

Christensen, D.L. (1987) The acrostic of Nahum once again: a prosodic analysis of Nahum 1:1–10. *Zeitschrift für die Alttestamentliche Wissenschaft*, 99, 409–15.

Cleaver-Bartholomew, D. (2003) An alternative approach to Hab 1,2–2,20. *Scandinavian Journal of the Old Testament*, 17, 206–225.

Clements, R.E. (1984) *Isaiah and the deliverance of Jerusalem*, JSOT Press, Sheffield.

Clements, R.E. (1986) The chronology of redaction in Ezekiel 1–24, in *Ezekiel and his Book: Textual and Literary Criticism and their Interrelation* (ed. J. Lust), Leuven University Press, Leuven, pp. 283–294.

Coggins, R. (1982) An alternative prophetic tradition? In *Israel's Prophetic Tradition: Essays in Honour of Peter Ackroyd* (eds R. Coggins, M.A. Knibb, and A. Phillips), Cambridge University Press, Cambridge, pp. 77–94.

Coggins, R. (1994) The minor prophets – one book or twelve? In *Crossing the Boundaries: Essays in Biblical Interpretation in Honor of Michael D. Goulder* (eds S.E. Porter, P. Joyce, and D.E. Orton), E.J. Brill, Leiden, pp. 57–68.

Coggins, R. (1996) Interbiblical quotations in Joel, in *After the Exile: Essays in Honor of Rex Mason* (eds J. Barton and D.J. Reimer), Mercer University Press, Macon, GA, pp. 75–84.

Coggins, R. (2003) Joel. *Currents in Biblical Research*, 2, 85–103.

Collins, J.J. (1974) Apocalyptic eschatology as the transcendence of death. *Catholic Biblical Quarterly*, 36, 21–43.

Collins, J.J. (1998) *The Apocalyptic Imagination*, 2nd edn., W.B. Eerdmans, Grand Rapids, MI.

Cooper, A. (1993) In praise of divine caprice: the significance of the book of Jonah, in *Among the Prophets: Language, Image and Structure in the Prophetic Writings* (eds P.R. Davies and D.J.A. Clines), JSOT Press, Sheffield, pp. 144–163.

Crenshaw, J.L. (1995) *Joel: A New Translation with Introduction and Commentary*, Doubleday, New York.

Cross, F.M. (1953) The council of Yahweh in second Isaiah. *Journal of Near Eastern Studies*, 12, 274–277.

Curtis, B.G. (2000) The Zion-daughter oracles: evidence on the identity and ideology of the late redactors of the Book of the Twelve, in *Reading and Hearing the Book of the Twelve* (eds J.D. Nogalski and M.A. Sweeney), Society of Biblical Literature, Atlanta, pp. 166–184.

Dangl, O. (2001) Habakkuk in recent research. *Currents in Research: Biblical Studies*, 9, 131–168.

Darnton, R. (2008) The library in the new age. *New York Review of Books*, 55 (10). http://www.nybooks.com/articles/21514 (accessed Nov. 28, 2008).

Davies, P.R. (1996) The audiences of prophetic scrolls: some suggestions, in *Prophets and Paradigms: Essays in Honor of Gene M. Tucker* (ed. S.B. Reid), Sheffield Academic Press, Sheffield, pp. 48–62.

Davis, E.F. (1989) *Swallowing the Scroll: Textuality and the Dynamics of Discourse in Ezekiel's Prophecy*, Almond, Sheffield.

Dearman, J.A. (1990) My servants the scribes: composition and context in Jeremiah 36. *Journal of Biblical Literature*, 109 (3), 403–421.

Deist, F. (1988) Parallels and reinterpretation in the book of Joel: a theology of the Yom Yahweh? In *Text and Context: Old Testament and Semitic Studies for F.C. Fensham* (ed. W.T. Classen), JSOT Press, Sheffield, pp. 63–79.

de Jong, M.J. (2007) *Isaiah among the Ancient Near Eastern Prophets: A Comparative Study of the Earliest Stages of the Isaiah Tradition and the Neo-Assyrian Prophecies*, E.J. Brill, Leiden.

De Vries, S.J. (1966) Acrostic of Nahum in the Jerusalem liturgy. *Vetus Testamentum*, 16, 476–481.

De Vries, S.J. (1995) *From Old Revelation to New*, W.B. Eerdmans, Grand Rapids, MI.

Dozeman, T.B. (1989) Inner-biblical interpretation of Yahweh's gracious and compassionate character. *Journal of Biblical Literature*, 108, 207–223.

Duhm, B. (1901) *Das Buch Jeremia*, J.C.B. Mohr, Tübingen.

Ellis, M. deJong (1989) Observations on Mesopotamian oracles and prophetic texts: literary and historiographic considerations. *Journal of Cuneiform Studies*, 41, 127–186.

Emerton, J.A. (1977) The textual and linguistic problems of Habakkuk II.4–5. *Journal of Theological Studies*, 28, 1–18.

Fischer, J.A. (1972) Notes on the literary form and message of Malachi. *Catholic Biblical Quarterly*, 34, 315–320.

Fishbane, M. (1985) *Biblical Interpretation in Ancient Israel*, Clarendon Press, Oxford.

Fisher, E.J. (1976) Cultic prostitution in the ancient Near East? A reassessment. *Biblical Theology Bulletin*, 6, 225–236.

Floyd, M.H. (1991) Prophetic complaints about the fulfillment of oracles in Habakkuk 1:2–17 and Jeremiah 15:10–18. *Journal of Biblical Literature*, 110, 397–418.

Floyd, M.H. (1994) The chimerical acrostic of Nahum 1:2–10. *Journal of Biblical Literature*, 113, 421–437.

Floyd, M.H. (1995) The nature of the narrative and the evidence of redaction in Haggai. *Vetus Testamentum*, 45, 470–490.

Floyd, M.H. (2000) *Minor Prophets, Part 2*, W.B. Eerdmans, Grand Rapids, MI.

Floyd, M.H. (2002) The מַשָּׂא (MAŚŚĀ) as a type of prophetic book. *Journal of Biblical Literature*, 121, 401–422.

Floyd, M.H. (2003a) Basic trends in the form-critical study of prophetic texts, in *The Changing Face of Form-Criticism for the Twenty-First Century* (eds M.A. Sweeney and E. Ben Zvi), W.B. Eerdmans, Grand Rapids, MI, pp. 298–311.

Floyd, M. H. (2003b) Deutero-Zechariah and types of intertextuality, in *Bringing Out the Treasure: Inner Biblical Allusion in Zechariah 9–14* (eds M.J. Boda and M.H. Floyd), T&T Clark, London, pp. 225–244.

Floyd, M.H. (2006) Introduction, in *Prophets, Prophecy, and Prophetic Texts in Second Temple Judaism* (eds M.H. Floyd and R.D. Haak), T&T Clark, New York, pp. 1–25.

Floyd, M.H. (2008) Traces of tradition in Zechariah 1–8: a case-study, in *Tradition in Transition: Haggai and Zechariah 1–8 in the Trajectory of Hebrew Theology* (eds M.J. Boda and M.H. Floyd), T&T Clark, London, pp. 210–234.

Foster, R.L. (2007) Shepherds, sticks, and social destabilization: a fresh look at Zechariah 11:4–17. *Journal of Biblical Literature*, 126, 735–753.

Fox, M.V. (1991) *The Redaction of the Books of Esther*, Scholars Press, Atlanta.

Fox, M.V. (2000) *Proverbs 1–9*, Doubleday, New York.

Fuller, R.E. (1996) The form and formation of the Book of the Twelve: the evidence from the Judean desert, in *Forming Prophetic Literature* (eds P.R. House and J.W. Watts), Sheffield Academic Press, Sheffield, pp. 86–101.

Glazier-McDonald, B. (1987a) Intermarriage, divorce, and the bat-'ēl nēkār: insights into Mal 2:10–16. *Journal of Biblical Literature*, 106, 603–611.

Glazier-McDonald, B. (1987b) Mal'ak habberît: the messenger of the covenant in Mal 3:1, in *Hebrew Annual Review*, vol. 11 (ed. R. Ahroni), Ohio State University Press, Columbus, pp. 93–104.

Glazier-McDonald, B. (1987c) *Malachi: the divine messenger*, Scholars Press, Atlanta.

Goldingay, J.E. and D. Payne (2006a) *Isaiah 40–55*, vol. 1, T&T Clark, Edinburgh.

Goldingay, J.E. and D. Payne (2006b) *Isaiah 40–55*, vol. 2, T&T Clark, Edinburgh.

Goldstein, E. (2007) On the use of the name of God in the book of Jonah, in *Milk and Honey: Essays on Ancient Israel and the Bible in Appreciation of the Judaic Studies Program at the University of California, San Diego* (eds S. Malena and D. Miano), Eisenbrauns, Winona Lake, IN, pp. 77–83.

Gosse, B. (1999) Les "Confessions" de Jérémie, la vengeance contre Jérusalem à l'image de celle contre Babylone et les nations, et Lamentations 1. *Zeitschrift für die Alttestamentliche Wissenschaft*, 111, 58–67.

Gosse, B. (2004) L'Influence du Psautier sur la présentation du prophète Jérémie en Jr 15, 10–21 et ses liens avec Jr 17,1–18. *Études Théologiques et Religieuses*, 79, 393–402.

Gray, J. (1961) Kingship of God in the prophets and Psalms. *Vetus Testamentum*, 11, 1–29.

Greenberg, M. (1983) *Ezekiel 1–20*, Doubleday, New York.

Greenberg, M. (1984) The design and themes of Ezekiel's program of restoration. *Interpretation*, 38, 181–208.

Greenberg, M. (1997) *Ezekiel 21–37*, Doubleday, New York.

Guillaume, P. (2007) The unlikely Malachi–Jonah sequence (4QXIIa). *Journal of Hebrew Scriptures*, 7. www.purl.org/jhs (accessed Aug. 8, 2009).

Gunkel, H. (1893) Nahum 1. *Zeitschrift für die Alttestamentliche Wissenschaft*, 11, 223–244.

Gutzwiller, K.J. (1998) *Poetic Garlands: Hellenistic Epigrams in Context*, University of California Press, Berkeley and Los Angeles.

Haag, H. (1975) בֶּן־אָדָם (trans. J.T. Willis), in *Theological Dictionary of the Old Testament*, vol. 2 (eds G.J. Botterweck and H. Ringgren), W.B. Eerdmans, Grand Rapids, MI, pp. 159–165.

Hallo, W.W. and Younger, K.L., Jr (eds) (2003) *The Context of Scripture*, 3 vols, E.J. Brill, Leiden.

Haran, M. (1963) The literary structure and chronological framework of the prophecies in Isa. xl–xlvii. *Vetus Testamentum*, 9, 127–155.

Haran, M. (1981) Scribal workmanship in biblical times. *Tarbiz*, 50, 65–87.

Hardmeier, C. (2005) King Josiah in the climax of the Deuteronomic History (2 Kings 22–23) and the pre-Deuteronomic document of a cult reform at the place of residence (23.4–15*): criticism of sources, reconstruction of literary pre-stages and the theology of history in 2 Kings 22–23*, in *Good Kings and Bad Kings* (ed. L.L. Grabbe), T&T Clark, London, pp. 123–163.

Herrmann, W. (2001) Das underledigte Problem des Buches Habakkuk. *Vetus Testamentum*, 51, 481–496.

Hillers, D.R. (1984) *Micah*, Fortress Press, Philadelphia.

Hillers, D.R. (1992) *Lamentations*, Doubleday, New York.

Holladay, W.L. (1960) Prototype and copies: a new approach to the poetry–prose problem in the book of Jeremiah. *Journal of Biblical Literature*, 79, 351–367.

Holladay, W.L. (1986) *Jeremiah 1: A Commentary on the Book of the Prophet Jeremiah, Chapters 1–25*, T&T Clark, Edinburgh.

Holladay, W.L. (1989) *Jeremiah 2: A Commentary on the Book of the Prophet Jeremiah, Chapters 26–52*, Fortress Press, Minneapolis.

Holladay, W.L. (2001) Reading Zephaniah with a concordance: suggestions for a redaction history. *Journal of Biblical Literature*, 120, 671–684.

Huffmon, H.B. (2000) A company of prophets: Mari, Assyria, Israel, in *Prophecy in its Ancient Near Eastern Context: Mesopotamian, Biblical, and Arabian Perspectives* (ed. M. Nissinen), Society of Biblical Literature, Atlanta, pp. 47–70.

James, W. (1958) *The Varieties of Religious Experience* (1902), Mentor, New York.

Janssen, E. (1956) *Juda in der Exilszeit: ein Beitrag zur Frage der Entstehung des Judentums*, Vandenhoeck und Ruprecht, Göttingen.

Janzen, J.G. (1980) Habakkuk 2:2–4 in the light of recent philological advances. *Harvard Theological Review*, 73, 53–78.

Japhet, S. (2004) The concept of the "remnant" in the Restoration period: on the vocabulary of self-definition, in *Manna fällt auch heute noch* (eds F.-L. Hossfeld and L. Schwienhorst-Schönberger), Herder, Freiburg, pp. 340–361.

Jeffers, A. (2007) Magic and divination in ancient Israel. *Religion Compass*, 1, 628–642.

Jenkins, A.K. (1989) The development of the Isaiah tradition in Is 13–23, in *Book of Isaiah / Le Livre d'Isaie* (ed. J. Vermeylen), Leuven University Press, Leuven, pp. 237–251.

Jeremias, J. (1970) *Kultprophetie und Gerichtsverkündigung in der späten Königszeit Israels*, Neukirchener Verlag, Neukirchener-Vluyn.

Jeremias, J. (1971) Die Deutung der Gerichtsworte Michas in der Exilszeit. *Zeitschrift für die Alttestamentliche Wissenschaft*, 83, 330–354.

Jeremias, J. (1983) *Der Prophet Hosea*, Evangelische Verlagsanstalt, Berlin.

Jeremias, J. (1988) Amos 3–6: from the oral word to the text, in *Canon, Theology, and Old Testament Interpretation* (eds G.M. Tucker, D.L. Petersen, and R.R. Wilson), Fortress Press, Philadelphia, 222–224.

Jeremias, J. (1996a) The interrelationship between Amos and Hosea, in *Forming Prophetic Literature* (eds J.W. Watts and P.R. House), Sheffield Academic Press, Sheffield, pp. 171–186.

Jeremias, J. (1996b) Die Anfänge des Dodekapropheton: Hosea und Amos, in *Hosea und Amos* (ed. J. Jeremias), J.C.B. Mohr (Paul Siebeck), Tübingen, pp. 34–54.

Jeremias, J. (1996c) Hosea 4–7: Beobachtungen zur Komposition des Buches Hosea, in *Hosea und Amos* (ed. J. Jeremias), J.C.B. Mohr (Paul Siebeck), Tübingen, pp. 55–66.

Jeremias, J. (1996d) Zur Eschatologie des Hoseabuches, in *Hosea und Amos* (ed. J. Jeremias), J.C.B. Mohr (Paul Siebeck), Tübingen, pp. 67–85.

Jeremias, J. (1996h) Völkersprüche und Visionsberichte im Amosbuch, in *Hosea und Amos* (ed. J. Jeremias), J.C.B. Mohr (Paul Siebeck), Tübingen, pp. 157–171.

Jeremias, J. (1996i) Zur Entstehung der Völkersprüche im Amosbuch, in *Hosea und Amos* (ed. J. Jeremias), J.C.B. Mohr (Paul Siebeck), Tübingen, pp. 172–182.

Jeremias, J. (1996j) "Zwei Jahre vor dem Erdbeben" (Am 1,1), in *Hosea und Amos* (ed. J. Jeremias), J.C.B. Mohr (Paul Siebeck), Tübingen, pp. 183–197.

Jeremias, J. (1996k) Grundtendenzen gegenwärtiger Prophetenforschung, in *Hosea und Amos* (ed. J. Jeremias), J.C.B. Mohr (Paul Siebeck), Tübingen, pp. 1–19.

Jeremias, J. (1996l) Das Proprium der alttestamentlichen Prophetie, in *Hosea und Amos* (ed. J. Jeremias), J.C.B. Mohr (Paul Siebeck), Tübingen, pp. 20–33.

Jeremias, J. (1996m) Die Rolle des Propheten nach dem Amosbuch, in *Hosea und Amos* (ed. J. Jeremias), J.C.B. Mohr (Paul Siebeck), Tübingen, pp. 272–284.

Jeremias, J. (1996n) Am 8,4–7: ein Kommentar zu 2,6f, in *Hosea und Amos* (ed. J. Jeremias), J.C.B. Mohr (Paul Siebeck), Tübingen, pp. 231–243.

Jeremias, J. (1998a) *The Book of Amos*, Westminster/John Knox, Louisville, KY.

Jeremias, J. (1998b) Neuere Tendenzen der Forschung an den Kleinen Propheten, in *Perspectives in the Study of the Old Testament and Early Judaism* (eds F. García Martínez and E. Noort), E.J. Brill, Leiden, pp. 122–136.

Jeremias, J. (2000a) Der "Tag Jahwes" in Jes 13 und Joel 2, in *Schriftauslegung in der Schrift* (eds R.G. Kratz, T. Krüger, and K. Schmid), Walter de Gruyter, Berlin, pp. 129–138.

Jeremias, J. (2000b) Tradition und Redaktion in Micha 3, in *Verbindungslinien: Festschrift für Werner H. Schmidt zum 65. Geburtstag* (eds A. Graupner, H. Delkurt, A.B. Ernst, and L. Aupperle), Neukirchener Verlag, Neukirchen-Vluyn, pp. 137–151.

Jeremias, J. (2002) Gelehrte Prophetie: Beobachtungen zu Joel und Deuterosacharja, in *Vergegenwärtigung des Alten Testaments* (eds R. Smend, C. Bultmann, W. Dietrich, and C. Levin), Vandenhoeck and Ruprecht, Göttingen.

Jeremias, J. (2004) Die Sicht der Völker im Jonabuch (Jona 1 und Jona 3), in *Gott und Mensch im Dialog: Festschrift für Otto Kaiser zum 80. Geburtstag*, vol. 1 (ed. M. Witte), Walter de Gruyter, Berlin, pp. 555–567.

Jeremias, J. (2007) *Die Propheten Joel, Obadja, Jona, Micha*, Vandenhoeck and Ruprecht, Göttingen.

Jones, B.A. (1997) *The Formation of the Book of the Twelve: A Study in Text and Canon*, Scholars Press, Atlanta.

Jones, B.A. (2000) The Book of the Twelve as a witness to ancient biblical interpretation, in *Reading and Hearing the Book of the Twelve* (eds J.D. Nogalski and M.A. Sweeney), Society of Biblical Literature, Atlanta, pp. 65–74.

Joüon, P. and Muraoka, T. (2006) *A Grammar of Biblical Hebrew*, Pontificio Instituto Biblico, Rome.

Kaiser, O. (1974) *Isaiah 13–39: A Commentary* (trans. J. Bowden), Westminster, Philadelphia.

Keefe, A.A. (2001) *Woman's Body and the Social Body in Hosea*, Sheffield Academic Press, Sheffield.

Kelber, W.H. (2007) Orality and biblical studies: a review essay, *Review of Biblical Literature*. www.bookreviews.org (accessed Apr. 2, 2008).

Kessler, J. (2002) Building the Second Temple: questions of time, text, and history in Haggai 1.1–15. *Journal for the Study of the Old Testament*, 27, 243–256.

Kessler, J. (2008) Tradition, continuity and covenant in the book of Haggai: an alternative voice from early Persian Yehud, in *Tradition in Transition: Haggai and Zechariah 1–8 in the Trajectory of Hebrew Theology* (eds M.J. Boda and M.H. Floyd), T&T Clark, New York, pp. 1–39.

Knights, C.H. (1995) The structure of Jeremiah 35. *Expository Times*, 106, 142–144.

Koch, K. (1976) *Amos: Untersucht mit den Methoden einer strukturalen Formgeschichte*, vol. 2, Neukirchener Verlag, Neukirchen-Vluyn.

Köckert, M., Becker, U. and Barthel, J. (2003) Das Problem des historischen Jesaja, in *Prophetie in Israel: Beiträge des Symposiums "Das Alte Testament und die Kultur der Moderne" anlässlich des 100. Geburtstags Gerhard von Rads (1901–1971) Heidelberg, 18.–21. Oktober 2001* (eds I. Fischer, K. Schmid, and H.G.M. Williamson), LIT Verlag, Münster, pp. 105–135.

Kratz, R.G. (2010) Rewriting Isaiah: the case of Isaiah 28–31, in *Prophecy and Prophets in Ancient Israel: Proceedings of the Oxford Old Testament Seminar* (ed. J. Day), T&T Clark, New York, pp. 245–266.

Kraus, H.-J. (1988) *Psalms 1–59: A Commentary*, Augsburg, Minneapolis.

Krüger, T. (1991) Literarisches Wachstum und theologische Diskussion im Jona-Buch. *Beiträge zur Namenforschung*, 59, 57–88.

Lambert, W.G. (1962) A catalogue of texts and authors. *Journal of Cuneiform Studies*, 16, 59–77.

Landsberger, B. (1965) Tin and lead: the adventures of two vocables. *Journal of Near Eastern Studies*, 24, 285–296.

Lange, A. (2006) Literary prophecy and oracle collection: a comparison between Judah and Greece in Persian times, in *Prophets, Prophecy, and Prophetic Texts in Second Temple Judaism* (eds M.H. Floyd and R.D. Haak), T&T Clark, New York, pp. 248–275.

Lapsley, J.E. (2000) Shame and self-knowledge: the positive role of shame in Ezekiel's view of the moral self, in *The Book of Ezekiel: Theological and Anthropological Perspectives* (eds M.S. Odell and J.T. Strong), Society of Biblical Literature, Atlanta, pp. 143–173.

Leclerc, T.L. (2007) *Introduction to the Prophets: Their Stories, Sayings, and Scrolls*, Paulist Press, New York.

Leonard, J.M. (2008) Identifying inner-biblical allusions: Psalm 78 as a test case. *Journal of Biblical Literature*, 127, 241–265.

Lescow, T. (1990) Dialogische Strukturen in den Streitreden des Buches Maleachi. *Zeitschrift für die Alttestamentliche Wissenschaft*, 102, 194–212.

Lescow, T. (1995) Die Komposition der Bücher Nahum und Habakuk. *Beiträge zur Namenforschung*, 77, 59–85.

Lescow, T. (1999) Die Komposition des Buches Obadja. *Zeitschrift für die Alttestamentliche Wissenschaft*, 111, 380–398.

Levenson, J. (1988) *Creation and the Persistence of Evil: The Jewish Drama of Divine Omnipotence*, Harper and Row, San Francisco.

Lichtert, C. (2005) La Prière de Jonas (Jon 2,3–10) comme élément narratif, in *Analyse narrative et Bible: Deuxième Colloque International du RRENAB, Louvain-la-Neuve, avril 2004* (eds C. Focant and A. Wénin), Peeters/Leuven University Press, Leuven, pp. 407–414.

Liebrich, L.J. (1956) The compilation of the book of Isaiah (part I). *Jewish Quarterly Review*, 46, 259–277.

Liebrich, L.J. (1957) The compilation of the book of Isaiah (part II). *Jewish Quarterly Review*, 47, 114–138.

Lohfink, N. (1961) Jona ging zur Stadt hinaus (Jon 4:5). *Biblische Zeitschrift*, 5, 185–203.

Long, B.O. (1973) 2 Kings III and genres of prophetic narrative. *Vetus Testamentum*, 23, 337–348.

Lundbom, J.R. (2004) *Jeremiah 21–36*, Doubleday, New York.

Lyons, M. (2009) *From Law to Prophecy: Ezekiel's Use of the Holiness Code*, T&T Clark, Edinburgh.

McKane, W. (1986) *A Critical and Exegetical Commentary on Jeremiah*, vol. 1, T&T Clark, Edinburgh.

McKane, W. (1996) *A Critical and Exegetical Commentary on Jeremiah*, vol. 2, T&T Clark, Edinburgh.

McKeating, H. (1994) Ezekiel, the "prophet like Moses"? *Journal for the Study of the Old Testament*, 61, 97–109.

McKenzie, J.L. (1967) *Second Isaiah*, Doubleday, New York.

McKenzie, S.L. (2005) Jonah and genre, in *How to Read the Bible*, Oxford University Press, Oxford, pp. 1–21.

Mackie, T. (2010) Transformation in Ezekiel's textual history, in *Transforming Visions* (eds W.A. Tooman and M. Lyons), Pickwick Publishers, Eugene, OR, pp. 249–278.

Malchow, B.V. (1984) The messenger of the covenant in Mal 3:1. *Journal of Biblical Literature*, 103, 252–255.

Mason, R.A. (1973) The use of earlier biblical material in Zechariah 9–14: a study in inner biblical exegesis. Dissertation. University of London.

Mason, R.A. (1977) The purpose of the "editorial framework" of the book of Haggai. *Vetus Testamentum*, 27, 413–421.

Mason, R.A. (1982) The prophets of the Restoration, in *Israel's Prophetic Tradition* (eds R. Coggins, A. Phillips, and M.A. Knibb), Cambridge University Press, Cambridge, pp. 137–154.

Mays, J.L. (1969a) *Amos: A Commentary*, Westminster, Philadelphia.

Mays, J.L. (1969b) *Hosea: A Commentary*, Westminster, Philadelphia.

Melugin, R.F. (1976) *The Formation of Isaiah 40–55*, Walter de Gruyter, Berlin.

Melugin, R.F. (1978) The formation of Amos: an analysis of exegetical method. *Society of Biblical Literature Seminar Papers*, 13, 369–391.

Merkur, D. (2005) Psychology of religion, in *The Routledge Companion to the Study of Religion* (ed. J.R. Hinnells), Routledge, London, pp. 164–181.

Meyers, C.L. and Meyers, E.M. (1987) *Haggai, Zechariah 1–8*, Doubleday, New York.

Meyers, C.L. and Meyers, E.M. (1993) *Zechariah 9–14*, Doubleday, New York.

Miller, J.M. and Hayes, J.H. (2006) *A History of Ancient Israel and Judah*, 2nd edn, Westminster/John Knox, Louisville, KY.

Moran, W.L. (1969) New evidence from Mari on the history of prophecy. *Biblica*, 50, 15–56.

Mowinckel, S. (1914) *Zur Komposition des Buches Jeremia*, Jacob Dybwad, Christiania.

Mowinckel, S. (1946) *Prophecy and Tradition*, Jacob Dybwad, Oslo.

Müller, A.K. (2008) *Gottes Zukunft: die Möglichkeit der Rettung am Tag YHWHs nach dem Joelbuch*, Neukirchener Verlag, Neukirchen-Vluyn.

Na'aman, N. (2002) The abandonment of cult places in the kingdoms of Israel and Judah as acts of cult reform. *Ugarit-Forschungen*, 34, 585–602.

Nakata, I. (1982) Two remarks on the so-called prophetic texts from Mari. *Acta Sumerologica*, 4, 143–148.

Nasuti, H.P. (2004) The once and future lament: Micah 2.1–5 and the prophetic persona, in *Inspired Speech: Prophecy in the Ancient Near East* (eds J. Kaltner and L. Stulman), T&T Clark, London, pp. 144–160.

Neef, H.-D. (1999) Vom Gottesgericht zum universalen Heil: Komposition und Redaktion des Zephanjabuches. *Zeitschrift für die Alttestamentliche Wissenschaft*, 111, 530–546.

Newsom, C.A. (1992) Response to Norman K. Gottwald, *Social Class and Ideology in Isaiah 40–55*. *Semeia*, 59, 73–78.

Nicholson, E.W. (1970) *Preaching to the Exiles: A Study of the Prose Tradition in the Book of Jeremiah*, Blackwell, Oxford.

Niditch, S. (1986) Ezekiel 40–48 in a visionary context. *Catholic Biblical Quarterly*, 48, 208–224.

Nissinen, M. (2000) Spoken, written, quoted, and invented: orality and writtenness in ancient Near Eastern prophecy, in *Writings and Speech in Israelite and Ancient Near Eastern Prophecy* (eds E. Ben Zvi and M.H. Floyd), Society of Biblical Literature, Atlanta, pp. 235–271.

Nogalski, J.D. (1993a) *Literary Precursors to the Book of the Twelve*, Walter de Gruyter, Berlin.

Nogalski, J.D. (1993b) *Redactional Processes in the Book of the Twelve*, Walter de Gruyter, Berlin.

Nogalski, J.D. (1999) The day(s) of YHWH in the Book of the Twelve. *Society of Biblical Literature Seminar Papers*, 38, 617–642.

Nogalski, J.D. (2003) Zechariah 13.7–9 as a transitional text: an appreciation and re-evaluation of the work of Rex Mason, in *Bringing Out the Treasure: Inner Biblical Allusion in Zechariah 9–14* (eds M.J. Boda and M.H. Floyd), T&T Clark, London, pp. 292–304.

Nurmela, R. (2006) *The Mouth of the Lord Has Spoken: Inner-Biblical Allusions in the Second and Third Isaiah*, University Press of America, Lanham, MD.

Odell, M.S. (2000) Genre and persona in Ezekiel 24:15–24, in *The Book of Ezekiel: Theological and Anthropological Perspectives* (eds M.S. Odell and J.T. Strong), Society of Biblical Literature, Atlanta, pp. 195–219.

Oswalt, J.N. (1986) *The Book of Isaiah: Chapters 1–39*, W.B. Eerdmans, Grand Rapids, MI.

Oswalt, J.N. (1998) *The Book of Isaiah: Chapters 40–66*, W.B. Eerdmans, Grand Rapids, MI.

Parker, S.B. (1993) Official attitudes toward prophecy at Mari and in Israel. *Vetus Testamentum*, 43, 50–68.

Parke-Taylor, G.H. (2000) *The Formation of the Book of Jeremiah: Doublets and Recurring Phrases*, Society of Biblical Literature, Atlanta.

Paul, S.M. (1991) *A Commentary on the Book of Amos*, Fortress Press, Minneapolis.

Peckham, B. (1993) *History and Prophecy: The Development of Late Judean Literary Traditions*, Doubleday, New York.

Person, R.F. (1999) II Kings 18–20 and Isaiah 36–39: a text critical case study in the redaction history of the book of Isaiah. *Zeitschrift für die Alttestamentliche Wissenschaft*, 111, 373–379.

Petersen, D.L. (1984) *Haggai and Zechariah 1–8*, Westminster/John Knox, Philadelphia.

Petersen, D.L. (1995) *Zechariah 9–14 and Malach*, Westminster/John Knox, Louisville, KY.

Petersen, D.L. (1998) The Book of the Twelve, in *The Hebrew Bible Today* (eds S.L. McKenzie and P.M. Graham), Westminster/John Knox, Louisville, pp. 95–126.

Petersen, D.L. (2000) A Book of the Twelve? In *Reading and Hearing the Book of the Twelve* (eds J.D. Nogalski and M.A. Sweeney), Society of Biblical Literature, Atlanta, pp. 3–10.

Pinker, A. (2006) Nahum 1: acrostic and authorship. *Jewish Bible Quarterly*, 34, 97–103.

Pinker, S. (2002) *The Blank Slate*, Penguin Books, New York.

Plöger, O. (1968) *Theocracy and Eschatology*, John Knox, Richmond, VA.

Pritchard, J.B. (1969) *Ancient Near Eastern Texts relating to the Old Testament*, Princeton University Press, Princeton.

Raitt, T.M. (1977) *A Theology of Exile*, Fortress Press, Philadelphia.

Redditt, P.L. (1995) *Haggai, Zechariah, Malachi*, W.B. Eerdmans, Grand Rapids, MI.

Redditt, P.L. (2008) *Introduction to the Prophets*, W.B. Eerdmans, Grand Rapids, MI.

Reicke, B. (1967) Liturgical traditions in Mic. 7. *Harvard Theological Review*, 60, 349–367.

Rendtorff, R. (1993) The composition of the book of Isaiah, in *Canon and Theology* (ed. R. Rendtorff), Fortress Press, Minneapolis, pp. 146–169.

Rendtorff, R. (2000) How to read the Book of the Twelve as a theological unity, in *Reading and Hearing the Book of the Twelve* (ed. J.D. Nogalski and M.A. Sweeney), Society of Biblical Literature, Atlanta, pp. 75–87.

Reventlow, H.G. (1987) Das Ende der sog. "Denkschrift" Jesajas. *Beiträge zur Namenforschung*, 38/39, 62–67.

Roberts, J.J.M. (1971) The hand of Yahweh. *Vetus Testamentum*, 21, 244–251.

Roberts, J.J.M. (1979) A Christian perspective on prophetic prediction. *Interpretation*, 33, 240–253.

Roberts, J.J.M. (1991) *Nahum, Habakkuk, and Zephaniah*, Westminster/John Knox, Louisville, KY.

Rofé, A. (1988) *The Prophetical Stories* (trans. D. Levy), Magnes Press, Jerusalem.

Römer, T. (2005) *The So-Called Deuteronomistic History*, T&T Clark, New York.

Rowland, C., Gibbons, P. and Dobroruka, V. (2006) Visionary experience in ancient Judaism and Christianity, in *Paradise Now: Essays on Early Jewish and Christian Mysticism* (ed. A.D. de Conick), Society of Biblical Literature, Atlanta, pp. 41–56.

Sasson, J.M. (1990) *Jonah: A New Translation with Introduction, Commentary, and Interpretation*, Doubleday, New York.

Scatolini Apóstolo, S.S. (2005) Ezek 36, 37, 38 and 39 in Papyrus 967 as pre-text for re-reading Ezekiel, in *Interpreting Translation: Studies on the LXX and Ezekiel in Honour of Johan Lust* (eds F. García Martínez, M. Vervenne, and B. Doyle), Peeters, Leuven, pp. 331–357.

Schaper, J. (2007) The "publication" of legal texts in ancient Judah, in *The Pentateuch as Torah: New Models for Understanding its Promulgation and Acceptance* (eds G.N. Knoppers and B.M. Levinson), Eisenbrauns, Winona Lake, IN, pp. 225–236.

Schaper, J. (2009) On writing and reciting in Jeremiah 36, in *Prophecy in the Book of Jeremiah* (eds H.M. Barstad and R.G. Kratz), Walter de Gruyter, Berlin, pp. 137–147.

Schart, A. (1998) *Die Entstehung des Zwölfprophetenbuchs*, Walter de Gruyter, Berlin.

Schart, A. (2000) Reconstructing the redaction history of the twelve prophets: problems and models, in *Reading and Hearing the Book of the Twelve* (eds J.D. Nogalski and M.A. Sweeney), Society of Biblical Literature, Atlanta, pp. 34–48.

Schart, A. (2003) Putting the eschatological visions of Zechariah in their place: Malachi as a hermeneutical guide for the last section of the Book of the Twelve, in *Bringing Out the Treasure: Inner Biblical Allusion in Zechariah 9–14* (eds M.J. Boda and M.H. Floyd), T&T Clark, London, pp. 333–343.

Schmidt, W.H. (1965) Die deuteronimostische Redaktion des Amosbuches. *Zeitschrift für die Alttestamentliche Wissenschaft*, 77, 168–193.

Schultz, R.L. (1999) *Search for Quotation: Verbal Parallels in the Prophets*, Sheffield Academic Press, Sheffield.

Seybold, K. (1985) *Satirische Prophetie: Studien zum Buch Zefanja*, Katholisches Bibelwerk, Stuttgart.

Seybold, K. (1989) *Profane Prophetie: Studien zum Buch Nahum*, Katholisches Bibelwerk, Stuttgart.

Seybold, K. (1991) *Nahum, Habakuk, Zephanja*, Theologischer Verlag, Zürich.

Shields, M.A. (1999) Syncretism and divorce in Malachi 2,10–16. *Zeitschrift für die Alttestamentliche Wissenschaft*, 111, 68–86.

Smelik, K.A.D. (1986) Distortion of Old Testament prophecy: the purpose of Isaiah 36 and 37, in *Crises and Perspectives* (eds J.C. de Moor, N. Poulssen, and G.I. Davies), E.J. Brill, Leiden, pp. 70–93.

Smith, P.A. (1995) *Rhetoric and Redaction in Trito-Isaiah: The Structure, Growth and Authorship of Isaiah 56–66*, E.J. Brill, Leiden.

Soggin, J.A. (1976) *Introduction to the Old Testament*, Westminster, Philadelphia.

Sommer, B.D. (1998) *A Prophet Reads Scripture: Allusion in Isaiah 40–66*, Stanford University Press, Palo Alto, CA.

Spronk, K. (1997) *Nahum*, Kok Pharos, Kampen.

Spronk, K. (1998) Acrostics in the book of Nahum. *Zeitschrift für die Alttestamentliche Wissenschaft*, 110, 209–222.

Stansell, G. (2006) Isaiah 28–33: blest be the tie that binds (Isaiah together), in *New Visions of Isaiah* (eds R.F. Melugin and M.A. Sweeney), Society of Biblical Literature, Atlanta, pp. 68–103.

Steck, O.H. (1985) *Bereitete Heimkehr: Jesaja 35 als redaktionelle Brücke zwischen dem Ersten und dem Zweiten Jesaja*, Verlag Katholisches Bibelwerk, Stuttgart.

Steck, O.H. (1989) Tritojesaja im Jesajabuch, in *The Book of Isaiah / Le Livre d'Isaie: les oracles et leurs relecteurs: unité et complexité de l'ouvrage* (ed. J. Vermeylen), Leuven University Press, Leuven, pp. 361–406.

Steck, O.H. (1991) *Der Abschluß der Prophetie im Alten Testament: ein Versuch zur Frage der Vorgeschichte des Kanons*, Neukirchener Verlag, Neukirchener-Vluyn.

Stromberg, J. (2008) Observations on inner-scriptural scribal expansion in MT Ezekiel. *Vetus Testamentum*, 58, 68–86.

Stromberg, J. (2011) *Isaiah after Exile: The Author of Third Isaiah as Reader and Redactor of the Book*, Oxford University Press, Oxford.

Stulman, L. (1986) *The Prose Sermons of the Book of Jeremiah: A Redescription of the Correspondence with Deuteronomistic Literature in Light of Recent Text-Critical Research*, Society of Biblical Literature, Atlanta.

Sweeney, M.A. (1991a) A form-critical reassessment of the book of Zephaniah. *Catholic Biblical Quarterly*, 53, 388–408.

Sweeney, M.A. (1991b) Structure, genre, and intent in the book of Habakkuk. *Vetus Testamentum*, 41, 63–83.

Sweeney, M.A. (1992) Concerning the structure and generic character of the book of Nahum. *Zeitschrift für die Alttestamentliche Wissenschaft*, 104 (3), 364–377.

Sweeney, M.A. (1995) Formation and form in prophetic literature, in *Old Testament Interpretation: Past, Present, and Future* (eds J.L. Mays, D.L. Petersen, and K.H. Richards), Abingdon Press, Nashville, pp. 113–126.

Sweeney, M.A. (1999) Zephaniah: a paradigm for the study of the prophetic books. *Currents in Research: Biblical Studies*, 7, 119–145.

Sweeney, M.A. (2000) Sequence and interpretation in the Book of the Twelve, in *Reading and Hearing the Book of the Twelve* (eds J.D. Nogalski and M.A. Sweeney), Society of Biblical Literature, Atlanta, pp. 49–64.

Sweeney, M.A. (2007a) Dating prophetic texts. *Hebrew Studies*, 48, 55–73.

Sweeney, M.A. (2007b) *I & II Kings*, Westminster/John Knox, Louisville, KY.

Thompson, M.E.W. (1993) Prayer, oracle and theophany: the book of Habakkuk. *Tyndale Bulletin*, 44, 33–53.

Tiemeyer, L.-S. (2008) Through a glass darkly: Zechariah's unprocessed visionary experience. *Vetus Testamentum*, 58, 573–594.

Tigay, J.H. (1985a) The evolution of the Pentateuchal narratives in the light of the evolution of the *Gilgamesh Epic*, in *Empirical Methods for Biblical Criticism* (ed. J.H. Tigay), University of Pennsylvania Press, Philadelphia, pp. 21–52.

Tigay, J.H. (ed.) (1985b) *Empirical Models for Biblical Criticism*, University of Pennsylvania Press, Philadelphia.

Tollington, J.E. (1993) *Tradition and Innovation in Haggai and Zechariah 1–8*, JSOT Press, Sheffield.

Tollington, J.E. (1999) Readings in Haggai: from the prophet to the completed book, a changing message in changing times, in *Crisis of Israelite Religion* (eds B. Becking and M.C.A. Korpel), E.J. Brill, Leiden, pp. 194–208.

Tooman, W.A. (2010) Transformation of Israel's hope: the reuse of Scripture in the Gog Oracles, in *Transforming Visions* (eds W.A. Tooman and M. Lyons), Pickwick Publishers, Eugene, OR, pp. 50–110.

Tov, E. (1985) The literary history of the book of Jeremiah in the light of its textual history, in *Empirical Methods for Biblical Criticism* (ed. J.H. Tigay), University of Pennsylvania Press, Philadelphia, pp. 211–237.

Tov, E. (1986) Recensional diffferences between the MT and LXX of Ezekiel. *Ephemerides Theologicae Lovanienses*, 62, 89–101.

Tov, E. (1992a) *Textual Criticism of the Hebrew Bible*, 2nd edn, Fortress Press, Minneapolis.

Tov, E. (1992b) Three fragments of Jeremiah from Qumran Cave 4. *Revue de Qumran*, 15, 531–541.

Troxel, R.L. (2008) *LXX–Isaiah as Translation and Interpretation*, E.J. Brill, Leiden.

Tucker, G.M. (1977) Prophetic superscriptions and the growth of a canon, in *Canon and Authority: Essays in Old Testament Religion and Theology* (eds G.W. Coats and B.O. Long), Fortress Press, Philadelphia, pp. 56–70.

Tuell, S.S. (1996) Ezekiel 40–42 as verbal icon. *Catholic Biblical Quarterly*, 58, 649–664.

Tuell, S.S. (2000) Haggai–Zechariah: prophecy after the manner of Ezekiel. *Society of Biblical Literature Seminar Papers*, 39, 263–286.

Tull Willey, P. (1997) *Remember the Former Things: The Recollection of Previous Texts in Second Isaiah*, Scholars Press, Atlanta.

Uehlinger, C. (2005) Was there a cult reform under King Josiah? The case for a well-grounded minimum, in *Good Kings and Bad Kings* (ed. L.L. Grabbe), T&T Clark, London.

Utzschneider, H. (1988) Die Amazjaerzählung (Am 7,10–17) zwischen Literatur und Historie. *Beiträge zur Namenforschung*, 41, 76–101.

Utzschneider, H. (1992) Die Schriftprophetie und die Frage nach dem Ende der Prophetie: Überlegungen anhand von Mal 1,6–2,16. *Zeitschrift für die Alttestamentliche Wissenschaft*, 104, 377–394.

van der Ploeg, J.P.M. (1972) Eschatology in the Old Testament. *Oudtestamentische Studien*, 17, 89–99.

van der Toorn, K. (1989) Female prostitution in payment of vows in ancient Israel. *Journal of Biblical Literature*, 108, 193–205.

van der Toorn, K. (2000a) From the oral to the written: the case of old Babylonian prophecy, in *Writings and Speech in Israelite and Ancient Near Eastern Prophecy* (eds E. Ben Zvi and M.H. Floyd), Society of Biblical Literature, Atlanta, pp. 219–234.

van der Toorn, K. (2000b) Mesopotamian prophecy between immanence and transcendence: a comparison of old Babylonian and neo-Assyrian prophecy, in *Prophecy in its Ancient Near Eastern Context* (ed. M. Nissinen), Society of Biblical Literature, Atlanta, pp. 71–87.

van der Toorn, K. (2004) From the mouth of the prophet: the literary fixation of Jeremiah's prophecies in the context of the ancient Near East, in *Inspired Speech: Prophecy in the Ancient Near East: Essays in Honor of Herbert B. Huffmon* (eds J. Kaltner and L. Stulman), T&T Clark, London.

van der Toorn, K. (2007) *Scribal Culture and the Making of the Hebrew Bible*, Harvard University Press, Cambridge, MA.

van Leeuwen, R.C. (1993) Scribal wisdom and theodicy in the Book of the Twelve, in *In Search of Wisdom: Essays in Memory of John G. Gammie* (ed. L.G. Perdue, B.B. Scott, and W.J. Wiseman), Westminster/John Knox, Louisville, KY, pp. 31–49.

Van Seters, J. (1997) *In Search of History*, Eisenbrauns, Winona Lake, IN.

Van Seters, J. (2000) Prophetic orality in the context of the ancient Near East, in *Writings and Speech in Israelite and Ancient Near Eastern Prophecy* (eds E. Ben Zvi and M. H. Floyd), Society of Biblical Literature, Atlanta, pp. 83–88.

Vasholz, R. (1980) Isaiah versus "the gods": a case for unity. *Westminster Theological Journal*, 42, 389–394.

Vielhauer, R. (2007) *Das Werden des Buches Hosea: eine radaktionsgeschichtliche Untersuchung*, Walter de Gruyter, Berlin.

Wahl, H.M. (1994) Die Überschriften der Prophetenbücher: Anmerkungen zu Form, Redakton und Bedeutung für die Datierung der Bücher. *Ephemerides Theologicae Lovanienses*, 70, 91–104.

Watts, J.W. (1996) Psalmody in prophecy: Habakkuk 3 in context, in *Forming Prophetic Literature* (eds J.W. Watts and P.R. House), Sheffield Academic Press, Sheffield, pp. 209–223.

Weigl, M. (2001) Current research on the book of Nahum: exegetical methodologies in turmoil? *Currents in Research: Biblical Studies*, 9, 81–130.

Weimar, P. (1985) Obadja: eine redationskritische Analyse. *Beiträge zur Namenforschung*, 27, 35–99.

Weimar, P. (1998) Zef 1 und das Problem der Komposition der Zefanjaprophetie, in *"Und Moses schrieb dieses Lied auf": Studien zum Alten Testament und zum Alten Orient* (eds M. Dietrich and I. Kottsieper), Ugarit-Verlag, Münster, pp. 809–832.

Weippert, H. (1973) *Die Prosareden des Jeremiabuches*, Walter de Gruyter, Berlin.

Weippert, M. (1991) The Balaam text from Deir 'Allā and the study of the Old Testament, in *The Balaam Text from Deir 'Allā Re-evaluated: Proceedings of the International Symposium Held at Leiden, 21–24 August 1989* (eds J. Hoftijzer and G. van der Kooij), E.J. Brill, Leiden, pp. 151–184.

Wellhausen, J. (1892) *Die kleinen Propheten*, 4th edn, Georg Reimer, Berlin.

Westermann, C. (1969) *Isaiah 40–66*, Westminster Press, Philadelphia.

Westermann, C. (1985) *Genesis 12–36: A Commentary* (trans. J.J. Scullion), Augsburg, Minneapolis.

Westermann, C. (1994) *Lamentations: Issues and Interpretation*, Fortress Press, Minneapolis.

Wildberger, H. (1991) *Isaiah 1–12* (trans. T.H. Trapp), Fortress Press, Minneapolis.

Wildberger, H. (1997) *Isaiah 13–27* (trans. T.H. Trapp), Fortress Press, Minneapolis.

Wildberger, H. (2002) *Isaiah 28–39* (trans. T.H. Trapp), Fortress Press, Minneapolis.

Williams, D.L. (1963) The date of Zephaniah. *Journal of Biblical Literature*, 82, 77–88.

Williams, M.J. (1993) An investigation of the legitimacy of source distinctions for the prose material in Jeremiah. *Journal of Biblical Literature*, 112, 193–210.

Williamson, H.G.M. (1990) The prophet and the plumb-line, in *In Quest of the Past: Studies on Israelite Religion, Literature, and Prophetism* (ed. A.S. van der Woude), E.J. Brill, Leiden, pp. 101–121.

Williamson, H.G.M. (1994) *The Book Called Isaiah*, Clarendon Press, Oxford.

Williamson, H.G.M. (1997a) Marginalia in Micah. *Vetus Testamentum*, 47, 360–372.

Williamson, H.G.M. (1997b) Relocating Isaiah 1:2–9, in *Writing and Reading the Scroll of Isaiah* (eds C.C. Broyles and C.A. Evans), vol. 1, E.J. Brill, Leiden, pp. 263–277.

Williamson, H.G.M. (2004) In search of the pre-exilic Isaiah, in *In Search of Pre-exilic Israel: Proceedings of the Oxford Old Testament Seminar* (ed. J. Day), T&T Clark, London, pp. 181–206.

Williamson, H.G.M. (2006) *Isaiah 1–5*, T&T Clark, London.

Williamson, H.G.M. (2010) Prophetesses in the Hebrew Bible, in *Prophets and Prophecy in Ancient Israel: Proceedings of the Oxford Old Testament Seminar* (ed. J. Day), T&T Clark, New York, pp. 65–80.

Willis, J.T. (1997) Isaiah 2:2–5 and the psalms of Zion, in *Writing and Reading the Scroll of Isaiah* (eds C.C. Broyles and C.A. Evans), E.J. Brill, Leiden, pp. 295–316.

Wilson, R.R. (1980) *Prophecy and Society in Ancient Israel*, Fortress Press, Philadelphia.

Wöhrle, J. (2006a) *Die frühen Sammlungen des Zwölfprophetenbuches*, Walter de Gruyter, Berlin.

Wöhrle, J. (2006b) The formation and intention of the Haggai–Zechariah corpus. *Journal of Hebrew Scriptures*, 6. www.purl.org/jhs (accessed July 16, 2009).

Wolff, H.W. (1974) *Hosea* (trans. G. Stansell), Fortress Press, Philadelphia.

Wolff, H.W. (1977) *Joel and Amos* (trans. W. Janzen, J.S. Dean McBride, and C.A. Muenchow), Fortress Press, Philadelphia.

Wolff, H.W. (1986) *Obadiah and Jonah* (trans. M. Kohl), Augsburg, Minneapolis.

Wolff, H.W. (1988) *Haggai: A Commentary* (trans. M. Kohl), Augsburg, Minneapolis.

Wolff, H.W. (1990) *Micah* (trans. G. Stansell), Augsburg, Minneapolis.

Wolters, A. (2008) "The whole earth remains at peace" (Zechariah 1:11): the problem and an intertextual clue, in *Tradition in Translation: Haggai and Zechariah 1–8 in the Trajectory of Hebrew Theology* (eds M.J. Boda and M.H. Floyd), T&T Clark, New York, pp. 128–143.

Yamauchi, E. M. (1973) Cultic prostitution: a case study in cultural diffusion, in *Orient and Occident: Essays Presented to Cyrus Gordon on the Occasion of his Sixty-Fifth Birthday* (ed. H.A. Hoffner), Kevelaer Verlag, Neukirchen-Vluyn, pp. 213–222.

Young, E.J. (1972) *The Book of Isaiah*, vol. 3: *Chapters 40–66*, W.B. Eerdmans, Grand Rapids, MI.

Young, I.M. (1998a) Israelite literacy: interpreting the evidence, part I. *Vetus Testamentum*, 48, 239–253.

Young, I.M. (1998b) Israelite literacy: interpreting the evidence, part II. *Vetus Testamentum*, 48, 408–422.

Yule, G. and Brown, G. (1983) *Discourse Analysis*, Cambridge University Press, Cambridge.

Zimmerli, W. (1958) Israel im Buche Ezechiel. *Vetus Testamentum*, 8, 75–90.

Zimmerli, W. (1979) *Ezekiel*, vol. 1: *Chapters 1–24* (trans. R.E. Clements), Fortress Press, Philadelphia.

Zimmerli, W. (1983) *Ezekiel*, vol. 2: *Chapters 25–48* (trans. J.D. Martin), Fortress Press, Philadelphia.

Scripture Index

Genesis

1:22, 28	238
4:1, 17	33
5:24	171 n.16
5:32	235
16:4	33
16:11–12	181
17:19	181
18:10, 18	65
21:6	181
22:17	34
25:26, 30	188 n.13
29:15–30	27
29:32, 34	188 n.13
31:38–39	101
32:12	34
38:18	33
38:21–22	32

Exodus

3:1	171 n.13
9:18, 24	107 n.11
10:2, 14	97
12:11	193
12:35	194
14:19	193
17:3–6	191
17:6	171 n.13
18:5	171 n.13
18:25	171 n.14
20:3	168
24:4–8	119
24:13	171 n.13
28:36–38	153
32:12	128–29
32:14	139 n.4
32:34	71 n.30
34:6–7	84–85, 107 n.13, 123 n.8, 127, 139 n.5, 171 n.13

Leviticus

18:4	233
25:25–26	206 n.5
25:47–55	206 n.5
26:5	240 n.15
26:22	232
26:36	240 n.15
26:45	240 n. 15
27:11–12	165

Numbers

4:30	227
16:34	171 n.14
22–24	10
22:11	188 n.12
26:55–56	61

Prophetic Literature: From Oracles to Books, First Edition. Ronald L. Troxel.
© 2012 Ronald L. Troxel. Published 2012 by Blackwell Publishing Ltd.

3:13–4:3	163, 166		Nehemiah	
4:4–6	167		13:1–3	198
4:5	85			

Psalms

			1 Chronicles	
7:1	121		2:55	70 n.18
9	123 n.5		3	140 n.20
20:2	48		3:17–19	136
24:8	109		4:21	70 n.18
40:9–10	101		6:41	160
44:24	194		29:29	12, 107 n.15
47:4	46			
53:6	48		2 Chronicles	
74	88 n.13		9:29	107 n.15
74:2	89 n.25		12:15	12, 107 n.15
80:8–18	96		13:22	12
89:13	58		16:9	153
89:35	46		21:12	107 n.15
103:5	205 n.2		36:10	140 n.20
118:16	58		36:15	223 n.14
128:5	48			
135:21	89 n.25		Ben Sira	
			49:7	88
Proverbs			49:10	81
1:1	16			
6:19	119		Esdras	
10:1	81		1:39–40	83
11:11	46			
12:17	119		4 Ezra	
14:5, 25	119		14:42–46	88
16:11	46			
19:5, 9	119		Josephus, *Contra Apionem*	
30:1	37, 81		1.40	88 n.22
30:15–16	40			
31:1	37		*Mart. Ascen. Isa.*	
			4:22	83
Ecclesiastes				
1:1	37		*Lives of the Prophets*	83
Ruth			Talmud	
2:20	206 n.5		*b. B. Bat.* 13b, 14b	81
3:9	206 n.5			
			Romans 1:16	124 n.16
Lamentations				
4:5	193		Galatians 3:11	124 n.16
4:13–15	193			
			Hebrews 10:38	124 n.16
Esther				
8:8–9	5			